T0316791

"Working people across America increasingly spend hours commuting to jobs in cities where they can no longer afford to live. Shaw shows how people are mobilizing to reverse this trend and describes how urban areas can and must stop the pricing out of the working and middle class."

Deepak Bhargava, President, Center for Community Change

"Shaw provides concrete strategies for how this generational divide over housing can—and must—be overcome."

Kim-Mai Cutler, Operating Partner, Initialized Capital, and former contributor, TechCrunch

Named in remembrance of

the onetime *Antioch Review* editor

and longtime Bay Area resident,

the Lawrence Grauman, Jr. Fund

supports books that address

a wide range of human rights,

free speech, and social justice issues.

The publisher and the University of California Press Foundation gratefully acknowledge the generous support of the Lawrence Grauman, Jr. Fund.

The publisher and the University of California Press Foundation also gratefully acknowledge the generous support of the Anne G. Lipow Endowment Fund in Social Justice and Human Rights.

Generation Priced Out

Generation Priced Out

WHO GETS TO LIVE IN THE
NEW URBAN AMERICA

Randy Shaw

With a New Preface

UNIVERSITY OF CALIFORNIA PRESS

University of California Press
Oakland, California

First paperback edition 2020
ISBN 978-0-520-35621-4 (pbk. : alk. paper)

The Library of Congress has cataloged an earlier edition as follows:

Names: Shaw, Randy, 1956- author.
Title: Generation priced out : who gets to live in the new urban America /
    Randy Shaw.
Description: Oakland, California : University of California Press, [2018] |
    Includes bibliographical references and index. |
Identifiers: LCCN 2018017667 (print) | LCCN 2018022222 (ebook) | ISBN
    9780520970991 (E-book) | ISBN 9780520299122 (cloth : alk. paper)
Subjects: LCSH: Housing—United States. | Middle class—United States—
    Economic conditions. | Generation Y—United States—Economic
    conditions.
Classification: LCC HD7293 (ebook) | LCC HD7293 .S4385 2018 (print) | DDC
    307.760973—dc23
LC record available at https://lccn.loc.gov/2018017667

Manufactured in the United States of America

26   25   24   23   22   21   20
10   9   8   7   6   5   4   3   2

To all those working for a more inclusive urban America

CONTENTS

Preface to the Paperback Edition ix
Acknowledgments xxix

Introduction 1

1 · Battling Displacement in the New San Francisco 11

2 · A Hollywood Ending for Los Angeles Housing Woes? 37

3 · Keeping Austin Diverse 74

4 · Can Building Housing Lower Rents? Seattle and
Denver Say Yes 103

5 · Will San Francisco Open Its Golden Gates to
the Working and Middle Class? 127

6 · Millennials Battle Boomers Over Housing 157

7 · Get Off My Lawn! How Neighborhood Groups Stop Housing 187

8 · New York City, Oakland, and San Francisco's Mission
District: The Fight to Preserve Racial Diversity 209

Conclusion: Ten Steps to Preserve Cities' Economic
and Racial Diversity 243

Notes 251
Index 277

PREFACE TO THE PAPERBACK EDITION

Generation Priced Out is a call to action for progressive cities to stop pricing out working- and middle-class residents. This preface offers me the opportunity to describe the progress that has been made, as well as the disappointments that have occurred, since the book's November 2018 publication.

Before the book came out, there had not been much talk about the generational divide over housing, the control boomer homeowners exercise over land-use policies, the elitism and negative environmental impacts of single-family-home zoning, the need for cities to combine new construction with stronger laws protecting tenants and rental housing, and the recognition of infill housing as essential for combatting climate change. These issues are now central to the national housing-policy debate.

Generation Priced Out highlights the rise of the YIMBY movement. Groups like A Better Cambridge, Minneapolis's Neighbors for More Neighbors, Seattle for Everyone, Portland for Everyone, AURA: An Austin for Everyone, Oakland's East Bay for Everyone, San Francisco's YIMBY Action, and YIMBY Democrats of San Diego County have nearly all continued to grow. These organizations have gained national attention, and new YIMBY groups are steadily developing, inspired by activists in other cities.

Generation Priced Out provoked spirited discussions about housing policy when I spoke in Austin, Berkeley, Boulder, Brooklyn, Cambridge, Culver City, Denver, Fremont, Irvine, Los Angeles, Minneapolis, Mountain View, New York City, Portland, Richmond (California), Sacramento, Seattle, and Walnut Creek. Foreign media were also interested in the book's recommendations, as I was interviewed by national media in Canada, Sweden, Germany, and Japan. A France-inspired "Night of Ideas" at the San Francisco Main Library featured a keynote, "What Kind of City Should SF Be in 2030?"

(drawn from my book title) asking who will get to live in the new urban America.

Activists like Portland's Madeline Kovacs, Seattle's Laura Loe, San Diego's Maya Rosas, Cambridge's Jesse Kanson-Benanav, Minneapolis's John Edwards (creator of Wedge Live!) and Neighbors for More Neighbors organizer Janne Flisrand, and San Francisco's Laura Foote (formerly Laura Clark) continue to work for greater affordability in local and/or state housing struggles.

Following the book's release I connected with many additional activists and groups who are making a difference on housing. These include Greg Anderson from Austin Habitat for Humanity; Abundant Housing LA and its managing director Leonora Camner; the activists with Open New York; Portland's Michael Andersen, Holly Balcom, and Tony Jordan; the team at the Seattle-based Sightline Institute; Darrell Owens of East Bay for Everyone; Alex Baca of Greater Greater Washington; Mark Richardson of Toronto's Housing Now; Diane Yentel, head of the National Low Income Housing Coalition; Michael Lane, deputy director of Silicon Valley at Home; and Bobak Esfandiari of SF YIMBY. These and many others are on the front lines of efforts to stop the pricing out of the non-rich from urban America.

PROGRESS ON INCREASING AFFORDABILITY

When I wrote *Generation Priced Out,* I knew that long-established exclusionary and elitist land-use policies could not be changed overnight. The forces working to stop housing, deny tenant and rental housing protections, and impose zoning restrictions that exclude the working and middle class would not go down without a fight. Yet despite this entrenched opposition, a new vision for urban America is gaining momentum.

Here are some examples.

Ending Single-Family Zoning

Single-family-home zoning bars cities from building the housing they need. Suburbia, not cities, was built on single-family zoning. But starting in the 1960s, primarily white homeowners in urban areas began to create restricted single-family-zoned neighborhoods to keep out renters, working-class residents, and racial minorities. Although many desirable communities were originally built with a mixture of housing types, suddenly only single-family homes were said to be consistent with neighborhood "character." In 1933, only 4 percent of Los Angeles had zoning restricted to single-family homes; today, the far-more populated city limits an unsustainable 75 percent of its buildable residential land to single-family homes or duplexes.

I've spent much of the past year railing against single-family zoning. I explained why it must be abolished on a two-minute video for NBC News' "Think" program. At book events I ask the audience if they like the lively street scenes of Paris, Vienna, or Barcelona. Nearly everyone nods. After all, Americans love Paris's narrow, walkable streets, sidewalk cafes, and the sheer energy at play. These charming European avenues are lined with six-story residential buildings. Single-family homes are rare. Europe's urban transit corridors are also filled with bicycle riders. Too few city streets in the United States even have unprotected bike lanes.

Yet the density that makes Paris or Barcelona streets so enchanting is illegal to build in many urban American neighborhoods. Many homeowners oppose not just the six-story residences on transit corridors common in Europe but any new housing that is not a single-family home. America's love affair with single-family homes deprives cities of lively, walkable streets. It also prevents cities from building enough housing to accommodate job and population growth. Cities that cannot build with sufficient density have steadily declining housing affordability, racial diversity, and economic inclusion. Single-family zoning also worsens climate change by forcing priced-out residents into long, greenhouse gas–emitting car commutes to get to jobs. Ending single-family-home exclusionary zoning furthers racial, environmental, and economic justice and is one of the key affordability strategies advanced in this book.

Fortunately, the tide against single-family zoning is turning.

A month after my book discussed Minneapolis's ambitious plans to increase housing density and described Councilmember Lisa Bender's critical role in this effort, the city drew national media attention by overturning single-family zoning. This action set a national precedent. Media began to question single-family-zoning land-use policies that cities had maintained for decades without controversy. People began asking why their city could not follow Minneapolis's lead and end a zoning practice rooted in racism and elitism. Progress soon followed.

In May 2019, Austin, whose powerful homeowner groups had killed a multi-year rezoning process in August 2018, enacted "Affordability Unlocked." This measure, initiated by Councilmember Gregorio Casar, effectively rezoned the city to allow six-unit buildings that are 50 percent affordable housing and eight-unit buildings that are 75 percent affordable. A shift to a pro-housing council majority in the November 2018 elections made the difference. In June 2019, Oregon kept up the momentum by ending single-family zoning and legalizing fourplexes statewide. Oregon's landmark victory reflected a sea change in the state's land-use politics since 2016. Another development discussed in *Generation Priced Out* is how environmental concerns have driven housing activism in Portland. Green housing activists have joined forces with Oregon's housing and social justice groups to create a powerful statewide coalition for more inclusive housing policies.

Cambridge spent much of 2019 debating legislation that would create a 100 percent Affordable Housing Overlay. Backed by the activist group A Better Cambridge, the overlay would allow four-story affordable buildings in most residential neighborhoods and up to seven stories along specific commercial corridors. It would also re-legalize the building of the triple-decker, a beloved housing type in the Greater Boston region. The debate over the overlay exposed the fault lines between Cambridge "progressives." Some who claimed to support new affordable housing opposed the overlay even though it would make such housing easier to build; they saw preserving single-family zoning as a higher priority. The overlay was attacked as a "major assault" on Cambridge neighborhoods that would reduce property values. One opponent's flyer showed a street of triplexes with a new six-story apartment building in the middle with the ominous words, "This Could Happen on Your Street . . ." The photo was from Jamaica Plains, not Cambridge.

The Cambridge City Council had a five-vote majority in support of the overlay, but Massachusetts is covered by a troubling state law that requires a supermajority for any zoning change that increases housing. Lacking the six votes needed on the nine-member council, the overlay was tabled in September 2019. Its fate depended on the November 2019 city council races, where A Better Cambridge put up a pro-overlay council slate against the rival Cambridge Residents alliance. In a huge victory for Cambridge's pro-housing forces, six candidates favoring the overlay won. Once enacted, the 100 percent Affordable Housing Overlay should become a model for other cities.

Massachusetts cities still have housing blocked by the state's supermajority requirement. A state Housing Choice bill was proposed that would restore majority rule, but while the bill won the support of a key committee at year's end, its passage was not assured. The bill if passed would make it a lot easier to build housing in Massachusetts. Unfortunately, Massachusetts law is not unique. Other cities and states also require a supermajority vote to increase housing. In Denver, which is as pro-housing as any major city, 20 percent of nearby property owners can submit a protest petition that then requires supermajority city council approval for a new housing project. Think about this. Why should a 20 percent minority be empowered to alter the traditional majority-vote process for cities to get more housing? You can build a football stadium in urban America without a supermajority local vote. Or open a liquor store. But the supermajority requirement to build housing is surprisingly common. It's among the special barriers cities and states have erected to keep tenants and people of color out of many neighborhoods. And as the debate over the Cambridge Affordable Housing Overlay shows, these supermajority requirements protect exclusionary single-family zoning from new affordable housing. These undemocratic requirements have no place in progressive cities and states that claim to promote racial and class diversity.

Despite the obstacles, I expect single-family-home zoning to end or be sharply restricted in most cities with high housing costs. Pressure to address climate change and the growing pro-housing political coalition will secure more diverse housing options. A key ally in this struggle is senior groups, including the powerful American Association of Retired People (AARP). AARP is backing "missing middle" housing—including duplexes, fourplexes, and small multiplexes—as a critical resource for the United States' rapidly aging population. The organization also supports much of the YIMBY movement's infill housing/increased density agenda. A green-YIMBY-senior alliance could bring an end to the dominance of single-family-home zoning in progressive cities.

Building More Housing

Cities need to create a lot more housing. This typically requires them to rezone streets to allow taller and/or denser buildings. YIMBY chapters often lead local and state rezoning battles, and support for more inclusive housing policies is growing steadily.

Generation Priced Out describes Seattle's ambitious Housing Affordability and Livability Agenda (HALA). This strategy to pair increased density with affordability restrictions reflects a policy often described as a "density bonus": builders get more units in exchange for making some of them affordable, with tenant protections. HALA was passed in March 2019 after being held up nearly a year by litigation. Seattle also enacted one of the nation's most aggressive accessory dwelling unit (ADU) laws. In-law apartments and backyard cottages, often known as ADUs, have become a major source of new housing supply in Los Angeles and other cities. ADUs break through the restrictions of single-family zoning and open upscale neighborhoods to the non-rich. Legalizing ADUs is essential for all high-housing-cost cities.

In the book I describe Portland's proposed Residential Infill Project (RIP), which would end single-family zoning and increase density in the city. It turned out that before Portland could vote on the RIP, Oregon's legislature legalized fourplexes statewide in 2019. The state law covers some of what Portland was moving towards, but the RIP would further increase density by streamlining the building of ADUs and eliminating minimum parking requirements for residences in single-dwelling zones. The RIP would also make it easier to develop missing-middle housing on many of Portland's unusually narrow lots. Portland city government takes its time on rezoning matters, and the city council is not expected to vote on the RIP until spring 2020.

Calling for Tech to Do More

I am routinely asked why tech doesn't fund housing for its workers. I believe cities should require tech to either build housing for their workforce or donate funds for construction. Tech began to move forward on its own housing efforts in 2019.

First, in January 2019, Microsoft committed $500 million for affordable housing in Seattle and the Puget Sound region. Of this, $225 million was slated for below-market loans, $250 million was earmarked for building housing for people earning 60 percent of the area's median income (roughly $50,000 for a couple), and the remaining $25 million was allotted to homeless organizations.

Later in January, the Chan Zuckerberg Initiative, cofounded by Facebook founder Mark Zuckerberg and his wife, Priscilla Chan, pledged to raise $540 million for affordable housing in the Bay Area. The funds will be used as loans, with the hope of creating 8,000 units in the next five to ten years. Chan stated, "Two or three years ago nobody [in tech] would say the word 'housing.' Nobody wanted to talk about it. It was just not our problem. Now, we're in a moment where Microsoft is standing up and saying we want to contribute and Facebook and Genentech are part of this partnership."[1] In June 2019 Google announced it was investing $1 billion to address the Bay Area housing crisis: $750 million toward converting the company's commercial land to residential use, and the balance for developing affordable housing. Facebook then followed its founder's donation in October 2019 by investing $1 billion for affordable housing, of which $225 million would build mixed-income housing on Facebook-owned land.

Tech contributions are long overdue and badly needed. But tech needs to do more to address an urban affordability crisis that directly impacts its workforce and home cities. The October 2019 Facebook contribution in particular raised questions about why cities are depending on voluntary donations from billion-dollar tech companies rather than requiring increased payments through taxes and other strategies. Tech contributions are no substitute for cities' ensuring that sufficient housing is built for incoming workers. In city after city, the failure to balance increased jobs with housing drives rising unaffordability. Since 2017, Facebook, Apple, Amazon, Netflix, and Google have leased 3.35 million square feet in Los Angeles. Housing these employees would require a lot of new construction as well as zoning changes to allow new multi-unit buildings where they are currently banned. But this has not happened.

In Culver City, Los Angeles's neighbor, Amazon has leased over 600,000 square feet and Apple over 200,000. The resulting new employees also need housing. Yet Culver City approved only fourteen new multi-family units in 2018 and averaged less than thirty-five new units per year from 2003 to 2017. That's fifteen years of inadequate new construction. It's easy to blame tech for driving up Culver City rents and home prices, but the city's failure to approve new housing to meet job growth is the real culprit. In November 2019, Culver City mayor Meghan Sahli-Wells acknowledged the city's past housing failures by backing a regional plan that requires the city to raise its housing production goal to 3,300 homes from 2021 to 2029. Culver City has become a positive pro-housing model since voters backed pro-housing politicians in the November 2018 elections.

Some felt that when New York City activists stopped Amazon from opening up a second headquarters in Queens in 2019 that the city had learned the perils of a steep jobs/housing imbalance. But this huge grassroots activist victory was primarily driven by local anger over Amazon getting billions of dollars in tax incentives. Google and Amazon both recently added thousands of New York City jobs in other neighborhoods without city officials raising concerns about the need for corresponding new housing. And soon after a key Queens politician helped kill the Amazon deal, he stopped a major housing development in his district.

Generation Priced Out urges cities to enact rent control, anti-rent gouging protections, and just-cause eviction laws. Historic progress was made in 2019. Oregon, New York, and California all greatly increased tenant protections. Statewide campaigns to lift rent-control bans were also underway in Colorado, Illinois, Massachusetts, Washington, and other states.

Oregon house speaker Tina Kotek (who also headed efforts to end single-family zoning) led the legislature to enact a statewide anti–rent gauging and just-cause eviction law in February 2019. The Oregon Housing Alliance, the Community Alliance of Tenants, and a broad coalition backed the new protections, which limit annual rent hikes to 7 percent plus inflation. Although tenant advocates sought a lower rent cap, the new state limit is a huge step forward, given that Oregon began 2019 with a ban prohibiting cities from adopting rent control. The new tenant protections will particularly benefit Portland, where the lack of just-cause eviction and rent caps has contributed to rising unaffordability and displacement.

New York has long allowed local rent controls. Over fifty cities have such laws, with New York City being the largest. But because local rent control has been controlled by the more pro-landlord New York state legislature, it has been extremely difficult for tenant groups to close loopholes and secure needed reforms. In June 2019, tenant advocates finally broke through. Following a statewide tenant campaign calling for "universal rent control," New York's state legislature adopted the Housing Stability and Tenant Protection Act. The measure greatly strengthened local rent-control laws and made it easier for cities to adopt such protections. Activists also won the permanent enactment of rent-control laws, ending the need for tenant groups to fight for their survival at the state level every four to eight years. New York cities will no longer need the state legislature's approval to enact and strengthen rent-control laws. The Housing Justice for All coalition did not win every reform it sought in 2019, but it helped close many of the loopholes that had steadily weakened and in some cases eliminated New York City's rent-control protections. The coalition has laid a strong groundwork for increasing tenant protections in future years.

Next to New York, California has the most cities with rent control and just-cause eviction laws. In 2019, Inglewood and Culver City, both of which border Los Angeles, passed such laws. The city of Alameda, Oakland's neighbor, and Sacramento, the state capital, also passed rent-control and just-cause eviction protections. These new rent-control cities in California fit a pattern. City officials initially responded to rising rents and displacement as a crisis that would soon pass. They refused to go beyond supporting non–legally binding landlord mediation and other strategies that did not adequately protect tenants. But when these weak measures failed, politicians in these cities saw no alternative to enacting rent-control and just-cause laws.

Until 2019, virtually every major gain for tenants in California was won locally. The state legislature was firmly controlled by Big Real Estate, which used the state body to preempt local tenant protections. In September 2019, this longstanding dynamic changed. California enacted AB 1482, the statewide Tenant Protection Act, which imposed a 5 percent plus inflation rent cap and statewide just-cause eviction. Sponsored by San Francisco assembly member David Chiu, the bill was strongly backed by Governor Gavin Newsom, who intervened in negotiations to strengthen the measure for tenants. AB 1482 is the biggest state legislation protecting tenants in California history.

AB 1482's passage reflects how California's affordability crisis is statewide and has spread among the middle class. Legislators who had previously opposed tenant bills took to the floor on AB 1482 to express anguish over stories of teachers, police officers, and construction workers sleeping in cars because they could not afford rents. AB 1482 was backed by a diverse coalition of groups ranging from the Alliance of Californians for Community Empowerment (ACCE) to California YIMBY, reflecting a growing consensus that California's housing crisis requires the "3P's": production of housing, protection of tenants, and preservation of affordable and rent-controlled housing. *Generation Priced Out* urges cities and state to adopt this multipronged solution to the affordability crisis.

Expanding Habitat's Mission

Generation Priced Out tells the story of a struggle to build a 123-unit, permanently affordable senior housing project that would be LGBTQ+ friendly in New York City's upscale Nolita neighborhood. Despite the fact that the site had long been planned for senior housing and the city had 200,000 seniors on affordable housing waiting lists, the project, known as Haven Green, faced vigorous neighborhood opposition. I ended my account with hopeful words from Councilmember Margaret Chin, the project's key backer.

But in 2019, the struggle for Haven Green got tougher. Opponents used their media connections to spin the housing into an attack on urban green space. Fortunately, Habitat for Humanity NYC, the project's co-developer, was prepared for opposition attacks. Led by Executive Director Karen Haycox and VP of External Affairs Matthew Dunbar, Habitat NYC worked hard to build support for the much-needed housing. Haven Green was also backed by housing groups like the Association of Neighborhood and Housing Development, Enterprise Community Partnership, and Open New York; the faith-based human service agency Vision Urbana; and other neighborhood groups and individuals. The project was approved by the city council in June 2019 by a surprising (given the opposition) 45–0 vote, with one abstention. While opponents sued to halt the project—an increasingly common strategy—the housing is moving forward. Many self-identified "progressives" fought this affordable senior housing, showing why many cities do not even propose such projects for upscale neighborhoods.

Habitat NYC's participation in co-developing Haven Green speaks to an encouraging expansion of the role of Habitat chapters in promoting new multi-unit housing. Long identified with providing affordable single-family homes, Habitat NYC made Haven Green its first rental-housing project. In Austin, Habitat has expanded into multi-unit projects because building single-family homes is no longer financially viable for housing low-income families. Austin Habitat's Greg Anderson is among the city's most outspoken advocates for rezoning neighborhoods to increase density. Habitat needs increased density to make its affordable projects financially feasible.

In 2019, Habitat for Humanity International launched Cost of Home, its first national advocacy campaign for housing affordability. In announcing the campaign, Habitat acknowledged how the worsening affordability crisis has led it to take on a larger role. "For more than 40 years, Habitat has been making safe, decent and affordable housing a reality, one family at a time," stated Jonathan Reckford, CEO of Habitat for Humanity International. "The challenge in front of us obliges us to do even more. Not only will Habitat lift our hammers to build affordable homes, we will lift our voices as one to declare that every family should be able to afford the cost of home."[2] The campaign commits Habitat over the next five years to mobilizing its local organizations, partners, volunteers, and community members across the country to help 10 million individuals meet their basic housing needs. It seeks to ensure that the one in six families paying more than 50 percent of their income for housing will no longer have to pay so much.

The campaign's message, "Habitat for Humanity is taking a stand," underlies the group's heightened focus on advocacy. Nor is the group shying away from controversial local zoning disputes. The campaign commits to challenging "barriers that make it difficult for people to find land for construction, build the home itself or be able to afford a place to live."[3] To this end, Habitat California backed SB 50, an ambitious planning and zoning bill to legalize fourplexes statewide and mandate increased density on transit corridors. In Oregon, Steve Messinetti, president and CEO of Habitat for Humanity Portland/Metro East, strongly endorsed HB 2001, a landmark 2019 bill that ended single-family home zoning in Oregon and opened the door to missing-middle housing. Nationwide, Habitat chapters are using their positive public image to promote increased density and affordability. As Habitat NYC's Matthew Dunbar put it after winning the struggle for Haven Green, "that's what spending political and social capital is for."[4]

Housing Policy Is Climate Policy

In addition to growing support for ending single-family zoning, building more housing, and increasing tenant protections, there has been great progress in identifying housing as a climate change issue. Green advocates, such as those in Portland and Seattle, are playing greater roles in promoting infill housing. As low-density housing triggers long car commutes, which undermine state climate change goals, housing policy is increasingly seen as a climate change issue.

In March 2019, Congressmember Alexandria Ocasio-Cortez sponsored a resolution for a Green New Deal. This led housing advocates to work to ensure that local, state, and federal Green New Deal proposals included sustainable land-use reform. In September 2019, the People's Action network of community groups released a national Homes Guarantee housing plan that would "embed goals and standards of the Green New Deal at every level."[5] There remains a generational divide, as many boomers identify green issues with preserving endangered species, reducing fossil fuels, and protecting the natural world—not with infill housing development. But progress is being made.

Urbanist Henry Kraemer, a Housing Fellow with the left-flank think tank Data for Progress, tweeted on June 24, 2019, that "'We don't have a housing scarcity problem' is tantamount to climate denial or anti-vax. It is willfully denying clear evidence from experts based on nothing but gut feeling & cultural signaling. It's also similarly dangerous." These strong words echo arguments in *Generation Priced Out*. The jobs/housing imbalance is real. Believing that cities can add jobs without building housing for new workers is akin to denying climate change. There cannot be a true Green New Deal without land-use reforms.

Building the YIMBY Movement

While the YIMBY movement is often wrongly portrayed as solely promoting market-rate housing, its members support many progressive housing issues. In 2019, the YIMBY movement prioritized building and rezoning for affordable housing. YIMBYs in the San Francisco Bay Area, Los Angeles, Seattle, Austin, and other cities were on the frontlines battling to open shelters for the unhoused. When HUD Secretary Ben Carson identified himself as a YIMBY, YIMBY groups pushed back, publishing articles explaining why his values were not theirs. California YIMBY also did as much as any group to promote AB 1482, the statewide Tenant Protection Act. The national YIMBYtown conference scheduled for Portland in April 2020 has two major themes: climate change and community stabilization. These themes reflect the core YIMBY value that "housing and climate movements can work together to achieve more energy-efficient, climate-resilient cities, from the Green New Deal to rethinking federal housing and land use, transportation, and infrastructure policies."[6]

Opponents of increased density and multi-unit housing see political value in labeling YIMBYs as "developer shills." Instead of aligning with YIMBYs to boost affordable housing, many so-called progressives have fought their plans, from the members of Bernie Sanders's Our Revolution groups in Cambridge who opposed the Affordable Housing Overlay to the "progressive" San Francisco supervisors who opposed placing limits on appeals that delay plans to build affordable and teacher housing. It's become clearer to me since *Generation Priced Out* was published how many local progressive politicians are dependent on political support from anti-housing luxury homeowners. Backers of exclusionary zoning and opponents of infill housing are worsening economic and racial exclusion. This fails the core definition of progressive social reform and further shows that housing politics requires reassessing traditional urban political identities.

Generation Priced Out urges YIMBYs to offer more unified support for inclusionary housing laws, which require private developers to include on-site affordable units (or payment of an in-lieu fee). Most YIMBYs support inclusionary laws but oppose cities setting affordability percentages so high that they would stop projects. This is a big issue in San Francisco, whose 20 percent inclusionary requirement is often treated as only a starting point for activists demanding greater concessions. San Francisco's heavily politicized housing approval process has also made the inclusionary percentage a backdoor strategy to stop projects. But the misuse of inclusionary requirements is fixable. Meanwhile, it's hard for housing advocates to build broad political coalitions with equity-oriented groups when proposed new housing includes no mandatory affordable units. Since inclusionary laws build political support for increased density and infill housing, they are a key component of cities' affordability toolbox.

ONGOING CHALLENGES

The progress since *Generation Priced Out* was originally released has been coupled with some letdowns, starting in my home state of California.

California's Missed Opportunity

California has the nation's least-affordable housing, highest number of unhoused people, and some of the longest car commutes. New homeless counts released in the summer of 2019 found at least double-digit increases in cities across the state, with Oakland's rising a whopping 47 percent. After Governor Jerry Brown spent most of his eight years refusing to address the housing crisis, in November 2018 California elected Gavin Newsom as governor. Newsom made housing the centerpiece of his campaign, vowing to build 3.5 million new units. He later reduced that goal but said he would at least quadruple the construction of new housing units, again raising the expectations of housing advocates.

Newsom's critique of the barriers to building housing was incorporated in State Senator Scott Wiener's SB 50. The bill preempted local zoning restrictions by allowing six-story buildings on or near transit corridors. It also legalized four-unit missing-middle housing statewide. SB 50 was backed by the California Federation of Labor, AARP California, environmental groups, and housing organizations. It was endorsed by the mayors of San Francisco, Oakland, San Jose, and Stockton and by many of the state's leading newspapers. But local politicians saw SB 50 as limiting their power over land use. The Los Angeles City Council unanimously opposed the bill, as did nearly all of the San Francisco Board of Supervisors. Beverly Hills and other primarily white, affluent, homeowner-dominated cities vigorously fought a measure that would bring renters into their neighborhoods.

SB 50 was building momentum until May 2019, when State Senate leader Toni Atkins abruptly shelved it. Atkins first claimed that the bill lacked the votes, but later said that she opposed SB 50's preemption of "local control." Governor Newsom did not stop Atkins from undermining California's key strategy for boosting its housing supply. SB 50's tabling was followed by the legislature's defeat of ACA 1, which would have given voters a chance to reduce the number of votes needed to pass affordable housing bonds from 66 percent to 55 percent. The two-thirds requirement, imposed in 1978 by the state's notorious Proposition 13, has cost the state billions of affordable-housing dollars. California Democrats controlled a two-thirds supermajority of the legislature, but ACA 1 could not get the votes needed to pass.

The legislature's failure to pass either SB 50 or ACA 1 brought negative public and media response to their inaction on housing. This led to some positive steps. First, Newsom added $2 billion to the state's affordable housing budget. Second, his administration required that the state mandate that cities, towns, and counties plan for the housing needs of residents—known as the Housing Element and Regional Housing Needs Allocation, or RHNA—be taken seriously for the first time. As a result of the pressure applied by the governor and activist groups like California YIMBY and Abundant Housing LA, RHNA housing projections for cities and counties became dramatically higher than in the past. Third, the legislature ended the session by passing arguably the nation's most sweeping ADU laws. The laws effectively ended single-family home zoning in California by allowing the building of an ADU and junior ADU on virtually every lot. The state ADU laws were a major if backdoor breakthrough in the campaign against single-family home zoning.

These actions help, but they collectively fall short of addressing California's drastic undersupply of housing. SB 50's raising of height and density limits on or near transit corridors—preempting local zoning restrictions—is critical to help the state closing its housing production gap. SB 50 must pass by January 30, 2020, or California will be left without a strategy to build housing for at least another year. As 2019 came to a close, pressure for action was growing; the California Department of Finance reported in November 2019 that permits for multi-family units like apartments were down in the first nine months of the year compared to the same period in 2018.

California must produce much more housing to meet population growth. Local governments have failed. Yet until 2019 no powerful coalition had emerged that was capable of winning state legislation to boost production. Too many state legislators hear only from homeowners who oppose new construction. They need to hear not just from constituents who support new construction but also from organizations representing labor, seniors, and environmentalists as well as individuals who are victimized by high housing costs and long commutes. San Diego, the nation's eighth largest city, has shown how the rise of pro-housing advocates can reshape politics. *Generation Priced Out* describes the emergence of YIMBY Democrats of San Diego, who have catalyzed stronger legislative support for housing. Candidates in the 2020 San Diego mayor's race have actively courted YIMBY support, and the group's housing activism is a model for other cities in high-housing cost states. This shows how dramatically political attitudes around housing can change when new voices are heard.

Homeowner Resistance

Addressing the housing crisis is also challenged by vehement homeowner opposition to shelter and housing for the unhoused. This occurs even in cities that passed funding measures for those purposes. *Generation Priced Out* describes how Los Angeles voters approved funding for new shelters and affordable housing in the November 2016 and March 2017 elections. But this has been followed by fierce resistance to specific projects, which has slowed approvals. Lawsuits have caused further delays. These postponements have increased construction costs and forced city officials to reduce estimates of the number of people who would be served by the bond and sales tax money. The result? Rising public cynicism over government programs to house the poor, even though opponents have created the delays.

Cities never should have empowered homeowners to decide who gets to live in their neighborhood. The exclusionary racial and class impacts are all too clear and have no place in progressive cities promoting inclusion and diversity.

Progressive Opposition

Adding to the challenges of building denser, more sustainable cities is opposition to new housing from self-identified progressives. They come in two varieties. The first are homeowners whose top political issue is preventing apartments from being built in their neighborhoods. Their support for elitist and even racist exclusionary zoning laws explains why such new apartment and missing-middle bans still exist in San Francisco, Los Angeles, Seattle, and nearly all blue cities other than Minneapolis and Portland. "Progressive" homeowners even oppose new 100 percent affordable apartments, as became clear with the "progressive" opposition to Cambridge's Affordable Housing Overlay.

The second group sees all-new market-rate housing as driving gentrification. Proponents argue this even though *Generation Priced Out* explains how most urban neighborhoods gentrified without any new "luxury" development. In fact, I cite a study of San Francisco that found only 10 percent of home sales over $1 million in the boom year of 2016 involved new construction.[7] This "progressive" opposition to infill housing, increased density on transit corridors, and any market-rate housing offers no hope for middle-class families seeking housing in over a dozen of the cities with high housing costs. Nor does it reduce greenhouse gas emissions caused by the long car commutes of people priced out of cities. Some anti-market-rate-housing activists have even aligned with anti-housing homeowners and reactionary groups like the nativist and anti-renter Livable California. New apartments for any income level cannot be built in most urban neighborhoods without the zoning changes that anti-market-rate "progressives" oppose. Let's be clear: Beverly Hills has not battled SB 50 and other pro-density measures in order to boost housing options for the working and middle class.

Lengthy Housing Approvals

Generation Priced Out highlights glacial housing approval processes as an overlooked factor in the crisis. in 2019, the problem got even worse. As construction costs rose nationally, many housing developments submitted for approval years earlier no longer made economic sense. A four-year gap between application and breaking ground makes projects vulnerable to changing market conditions—yet in San Francisco this lengthy time frame is standard practice. Expediting housing requires taking politics out of the approval process. Seattle's planning commission does not vote to approve projects that are consistent with zoning. It is a technical rather than a political body. Seattle's approval process is twice as fast as San Francisco's, where every project must be approved by the planning commission and could then be subject to an appeal vote by the Board of Supervisors.

San Francisco allows virtually every building permit to be appealed. This triggers automatic delays in projects, which must await a public hearing on the claim. Any resident can file an appeal; they don't need to have a connection to the property at issue. San Francisco even protects the right to file frivolous appeals. *Generation Priced Out* describes how any member of the public in San Francisco can hold up a project for months by writing a check for $617 and filing an appeal for discretionary review. In 2019, San Francisco mayor London Breed proposed a charter amendment for the November 2019 ballot to prevent such appeals for affordable and teacher housing, but none of the "progressive" supervisors backed the reform and it failed to reach the ballot. The challenge is that luxury homeowners typically file these appeals, and most city supervisors are dependent on their votes for election. As a result, protecting homeowners' public input rights takes precedence over ensuring that sufficient housing gets built.

THREE KEY STEPS FOR DIVERSIFYING URBAN AMERICA

Since *Generation Priced Out*'s release, the importance of three areas in boosting affordability has become clearer.

Expanding the Pro-Housing Movement

We need a broader pro-housing movement. It's great to see YIMBY chapters emerging in Raleigh and Durham, Denver, Central New Jersey, and other once-affordable cities across the nation. But too many cities threaten to price out the working and middle class. This is true even for cities and neighborhoods that do not appear at risk of an affordability crisis. The post-2012 era showed how quickly housing prices can skyrocket even in longtime affordable cities and neighborhoods. Thus groups pushing affordability must form before this exclusionary process begins.

How to get a group started? Some of the activists I write about, like Cambridge's Jesse Kanson-Benanav and San Diego's Maya Rosas, went from being isolated advocates to helping build powerful pro-housing organizations. Every city with an affordability crisis has people who can do the same. If you think your city will not change its opposition to new housing or tenant protections, *Generation Priced Out* shows otherwise. Consider how Portland started 2019 being barred by state law from enacting rent control or just-cause eviction laws. Yet within a few months the Oregon legislature had enacted a statewide version of both. Organizing and activism are making a huge difference in stopping the pricing out of the non-rich from urban America; we just need to see this in more cities.

Electing Pro-Housing Politicians

Generation Priced Out emphasizes the importance of electing pro-housing politicians. I describe how councilmembers like Minneapolis's Lisa Bender, Austin's Gregorio Casar, Portland's Chloe Eudaly, and New York City's Margaret Chin, along with San Francisco's mayor Ed Lee, played essential roles in advancing affordability. Many politicians I do not specifically mention in the book have also had a major impact, including Cambridge city councilmember Denise Simmons and mayor Mark McGovern, Denver councilmember Chris Hinds, Oregon house speaker Tina Kotek, Seattle councilmember Teresa Mosqueda, Culver City councilmember Alex Fisch and mayor Meghan Sahli-Wells, San Francisco state legislators Scott Wiener and David Chiu and mayor London Breed, and California state senator Nancy Skinner, who represents Berkeley and the adjacent East Bay. Far more politicians are pushing for affordability solutions, and the list is steadily expanding.

But progress depends on having more pro-housing urbanists run for office. Urbanist Sarah Kate Levy, who would become the first member of Los Angeles's fifteen-member city council to back upzoning over homeowner opposition, is running for a council seat in 2020. Urbanist Sarah Iannarone is running for mayor of Portland in 2020. The Seattle City Council had two strong housing/urbanist candidates running in 2019: Tammy Morales and Shaun Scott. Morales, who interviewed me about *Generation Priced Out* before my December 2018 visit to Seattle, won election, while Scott lost narrowly. Seattle's roughly 55 percent November 2019 election turnout was higher than usual for those contests, but it was far below the 70 percent turnout for the 2018 election or the roughly 80 percent turnout in November 2016. Seattle's 2019 electorate, as was the case for the off-year elections in other cities, was also disproportionately made up of older, white voters. Electing urbanist, pro-renter, and pro-housing candidates requires that younger, lower-income and more racially diverse residents vote. *Generation Priced Out* urges cities to align local elections with state and national cycles.

Strong urbanist candidates won in Cambridge, Boulder and Seattle in November 2019 despite the lack of younger voters but the significantly higher turnout in November elections can mean the difference between victory and defeat for strong urbanist candidates like Shaun Scott. Urbanists need to maximize their political power, and that requires aligning local elections with state or national.

Electing pro-housing candidates is essential to improve affordability. Minneapolis ended single-family zoning in 2018 because voters elected candidates committed to that goal. Austin passed "Affordability Unlocked" because voters elected a pro-housing council majority. In contrast, the Silicon Valley city of Cupertino (home to Apple) elected an overtly anti-housing council majority in 2018 and quickly became a national poster child for promoting exclusionary housing policies. The anti-housing Boulder policies I describe in the book reflect a longstanding council majority that promotes this agenda; fortunately, a slate of urbanist candidates ran in the November 2019 election and won four of the six council seats (all of which have four-year terms). If Boulder can see a shift toward a more pro-housing electorate, it can happen in your city.

Urbanist candidates in council and mayor's races inject housing affordability, infill housing, bike lanes, public transit, and parking requirements into city policy debates. Even if these candidates lose, their presence pays dividends by forcing their opponents to address urbanist concerns. This dynamic is even more important at the national level. There has not been a single presidential election in the United States since widespread homelessness began in 1982 where the housing affordability crisis has been a campaign issue. In November 2000, I wrote a magazine story—"There's No Place Like Home"—about how the Bush, Gore, and Nader presidential campaigns ignored the housing crisis. I could have written the same story, changing only the candidates' names, in 2004, 2008, 2012, and 2016. As a result of housing's exclusion from the national political debate, even Barack Obama's two terms failed to meaningfully increase spending on affordable housing. In 2019, the National Low Income Housing Coalition assembled a national campaign to ensure that candidates addressed the housing crisis. The Our Homes, Our Votes: 2020 coalition has pushed Democratic presidential candidates to announce strong pro-housing policies. All of the leading candidates have done so. This means that if a Democrat wins the presidency, they will begin their term in 2021 with a ready-to-go national affordability strategy. That strategy, coupled with a public commitment to implement it, will facilitate the dramatic action on housing affordability that millions of Americans desperately need.

Treating the Housing Crisis as an Emergency

The third main area, which I see as even more important since writing *Generation Priced Out,* involves framing the affordability crisis as an emergency. In early 2019, I heard San Franciscans urging the board of supervisors to formally declare a "housing emergency." This seemed fitting, as that is how the city's affordability crisis is regularly described. But San Francisco declared a housing emergency in 1979. It has never gone away. Despite the ongoing and worsening crisis, San Francisco has never acted with a sense of urgency toward building needed housing. Declaring a housing emergency in urban America is more often a substitute for action. Cities are still operating on housing autopilot.

We recognize a medical emergency by allowing ambulances to speed through red lights. How would such an approach address the housing emergency? Enacting the "Ten Steps to Preserve Cities' Economic and Racial Diversity" outlined in this book's conclusion would make a huge difference. In addition, cities would begin to address the jobs/housing imbalance by conditioning new office building approvals on accompanying new housing. Apartments would be legalized citywide and transit corridors would be upzoned to at least six stories. The housing approval process would be expedited to give builders an up or down decision on their project within a year. Politicians, their appointees, and self-interested homeowners would no longer have the discretion to stop housing. Many other policies could be quickly implemented if we treated housing affordability like a true crisis.

In 1999, I co-authored a national study, "There's No Place Like Home: How America's Housing Crisis Threatens Our Children." It focused on the negative health and education impacts on kids growing up without safe and affordable housing. Today, the lack of affordable housing is even worse, impacting tens of millions of Americans. *Generation Priced Out* pushes urban America to act.

ACKNOWLEDGMENTS

This book emerged from a phone conversation I had with my longtime University of California Press editor Naomi Schneider on the day following Oakland's Ghost Ship fire. We got to talking about the tragedy of young artists living in dangerous housing due to the high cost of Bay Area rents. She asked if I were interested in writing a book about a generation priced out of big cities. This is the result.

Thank you to everyone who gave their time to be interviewed for this book. I particularly appreciate those who shared their personal stories of how they have been impacted by eviction, displacement, and/or otherwise being priced out. Thanks to the elected officials who took time to talk: Austin's Gregorio Casar, Minneapolis's Lisa Bender, New York City's Margaret Chin, and San Francisco's then-Mayor Ed Lee. Lee died suddenly on December 12, 2017. I spent years talking housing policy with him and regret that he will not get the chance to read this book.

My Tenderloin Housing Clinic colleagues Raquel Fox and Steve Collier offered insights on their cases, and Stephen Booth provided valuable feedback. THC attorney David E. Tchack provided invaluable help with translation for interviews in Austin and Los Angeles. THC paralegal Cynthia Price formatted my text into a manuscript and created the index. My longtime friend and THC co-founder and current board president Chris Tiedemann provided valuable feedback on chapters, as did former THC community organizer Rio Scharf. My wife, Lainey Feingold, reviewed more chapters than anyone and significantly improved the book.

Rick Jacobus was the first person I met with to discuss *Generation Priced Out*. He offered valuable insights and suggested cities to write about. Jerry Jones lined up tenants for me to talk to in Los Angeles. Heather Baker and

Angela Ryan graciously shared their experiences with me about the Oakland artist housing scene. Shoshana Krieger, Victoria Jara, and Stephanie Trinh went the extra mile to get me people to interview in Austin, as did Celia Weaver for Crown Heights and Nick Licata for Seattle. Tyler Anderson connected me to the mariachis facing eviction in Los Angeles's Boyle Heights. Sam Moss connected me to Pete Gallegos for my interview on San Francisco's Mission District, and Laura Loe linked me to YIMBYs in other cities. Sam Dodge put me in touch with his family in Seattle, and Erin House connected me to a spokesperson for Seattle for Everyone. AnMarie Rodgers, Tammy Hung, Denise Pinkston, Roland Li, Todd David, and my old pal Joseph Lindstrom provided helpful information. I also benefited hugely from years of bouncing housing ideas off of Mayor Lee's top housing advisor and my former co-worker, Jeff Buckley.

Stories by Mike Rosenberg of the *Seattle Times* and too many other reporters to name were enormously helpful. The contributions of these reporters can be seen throughout the text and endnotes.

As always, this book could not have been written without the support of my wife, Lainey Feingold. She and my children, Anita and Ariel Feingold-Shaw, create the stable foundation that allows a writing life. I also thank my father-in-law, Saul Feingold, for a lifetime of encouragement of my work.

Introduction

When Heather Baker walked into the Oakland warehouse known as the Ghost Ship in November 2016, it "looked like a gypsy dream."[1] The artist live-work space was filled floor to ceiling with furniture and art projects. A large two-story open space was the setting for regular weekend concerts. A friend had just moved into the building and knew that Baker was looking for cheap housing. Since she was an artist he suggested she visit the Ghost Ship and check it out.

Baker had lived in Oakland's Temescal neighborhood through the 1990s, paying $725 for a large one-bedroom apartment with a garden. After attending Oakland's Mills College she left the city in 2000, returning sixteen years later. Baker came back to a dramatically changed city. Rents had more than doubled for apartments that were not as nice near her former home. She discovered "legal live-work housing was way more expensive than apartments." The Ghost Ship was cheaper because it was not legal to live there.

Despite the appeal of the low price, Baker decided not to move into the Ghost Ship. She instead accepted an offer to stay in a room in a legal live-work space while she looked for a permanent home. A month later, the Ghost Ship was engulfed in flames.

On December 2, 2016, at 11:20 p.m., when the Ghost Ship was packed with musicians and concertgoers, a fire broke out. Thirty-six people were killed, all but one visitors to the warehouse for the evening's music. All of the residents were displaced. The friend who had suggested Baker consider moving into the space lost all his possessions in the blaze. Another friend jumped out of a second-story window and survived.

It seemed impossible that so many talented and creative young people could have their lives cut short by attending a concert in a building that lacked legally required fire exits. In the search for answers as to how a warehouse could openly house residents and hold public events without the legal right to do either, one theme emerged: Oakland's young, upcoming creative class was living in unsafe buildings because their generation had been priced out of safe and affordable housing.

Media headlines on the tragedy spoke volumes: "Ghost Ship Tragedy Puts Focus on Plight of Oakland Artists Dealing with Soaring Bay Area Housing Costs"; "Rising Prices in Oakland Push Artists into Risky Housing"; "After a Tragedy, Reckoning with Oakland's Affordability Crisis"; "Housing Crisis, Not Ravers, Is Responsible for the Oakland Fire"; and "Take Note, California: Oakland Tragedy Shows the Cost of Too Little Housing Construction." Like New York City's Triangle Shirtwaist fire of 1911, which killed 146 workers and brought pressure for workplace protection for sweatshop workers, the Ghost Ship tragedy highlights the housing affordability crisis afflicting many of the nation's cities.

The message I took from the Ghost Ship is that cities must act far more urgently to stop the pricing out of working- and middle-class residents. This book offers a blueprint for making that happen.

The Ghost Ship tragedy occurred in Oakland, but urban housing unaffordability and rising inequality in cities is a national story. New York City's once working-class and then gay Chelsea district now has a skyline dominated by luxury condo towers. In some, each unit has its own swimming pool. Chelsea joined Williamsburg, the Lower East Side, Fort Greene, and other longtime working-class New York neighborhoods in pricing out the middle class. In Los Angeles, the working-class and ethnically diverse neighborhoods of Boyle Heights and Highland Park long resisted the city's trend toward housing unaffordability. But both neighborhoods are now battling to stave off gentrification. San Francisco's fabled North Beach and Haight-Ashbury neighborhoods long housed poets, musicians, and representatives of the city's counterculture; today, you need the salary of a bond trader or corporate attorney to afford a vacant one-bedroom apartment in either community.

The pricing out of the middle class used to be a story only heard in San Francisco, New York, and affluent sections of other cities. But times have changed. Seattle's housing prices are rising as fast as anywhere. Austin's boom times have left working- and middle-class Latino and African American families behind. Long-affordable Portland is a housing bargain no more. Those seeking housing in Los Angeles often must choose between living in a converted garage, renting a living room in a flat, or commuting an hour or more to their job. Boulder's housing prices nearly rival San Francisco's. Denver has undergone a housing construction boom that has yet to reduce prices for the non-affluent. Berkeley and Cambridge are best known as college towns, but their housing prices are exorbitant. San Diego is no longer a coastal bastion of middle-class affordability. The unaffordability of desirable, high-employment cities now defines urban America. A generation of young people find themselves unable to live in cities that have long been open to all.

The pricing out process often intersects race and class. In Austin, Texas, the city's Latino families endure slum housing and are frequently displaced as their buildings are demolished and replaced with upscale housing. San Francisco's Mission District struggles to preserve the dominant Latino culture that put the neighborhood on the national map. The Black Panthers helped build Oakland's identity as the leading African American city on the West Coast; now the city's African American population is declining, priced out by soaring rents and home prices.

Something is very wrong with this picture.

When did it become acceptable for America's politically progressive and culturally diverse cities to price out the non-rich? And why are progressive cities—those that back minimum-wage hikes, LGBTQ rights, health care for all, and greater racial and gender equity—allowing and often promoting increased housing inequality? That the Ghost Ship tragedy occurred in Oakland, long an affordable refuge for those priced out of San Francisco, shows how desperate urban unaffordability has become. When urban America cannot offer affordable housing to artists in cities like Oakland, its future as a nucleus for our creative class is at risk.

I have been on the front lines of the housing crisis for forty years. From my office at San Francisco's Tenderloin Housing Clinic I regularly see longtime residents facing displacement. They despair over being forced to leave their home, neighborhood, and city if we cannot stop their eviction. Tenants should not have to live with such fear. Decades of misguided land-use policies have plunged urban America into a deep affordability crisis; cities must now embrace the right policies to find their way out. Cities have the ability to preserve and expand housing for low-income residents and the working and middle class; achieving that is a question of political will.

Addressing the urban affordability crisis has been hampered by policy conflicts. Many blame rising housing prices on cities' long failure to build enough homes. They see boosting the supply of housing units as the primary goal. Others see the affordability crisis as driven by the lack of strong tenant and rental housing protections. They dispute the value of increasing supply because most new housing does not serve those with low incomes.

This often heated conflict between these perspectives creates the false impression that they are mutually exclusive. They are not. Cities can and must expand housing opportunities for the middle-class *and* strengthen tenant and rental housing protections. Cities can and must promote deeply affordable housing for low-income residents *and* change zoning laws to allow multi-unit buildings in single-family-home-zoned neighborhoods. Cities must also join groups like the National Low-Income Housing Coalition (NLIHC) to demand more federal housing assistance for those unable to afford market rents. There is no "one size fits all" solution to stopping the pricing out of the working and middle class from the new urban America; to the contrary, this book offers multiple, comprehensive policies to achieve this goal.

This book argues that cities must address the housing needs of those of all income levels. Improving urban affordability also requires thinking differently about the housing crisis in four key ways.

First, there is a generational divide between millennials and boomers over the urban affordability crisis. Millennials are often the victims of inflated housing costs caused by city zoning laws—pushed by many boomers—that artificially restrict the housing supply. This leads many in the younger generation to support building a lot more housing of all types and in all neighborhoods. Many boomers, in contrast, have enjoyed soaring home values by preventing the construction of new housing in their communities. This millennial-boomer conflict is occurring across America's high-housing-cost cities.

Second, urban gentrification is neither inevitable nor unstoppable, despite what some may claim. Political decisions caused gentrification to emerge, spread, and intensify. Cities put the interests of real estate speculators and existing homeowners ahead of the preservation of a vibrant working and middle class. Fortunately, as detailed in this book, support for a far more inclusive set of political and policy decisions is growing across urban America. These can slow if not stop the pricing out of the urban working and middle class. Even hyperexpensive cities like New York and San Francisco can become more economically inclusive.

Third, neighborhood activism is the long-overlooked villain in cities pricing out the non-affluent. A movement that emerged in the 1970s to preserve working- and middle-class neighborhoods against the threats of urban renewal now too often works against that goal. Preserving a neighborhood's status quo is not progressive when it denies housing to all but the rich. Neighborhood activists worsen the housing crisis by stopping the new working- and middle-class housing opportunities essential for preserving economic diversity.

Fourth, the urban housing crisis must be seen in the larger environmental context. Rising urban population and job growth means people either live in the cities where they work or get priced out and often live a one- to two-hour driving commute away. Such commutes worsen climate change yet many who identify as environmentalists fail to see that opposing infill housing undermines green goals. Expanding urban housing for the working and middle class in cities advances social and economic justice and is the best strategy for combating climate change.

When it comes to preserving economic diversity, progressive cities have gone off track. Many of our bluest cities, the progressive bastions, price out the working and middle class. Most books blame their removal on "evil" developers, "bought-off" politicians, and real estate interests. But the pricing out process could not have happened in San Francisco, Berkeley, Los Angeles, Boulder, Cambridge, Seattle, Portland, Minneapolis, Austin, New York, and other blue cities without progressive support. No progressive city posts "Priced Out: Only the Affluent Allowed" signs in its neighborhoods. But that is where urban land-use policies have led.

I know from personal experience that new laws and policies can help protect the working and middle class. In 1992, I co-authored the first pro-tenant ballot measure to ever win in San Francisco. It slashed how much landlords could annually raise rents by more than half. This has saved the city's tenants tens if not hundreds of millions of dollars. It may be the biggest transfer of wealth from landlords to tenants in urban history. In 1994, I authored a charter amendment passed by voters that overhauled city housing code enforcement. San Francisco's enforcement of safe and healthy housing for tenants has become a national model.

At the state level I helped restore $250 million annually for California's renters' tax credit and led the campaign to exempt single-room occupancy hotels (SROs) from the state's Ellis Act, which preempts local just-cause eviction laws. In March 1999, I co-authored a widely covered report, "There's No Place Like Home: How America's Housing Crisis Threatens Our Children," that urged increased federal funding for affordable housing. I later joined Sister Bernie Galvin in coordinating the "Religious Leaders' National Call for Action on Housing," an open letter to President Bill Clinton calling for increased federal housing aid. The *New York Times* described the over 300 signers from 48 states as "an unusually broad group of religious leaders." The

Clinton Administration credited the "National Call" with securing 60,000 additional Section 8 vouchers from Congress.[2]

In 1980, I co-founded San Francisco's Tenderloin Housing Clinic (THC), where I have been executive director since 1982. THC leases and manages more than twenty SROs and is San Francisco's leading provider of permanent housing for homeless single adults. THC's attorneys have provided comprehensive legal assistance to tenants for four decades and represent the vast majority of San Francisco tenants facing no-fault evictions. THC also directly enforces laws protecting SROs from conversion to nonresidential uses; protecting SROs is a critical city strategy for promoting economic and racial diversity.

When I arrived in the Tenderloin in 1980 it was assumed that the gentrification of this low-income community located between Union Square and Civic Center would soon occur. But thanks to proactive strategies available to many other neighborhoods across urban America, the Tenderloin remains primarily working class and low income to this day. Its resistance is a lesson for activists in other cities who are told that battling the pricing out of the working and middle class is futile.

The Ghost Ship tragedy was a wake-up call. The working, creative, and middle classes provide the cultural richness and civic engagement that underlie successful cities. Pricing out these groups displaces the parents who run and join PTAs, coach youth soccer and softball, and volunteer at neighborhood events. The working and middle class made our big cities great. Urban America still needs them.

. . .

Starting with Teresa Dulalas's remarkable fourteen-year fight to stay in her family's South of Market home, chapter 1 tells the stories of seniors, people with AIDS, and working families battling displacement from their San Francisco homes and neighborhoods. Tenants resisting eviction have long been a critical dimension of San Francisco's housing crisis. These struggles show that the city's working- and middle-class tenants are fighting to stay in the increasingly expensive city; their successes are inspiring others.

Chapter 2 discusses Los Angeles's post-2009 transformation into a high-housing-cost city. The rapid spread of the city's affordability crisis has put at risk even the longtime working-class neighborhoods of Boyle Heights and Highland Park, both of which had remained affordable for decades. In Boyle Heights, speculators sought to displace mariachis, the musicians who culturally define Boyle Heights and its central hub, Mariachi Plaza. Controversial tactics employed by Boyle Heights' anti-gentrification activists have played a key role in resisting tenant displacement. Highland Park shows how quickly a longtime working-class neighborhood can be gentrified in the absence of proactive strategies to protect its affordability. Highland Park, Boyle Heights and other former working-class Los Angeles neighborhoods were particularly vulnerable to upscale transformation due to the city's prolonged failure to build much affordable housing.

Los Angeles's housing crisis has primarily profited two groups: homeowners and landlords. Homeowner opposition to new apartment buildings is so widespread that it even occurs in progressive neighborhoods like Venice. Meanwhile, politically powerful landlords have prevented the enactment of stronger tenant protection and rental housing preservation laws. I describe in this chapter how a broad pro-housing movement with support from Mayor Eric Garcetti is charting a far more inclusive course for the city. New strategies are expanding working- and middle-class housing opportunities, a sharp contrast from the days when these groups were continually priced out. Los Angeles still has the nation's worst homeless problem and rising unaffordability, but it is moving in the right direction.

Chapter 3 examines fast-growing Austin, Texas. "Keep Austin Weird" is its mantra, but beneath its progressive image lurks a disregard for tenants' rights that worsens racial and economic inequality. I tell the stories of tenants victimized by Austin's failure to ensure safe and healthy housing, and I describe how displacement and demolitions have reduced its racial diversity. As in Los Angeles, Austin's powerful homeowner groups have long used single-family-home zoning restrictions to bar tenants from their neighborhoods. This excludes the working and middle class and many families of color from the city's high-opportunity communities.

As Austin's thriving economy has increased its racial and economic segregation, a large and diverse coalition has begun pushing Austin to become more inclusive. Along with rising young politicians like councilmember Greg Casar, this coalition is promoting housing policies far more consistent with Austin's progressive reputation. An opportunity to implement more inclusive housing policies emerged in recent years, when Austin undertook a once-in-a-generation rewriting of its land-use policies (a process known as CodeNext). The battle over CodeNext has become the defining issue in Austin's November 2018 mayor's race, as the city decides whether a new generation of working- and middle-class residents gets to live in Austin, or whether the city becomes a future home primarily for the rich.

In chapter 4, I describe how Seattle and Denver have built a lot of new housing in an effort to expand affordability. While cities cannot simply build their way out of the housing crisis, expanding housing supply is essential amid rising population and job growth. Housing prices in both cities have risen sharply in the past decade but they are far below what they would have been absent the increased supply. Seattle for Everyone, a diverse coalition of labor, environmentalists, and private and nonprofit developers, has helped implement a citywide housing plan—the Housing Affordability and Livability Agenda (HALA)—that increases affordable housing by upzoning neighborhoods to add height and density. HALA should be a national model for other cities. Denver's housing construction boom has primarily reduced rents in downtown projects targeting high-income renters. Denver has a golden opportunity to expand housing opportunities for the working and middle class by using publicly owned land near transit stations to dramatically increase affordable housing.

Chapter 5 explains why San Francisco went from the late 1970s through 2012 without building much housing. I tell the story of Irish builders who have spent decades battling long approval processes, neighborhood opposition, and years of rezoning meetings in order to build. The city's failure to build anywhere close to enough housing necessary to match population and jobs growth has greatly contributed to its acute housing shortage and unaffordability.

After Mayor Ed Lee took office in 2011, however, San Francisco's approach dramatically changed. Lee pushed the city to build 5,000 units annually, more than double the average built in the thirty previous years. Lee's pro-housing agenda changed the city's culture around building housing. In the face of rising unaffordability, San Francisco implemented the nation's most comprehensive program for protecting tenants and preserving and expanding housing for the working and middle class. It will take years for San Francisco to make up for over three decades of housing policy that priced out the working and middle class, but the city is moving in the right direction.

Chapter 6 highlights the generational conflict between millennials and boomers over housing. Millennials (those born between 1981 and 1996) are the generation most impacted by today's high rents and home prices. Many support building housing, increasing density, and opening up single-family-home-zoned neighborhoods to more affordable two- to four-unit buildings. Boomers (born in 1946 to 1964) typically bought homes or secured rent-controlled housing when cities were far more affordable. Their home values have jumped due to the lack of housing supply. Many oppose the new housing and less restrictive neighborhood zoning that millennials see as essential for a new generation of the non-rich to live in our cities. Members of Generation X (those born in the years from 1965 to 1976) typically have housing views shaped by whether they came of age before housing prices became unaffordable in their city.[3]

Chapter 6 goes on to describe how pro-housing millennials and their allies in Austin, Boulder, Cambridge, the East Bay, Portland, San Diego, San Francisco, and Seattle are shifting urban politics to promote rather than oppose new housing. It also describes how instead of sympathizing with millennials forced to pay skyrocketing rents (often on top of paying off huge student loans), many boomers blame young workers, particularly those in tech, for causing the housing crisis. While such boomers mock millennials for allegedly squandering money on hipster luxuries like avocado toast, their real goal is to derail a rising political movement that supports building urban housing for all income levels.

Chapter 7 addresses a chief cause of the pricing out of the working and middle class from urban America: neighborhood groups preventing the construction of new multi-unit housing. The neighborhood preservation movement emerged in Berkeley in 1973 as a progressive response to threats to middle-class neighborhoods from urban redevelopment. But today's neighborhood associations work to exclude the non-rich from these communities. Preserving neighborhood "character" now keeps tenants and racial minorities out.

I describe how affluent neighborhood groups have fought affordable senior housing in New York City's upscale Nolita neighborhood and in San Francisco's affluent Forest Hill. I also detail how Berkeley twice went to court to stop a small three-unit project on a site zoned for four units. I show how Minneapolis homeowners went all out to stop new market-rate rental housing—in an 80 percent renter neighborhood.

Boomer homeowners who oppose new housing in their neighborhoods get more than increased property values by limiting supply: they are the chief recipients of federal housing assistance, via the mortgage interest deduction. In California, boomer homeowners also disproportionately benefit from having their property taxes restricted by Proposition 13, which passed in 1978. Prop. 13 severely limits property taxes on longtime owners while shifting the state's tax burden to the millennial buyers of new homes. New buyers pay two to three times the property taxes, and often more, than is levied on the longtime owners of the house next door, which is of equal market value.

Chapter 8 highlights how the pricing out of the urban working and middle class also reduces racial diversity. New York City's Crown Heights is a historically African American neighborhood at risk of gentrification. A block-sized city-owned parcel at the Bedford Union Armory gave Mayor Bill de Blasio a perfect opportunity to build hundreds of new affordable housing units, but de Blasio instead supported building luxury condominiums on the site. I describe the powerful battle waged by longtime residents of Crown Heights and community groups to "Kill the Deal." The Crown Heights struggle shows how even politically progressive cities like New York often take actions that further, rather than slow, the pricing out of working people.

On the other coast, Oakland's challenge is to maintain its historically African American population amid steadily rising rents. Oakland's racial and ethnic diversity draws young people, many of whom are part of the generation priced out of San Francisco. But this influx has increased housing demand and rents, leaving Oakland less affordable to African American working- and middle-class residents. Oakland has adopted a "Roadmap to Equity" to promote diversity; this chapter assesses its progress and prospects for future success.

I end chapter 8 by discussing San Francisco's Mission District. The neighborhood, seen as ground zero for gentrification, has struggled to maintain its Latino population. Mission activists have used controversial but effective tactics to preserve the neighborhood's dominant Latino culture in the face of tech booms and rising citywide affluence. Grassroots activism is protecting the Mission's diversity.

The conclusion provides ten proven strategies cities should adopt to expand economic and racial diversity. These strategies, drawn from the cities discussed in the book, show that expanding housing for low-income, working-, and middle-class residents is a winnable fight. A new generation is building momentum across America's high-housing-cost cities for more inclusive housing. Many in this generation grew up in big cities. The working and middle class built these cities; their contributions are the bedrock of urban life. Housing policies promoting their exclusion created our affordability mess, and implementing inclusive policies will get us out of that mess.

There should not be a new generation of working people priced out of living in many of the country's most desirable cities. People increasingly agree. That's why enthusiasm for expanding housing opportunities is growing. It is my hope that this book contributes to this momentum by promoting policies that support working- and middle-class people who want to live in the new urban America.

1

Battling Displacement in
the New San Francisco

We don't have enough places to live, and too many can't afford the places that exist. . . . And communities of color are feeling this impact the hardest. . . . If we stay on the path we're on, we'll end up like San Francisco where the average house price is $1,150,000 and only the well-to-do and those being subsidized can live. . . . No middle-class, no working class, no creatives and artists.

Austin mayor Steve Adler, State of the City Address, 2017

Can Portland avoid repeating San Francisco's mistakes?

The Atlantic, May 17, 2016

Will Seattle really become the next San Francisco?

Seattle Times, July 28, 2016

How did San Francisco replace New York City as the poster child for urban unaffordability? Why did the nation's most politically progressive big city become "the US capital of insane housing prices"? A city with a "deranged housing market" where a "one-bedroom apartment rents for more than a 13-bedroom 20th century palace with a pool in Spain"?[1]

These are great questions. I co-founded the Tenderloin Housing Clinic (THC) in the fall of 1979 to address the growing crisis. In addition to helping Tenderloin tenants, THC became the city's eviction defense center for tenants facing the loss of their homes due to nonpayment of rent.

In those days the daily parade of people clutching their court eviction papers in my office was overwhelmingly low-income. Yet those displaced from their homes could usually find other housing in San Francisco. Now they have a better chance of winning the lottery than of securing non-subsidized housing in most neighborhoods.

Today, working- and middle-class tenants have been priced out of much of the city. It's not just that studios start at $1,800 and one-bedrooms at

$3,300; rather, apartments require up-front payments of the last month's rent and a security deposit. Those unable to afford this move-in cost of $6,000–$9,000 cannot meet the financial requirements for living alone in a San Francisco apartment.

So how do teachers, service workers, and others desiring to live in San Francisco find housing? First, they respond to ads for a vacant bedroom in an already occupied unit. This requires competing with other applicants through an interview process. And if they get selected and the master tenant then moves, the landlord can raise the price of the unit to the current market rate.

Second, they can move to a single-room occupancy hotel, or SRO. These typically do not have steep move-in requirements. A typical 140-square-foot SRO room with private bath rents for $1,800 and up. Many SROs appealing to a more affluent market now include microwaves in the rooms and/or common kitchens.

Third—and this has become the most popular option—they can look for apartments outside the city that they can afford. But as I discuss later, Oakland, long the place where those priced out of San Francisco ended up living, is no longer affordable either.

Never in San Francisco's history has it been harder for a working- or middle-class family to get housing. And having been on the front lines of the crisis almost from the very start, I can say that no politician, community organization, or corporate interest wanted this to happen.

To the contrary, as the housing crisis worsened through the 1980s, San Francisco's divergent political camps were unified around one goal: ensuring the city did not follow the path of New York City. While progressives denounced the city's downtown high-rise boom as "Manhattanization," the real estate industry sent out mailings showing fires and dilapidated buildings in the South Bronx as a preview of what San Francisco would become if strong rent-control laws were passed.

Nobody wanted San Francisco to replace New York City as the national cautionary tale for misguided housing policies, but that is what occurred. And it has had a steep human cost.

SAN FRANCISCO'S HISTORIC AFFORDABILITY

It seems hard to believe from today's vantage point, but until the late 1970s San Francisco had always been affordable despite its panoramic bay views, striking hills, temperate climate, and historic architecture. San Francisco always had posh Nob Hill and Pacific Heights, but middle-class families had no problem buying houses in most neighborhoods.

At the dawn of the 1970s, there was not a shred of evidence that by decade's end San Francisco would begin the long trajectory of becoming a high-priced city. The Haight-Ashbury was three years beyond the Summer of Love. The neighborhood housed hippies and its rents and home prices were cheap. Bohemian North Beach was filled with poets and artists. The redevelopment agency's notorious urban renewal plans had not yet demolished South of Market's "Skid Row" or the predominantly African American Fillmore neighborhood.

Investment property in San Francisco was incredibly cheap. In 1975, Paul Boschetti, an Italian immigrant working in San Francisco as a United Airlines mechanic, was convinced by a co-worker to invest in apartment buildings. He bought a sixteen-unit apartment building with seven retail spaces in the Hayes Valley neighborhood for $150,000. The building was in the city's heroin hub. Gang killings were so common that one occurred in front of Boschetti's building while he was working inside. Boschetti kept his retail spaces boarded up to prevent having to constantly repair broken windows. He got the property at a low price and charged low rents due to the neighborhood's problems. Boschetti remembers the area was so unsafe "they were giving properties away."[2]

On the other side of town, Latino immigrants were moving in large numbers to the Mission, long a working-class Irish neighborhood. Blue-collar workers had their choice of homes to buy or flats to rent in Noe Valley, the Castro, or Bernal Heights; the Inner Sunset and Inner Richmond were just as affordable.

Yet seemingly overnight, San Francisco's housing market changed.

THE CRISIS BEGINS

San Francisco's housing affordability crisis was caused by the convergence of five factors:

- the boost in the city's economy driven by San Francisco's new reliance on tourism and finance;
- a rising gay and lesbian migration into the nation's most tolerant city for those of nontraditional sexual orientation;

- the demolition of thousands of low-cost units due to urban renewal in the South of Market and Fillmore neighborhoods;
- young workers often described as yuppies (young urban professionals) choosing to live in San Francisco rather than the suburbs, where prior generations of white-collar workers lived;
- increased immigration from Central America and Southeast Asia.

Looking back on these simultaneous developments, it is easy to understand how the city got started on a road toward unaffordability. Thousands more people were seeking housing in a city where supply not only did not stay the same but actually declined. It was the perfect recipe for a housing crisis.

At first, San Francisco's liberal political establishment ignored rising concern over rent hikes and evictions. Supervisor Harvey Milk was the only elected official to back a pro-tenant measure on the November 1978 ballot, in an election held less than a month before Milk and Mayor George Moscone were assassinated at city hall.

But by the spring of 1979 public outrage over rent hikes forced the hand of Mayor Dianne Feinstein and the politically moderate board of supervisors. In April 1979, the board, which included two Republicans, found "there is a shortage of decent, safe and sanitary housing" in San Francisco, "resulting in a critically low vacancy factor."[3] After declaring a moratorium on rent increases, in June 1979 the board unanimously adopted an emergency rent stabilization ordinance regulating rents and evictions.

San Francisco's housing crisis had officially begun. And forty years later it has gotten even worse. Today, working- and middle-class people are priced out from renting or buying in most San Francisco neighborhoods. The city also has a persistent and visible homeless crisis despite providing the most permanent housing for homeless persons per capita of any major city.

On June 9, 1981, the *New York Times* reported in "Changing San Francisco Is Foreseen as a Haven for Wealthy and Childless" that San Francisco "was crowding out middle-income people and could soon become a place only the elite can afford." Yet San Francisco's then-mayor Dianne Feinstein promoted policies that encouraged this trend. Rents for two-bedroom apartments more than doubled during the Feinstein years, rising from $435 a month in 1979 to $900 in 1987. Rising housing demand actually led to bigger rent hikes in the decade *after* the passage of a weak rent-control law in 1979 than in the preceding decade.[4]

THE LATE 1990s DOT-COM BOOM

San Francisco's affordability problem went from bad to extreme around 1996, when the tech-driven dot-com boom began impacting housing prices. The city suddenly faced a real estate explosion that remains unprecedented.

Between 1990 and 2000, the median monthly rent jumped from $643 to $977 a month, a 52 percent increase. Over that period, the number of units renting from $250 to $749 a month decreased by over 50 percent, from 132,278 to 63,849. Meanwhile, the number of units renting for $1,000 or more a month skyrocketed from 24,070 to 90,247, an astronomical 275 percent increase.[5]

From 1995 to March 1997 alone, rents on vacant apartments in San Francisco rose 50 percent. The number of owner move-in evictions more than tripled in 1997, rising from an average of 400 per year in 1990–1995 to over 1,300 that year (the rise was partially attributable to owner-occupied buildings of four units or fewer being exempt from rent control until 1995). The vast majority of those evicted for owner move-in and other no-fault evictions during these years were long-term tenants paying well below market rents.[6]

The dot-com boom brought thousands of affluent Silicon Valley workers into a San Francisco housing market whose supply remained relatively fixed. Most of these tech workers lived in San Francisco because the South Bay cities where they worked were not building housing for their workers either. This failure negatively impacts the San Francisco housing market to this day.

POST-BOOM SAN FRANCISCO

San Francisco's housing prices rose steadily from the mid-1990s until the national financial crisis put a stop to most real estate activity in the fall of 2008. But the respite was brief. The national economy's revival in 2011 and San Francisco's new tech boom brought back the rising prices and evictions of the dot-com era.

Most San Francisco residents are tenants. The displacement of long-term tenants has come to define the city's housing crisis. The impact of these evictions goes far beyond those actually displaced; tens of thousands of renters fear that one day they will come home to an eviction notice that seeks to remove them from their home, neighborhood, and the city they love.

The stories of Teresa Dulalas and other San Francisco tenants set forth below reveal the human costs of a city in which renters are continually priced out. I've been touched by many of these stories, as THC attorneys represent the vast majority of tenants in San Francisco's high-profile eviction cases. I sometimes feel akin to an emergency room physician as the victims of rising unaffordability and civil strife come to our office seeking help. Their experiences are also stories of resistance and show the power of fighting back. Contrary to what many believe, displacement can be stopped. And San Francisco can still increase housing opportunities for the working and middle class.

San Francisco tenants will not be moved. Those targeted for removal, like Teresa Dulalas and her family, never gave up fighting to stay in their homes. They always insisted that they had the same right as rich people to live in San Francisco.

This resistance has kept the dream of a more affordable San Francisco alive.

It's a question of political will.

TERESA DULALAS: "MOVING WAS NOT AN OPTION"

Teresa Dulalas's tenancy began in 1979, soon after San Francisco's housing crisis started. She moved with her parents to an apartment in a South of Market Victorian in 1979. Theirs was one of three flats located at 1353–1355–1357 Folsom Street. The three-story 1912 building is above a garage that has two parking spaces and storage. There is a communal backyard. The three flats are quite spacious; each has four large bedrooms and hardwood floors.

Dulalas and her family had previously lived one block away. The family liked their new home because it was bigger and still part of the neighborhood's active Filipino community. Two years earlier, the mass eviction of elderly and working-class tenants at the International Hotel in the heart of the city's Manilatown had garnered international attention. As many as 10,000 Filipinos had once lived in the five-block stretch of Kearny Street from Bush to Jackson that included the I Hotel. The evictions were the culmination of a process that led to the disappearance of the Manilatown neighborhood, and the center of the Filipino community shifted south of Market Street.

Dulalas's flat was located in a section of the South of Market (SOMA) neighborhood that was still very affordable. On the eastern side of SOMA, adjacent to downtown, the San Francisco Redevelopment Agency had demolished thousands of similar Victorians as part of its urban renewal efforts in the 1960s and 1970s. But western SOMA was a different world. Filipino immigrant families lived in alley flats and along the major thorough-fares that ran through the neighborhood. Western SOMA had a strong sense of Filipino community identity that continues to this day.

Unlike many San Francisco tenants, Teresa Dulalas and her family faced no steep rent hikes or eviction threats through the 1980s. They had such a good relationship with their Italian-American immigrant landlord that they called him Uncle Randy. Parts of SOMA were becoming trendy, but theirs had yet to be targeted by the speculators who had begun transforming other longtime working-class neighborhoods like Noe Valley, the Castro, and Haight-Ashbury. These communities were already seen as gentrified by the end of the 1980s.

In 1991, the Dulalases were joined at the three-unit building by Ricardo Samaniego. Samaniego's brother, Carlos, had moved into the unit a year earlier (their mother, Maria, would join them in 2001). Samaniego was a tow truck operator, a busy profession in San Francisco. The Samaniegos, like the Dulalases, were working-class families with multiple generations living in the same flat. Having multiple generations under one roof is quite common in San Francisco's immigrant communities. It helps explain why so many immi-grant tenants never move once they find a family home, and why their poten-tial displacement is so wrenching.

No Heat, No Water

In 2001, after the death of the longtime owner, a speculator couple named Hung and Judy Cheng bought the Dulalases' Folsom Street home. The ten-ants' problems soon began.

The Chengs owned six buildings in the city. Hung Cheng was a licensed contractor in the business of demolishing buildings and/or renovating them for resale. Cheng's practice was to buy only vacant buildings. He bought the Folsom Street building because he was in a rush, for tax reasons, but went on to treat the property as if it were vacant. The Chengs did not even bother to tell the Dulalases or the other tenants how to contact them.

From the very start, tenant complaints about lack of heat, plumbing leaks, a pigeon infestation, and other problems were ignored. In October 2001, Teresa Dulalas called the Public Utilities Commission and asked why her building suddenly had no water. She was told that the owner she knew as Uncle Randy had called to shut the water off.

"I was shocked," Dulalas remembers. "I told them Uncle Randy had died and I didn't know that someone who died could rise from the dead and call the PUC to turn off the water." The person she was talking to hung up.

Dulalas then followed a pattern she would continue for the next decade: she turned to SOMA's tight-knit Filipino community for guidance. "We didn't know about tenants' rights so we asked community people what to do." She met with the South of Market Community Action Network, known as SOMCAN. Angelica Cabande, SOMCAN's longtime leader, referred her to the Tenderloin Housing Clinic for legal representation. THC Attorney Dean Preston met with Dulalas and advised her to address the immediate crisis by opening an account in her name and paying the water bill for the entire building. It worked. This began over a decade of THC's legal representation of Dulalas and her building, first by Dean Preston and then Raquel Fox.

The lack of water reflected a larger problem of landlord neglect. The Department of Building Inspection issued housing citations for several months beginning in November 2001. They were ignored by the landlord. Living conditions got so bad that the Dulalas family thought the owners had abandoned the property. Teresa Dulalas's elderly parents particularly suffered from the lack of heat and the owners' neglect.

This was likely the landlord's goal. San Francisco has the nation's most aggressive housing code enforcement, but some landlords still try to get tenants out by making living conditions so miserable that their health forces them to move. These landlords figure that the cost of paying housing fines is far less than the huge profits gained from ousting long-term tenants paying below-market rents and re-renting their units at market rates.

But if the Chengs thought that refusing to maintain the Folsom Street building would get the tenants to move, they bought the wrong property. My office filed a lawsuit on behalf of Dulalas and her family against the Chengs for money damages and injunctive relief. On May 31, 2002, attorneys Dean Preston and Raquel Fox obtained a court order requiring the owners to provide heat and make necessary repairs. The lawsuit was eventually settled. The tenants won compensation for living in such bad housing, long-overdue repairs were made, and the Chengs' strategy to displace their tenants was left in the dust.

The Chengs sold the building to Joe Nim Chan and Alda Chan on March 12, 2004. For the tenants it was like going from the frying pan into the fire. The new owners immediately obtained the names of all the tenants in the building for what they claimed were insurance purposes. Every tenant soon received an eviction notice under the state's Ellis Act, leaving little doubt that the Chans purchased the building to convert the units into tenancies in common (TICs) and re-sell them.

Dulalas Resists Eviction

When Teresa Dulalas and her fellow tenants were served the Ellis eviction notices, she felt "I have to protect my family. We'd lived in our home for so long. Now we couldn't be certain that this would still be our home. I felt we had to rally the tenants together to fight for our family. We lived so long with the other tenants that we saw them as family too."[7]

The Ellis Act, California Government Code 7060, preempts local eviction protection laws. It requires the owner to "go out of the rental housing business," but court rulings have given owners the right to then sell the tenant's former unit as a tenancy in common. Once described as the "neutron bomb" for evictions because it removes tenants while keeping vacant buildings intact, the courts turned the Ellis Act into a powerful weapon that real estate speculators use to displace elderly and vulnerable tenants throughout California.[8]

The Dulalas family had experienced bad landlords before the Chans, "but we never expected to get an Ellis Act eviction. I had to keep telling myself, 'Protect. Protect the people you love.' I prayed so much. I know that life is never a smooth journey but did not think we could ever lose our home."

After the initial shock, Dulalas's resolve kicked in: "I was seeing the goal of victory. I didn't want to lose. You can't think of losing when you are talking about your family's life." Dulalas recalled that she and the other tenants were really worried about the eviction notices until attorney Dean Preston "told us tenants had rights. Once we learned that we could beat this in court it strengthened our resolve. I felt that with Dean, Raquel, and the community behind us we would win."

When the Ellis eviction notices were issued, the building housed over twenty people, including seniors and young children. Teresa Dulalas's father, Uldarico Barclay, had retired from his state job in 1999. He and his wife,

Lolita, lived with their children and Dulalas's children in the affordable, rent-controlled flat. Owner Alda Chan suggested to Dulalas that she "could always move her parents to an assisted living home." This outraged Dulalas. She recalled telling Chan, "We Filipinos are not like that. That's against our community values."

Amparo and Romulo Garcia, both seventy-two years old, lived with their son Hector in another apartment in the building. Hector worked for a local landscaper and his parents were retired. The third apartment housed the Mexican immigrant family of Maria Samaniego, age sixty-two, her son Ricardo, and other family members. Three working-class families now faced losing their longtime homes. None could afford to relocate in the city at the current market rents. Their potential displacement symbolized how blocks, neighborhoods, and ultimately cities change.

The Folsom Street tenants were also getting community support. Ellis Act evictions were becoming all too common in SOMA, and groups like the San Francisco Tenants Union were building grassroots opposition to them. This led to a May 4, 2004, rally at the Folsom Street building organized by tenant activists on behalf of Dulalas and the other tenants. At the rally Teresa Dulalas thanked fellow tenants and activists for supporting her effort to save her home and for calling attention to the harmful effects of Ellis Act evictions: "I moved here with my parents and brother when we were very little. Now I'm married and have three young children and I still live here. We don't want to move."[9]

In August 2005, THC attorneys Dean Preston and Raquel Fox got the Ellis eviction notices thrown out by the court due to a technical defect. Because Dulalas's parents were seniors (her father was seventy and her mother sixty-seven), the owners would have to issue another one-year Ellis notice. In December 2005, the Ellis notices for the other tenants on the property were thrown out for the same defect. This required the issuance of new one-year Ellis notices as well.

With huge potential profits looming if they could vacate the Folsom Street property, the Chans quickly issued new Ellis notices. A year later new eviction lawsuits were filed against Dulalas and her parents, Ricardo Samaniego and his family, and the Garcias. On September 21, 2007, THC attorneys Raquel Fox and Steve Collier again got the court to throw out the eviction notices on procedural grounds. The tenants' skilled legal representation had stopped the evictions once again. The Chans issued a third round of Ellis notices but then changed course and resumed accepting the tenants' rent.

After almost six years of nonstop battles with their landlords, Teresa Dulalas and her fellow tenants were safe from eviction. But these battles take their toll. Dulalas had tried to shield her children from the potential loss of their home but eventually had to tell them. She recalled, "My kids are very strong. They were connected to the community and did not want to move. They were worried over being uprooted. I kept telling them that 'Moving was not an option.' My parents were constantly anxious. I kept assuring them that we would not be moving anywhere." Dulalas's confident attitude masked her own inner fears. She told me, "I cried in my bedroom at night because I didn't want others to see that I was worried."

Many tenants find the stress of these conflicts too much to take and prefer to move rather than continue fighting eviction. The tight-knit family networks at the Folsom Street building helped the tenants cope with the emotional turmoil of their housing situation. Some landlords try to evict time and time again just to wear out vulnerable tenants. Tenants with health problems are often targeted because speculators see them as particularly vulnerable. Jeremy Mykaels had full-blown AIDS when he got an Ellis eviction notice to vacate the home he had lived in for nineteen years. He described the stress it caused: "It's a pretty high level of anxiety not knowing what's going on with your future and at the same time dealing with . . . [your] own health. . . . The citizens of San Francisco need to realize what's going on."[10]

Teresa Dulalas and her fellow tenants would find their break from eviction threats short-lived. In January 2012, Sergio Iantorno, doing business as Golden Properties, bought the Folsom Street building. He quickly sought to triple the rent. The tenants successfully challenged the rent increase, so on November 26, 2012, Iantorno sent the tenants a letter offering to pay them to move. They rejected the buyout. Two months later, the owner again made a buyout offer. The tenants rejected that as well.

His prior attempt at tripling rents having failed, in mid-summer 2013 Iantorno sought a San Francisco Rent Board determination allowing the tenants' rents to be significantly raised. Once again, Dulalas and her fellow tenants fought back. After they provided the full rental history of their tenancies, Iantorno dropped the rent board petition.

Unsuccessful at getting the tenants out by other means, on December 30, 2013, Iantorno did what many other owners have done when tenants resist moving: he issued Ellis Act eviction notices for the building. This was the fourth set of Ellis notices the building's tenants had received since 2005.

Dulalas had been almost constantly fighting off landlord efforts to get her out of her home since the heat and water were cut off to her unit in 2001.

By 2015, Teresa Dulalas deserved a break from battling her landlord. She was fifty-five years old. She had a heart condition and had survived a cancer scare that required surgery. Her three children had all been raised at 1357 Folsom. Her father still lived there. He was now an eighty-two-year-old widower with prostate cancer and was undergoing chemotherapy. They were joined by Teresa's mentally disabled brother, Joseph Barclay; her brother Luciano Barclay, a low-income worker; her daughter Daynelita Dulalas, a full-time college student; her daughter Marti Dulalas, who would be studying in Japan for the next two years; and Teresa's eighty-seven-year-old aunt Felisa Barclay, who moved into the home in 2002–2003 and regularly spent time in the Philippines.

In 2015, the Dulalas family paid monthly rent of $560.45 for 1357 Folsom Street, a large four-bedroom flat. Ricardo Samaniego and his family had moved into 1353 Folsom in 1991, and their rent in 2015 was $910.00. Similar four-bedroom flats on the open market were renting for $5,000 to $7,000 per month. The rents in Dulalas's building seem remarkably low in San Francisco's current market, but they reflect the success of rent-control and just-cause eviction laws expressly designed to keep long-term tenants in their homes. All of the owners of the Folsom Street building paid a relatively low price for it because the tenants paid below-market rents, yet each sought to reap huge profits by getting the tenants out.

Speculators in San Francisco seize on opportunities to buy buildings at a bargain due to below-market-rent tenants on the premises. After purchase, speculators either move to get the tenants out so they can re-rent the units, or they use the Ellis Act to vacate the building and then sell the units to buyers as TICs. Speculators tried both approaches with Teresa Dulalas and her fellow tenants. The huge gap between what the Folsom tenants paid and market rents led landlord after landlord to try to get the residents of out of their homes. If they had succeeded, the profits would have been enormous.

Because nearly all of those trying to displace long-term tenants are speculators whose profits come from quickly flipping properties, time is of the essence. Some only have short-term financing that requires a quick turnover; others lack the capital to pay attorneys for lengthy litigation. When tenants like Teresa Dulalas or Ricardo Samaniego resist, many landlords start to recognize that this was not the quick route to easy profits that they anticipated. And they often rethink their strategy.[11]

That realization is what led Sergio Iantorno, the Folsom Street building's landlord, to reconsider his Ellis evictions in that building and others he owned. And fortunately, San Francisco had come up with a win-win option for owners like Iantorno who wanted to drop their Ellis Act evictions: a proactive, anti-displacement strategy called the Small Sites Acquisition Program (SSP).

The SSP funds nonprofit groups to buy properties to protect existing tenants from eviction. The program keeps middle- and working-class families in the city, enabling them to stay in their homes and in the neighborhoods where they have built a community. Housing acquired through the SSP is permanently affordable.

The SSP was launched by San Francisco Mayor Ed Lee in 2014. Over a decade earlier, I had joined with the late San Francisco Tenants Union leader Ted Gullicksen in asking then-mayor Willie Brown's administration to buy small buildings whose tenants faced eviction. But because the nonprofit housing sector was geared toward larger properties with vacant units, the mayor's housing director would not go along. Hundreds of working- and middle-class tenants who could have been saved by the SSP were instead displaced.

After Iantorno issued the eviction notices for Folsom Street in 2014, Teresa Dulalas was at a SOMCAN event where she reached out to the director of the San Francisco Community Land Trust (SFCLT), Tracy Parent, asking her to buy her building: "I told her that we are facing eviction again. Please see if you can help us."

The SFCLT purchase of Dulalas's building was announced in February 2016. It was one of five Iantorno properties acquired through the SSP. When Dulalas got the news that the sale was happening, she told me she "broke down and thanked God and everybody. I felt God had sent Dean Preston and Raquel Fox as angels to protect us. I knew we could not give up when we loved the city and the neighborhood and our family. I had the most wonderful team and I trusted everybody." Dulalas could not be happier with the building since SFCLT's purchase. SFCLT got a grant to make upgrades and Dulalas describes the once unmaintained property as "beautiful. It is way better than when we first moved in back in 1979."

Dulalas's long struggle to stay in her home had a wonderfully happy ending. But many tenants are not so fortunate. Their stories go to the heart of the human cost of San Francisco's affordability crisis.

DISPLACING THE ELDERLY

Lola McKay

Lola McKay was the first tenant whose eviction drew major media attention in the dot-com era. McKay lived in her Noe Valley apartment for forty years prior to real estate speculator John Hickey issuing an Ellis eviction notice for the building. The other tenants moved, but the feisty McKay told the landlord "Hell no!" She became the first San Francisco tenant whose Ellis eviction made national television, and local media were all over the story.[12]

McKay and her original longtime landlord were friends. She never bothered asking for repairs but simply made them herself. McKay painted and carpeted her unit and installed a new stove, refrigerator, bathtub, and toilet. She planned on living the rest of her life at 57 Alvarado Street, but after her landlord died, Hickey bought the property. Hickey issued eviction notices in January 1999, eager to sell the building's four units individually as tenancies in common. He could have sold the three vacant units and allowed McKay's case to languish, but that's not the mentality of those evicting seniors for profit.

Hickey had lost his real estate broker's license for unethical dealings and was evicting McKay while under indictment for mail and securities fraud. He would soon go to prison for elder abuse. In September 1999, McKay agreed to a settlement whereby she would move a year later. But before she could be displaced she died, in March 2000, still in her longtime home. "She always said she didn't want to leave unless it was in a casket, and I guess she got her wish," said her attorney, Raquel Fox. "She was a strong-willed old lady."[13]

At the time of McKay's eviction, the Ellis Act required only that seniors get sixty days' notice for eviction. McKay's story inspired state senator John Burton to get the law changed to require one-year notices for senior and disabled tenants, a big advance for this vulnerable population.

Grace Wells

If anyone thought that the bad publicity generated by Lola McKay's eviction would deter other senior evictions, the displacement of eighty-five-year-old Grace Wells proved otherwise. Wells had lived in the Western Addition since 1942, and in her apartment at 908 Page since 1989. She survived the San Francisco Redevelopment Agency's mass displacement of the Fillmore

District's African American residents in the 1960s and 1970s but could not overcome a new landlord's strategy to displace her. June Croucher bought the building in 2000 and in her 2002 eviction notice claimed she needed to evict Wells in order to combine the building's two units into a mansion for her own use. The unit above Wells was vacant and Croucher could have lived there, but she insisted she needed both units.

Since city law protected elderly tenants like Wells from owner move-in evictions and further requires that owners seeking such evictions choose a vacant unit if available, as one was in this case, Croucher faced a challenge in displacing Wells. So Croucher did what San Francisco landlords do when the city has taken away the local strategies to implement an immoral eviction: she issued an Ellis eviction notice to Wells.

Like many senior tenants targeted for eviction, Grace suffered from health problems. She had arthritis, diabetes, and a heart condition. Grace was skeptical about Croucher's intentions from the start. "They want to make the house into one big building and the lady said she's going to stay here and build a family. But you need a baby to start a family."[14]

The media fell in love with Grace, whose potential eviction angered them. In a November 2002 interview with *POOR Magazine* she stated, "I've lived in this area for a long time. I came to San Francisco in 1942 and have always lived in this area. Now they are expecting me to move and with the cost of rent it will be hard on me, not on them." Grace wore a neck brace at the time and her hands trembled. "Do you see my hands? My hands are all crippled. It's challenging. I'm trying to live nice and comfortable, but I have terrible arthritis and of course I can't leave here."

As with the attempted eviction of Teresa Dulalas and many others, tenant activists and senior groups rallied to support Grace Wells. Grace had no family, so this support meant a lot. "I appreciate them trying to help me because it is so hard. It is hard trying to pack when you're old with arthritis." Tenderloin Housing Clinic attorney Dean Preston, who represented Wells, told the crowd that Croucher had "made life hell" for his client: "Croucher has served Grace two eviction notices and decreased Grace's services in her home—including cutting off her heat this winter."

Ted Gullicksen of the San Francisco Tenants Union, which organized a rally in support of Wells, noted the broader implications of her eviction. "We're here to say, 'You don't have the right to take away someone else's home because you have lots of money and the tenant doesn't.' We'll be back and we'll keep coming back until we stop this eviction." Reflecting the changing neighborhood that now priced out working- and middle-class residents, Gullicksen stated, "This neighborhood has been gentrified to an extraordinary degree in recent times. On a small block around the corner on Scott Street, 75–95% of the tenants have been displaced by owner-move-in and Ellis evictions over the past year and a half."[15]

Speaking for many in the media, a reporter interviewing Wells observed, "I left the apartment in a daze, wondering how a woman of such genuine personal appeal could be so obviously discarded. I had to ask myself, what in the world could Mrs. and Mr. Croucher be thinking in demanding the eviction of Grace Wells?"[16]

In April 2003, Grace Wells reached a settlement requiring her to vacate her apartment by March 2004 in exchange for undisclosed financial compensation. Plans to take Wells's case to jury trial were subverted by one of the city's many pro-landlord judges, who took away Wells's key legal defenses in pre-trial motions. Attorney Preston called the settlement a "great success" for Wells given the circumstances.

GAY DISPLACEMENT IN THE CASTRO

Gregory Gill

Among the most troubling features of San Francisco's housing crisis is its pricing out of the working and middle class from the historic gay neighborhood of the Castro. The city's LGBTQ movement was launched in the Tenderloin in the 1950s and 1960s; by the late 1970s the Castro had become the city's gay male mecca. Harvey Milk opened his camera shop on Castro Street and the area became identified with gay bars, bathhouses, and an openly gay lifestyle. Two of the gay men drawn to the affordable district in the 1970s were Gregory Gill and Jeremy Mykaels. Both would be displaced under the state's Ellis Act.

Gregory Gill lived in his one-bedroom Castro apartment for twenty-one years before receiving an Ellis Act eviction notice in 1998. Gill had AIDS, but this did not protect him from eviction. A gay African American from a conservative part of Indiana, Gill had grown up "20 miles from the grand dragon of the Ku Klux Klan" and was the only black and the only gay person in his high school. He said, "When I moved [to San Francisco] it was like I'd finally made it to Oz."[17]

Because he moved into the unit before Castro rents skyrocketed and was protected by rent control, Gill paid only $516 in monthly rent. His landlord called the rent "dismally low" and Gill suspected that his low rent was the chief reason the landlord wanted him out.

Steve Collier of THC represented Gill. Diagnosed with AIDS and living on a disability check of only $600 a month, Gill feared his eviction meant either homelessness or a return to Indiana. Collier negotiated a financial settlement for Gill, who ultimately left his longtime home for Palm Springs.

Jeremy Mykaels

Jeremy Mykaels also moved to the Castro in the 1970s. He moved to his apartment in a three-unit building at 460 Noe Street in 1995. Unable to fulfill his dream of becoming a rock star, Mykaels worked in the tech field until he was diagnosed with full-blown AIDS in 2001 and went on permanent disability. When Mykaels's building was sold to three real estate speculators from Union City in 2012, his health problems were soon joined by the threat of an Ellis Act eviction.[18]

Mykaels fit the profile for other vulnerable San Francisco tenants: he was a long-term tenant over sixty years of age paying below-market rent in a small building whose units could be sold off as tenancies in common and potentially converted to condominiums. When the attorney for the new owners offered to buy out Mykaels's tenancy as an alternative to evicting him under the Ellis Act, Mykaels instead chose to fight. To get his story out, he started the website EllisHurtsSeniors.org and posted signs in his windows reading, "Boycott this property. Do not buy properties where seniors or disabled tenants have been evicted for profit by uncaring real estate speculators using and abusing the Ellis Act."

Working with Tommi Avicolli Mecca at Housing Rights Committee of SF and the San Francisco Tenants Union, Mykaels joined a Christmas 2012 rally at Market and Castro for people going through evictions. For Mykaels it "was the first time I publically came out and said anything." In the summer of 2013 the direct action group Eviction Free Summer (now Eviction Free San Francisco) went to the houses of Mykaels's landlords and demanded they drop the eviction. This was followed by a big rally at Mykaels's home in October. Even elected officials not typically aligned with tenants were outraged by Mykaels's eviction, which had come to symbolize public concern over the displacement of longtime gay residents from the Castro. This was a neighborhood that was once a refuge for gays; now speculators sought to profit by evicting a long-established Castro tenant with AIDS.

Mykaels expected he would have to vacate his home by September 10, 2013, but Steve Collier, who also represented Gregory Gill, got the case thrown out due to procedural defects. By this time Mykaels had spoken out at a San Francisco Board of Supervisors meeting on legislation to increase compensation for Ellis Act evictees, and had become a regular focus of media stories. He even sang a new version of the song "San Francisco" at one of the rallies: "San Francisco, please don't abandon me / you've always been fair, you see / and I've paid my dues / San Francisco, now that I'm turning gray / please don't take my home away, too."[19]

But the stress of battling to save one's home takes a toll. Mykaels wrote in 2014:

> There's a level of anxiety. Part of me is saying, "Are they going to try some other way to get me out?" If they re-Ellis me I'll have a whole other year here, or are they trying to find some other maneuver to get me out? It's a pretty high level of anxiety not knowing what's going on with your future and at the same time dealing with . . . [your] own health. . . . Still, I have to fight this, to preserve what has been my home for so long and to serve as a rallying call for others going through similar struggles.[20]

As occurred with Teresa Dulalas's South of Market building, Mykaels's resistance led the speculators seeking to evict him to finally sell the property. When the new owner offered a buyout as an alternative to issuing a new owner move-in eviction, Mykaels realized that after two years of fighting for his home, it was best for his health to move. His confidential buyout did not enable him to stay in the now extremely expensive Castro neighborhood. On May 14, 2014, Mykaels left his city of four decades and moved south to Desert Hot Springs.[21]

NORTH BEACH EVICTIONS

Longtime tenants living in the once bohemian stronghold of North Beach have been particular targets of Ellis Act evictions. One of the earliest cases involved a six-unit building at 121 Varennes. Jean Dierkes-Carlisle, a painter and photographer, was sixty-six years old and had lived in her apartment for sixteen years when she and her fellow tenants got Ellis eviction notices. Her rent was $437 a month, far less than the market rate. Her fellow tenants Roger Strobel, Ronald Sauer, and Margery Perturis also had roots in the area's artist community. Their eviction notices led renowned North Beach poet and painter Lawrence Ferlinghetti, City Lights bookstore co-owner Nancy Peters, and other artists from around the city to hold a benefit for the tenants on January 10, 1999. It was then learned that ninety-year-old Peter Macchiarini, a Modernist sculptor and jeweler whose creations were worn throughout the world, was also being evicted from his longtime North Beach home.

North Beach quickly became ground zero for Ellis Act evictions. Its preponderance of buildings with six or fewer units and its many long-term tenants paying below-market rents made the neighborhood ripe for speculator evictions. Starting in 2002, a speculator team of W. B. Coyle and Gary Rossi operating under different corporate names invoked the Ellis Act to evict all tenants from 1815 Stockton, 1427 Grant, 768 Green, 333 Greenwich, and 424 Francisco. These buildings contained dozens of rent-controlled housing units, now lost forever thanks to Rossi, Coyle, and the people who bought TICs from them.

The Ellis Act was supposedly passed to allow landlords to go out of the rental housing business. Its sponsor said the law could only be used to create a vacant building. Instead, courts allow buyers to purchase a property and "go out of the rental business" on their first day of ownership. They can then sell off the rental units as TICs. San Francisco enacted laws in the late 1990s under Mayor Willie Brown to restrict the conversion of rental housing to TICs, but the local court threw them out. Such laws were said to "impermissibly interfere" with owners' rights under the Ellis Act.

VICTORY AT JASPER PLACE

North Beach has had some notable victories in Ellis cases. In 2008, eight long-term Chinese American tenants living in six units at 152–162 Jasper Place received Ellis notices. The tenants ranged from sixty-nine to eighty-nine years of age. One was a World War II veteran. Another, Wing Hoo Leung, would later become the longtime president of the Community Tenants' Association, a powerful Chinatown-based group that is the largest tenant membership organization in San Francisco. One tenant moved out right after getting the eviction notice. Another responded by committing suicide. His mother still lives there, but has lost forty pounds since her son's death.

Wing Hoo Leung immigrated to the United States from China in 1992. A retired clothing salesman, he had lived at Jasper Place with his wife for fifteen years. Leung told a colleague of mine in 2009 (with organizer Tammy Hung translating), "My life was very peaceful and happy before 2008," which was when the landlord who had bought the property a year earlier served him with the Ellis notice. "After that, all of us felt hopeless and helpless. I lost all my appetite—I could not eat or sleep. With my SSI income at $800 a month, I could not afford anywhere else to live. Even an SRO unit in Chinatown would cost about $700 a month."[22]

As vice president of the tenants' association, Leung attended rallies on behalf of tenants facing eviction. But this did not prepare him for the stress of dealing with his own potential displacement. When Daniel Chu, who was born in the building and lived there for forty-two years, hung himself after the Ellis notice arrived (he had also just lost his job), Leung was the first tenant who arrived at the scene when Chu's mother called for help. "Words cannot describe how I felt. We are all sad at the death of her son," Leung said.

The building's owner soon learned it was a mistake to try to evict members of an activist tenant and neighborhood organization. Jasper Place tenants and their supporters fought back hard. They picketed in front of their owner's Shabu House restaurant in the Richmond District. The Jasper Place block was shut down for a public rally on the tenants' behalf. Local and state politicians joined over a hundred seniors and their supporters at the festive event. I recall feeling that the landlords had no idea what they had gotten themselves into when they issued an Ellis notice to Wing Hoo Leung.

A turning point came when Steve Collier, my Tenderloin Housing Clinic colleague who was representing the tenants, discovered that the owners had secured financing for the property using less than accurate information. When he confronted them with the facts, they decided it was better to withdraw their Ellis eviction notices than get into trouble with their lender. As a result, in April 2010 the evictions were dropped.

This not only proved an inspiring victory for Chinatown and North Beach tenants, but for all of the renters from across the city who had rallied and protested on the Jasper tenants' behalf. The case propelled Wing Hoo Leung to not only join CTA but to serve as its president from 2011 on.

The attempted evictions at Jasper Place spawned legislation deterring Ellis evictions in North Beach. The neighborhood notoriously lacked street parking, and parking garages rented for hundreds of dollars per month. Since potential TIC buyers wanted parking with their units, district supervisor

David Chiu sought to discourage this market by restricting the building of new garages in North Beach buildings that had experienced Ellis evictions. Without parking, the TIC market in North Beach slowed, reducing Ellis evictions. The law banning new parking garages has helped slow the displacement of working- and middle-class tenants from North Beach ever since.

San Francisco has so many seniors and longtime tenants who have been evicted under the Ellis Act because city laws prevent their eviction on other grounds. The city now does an outstanding job preventing no-fault tenant evictions, but for many years this was not the case.

SAVING ARTIST LIVE-WORK LOFTS IN MID-MARKET

When Xi'an Chandra Redack moved into 1049 Market Street in 2004, it was the first time since coming to San Francisco in 1982 that she could afford to live alone. This was important to Redack because she was a musician who could now fully concentrate on the creative process of composing music on the guitar. She told me that "it wasn't until I moved here that I could do serious work." Redack, who is African American, became part of a three-woman music group called Mocha Blue, combining her music with a full-time paying job for the well-known Rainbow Grocery Cooperative, a health food market.[23]

Redack's building at 1049 Market Street is an eighty-six-unit, six-story structure in the heart of San Francisco's Mid-Market neighborhood (which became Twitter's headquarters in 2012). A mixed neighborhood, it is home to transit, farmer's markets, street artists, theaters, restaurants, large and small businesses, and political demonstrations; 1049 Market has been a longtime home for those working in the arts.

Redack's unit was typical, featuring a loft bed, a sink, and shared bathrooms down the hall. The top floor of the building had long been permitted for live-work lofts, while Redack's third-floor space and the rest of the building housed artists without the owner having obtained city housing permits.

Redack loved the Mid-Market area. She had lived in upscale Noe Valley, Alamo Square, and other parts of the city and preferred Mid-Market over all of them. So when she came home one day in the fall of 2013 to find an eviction notice, she immediately began the fight to stay in her home. She and fellow tenant Benjamin Cady went to the Housing Rights Committee of

San Francisco and were advised by staffer Tommi Avicolli Mecca to go to the Tenderloin Housing Clinic for legal representation.

The landlord had issued eviction notices to thirty-nine units on the first five floors. City officials, tenants, and Avicolli Mecca attended a meeting with THC attorney Steve Collier in the group's Hyde Street office; thus began the five-year struggle by 1049 Market tenants to stay in their homes.

Landlords often allow artists to live in spaces that do not meet conventional housing or building codes, evicting them when higher-paying tenants become available. But the tenants at 1049 Market wanted to fight to stay in their homes. Their struggle is a case study in how cities can preserve affordable artist live-work units rather than close them down.

As tenants in San Francisco, Redack and the other residents were protected by the city's rent-control and just-cause eviction laws. The latter required the owner to have a legal "just cause" to evict them. The cause given in the fall 2013 notices was to demolish and permanently remove the units from housing use. While many tenants vacated their units pursuant to these notices, others remained. In a building filled with dancers, clothing designers, photographers, and other types of artists, most faced a chilling reality: if they got evicted they would likely be priced out of San Francisco entirely.

The tenants also had political support. Mayor Ed Lee made it clear to his staff that he wanted them to work with city agencies to ensure that there were no building, planning, or housing code issues that would prevent the 1049 Market tenants from staying in their homes. The Housing Rights Committee continued to support the tenants by holding meetings, speaking on the tenants' behalf at city hall, directing media inquiries, and connecting the tenants' struggle to activist events.

But the biggest help the city gave the 1049 Market tenants was funding their free representation. San Francisco contracts with the Tenderloin Housing Clinic to represent tenants facing no-fault evictions. THC Attorney Steve Collier represented the 1049 Market tenants from 2013 through 2018 at no cost to them. His vigorous representation kept both administrative and legal proceedings going for years. After Collier got the 2013 eviction notices seeking removal of the units from housing use thrown out by the court in early 2016, the landlord followed the strategy used against Teresa Dulalas and other San Francisco tenants: he issued eviction notices under the state Ellis Act, which were filed in February 2016 against the twenty-three remaining tenants.

The Ellis evictions were heavily litigated. By the time the case was sent to trial in March 2018, the owner faced a four-week jury trial that he was in no way assured of winning. The trial judge helped the parties reach a settlement: all of the tenants would move to the second floor, which would then be purchased by the Tenderloin Housing Clinic (with city funds) as an affordable live-work condo for artists.

It was a remarkable victory that should be a model for other cities' efforts to preserve artist live-work housing. For Xi'an Chandra Redack, it justified all of the meetings, press interviews, depositions, and stress that accompanied the prospect of losing her longtime home. The outcome at 1049 Market again shows that urban America can preserve living spaces for artists; doing so is a question of political will.

INCENTIVIZING EVICTIONS

In the 1980s San Francisco actually created incentives for tenant displacement. Consider my experience representing Richard Rouleau, which started in 1986. Rouleau lived in an apartment at 250 Taylor Street across from Glide Memorial Church. If you had been brought blindfolded into Richard's apartment you would have thought you were in Pacific Heights. It was right out of an upscale design magazine. Richard had remodeled the unit at his own expense and selected the hippest of furniture. A self-described "gay boy," Richard attended design school to fulfill his dream of becoming an interior decorator.

Richard and his fellow tenants contacted me because their landlord, notorious slumlord Robert Imhoff of Landmark Realty, had issued eviction notices for the entire building. The rent law at the time allowed owners to permanently displace tenants in order to undertake the "substantial rehabilitation" of their building. The problem was that Mayor Feinstein's landlord-controlled rent board allowed landlords to meet the "substantial rehabilitation" threshold with mere cosmetic improvements. After letting 250 Taylor Street fall into decline, Imhoff planned to use this loophole to evict all the tenants and exempt the building from rent control.

Rouleau's building was filled with single mothers, immigrant families, retired seniors, and the type of working people that in the 1980s San Francisco housing market were at risk. Rouleau's beautiful apartment did not need any renovations, and Imhoff later testified at a trial that the building's problems were merely "maintenance items."

The tenants battled to stay in their homes with protests, public hearings, a jury trial, and multiple lawsuits. My clients ended up well compensated. All won the right to return to 250 Taylor Street at their old rents and with life-time leases once the renovation was complete. But we could not stop city law from exempting the building from rent control.

Richard Rouleau was one of only two tenants who declined a buyout of their right to return. The other, Anthony Florio, was an immigrant banquet waiter who had battled for freedom in his native Yugoslavia. Florio returned to 250 Taylor after waiting more than five years for Imhoff to complete the renovation; his rent was less than 25 percent that being charged new tenants. Sadly, Richard Rouleau did not make it to the building's long-delayed reopening; he was among the thousands in the San Francisco of the 1980s who died of AIDS.[24]

USING PASS-THROUGHS TO CIRCUMVENT RENT CONTROL

The 1980s also saw many working- and middle-class tenants forced out due to huge "capital improvement" pass-throughs. Owners bought a rundown building at a bargain price, fixed it up, and then were allowed to "pass through" the costs of these upgrades to tenants.

It was a speculator's dream. They got an upgraded building and got rid of long-term tenants unable to pay rent hikes that often exceeded $100 per month.

I worked out deals for tenants in dozens of buildings in the 1980s so that high capital improvement pass-throughs did not displace them. I also began challenging building permits at the San Francisco Board of Permit Appeals (now Board of Appeals). This forced a public hearing in which we would ask the board to either deny the permit, condition approval on no evictions, and/ or condition approval of the permits on not allowing tenant pass-throughs.

But many tenants moved upon getting the capital improvements notice, which under the law was served on tenants before the rent board even approved the amount. Tenants wanted to avoid the risk of getting an eviction on their record should they wait until the pass-through amount was due.

Capital improvement pass-throughs caused the most harm in the Haight-Ashbury, Noe Valley, the Castro, and other neighborhoods where Victorian flats were transformed into upscale housing. That's because the renovation costs were divided among only a handful of units, rather than the fifty-plus units in large-building areas like the Tenderloin. This sent rents into the stratosphere.

2

A Hollywood Ending for Los Angeles Housing Woes?

In the HBO series *Insecure,* co-creator and star Issa Rae (author of the best-selling *Misadventures of Awkward Black Girl*) plays a character also named Issa Rae. The fictional Rae spends the first two seasons living in a spacious one-bedroom apartment in Inglewood, just outside Los Angeles. She is a UCLA graduate working for a nonprofit tutoring program for middle-school students of color. Rae lives in a two-story apartment building named "The Dunes," which has balconies, a courtyard, flowering plants, and a swimming pool.

During season two, Rae's building changes ownership. The new owners begin making upgrades, and Rae comes home one night to a notice from her landlord raising her rent to $1,200. When she tells a friend that she "wants to live by herself," the friend laughs: "You ain't got no money. You can't live anywhere but way the fuck out. I'm talking Lancaster [a suburb forty-five miles from Los Angeles] and West Covina." In the background a song plays with the lyrics, "She wants to move to the city but not the side that's gentrified."

In the season finale, Rae takes a long last look around her apartment before leaving. She tells her former boyfriend that "it's gonna make some young white couple really happy one day." Rae's displacement occurs as Inglewood is undergoing a rebranding. Rae's friends note that a Popeye's Chicken is now a Pinkberry Frozen Yogurt, part of traditionally African-American Inglewood's transformation into a hip "ITown."

Rae's series is fictional, but the housing crisis her character confronts is all too real for many Los Angeles residents. Consider Areli Hernandez, who grew up in the Canoga Park neighborhood of Los Angeles. She graduated from Cal State Northridge in 2007 and since 2011 has been an executive assistant at a nationally known nonprofit based near downtown, close to MacArthur Park. Hernandez lives with her parents in the San Fernando Valley neighborhood of Tarzana, an hour's drive from her job. She would like to live in an apartment on her own but cannot afford it. "I'm at the mid- to upper-end of the salary range for executive assistants, and there is nothing affordable any closer to my job. I can't imagine how people who have families or entry-level jobs find any place to live they can afford."[1]

The organization Hernandez works for has over fifty employees. Only two live near the MacArthur Park neighborhood. The rest of her co-workers live "in places like Whittier near Orange County, Pasadena, or Long Beach. One worker lives in Lancaster. She crashes on a couch during the week and goes home on weekends. I found a place in North Hollywood for $1,600 but it required last month's rent and security deposit. I didn't have the $4,800 move-in costs. I could afford a backyard unit or converted garage, and there are single rooms that can be rented for $1,600 that are part of multiple units [created when landlords divide flats into separate rentals]. I have a much better situation living with my parents."

Hernandez's parents bought a house in the San Fernando Valley city of Reseda in Los Angeles County in 2005. When the housing bubble burst in 2008, half the homes on their block were foreclosed. Theirs was among them. They were fortunate to get a very good deal on a three-bedroom condo in Tarzana for $1,500 a month; two-bedroom units in the complex now rent for $1,700 and up.

Hernandez noticed in recent years "there was a lot of bulky furniture on the street in Tarzana. I then started noticing this in other LA neighborhoods. I talked to one man and he said he was moving to a smaller place and his couch would not fit. People have to downgrade their living situations and when furniture cannot fit into their new place they leave it on the street and call 311 for the city to pick it up."

This is what Los Angeles has become: a city where college graduates with jobs that pay well cannot afford an apartment anywhere near those jobs. Areli Hernandez is committed to spending her life in Los Angeles but recognizes that she will never be able to afford her own place without combining resources with others. And as she recognizes, those earning lower salaries have fewer housing options. Los Angeles is a city where the working and middle class seeking quality housing has been steadily priced out.

As Areli Hernandez observed, many of those priced out of regular apartments in Los Angeles end up living in converted garages. Mary Paz Ruiz is among them. Mary moved to Los Angeles in 2002 and used to live in a house with a backyard and two bedrooms. But in 2011 the owner raised the rent from $950 to $1,500. This forced her to move. Ruiz now lives with her husband and daughter in a converted garage in Pacoima in the San Fernando Valley. The family pays $1,100 a month for a space that includes a combined kitchen/living/dining room, a bedroom, and a bathroom. The garage houses two other families with separate entrances to their spaces.

Ruiz is a housekeeper whose work takes her to homes throughout Los Angeles, Hollywood, and Beverly Hills. The latter requires a 1.5-hour car commute each way. Her husband works full-time pruning and trimming trees. Yet their combined income does not enable them to afford a regular apartment.

Maru Galvan lives in a nice three-bedroom apartment in Van Nuys but must rent out a bedroom to help pay the rent. Galvan is a community organizer whose husband has a carpentry business specializing in kitchen renovations for well-to-do homeowners. They are among the fortunate tenants who moved into their apartment before rents skyrocketed. Because of that, in 2017 they were paying $1,400 for their three-bedroom unit, while two-bedroom units were going for $1,500. "I have a lot of friends who rent out rooms in their apartments to get by. There are a lot of ads for renting a bedroom for $700 to $800 per month. Many immigrants can only afford to rent a converted living room, which goes for $300 to $400."[2]

While group households have long been common in the rental market, the renting of living rooms as bedrooms—where the tenant has no door and no privacy—was not widespread in Los Angeles until the current crisis. Working people living in living rooms and garages is what happens when a city fails to build anywhere near enough housing to meet job and population growth.

Like many priced out from living anywhere near their workplace, Galvan has a daily one-hour driving commute to work. She has tried to find housing closer to her job but, like Areli Hernandez, could not come up with the required move-in costs. An apartment she liked and could afford required a $4,000 up-front payment; few working people can advance that amount.

The experiences of Areli Hernandez, Mary Ruiz, Maru Galvan, and others whose stories are told below reflect the human cost of Los Angeles's housing crisis. This crisis seemed to emerge suddenly, but it followed decades of misguided housing policies for which the city's working and middle class is now paying the price.

A CHANGING LA

I grew up in Los Angeles's Westside in the 1960s and 1970s. In those days, many residents only went downtown for Dodger games, the theater, or special events. High-rise buildings were rare. The Westside's only towers were in Century City, a new development that garnered national publicity as the site of a mass protest in 1967 against the Vietnam war and President Lyndon Johnson. The *Los Angeles Times* headline, "10,000 in Melee," described the Los Angeles Police Department's violent attacks on protesters. The event was later described as "irrevocably changing the city and its politics."[3]

What has most changed in Los Angeles are its population and demographics. In 1970, the city had 2.8 million residents; by 2017, that had risen to over 4 million. Latinos became a demographic majority in 1991, and immigration drove population growth. Long described as "seventy-two suburbs in search of a city," Los Angeles now has a downtown filled with office buildings and residential towers. Downtown has finally become the business and cultural hub that the city's elite long sought; the area also serves as the most visual reminder of the city's acute homeless crisis.

Los Angeles has also been transformed into a high-housing-cost city.

Los Angeles always had upscale neighborhoods, but even these usually included affordable apartments for middle-class families. In the 1980s, when rising home prices on the city's Westside began pricing out the middle class, these families could still buy houses in such desirable neighborhoods as Silver Lake, Hollywood, Eagle Rock, Mar Vista, or throughout the San Fernando Valley.

Los Angeles in the 1980s did not experience the sharply rising rents and rapid gentrification felt by San Francisco and New York City. Nor did 1990s Los Angeles endure the dot-com boom that forever worsened San Francisco's affordability. Los Angeles did not have an affordability crisis like those of San Francisco and New York until the post-2009 economic resurgence; this has made the dramatic price hikes even more of a shock to residents.

Los Angeles's downtown development boom, economic growth, and increased population all occurred without the city building much housing. Nor did the city enact critical tenant and rental housing protections to ensure affordability. Together, these failures took their toll. Seemingly overnight, working- and middle-class people were priced out of long-affordable neighborhoods. Even historically working-class communities like Boyle Heights and Highland Park were targeted by speculators for upscale transformation.

By 2014, Los Angeles had become an affordability nightmare. That year, Harvard's Joint Center for Housing Studies found Los Angeles was the least affordable rental market and the second least affordable region for middle-class home buyers in the country.[4] Los Angeles housing prices rose four times faster than incomes from 2000 to 2014, and the situation was far worse for renters: from 2000 to 2010, rents increased 31 percent in real terms, while incomes rose only 1.2 percent. Los Angeles's population growth from 1980 to 2010 exceeded housing growth by a whopping 42 percent, making the situation ripe for an affordability problem: Los Angeles was neither building enough housing nor adequately protecting its existing rentals.[5]

As Los Angeles's housing crisis was exploding, the city's inaction let it get even worse. The 2017 "State of the Nation's Housing" report from Harvard's Joint Center for Housing Studies placed Los Angeles second only to Miami in the percentage of its renter households (57 percent) paying over 30 percent of their income for rent. The rental listing site Zillow found that average renters in Los Angeles's African-American and Latino neighborhoods paid a very unhealthy 60 percent of their income for housing. Paying 60 percent of your income for rent is not sustainable. It means that one missed paycheck or an unexpected medical expense can quickly put a tenant out on the street. This steep rent burden helps explain why Los Angeles's homeless population has risen in recent years.[6]

When Eric Garcetti was elected mayor in 2013, it became his job to address the city's housing crisis. He had a big challenge ahead. On January 11, 2015, the *Los Angeles Times* editorial board wrote, "L.A. has a serious housing crisis and it's time for city officials to do something about it." The *Times* stated, "Garcetti and the City Council must make housing affordability a higher priority in 2015, in tandem with raising the minimum wage. That means increasing the supply of both market-rate and subsidized units, for rent and for sale. It means making it easier to build housing, but also requiring developers to set aside units for low-income residents in exchange for permission to build bigger, taller projects. It means preserving the number of affordable apartments by adopting a 'no net loss' policy that ensures subsidized units don't disappear when buildings are demolished and replaced."[7]

The *Times* did not mention that its proposals had been long recommended by Los Angeles housing advocates. Nor did the newspaper explain or identify the political forces that prevented the policies from being implemented.

This chapter describes these political forces, which include powerful homeowner associations and landlord groups whose policies caused Los Angeles's extreme housing crisis. Los Angeles's affordability crisis was not inevitable. Homeowner associations used exclusionary zoning to create an acute housing shortage. Landlords prevented the passage of new laws that would have slowed if not stopped tenant displacement and neighborhood gentrification. Both groups saw the value of their own real estate skyrocket at the expense of everyone else.

This chapter describes how Los Angeles is trying to replace housing policies promoting exclusion with those advancing affordability. Can the Garcetti-backed broad-based pro-housing coalition overcome the powerful forces that have priced out the city's working and middle class? I begin answering this question by describing what has happened in the longtime working-class neighborhoods of Boyle Heights and Highland Park. These two neighborhoods were not on anyone's gentrification radar prior to 2009, but the former is now under siege while the latter has been rapidly transformed. Their battle against displacement and gentrification reflects the failure of past city policies and the urgent need to chart a more inclusive future.

THE FIGHT FOR BOYLE HEIGHTS

When I was growing up in Los Angeles I only knew of Boyle Heights because a family friend grew up there. He was part of the neighborhood's pre–World War II era, when Boyle Heights was a primarily Jewish community (many residents had moved there from New York City, which is why a main street is named Brooklyn Avenue). By 1930, 10,000 Jewish families lived in Boyle Heights; the mobster Mickey Cohen began his crime career there. As the neighborhood's Jews moved west, Latinos took their place. In 1949, a Latino-Jewish coalition in Boyle Heights elected Ed Roybal as the first Latino on the Los Angeles City Council. That historic victory, a result of grassroots outreach by Roybal's campaign manager, Fred Ross, became a milestone for Latino voting.[8]

In 2000, 94 percent of Boyle Heights' 100,000 residents were Latino. This increased to 95 percent in 2011. Boyle Heights' median household income in 2000 was only $33,235, making it one of the poorest neighborhoods in Los Angeles. Yet by 2014 it was being eyed for gentrification.[9]

The Next Hot Spot

Boyle Heights' proximity to downtown long protected its working-class character. White people with money did not want to live near downtown, which for decades had little housing targeted at upscale young residents. But as Los Angeles transformed its downtown into a cultural and employment hub (rebranded as DTLA), hipsters and young professionals took notice. As other Los Angeles neighborhoods became unaffordable, Boyle Heights became an attractive housing option for those priced out. It was within walking distance from the revitalized and now hipster Arts District. It also had a station on the Gold Line Metro rail in a city where public transit can be hard to find. Boyle Heights' Metro station was only three stops from the city's chief transit hub at Union Station. This meant residents who once avoided living downtown due to clogged traffic could live in Boyle Heights and ride public transit to their jobs across the city.[10]

Boyle Heights was vulnerable to gentrification not only because of its location, but also because of the primarily one-story commercial buildings surrounding Mariachi Plaza, the neighborhood's hub. If four- to eight-story rent-controlled apartment buildings circled the plaza, speculators would have a difficult time politically trying to demolish them and then build upscale housing or mixed-unit developments; Los Angeles would not allow this. But leaving the escalator at the Mariachi Plaza / Boyle Heights Metro station and walking toward Mariachi Plaza, one sees a stretch of primarily one- and two-story commercial buildings, not taller apartments.

All are local-serving businesses. On the corner, at 1812 East 1st Street, is Cerda's Upholstery, which has repaired sofas, benches, and other items since 1967. Next door is Yeya's Restaurant, at 1816 East 1st Street, known for its tacos, chilaquiles, and carne en su jugo. At 1818 East 1st Street is Un Solo Sol, a Latino American vegetarian and vegan-friendly restaurant featuring papusas. House of Trophies is next, and adjacent to that the trail of restaurants and small businesses continues.

This low-rise landscape of owner-run businesses gives Boyle Heights a small-town feel and sense of community. It is what Boyle Heights residents love about the area. But this lack of multi-story rent-controlled buildings or historic structures makes stopping future demolitions more difficult. In a city with a huge housing shortage, many see one-story commercial structures as an inefficient land use. Plans to replace them with a taller mixed housing/ retail complex will be promoted as bringing jobs, badly needed housing, and "progress" to a long-overlooked neighborhood. But as of mid-2018 Los Angeles did not require on-site affordable housing units as a condition of development, so such taller mixed-use projects offered little or no housing opportunities for the working or middle class. That's why Boyle Heights' landscape of one-story neighborhood-serving businesses increased its vulnerability to gentrification.

In November 2014 the Metro itself spread fears of an upscale transformation of Boyle Heights when it planned to build an eight-story medical office building and a three-story complex with a gym and ground floor retail/food at 1804 East 1st Street. This led the real-estate site Curbed LA to ask on January 2, 2015, "Will Boyle Heights Be L.A.'s Gentrification Hot Spot of 2015?" In addition to the proposed medical plaza, the article pointed to a new residential development planned for the site of a former Sears store in the neighborhood, the installation of a fence in front of a single-family home, and the hanging of a banner—"¡Ya Basta! Boyle Heights Says No to Gentrification"—on a building outside Mariachi Plaza, the neighborhood's central public space. The article also noted that in May 2014 a real-estate firm marketed a bike tour of Boyle Heights that would "be followed by 'artisanal treats' around this 'walkable and bikeable' neighborhood." After a furor, the tour was canceled.[11]

But strong community resistance to the Metro's medical office building plan quickly doomed the project. "We've already lost Echo Park, Silver Lake, downtown and now we're being squeezed out by prices," a Boyle Heights resident testified at a public hearing on the project. The exterior walls of J & F Ice Cream, one of the buildings that would be destroyed by Metro's plans, featured two-story murals of mariachi players; some mariachis asked the Metro if the erasure of the murals was part of a broader agenda to exclude them from the plaza.[12]

Curbed LA concluded after the Metro's plan was defeated that "Boyle Heights Is Winning Its War against Gentrification." But the Metro's ambitious plans had clearly already boosted speculator interest in the neighborhood. Real estate purchases intensified as speculators followed the familiar strategy of purchasing buildings, renovating them, and then charging much higher rents to the new more upscale tenants. Curbed LA correctly described the defeat of the Metro plan as "Boyle Heights' biggest victory yet in its impressively successful war against gentrification," but the battle had just begun. More ominous was that the median rent for apartments in Boyle Heights was rising; it went from $1,572 in 2010 to $2,242 in 2017.[13]

In August 2017, three storefronts on Mariachi Plaza were put up for sale. All had been part of the Metro's failed 2014 plan. They include J & F Ice Cream, Santa Cecilia restaurant, and the lending library Libros Schmibros. The $6.2 million sales price assumes a new construction on the site: a project whose future businesses will have to generate a lot more money to make the rent than can be earned from selling ice cream cones or managing a lending library for Latino working families.[14]

I know from my nearly forty years working in San Francisco's low-income Tenderloin neighborhood how real estate interests try to rebrand communities as the "next hot spot." The idea is to get people thinking differently about neighborhoods that have long resisted gentrification. In the Tenderloin's case, efforts to rebrand the neighborhood as "Union Square West" began in the 1980s and have continued to be revived in recent years. But they have gone nowhere because of the Tenderloin's preponderance of large apartment buildings and SRO hotels, its high percentage of nonprofit and subsidized housing, and its land use and tenant protections. In Boyle Heights, however, the long-term affordability of the neighborhood was at risk. The marketing of the community as "walkable and bikeable" understandably raised concerns that speculators saw big profits in future displacement and gentrification.

Evicting the Mariachis

Mariachi culture has long defined Boyle Heights. It explains the massive resistance to building medical offices on Mariachi Plaza, and why a proposed Mariachi 5K run was derailed by opponents of gentrification. At the beginning of 2017, mariachi musicians living in a non-rent-controlled building at 1815 East 2nd Street were given huge rent increases that would cause their eviction. Many in the community saw the potential displacement of these key cultural figures as part of the larger landlord strategy to transform the neighborhood, which it certainly was.

In January 2017, Arturo and Estela Ruvalcaba got a notice from their landlord raising the rent on their two-bedroom apartment from $1,175 to $1,825 a month, effective April 1. Because the building was constructed after

1979, California's Costa-Hawkins law prevented it from being covered by rent control. The Ruvalcabas were among several tenants handed such increases. If they took effect, all of the tenants would be priced out of their homes and have to move. Arturo Ruvalcaba, who was forty at the time, had been playing the violin professionally for twenty-four years and was a mariachi musician, as were members of four of the other families. Their apartment building was conveniently located next to the open space known as Mariachi Plaza.

Mariachi musicians have a long history in Boyle Heights. They have defined the neighborhood's culture. Ruvalcaba estimates that there are roughly 200 mariachis in the area. Following the tradition in Mexico City, where mariachi musicians gather at Plaza Garibaldi to get gigs, the Boyle Heights mariachis find work by meeting people at Mariachi Plaza. Musicians like Arturo Ruvalcaba could get jobs through the Internet or by phone, but that is not the cultural tradition. Likewise, the people who prefer to find musicians by coming to the plaza rather than going through Yelp are also part of this tradition.

"If I don't have close access to the plaza I can't get jobs," Ruvalcaba told me. "My livelihood depends on me being there. I won't be able to get work otherwise." The Ruvalcabas had had no indication that their landlord would suddenly jack up the rent. The family had lived in the building for three years; Ruvalcaba had lived there for six years before that, spending two years in Mexico and returning to Boyle Heights. He moved back to the building because it was only a block from the job opportunities offered daily at Mariachi Plaza.

"I have been feeling very stressed since getting the rent increase. I don't know what is going to happen," said Ruvalcaba. As with so many families facing displacement, the Ruvalcabas are very worried about finding new schools for their two sons in the middle of the school year. "They currently can walk to school, but that will not be the case if we have to move."

Battling to save one's home is extremely stressful. As the stories of Teresa Dulalas and other tenants showed in chapter 1, the stress alone can take its toll. For Arturo Ruvalcaba, it was not only his home that was at risk but his livelihood. He also feared that "if they succeed in driving out all of the mariachis from the Boyle Heights neighborhood, then the Plaza of Mariachis will cease to exist."

Ruvalcaba's concerns were echoed by Margarita Perea, whose husband Pedro Zuniga has been a mariachi musician for thirty-five years, playing the violin and trumpet. As of 2017 the couple had lived in Boyle Heights for twenty years. They had spent the last five with their now-teenaged daughter at 1815 East 2nd Street. In January the landlord raised their rent from $945 to $1,495 a month. The increase would force them to leave, though Perea confessed she has not even begun to think about where she would move. "It would have to be far away to get something affordable. My husband would have no way to earn a living being that far from the plaza." Perea sees Boyle Heights as changing: "There's the selling of a lot of buildings and the mariachi community is being displaced."[15]

According to Catherine Kurland, co-author of *Hotel Mariachi: Urban Space and Cultural Heritage in Los Angeles,* displacing the mariachis would be an "irreversible loss" to the neighborhood.[16] Yet the owner of Arturo's building sees dollar signs in preserving a cynical version of mariachi culture. The building from which the mariachis are being evicted is undergoing renovation and will be renamed Mariachi Crossing. If there were a Hall of Shame for gentrification's outrages, this renaming would be among the first inductees.

"I think it's particularly ironic in this case and terrible . . . [that] the company that bought this property is branding itself, choosing the mariachi name and logo, they're next to the Mariachi Plaza and they're using mariachi in their corporate marketing," said Tyler Anderson, an attorney for the Los Angeles Center for Community Law and Action who represented many of the tenants who received eviction notices due to their failure to pay the steep rent hikes. "But the actual mariachis who live and work there . . . are going to leave and lose their jobs."[17]

In a time of rapid change, Boyle Heights' mariachi culture offers a soulful connection to the past. Arturo Ruvalcaba, Pedro Zuniga, and their fellow mariachis maintain this connection. Theirs is a legacy that the landlord sought to erase.

Changing Boyle Heights

Francisco Gonzalez moved to the apartment building where Arturo Ruvalcaba and the other mariachis lived in 2005. He too got a notice from the landlord in January 2017, raising his rent from $900 to $1,500 a month, which would force him to move. I asked Gonzalez why only seven of the twenty-four units in the building received rent increases, and he said that the manager "verbally told other tenants that they would eventually get increases by the end of the year."[18]

Gonzalez was not completely surprised by the landlord's action. "A year or two ago the new owner of a building across the street evicted all of the tenants. It's been vacant ever since. Dozens of families in the neighborhood have also gotten evicted. Schools are being closed because their students are being forced to leave the neighborhood."

Gonzalez feels that as recently as five years ago, "It was easy for us if a landlord raised your rent. You could just move to another place in Boyle Heights at the same rent you were paying. Now the whole scenario has changed. Rents have gotten so expensive that for me to get a one-bedroom apartment at the $900 I currently pay I would have to move more than ten miles away. The only cheaper places are in garages or those in rundown condition."

He sees the change in the neighborhood as connected to the opening of the Mariachi Plaza Metro station in 2009. "We thought it was good for us. We didn't realize it would make it easier for upscale residents attracted to downtown to live in Boyle Heights."

Gonzalez had never been an activist until he joined other tenants in protesting the rent increases. The stakes for him are high: "When you live in a community for twelve years, you are emotionally connected. I feel safe and secure in Boyle Heights. When I walk my dog through the streets I know people by name and they know me. I know the neighbors in my building, on my block, and a lot of people within a one-mile radius. Boyle Heights is a very tight-knit community. I would lose all of this if I have to move far from the area."

Gonzalez has met some of the newcomers to his building. All are white. "They are nice people. They come from out of state and were not aware of what was going on in the building. Now they see the posters protesting evictions and say they wouldn't have moved in if they had known."

In defending the rent hikes, the owner's agent cited "new HVAC units, new fencing and gates, new on-site laundry facilities, improved trash collection, roof repairs, new exterior paint and landscaping and improved exterior lighting throughout." These are primarily the type of discretionary cosmetic improvements that San Francisco landlords used in the 1980s to hike rents and displace long-term rent-controlled tenants. Unfortunately, Gonzalez and his fellow tenants are not under rent control. Rents on their homes can be raised an unlimited amount for no reason other than landlord profits. Creating vacant units allows unlimited rent hikes even for rent-controlled housing, which helps explain why Boyle Heights' median apartment rents have risen over 40 percent in the past three years.[19]

Two affordable housing developments had opened up in Boyle Heights in recent years. Gonzalez and some of his fellow tenants applied twice for residency. The first was a fifty-unit building and Gonzalez was on a waiting list with 450 others. The second was a similar sized building, and the waiting list cut off after 400.

Francisco Gonzalez and his fellow tenants played by the rules. But they share the view that more aggressive action is needed to save the historic working class character of Boyle Heights.

Opposing Art Galleries

The potential transformation of Boyle Heights raises a critical question: What strategies and tactics should neighborhoods use to combat displacement and gentrification? Ideally, what happened in my own Tenderloin neighborhood in San Francisco would be a model: nonprofit groups purchased real estate and took it off the speculative market, strong tenant and rental housing protections were enacted, and all of this occurred before the threat of upscale transformation was at the community's door. But these options are not politically feasible in many cities and neighborhoods, and/or were not undertaken before it was too late. When the threat of displacement and gentrification came to Boyle Heights, key structural strategies that would have protected the community were not in place. This left activists little choice but to engage in more confrontational tactics to protect the community's working-class character.[20]

In 2016 the group Defend Boyle Heights (DBH) launched a campaign against the arrival of upscale art galleries in the still low-income neighborhood. Activists protested at gallery openings and called for all galleries to leave the neighborhood (among its chief targets was the PSSST gallery, which closed in February 2017). DBH sought to stop "artwashing," described as "using artists' presence in a neighborhood as a way to dress up a formerly neglected area and rebrand it as highly desirable." In July 2016 DBH joined other activists to form the Boyle Heights Alliance against Artwashing and Displacement. The new coalition called for "all art galleries in Boyle Heights to leave immediately and for the community to decide what takes their place." In December 2016 DBH issued a statement declaring, "As these art galleries, which range from either being ignored or hated by most of our community, continue to occupy Boyle Heights, low-income working class renters of color continue to be mercilessly displaced by new landlords and developers who are raising rents for the incoming wave of white and more affluent renters and homeowners, in particular those living close to the new art galleries. This isn't an exaggeration. This is our community's reality."[21]

Critics of DBH's targeting of galleries seemed unconcerned about what brought hipster art establishments to the working-class Latino Boyle Heights neighborhood just as it was facing threats of gentrification and displacement. The galleries certainly did not arrive to help preserve the existing Latino community. To the contrary, the galleries were part of a broader real estate campaign to convince a white, upscale demographic that Boyle Heights was a good place for them to live. The PSSST gallery, ultimately forced to close, was co-founded by a real estate agent. Was his primary agenda art or gentrification?

Artists are not the vanguard of neighborhood gentrification. Most artists are low income. They are far more likely to be the victims of displacement than the cause. The conflict in Boyle Heights was not about local artists opening a gallery to sell their wares to the existing neighborhood. Nor was it about galleries opening in a neighborhood already protected from gentrification. Instead, the galleries were part of a larger plan that put tenants like Francisco Gonzalez, Arturo Ruvalcaba, and many others at risk.

Coffee Wars

The criticism directed at activists for opposing art galleries escalated when they targeted the opening of a hipster café called Weird Wave Coffee. It opened on a street named after United Farm Workers and Latino leader Cesar Chavez. Activists attacked the business on social media even before it served its first espresso on June 15, 2017. After it opened, activists held protest rallies outside the business, waving posters, including one that used an expletive to describe "White Coffee" and another that said "AmeriKKKano to go." They passed out fliers with a parody logo that read "White Wave." In July, the café's glass front door was broken, and the café was later vandalized. Many blamed activists. Leonardo Vilchis, director of Union de Vecinos, a group leading efforts to stop displacement in Boyle Heights, was undeterred: "It's a threat to local businesses and it's one more sign of gentrification that we need to defeat. Otherwise this neighborhood is going to end up just like Highland Park."[22]

Activists' attacks on Weird Wave Coffee greatly increased media attention on the gentrification struggle in Boyle Heights. Most stories cast the activists in a negative light. They were accused of resorting to "race-based attacks" and "vandalism" in the battle over gentrification. Councilmember José Huizar criticized "destroying property or violence of any kind, or targeting people solely based on race," saying "that goes against everything Boyle Heights stands for." Soon after making that comment Huizar killed a forty-nine-unit supportive housing project for veterans and the formerly homeless planned for Boyle Heights, which seems far more inconsistent with "everything Boyle Heights stands for" than someone breaking a glass door to a café. (Under pressure, in March 2018 Huizar reversed five years of opposition and allowed the housing to move forward.)[23]

The media used comments from café patrons and nearby business owners to define the anti-gentrification activists as opposing "change" and "progress." That they were only opposed to a type of change that displaced longtime residents was not pointed out, nor did the media question whether it was "progress" to promote displacement and gentrification. The media instead accepted the "inevitability" of the community's transformation.[24]

Even the *Los Angeles Times* criticized the Boyle Heights' activists' tactics. The paper stated in a July 20, 2017, editorial, "Activists would do more for their cause if they'd stop focusing on running new businesses out of town and alienating people with offensive racial comments, and take their signs instead to City Hall to demand more policies that help protect longtime residents and businesses in Boyle Heights from being forced out of their neighborhood." That tenant activists in Los Angeles had long demanded action from city hall without getting results was ignored. It was as if activists were protesting businesses to the exclusion of other strategies.[25]

"By All Means Necessary"

Claims that Boyle Heights activists "hurt their cause" through aggressive tactics is a common response to activist strategies that often prove quite effective. A Gallup poll taken in May 1964, shortly after the 1963 March on Washington, DC, found that 74 percent of Americans believed that "mass demonstrations by Negroes" would "hurt the Negro's cause for racial equality."[26] I discuss in *The Activist's Handbook* how the AIDS activist group ACT UP was strongly criticized for its "by all means necessary" approach, but its aggressive tactics worked. The same was true for Earth First! activists who took the radical step of sitting in old-growth trees to stop them from being chopped down. As one Earth First! activist put it, "Society doesn't want a crisis dealt with through crisis tactics." The same holds true for those trying to stop displacement and gentrification in urban neighborhoods.[27]

Suppose Defend Boyle Heights, the LA Tenants Union, and other activists groups battling displacement and gentrification in Boyle Heights had limited their opposition to media-approved tactics. What message would that have sent to tenants like Francisco Gonzalez who went to these groups for help? It would have said that these groups put the interests of outsiders ahead of those of the tenants. That's not a good strategy for building the support base necessary to overcome landlords evicting mariachis and other tenants in Boyle Heights. With the future of economically and racially diverse Boyle Heights at risk, crisis tactics were required.

On December 12, 2017, the LA Tenants Union and Union de Vecinos joined other supporters in holding a protest and setting up a camp outside the West Los Angeles mansion of landlord B.J. Turner. Members of the Los Angeles chapter of the Democratic Socialists of America (known as DSA-LA) then followed this by setting up tents outside Turner's home, chanting and marching through the following morning. When the tenants and their supporters returned to Turner's house the next weekend, the landlord realized that they weren't going to give up. Turner offered to negotiate a resolution of the evictions. The agreement reached on February 12, 2018, stopped the evictions. It also provided that after an initial increase of 14 percent, annual rent increases would be limited to 5 percent through June 30, 2021. Future rent hikes would be subject to collective bargaining, with the LA Tenants Union expressly granted the right to participate on the tenants' behalf. The tenants facing eviction also got six months of back rent forgiven, which for some exceeded $7,000.

Overall, the Boyle Heights mariachis won a remarkable victory. Tenant Francisco Gonzales "hoped it would be a model for other people in other buildings, so that they have hope even when they don't have rent control." The outcome vindicated the tenants' steadfastness in the face of losing their homes and the commitment of their supporters. It was also a tribute to strong legal work by attorneys Tyler Anderson and Noah Grynberg, co-directors of the Los Angeles Center for Community Law and Action, who kept the eviction cases going long enough to bring the landlord to the negotiating table. The mariachis' victory shows that Boyle Heights' struggle against gentrification and displacement remained a winnable fight, and that tenant organizing and community support for tenants are essential in at-risk communities. A powerful message was sent to speculators that they should think twice before trying to make a quick profit by evicting tenants in Boyle Heights.[28]

Fortunately, Boyle Heights' battle to preserve its working-class character is also making progress on other fronts. The area around Mariachi Plaza includes a 14,000-square-foot city-owned site projected for future affordable housing. Joining it is a four-story affordable project owned by the Metro on the southwest corner of Boyle Avenue and 1st Street, the Santa Cecilia Apartments. Boyle Heights will also now have (after Councilmember Huizar dropped his five years of opposition) forty-nine units for veterans and homeless people operated by A Community of Friends on a vacant lot on 1st Street next to the El Mercado shopping center. So after years in which little affordable housing was built in the neighborhood, projects are moving forward before it is too late.[29]

Boyle Heights is aggressively resisting the pattern of displacement and gentrification that has spread across Los Angeles in recent years. But pressures remain. In May 2018 the Starz cable network premiered *Vida,* a series focusing on two Latina sisters returning home to Los Angeles after their mother's death. As described in a *New York Times* review, one of the sisters "is staying in Boyle Heights, a Hispanic Eastside neighborhood that's being pushed to become like Silver Lake—more expensive, more Anglo—by gentrifiers and investors. It's the sort of place where locals eat at a longstanding birria (stewed goat) restaurant while a white woman shoots a video on the sidewalk about 'discovering' it." It's no wonder that Boyle Heights' activists saw Highland Park's experience as a cautionary tale.[30]

HIGHLAND PARK'S WORKING-CLASS EXODUS

Highland Park is a longtime working-class Latino neighborhood that shares much of its political representation with Boyle Heights. Like Boyle Heights, it was once a Jewish neighborhood; its Temple Beth Israel, built in 1923, is the second-oldest synagogue in Los Angeles. Highland Park is smaller (60,000 vs. 100,000 residents) and less exclusively Latino (72 vs. 94 percent) than Boyle Heights, but both neighborhoods seemed safe from the displacement and gentrification that the Los Angeles housing crisis was spreading—until it came without much warning to their front doors.

As recently as 2009 Highland Park was best known for gang violence. But like Boyle Heights the neighborhood offered opportunities for gentrification. For example, Highland Park also has a stop on the Metro Gold Line. This facilitates commutes for residents working across the city. The neighborhood's biggest selling point is its history. It features the now highly desired 1920s- and 1930s-era Craftsman homes, part of the architectural legacy of the Arts and Crafts movement. Many have undergone major interior renovations to meet the needs of today's upwardly mobile owners. The Highland Park–Garvanza Historic Preservation Overlay Zone is the largest in Los Angeles, with over 4,000 structures.

Whereas Boyle Heights was vulnerable to gentrification because of its one-story commercial buildings, Highland Park was attractive due to its historic character. Consider this depiction in a local public television documentary: "One can argue that Los Angeles came of age in Highland Park, with artists, writers, and intellectuals such as [journalist and preservationist] Charles Lummis creating the vocabulary on which we now rely when we try to explain what Los Angeles was and could be. . . . Now, the DIY, bohemian ethos that grew out of the neighborhood's early days is alive in the area again, while its diverse residents are coming to terms with what it means to live here and care for the shared built environment."[31]

In 2013, the real estate website Redfin named Highland Park the hottest neighborhood in the United States. A year later, the National Public Radio show *Marketplace* used Highland Park as a case study on gentrification. I grew up in Los Angeles without ever hearing of Highland Park; now it was on the national stage because of its upscale transformation. In one of national media's most thorough investigations of urban gentrification, *Marketplace* listeners learned that while Highland Park was affordable only a decade ago, it was now pricing people out. House flipping and upscale renovations had become part of the community landscape. Residents identified gentrification with "coffee shops, flipped houses, paved streets, bike lanes, more dogs, new parks, higher prices, hipsters." Longtime working-class Highland Park was becoming part of the "gentrification industrial complex."[32]

The *Marketplace* series did not suggest that Highland Park could slow rising unaffordability by building affordable housing. Instead, *Marketplace* portrayed Highland Park gentrification as "driven by deeper forces— structural changes in our economy, trends like the widening gap between people who have access to money and people who don't." The "pursuit of profit also drives gentrification."

Structural forces certainly created an opening for gentrification. But *Marketplace* never explained that Highland Park's gentrification was not "inevitable." Why? Probably because the reporters thought the neighborhood's upscale transformation could not be stopped. They were also likely unaware of strategies that could have either avoided this outcome or slowed its momentum.

"Deeper forces" were less of a factor in gentrifying Highland Park than Los Angeles's failure to build or purchase housing in the neighborhood affordable to the working and middle class. Los Angeles also lacked key tenant and rental housing protections that slow the displacement process. By not expanding its housing supply in response to the city's rising population or adequately protecting tenants, Los Angeles subjected Highland Park to the rising prices on existing houses associated with gentrification.

Highland Park is among the most troubling examples of Los Angeles's housing crisis. In less than a decade it was so transformed that its prior history as a working-class, affordable neighborhood had been completely erased. The January 21, 2018, *New York Times* travel section featured Highland Park as a "relatively unknown and quiet residential part of the city" that has been transformed by "20- and 30-somethings, lured by the neighborhood's affordable rents and proximity to downtown." It was as if the gentrification of Highland Park had never happened. Absent successful struggles in Boyle Heights the same could happen to that community. Who is primarily profiting from this crisis at everyone else's expense? Anti-housing home owners and landlords.[33]

HOMEOWNER GROUPS: "THE MOST POWERFUL SOCIAL MOVEMENT IN LA"

The chief obstacle to building housing in Los Angeles has long been the city's powerful homeowner associations. In his legendary 1990 book *City of Quartz: Excavating the Future in Los Angeles,* Mike Davis described Southern California's affluent homeowners, "engaged in the defense of home values and neighborhood exclusivity," as the area's "most powerful social movement." Many of Los Angeles's most politically powerful homeowner groups represent those living in the exclusive communities bordering Sunset Boulevard, home of the Sunset Strip. Davis describes the slow-growth movement led by Los Angeles homeowners as "Sunset Bolshevism."[34]

The power (and selfishness) of Los Angeles homeowners became enshrined in state policy with the passage of Proposition 13 in 1978. Proposition 13 was sold by San Fernando Valley realtor Howard Jarvis as a "Homeowner Revolt" against excessive property taxes. Proposition 13 sharply reduced property tax hikes for longtime homeowners, shifting the cost of funding public services to a younger generation of new buyers. Proposition 13's skewed property tax system has dramatically reduced California's funding for public schools, health care, housing, and other public sector needs.

Los Angeles went decades without building multi-unit housing because homeowner associations did not want tenants as neighbors. Zoning laws barred new apartment buildings. As a result, nearly half the city is zoned exclusively for single-family homes. Building apartments that would bring working and middle-class families into these neighborhoods is illegal; it is a classic example of the use of exclusionary zoning to promote racial and class segregation. By limiting housing supply, homeowners also raised their own property values at the expense of working- and middle-class families, who were denied the ability to buy into the Los Angeles market. In 2016, the real estate site Trulia found that median first-time homebuyers in LA had to spend an astonishing 88.1 percent of their income in order to purchase a simple starter home. It concluded that "home buying in Los Angeles is pretty much impossible right now for many people. . . . Not only are there fewer homes available to buyers of all income levels, those just starting out or making their first foray into home ownership are worse off than they've been in years."[35]

Despite the pricing impact on future generations, Los Angeles homeowners continue to prevent multi-unit housing from being built. This is even true in the wealthy and progressive neighborhood of Venice.

Venice: Wealthy Residents Say No

I grew up around Venice, California, in the 1960s and 1970s, when it was at the heart of the Los Angeles counterculture. Venice was known for rundown canals, weightlifting at Muscle Beach, and later for its beach boardwalk. Despite rising housing prices due to the nearby beach Venice always had a dangerous side. Crime was higher than in adjacent Santa Monica (which is its own city), and homelessness was a noticeable problem years before it expanded through much of Los Angeles.

Today, Venice is very different. Muscle Beach and the boardwalk are still there, and the homeless numbers are even higher. But Google opened offices in 2011 and Snapchat followed in 2015, accelerating the neighborhood's upscale transformation. The Venice canals have been beautifully restored. Houses along the canal are now generally owned by millionaires, many of whom rent them out for over $10,000—and as much as $19,500—per month. Venice's Abbott Kinney Boulevard has some of the city's best restaurants and is among the most upscale streets in LA. In the space of less than a decade, Venice has priced out all but the rich from most of its housing.

In many cities, homeless tent encampments are erected under freeway overpasses or other out-of-the-way areas. Not so in Venice. Google's hip, 100,000-square-foot Venice campus on Main Street includes the Frank Gehry–designed "Binocular Building" (which really looks like binoculars). It is one of three buildings making up an extraordinary state-of-the-art office complex. Yet behind Google is a homeless encampment covering two sidewalks. I saw the encampments in 2017 during my annual visit to the Venice and Santa Monica beaches. The sidewalk directly across the street from the now upscale Rose Café was almost impassable. Nearby is the organic eatery Gjuna, which TripAdvisor ranked seventeenth out of 8,692 restaurants in Los Angeles.

A neighborhood filled with upscale businesses and restaurants impacted by homeless persons would be expected to offer support for housing and other services aimed at helping people get off the street. A neighborhood with a progressive counterculture legacy like that of Venice should be the last to oppose new housing for low-income people. This is probably what the city thought when it proposed building 136 supportive housing units for low-income people on an unsightly city-owned parking lot. The lot is near the canals in the median of Venice Boulevard, between Dell and Pacific Avenues. Nearby homeowners should have been thrilled to see the rundown space transformed into new housing with attractive landscaping. But many Los Angeles homeowners, even in "progressive" Venice, oppose building any multi-unit housing in their neighborhood, and for decades they have been remarkably successful in preventing such construction.

Building supportive housing in Venice makes perfect sense. The term refers to housing with on-site supportive services, and it is *the* key strategy for reducing homelessness among single adults. It ensures that those entering housing after years on the street get the services they need to stay housed. My organization is San Francisco's largest supportive housing provider for homeless single adults, and I know firsthand that the strategy works.

Despite a longstanding homeless problem, Venice had not built any new supportive housing since the 1990s and there had been only two instances in which existing housing was rehabilitated as supportive housing. When the parking lot site was proposed, Venice had only forty-two units of permanent supportive housing. In 2017, the *Wall Street Journal* reported that Venice is the hardest place in the entire country to build housing. Venice had roughly 700 *fewer* housing units in 2015 than in 2000. From 1960 to 2010, the Los Angeles metro area added two million housing units. Venice added virtually none. Los Angeles added 1.3 million new residents during this fifty-year period, but the population in the main part of Venice actually declined 20 percent. Venice has been so effective at stopping housing construction that its zoning laws now allow half the number of new units to be built as was allowed in the late 1950s—all while Los Angeles's population has skyrocketed.[36]

When Los Angeles did an RFP (request for proposal) for building supportive housing on the Venice parking lot site, the nonprofit organization Venice Community Housing (VCH) partnered with the Hollywood Community Housing Corporation and the team was selected to develop a proposal. Becky Dennison is VCH's executive director. Since assuming the position in January 2016 Dennison has led efforts to finally get Venice to take action to house homeless persons. VCH's proposal for the site includes sixty-eight studios and one- and two-bedroom apartments for currently homeless persons, and another sixty-eight units for low-income artists and low-income families.

Dennison told me that her group had not acquired other sites in Venice because land is simply too expensive. That the parking lot is city owned avoided that problem. Cities striving to maintain economic and racial diversity must use city-owned property—like the Elizabeth Street site in Nolita or the Bedford Union Armory in Crown Heights discussed later in this book— to build affordable housing. This is essential for slowing urban inequality.[37]

Dennison came to VCH after fifteen years at the Los Angeles Community Action Network (LACAN). LACAN is based in the city's Downtown and South Los Angeles neighborhoods, which may be the only part of the city with a larger homeless problem than the one Venice has. Dennison's been around poverty advocacy long enough to know how to win these fights. I quickly learned this when I expressed surprise that VCH would retain all of the parking at the site, which required additional private fundraising. But Dennison correctly recognized that the housing battle was tough enough without having to also fight neighbors over reduced parking.

Dennison takes nothing for granted, is always up on the facts, and knows the importance of preempting opposition. She took a page from the playbook of legendary UFW organizer Fred Ross by arranging over fifty house meetings in Venice to educate people about permanent supportive housing. House meetings offer a more informational setting than what the *Los Angeles Times* described as "a series of raucous community meetings" that took place in the fall of 2016. These devolved into attacks on the project, on Los Angeles councilmember Mike Bonin for supporting it, and on the very idea that a city-owned parking lot in a wealthy area should be used to house the non-rich.[38]

John Moore, described by the *Times* as "a shaggy-haired, full-bearded surfer, Venice resident and launcher of 'ethically minded' brands and fashion lines," personifies how those profiting from Venice's counterculture image seek to exclude low-income people from their community. As the *Times* puts it, "His family's lifestyle—crafting, tandem skateboarding and eating on pillows in the backyard—has been celebrated as 'haute bohemian' in online video and photo spreads. But Moore, 42, who came up with the name for Abercrombie & Fitch's Hollister brand, draws the line at a proposal to house homeless people blocks from his property."

Moore stated at a September 2016 community meeting, "I will help you come up with a solution that is not putting people in my alley, in my front yard, that could potentially devalue my home and put me and my children in jeopardy." It was not that long ago when such comments were made about people who looked like Moore, but that irony was no doubt lost on the millionaire surfer.

According to the *Times,* only two African-American speakers were at the September meeting. Attorney Gloria Dabbs-Mann backed the project, noting, "I grew up here. There were black people, white people, brown people, Native Americans—everybody lived here and it made me a better person."[39]

Many opponents insisted that they supported housing for homeless persons, but that VCH had picked the wrong neighborhood and/or the wrong site. Christian Wrede of Venice Vision, a group formed to oppose the project, appeared with Dennison on a radio show to discuss the issue. Wrede said his group supports new housing and services for the homeless. What it finds "troublesome" are councilmember Bonin's plans to "transform Venice into a hub for delivery of services to the homeless on the Westside." That Venice has long been the homeless "hub" of the Westside without providing supportive housing, or even emergency shelters for homeless single adults, has not stopped opponents from viewing the neighborhood as over saturated.[40]

Like many opponents, Venice Vision opposes real solutions to the housing crisis while promoting false alternatives. For example, its website states that it opposes VCH's project because "building expensive permanent housing on city-owned properties ... [has] little to do with ending homelessness or providing services." But that's precisely what supportive housing does. Instead, the group feels money should "immediately be put to use by rehabilitating existing structures." Where there is a vacant 136-unit structure ready to be renovated for low-income housing is not explained.

Venice also has less progressive opponents of low-income housing, like Mark Ryavec, president of the Venice Stakeholders Association. Ryavec, who ran for city council and lost to Bonin in March 2017, is unhappy about the many units in VCH's project set aside for people with disabilities. He told *LA Weekly,* "Frankly, what you're doing is putting an insane asylum in a residential neighborhood. And I fully understand any residential neighborhood saying, no, we don't want that." Ryavec continued, "We don't want a Soviet-era apartment project—simply three levels of dense apartments over one level of parking. This is not attractive; this lowers our property values."[41]

Opposition to Housing the Homeless

Homeowner opposition to supportive housing in Venice occurred as Los Angeles voters were passing landmark funding measures to address the city's worsening homeless crisis. In November 2016, 77 percent of Los Angeles voters approved Proposition HHH, a $1.2 billion dollar bond to build 10,000 supportive housing units for homeless persons over the next decade. In March 2017, voters passed Proposition H, a quarter-cent sales tax hike projected to raise $355 million for homeless services over the next decade. But supporting new funding for housing homeless persons does not necessarily reduce neighborhood opposition to specific projects. When the Los Angeles County Board of Supervisors approved a $1 billion spending plan for the Proposition H funds in June 2017, Supervisor Kathryn Barger noted, "The good news is we have the money, the bad news is we now have to address the issue of 'not-in-my-backyard.'" Councilmember Marqueece Harris-Dawson also foresaw difficulties: "We did the glitzy part, but now we have to get the work done, brick by brick, block by block. I predict we'll hit a wall—that we'll get stuck."[42]

Mayor Garcetti sought to discourage neighborhood opposition to homeless housing when he met with representatives of neighborhood councils only a month after the passage of Proposition H in March 2017. Garcetti described the outreach as part of his "'YIMBY campaign,' as in, Yes in My Back Yard. If you keep saying, 'No, I'm for this in the abstract but I don't want it here,' or, 'This isn't the right location,' or 'I'm liberal but . . .,' then we'll never solve the problem. The choice is whether the homeless people that are already in your neighborhood, will they be on the street, or will they be housed and helped?"[43]

Garcetti's concerns were amplified in December 2017 when the city council approved regulations for spending Proposition HHH bond funds that required a "letter of acknowledgement" from the city councilmember in whose district a project would be built. A tradition of giving councilmembers veto power over projects is how Councilmember Huizar delayed the forty-nine-unit supportive housing project in Boyle Heights for so long. Now this tradition became a legal requirement for disbursement of Prop HHH funds.

This veto power, which enabled neighborhood groups to pressure councilmembers not to issue the required letters, quickly became a problem. In February 2018, the Los Angeles housing department rejected funding for two supportive housing projects that lacked the required letter, including a fifty-one-unit development in South Los Angeles, where homelessness is particularly acute. A March 12, 2018, *Los Angeles Times* story on the letter requirement incited a storm of anger over the practice. Assembly member David Chiu from San Francisco introduced state legislation (Assembly Bill 2162) preventing local governments from giving a single elected official the power to veto affordable housing projects. That such state intervention would be necessary reflects Los Angeles's strong neighborhood opposition to new low-income housing. Responding to public and media anger over the letter requirement, the city council voted unanimously to pledge that each member would support a minimum of 222 housing units for homeless people in his or her district. This would create at least 3,330 units over three years, helping the city meet its stated goal of building 10,000 units for homeless residents over a decade.[44]

I asked Becky Dennison if she thought Mayor Garcetti should be doing more to help nonprofit projects overcome neighborhood opposition. Dennison said she appreciates the mayor's meeting with the councils and going on the radio to back housing. She also thinks Garcetti could make "a big difference" if he came to community meetings and public hearings to demonstrate his backing of supportive housing projects. She notes that the mayor has not generally engaged in these "heated public discussions," and that this leaves nonprofit housing groups engaging with angry neighbors on their own.

It's a good point. San Francisco mayors never attend community meetings with neighbors opposed to new housing. But given the crisis, popular mayors like Eric Garcetti may need to be more directly engaged. After all, new funding to address homelessness only matters if housing actually gets built.

With councilmember Bonin's strong support and Dennison's activist skill set, VCH's 136-unit supportive housing project is projected to obtain final approvals by June or July of 2019. Building affordable housing is a long process. That's why fifteen months after Prop HHH's November 2016 passage only two projects with bond funding had broken ground. The Los Angeles City Council passed an ordinance in spring 2018 to expedite the approval process for homeless housing, which will certainly help. The success of the Venice supportive housing development could reduce fears about future projects in Venice and help build backing for supportive housing in less progressive communities. How wonderful if a project in long-resistant Venice facilitated the expansion of supportive housing throughout Los Angeles.

Anti-Housing Ballot Initiatives

Los Angeles homeowners' longtime opposition to building new apartments goes well beyond concern over low-income housing. Mike Davis has described the agenda of Los Angeles's homeowner groups as follows: "The master discourse here is homeowner exclusivism, whether the immediate issue is apartment construction, commercial encroachment, school busing, crime, taxes or simply community designation."[45]

Many attribute Los Angeles homeowners' enormous power to stop housing to the passage—by a whopping 70 percent—of Proposition U in 1986. The large victory margin for the "Initiative for Reasonable Limits on Commercial Building and Traffic Growth" was no surprise. Prop U was seen by many as a referendum on traffic. Los Angeles residents hate traffic. Many spend hours in freeway gridlock each day and dread their commutes. Since commercial buildings were associated with increasing traffic, any ballot measure promising to limit such development—and hence traffic growth— was a winner.

Proposition U was also fueled by Westside outrage over the sudden spread of high-rise towers in Westwood and elsewhere. I shared this anger. I returned home from Berkeley, where I had gone for college in 1974, to see multiple new towers at the intersection of Wilshire and Westwood. Their construction even demolished the historic coffee shop Ships. Known for its iconic Googie architecture, Ships served over 50 million customers in its three Los Angeles locations from 1956 to 1996. I regularly went to the Wilshire Ships. We saw

Ships as a Los Angeles icon that would always be there. We were wrong. The Westwood Ships closed on September 20, 1984, and construction of a twenty-story office building began the next day. No wonder Westside neighborhood coalitions like Not Yet New York strongly backed Proposition U. High-rises in the area near UCLA known as Westwood Village changed the neighborhood's longtime feel.

But Proposition U also halted housing. Housing was not mentioned in Proposition U's title and ballot language. But Prop U effectively downzoned 70 percent of the city's commercially zoned land and cut in half the size of housing that could be built on commercial sites in residential districts. This sharply reduced the number of housing sites. One critic concluded that "of the 29,000 acres zoned for commercial and industrial uses throughout L.A., 70 percent saw their development capacity sliced in half.... Prop U didn't just mean less office, retail, and manufacturing space, but fewer homes as well."[46]

Proposition U laid the groundwork for restrictions on new housing that continued for decades. Led by powerful coalitions of upscale neighborhood groups like the Federation of Hillside and Canyon Associations (founded in 1952), the slow-growth movement demanded total control over what got built in neighborhoods. As Mike Davis describes, fed up with "token" representation on advisory boards, "They demanded completely elected community planning boards of local residents, invested with 'implementation power.'" Neighborhood groups wanted up or down votes by local homeowners only to be overridden by a four-fifths vote of the planning commission.[47]

Although the city council rejected this radical plan for homeowner control, it gave in to the Hillside federation's policy demands in 1987 by enacting fifty "interim control ordinances." These temporarily halted certain kinds of construction, including new apartments and mobile home parks. In other words, homeowner groups secured "interim" ordinances excluding new working- and middle-class residents from their neighborhoods. The interim prohibitions killed most new housing in Los Angeles, despite rising population and job growth.

The year 1987 also saw a court ruling in an environmental lawsuit brought against the city of Los Angeles by homeowners associated as the Friends of Westwood. The ruling, little noticed at the time, had enormous implications for the city's housing market. It effectively subjected nearly all housing projects in Los Angeles with fifty or more units to the cost and delays associated with a full environmental review under the California Environmental

Quality Act. This added level of cost and delay would apply even when, as in the Westwood case, the proposed housing met applicable zoning laws.[48]

From 1980 to 2010 the Los Angeles metro area built barely more than a third of the housing units that other urban areas constructed. The city added 160,000 new residents from 2010 to 2015 but only 25,000 housing units. Assuming three residents per household, this left the city over 28,000 units short. This resident/housing imbalance had predictable results: Los Angeles entered 2017 with arguably the nation's worst affordable-housing crunch and with a homelessness crisis that the *Los Angeles Times* deemed a "national disgrace."[49]

Homeowners Worsen the Crisis

In 1999, homeowner groups won voter approval of a Neighborhood Council System and a Department of Neighborhood Empowerment within city hall. The city charter now ensured "each neighborhood council receives early warning of upcoming city decisions and has the opportunity to be heard." By 2017 there were ninety-seven neighborhood councils.[50]

Unfortunately, "neighborhood empowerment" in Los Angeles and elsewhere too often means promoting opposition to new apartments. A 2007 University of Southern California study found that neighborhood councils were typically wealthier and whiter than their constituents. They were also far likelier to identify land-use issues as their top priority, with land-use matters constituting 49 percent of the councils' issue-based activities. Paavo Monkkonen, associate professor of urban planning at UCLA, wrote a white paper in 2016 connecting eight neighborhood councils to their most common reasons for opposing multi-unit housing. Based on minutes from meetings in 2015, the reasons most cited were "inconsistency with neighborhood character" and the developer's alleged "lack of engagement with the community." In gentrifying areas like Highland Park and at-risk Boyle Heights, opponents also raised issues of excessive density and potential displacement.[51]

These councils used their political clout to restrict new working- and middle-class housing citywide. This accelerated risks of gentrification and displacement not only in Boyle Heights and Highland Park but also in Pico-Union, Echo Park, and other neighborhoods. Residents in all of these neighborhoods fell victim to a cruel game of housing musical chairs: when the music stopped, there were two, three, five, or even ten times the number of people seeking housing as there were available units.

People priced out of their preferred Los Angeles neighborhood have two choices. First, they can leave the city altogether. For many this is not an option given their workplace location or the draw of living in a cultural metropolis like Los Angeles. Second, they can find housing they can afford somewhere within a two-hour commute. For Mary Ruiz (discussed above), this meant living in a converted garage in the San Fernando Valley. Those with more resources might move to a neighborhood they do not know but have been told is changing for the better, like Boyle Heights or Highland Park. This is how Los Angeles's failure to build housing has spread gentrification and displacement across the city. Rising prices in one neighborhood shift those priced out to the next most affordable community. These new arrivals then create a "hot" housing market in that community, boosting prices for landlords and home sellers. This in turn encourages landlords and speculators to displace existing residents in order to obtain tenants paying the new market rents. Once the process is well under way in one once-affordable community, it repeats itself in the next.

This is what Los Angeles's anti-housing homeowner "revolution" has wrought. And when the city's failure to build housing was compounded by the absence of key tenant and rental housing protections, the displacement and pricing out crisis got even worse.

LANDLORD POWER IN LOS ANGELES

Along with the city's prominent homeowner associations, Los Angeles landlord organizations have enormous political power. The city's housing crisis has been hugely profitable for residential landlords; in a market of rising rents and inadequate tenant protections, where even rent-controlled tenants sacrifice an unhealthy percentage of their incomes for rent, residential landlords have been the big financial winners.

Los Angeles landlords have a well-oiled political machine. The Apartment Association of Greater Los Angeles, founded in 1917, serves smaller landlords. The group represents landlords in 120 cities and proudly claims on its website that it is "always on watch to defend the rental housing industry." The huge landlords, those owning hundreds of units or more, are represented by the California Apartment Association (CAA).

CAA has lobbyists at the state and local levels and is very engaged at both. The group's opposition to increased tenant and rental housing protections, promotion of real estate speculation, and attacks on existing affordable housing laws has made CAA the driving force behind Los Angeles's pricing out of the middle class. CAA is a major donor to politicians across the state. Its members' profits from skyrocketing housing costs help fund a political operation designed to keep rents rising.

Los Angeles offers a dream political environment for real estate interests for a number of reasons. Political power is much less centralized. It takes eight votes on the fifteen-member Los Angeles City Council to enact the strong tenant and rental housing protections that the city's low-income, working-, and middle-class residents need—and that has proved a heavy lift for tenant advocates. It is not easy to get eight votes for pro-tenant measures when each of the fifteen council members represents nearly 300,000 people (a San Francisco Supervisor represents less than 80,000). Large voting districts put a premium on campaign donations from real estate interests. Tenants are politically strong in some districts but real estate offices and influential landlords are everywhere. Winning a council majority for tenant legislation requires that advocates get the votes of politicians whose own districts lack a strong renter base (and whose voting constituency is primarily homeowners). Jerry Jones, policy director of the Inner City Law Center, notes that many councilmembers eventually run for higher office. Landlord and real estate industry money can fund their future campaigns.

Los Angeles's sprawling size also makes building tenant power challenging. Neighborhoods that suddenly face tenant displacement typically lack the tenant counseling and organizing groups that are found in cities like San Francisco. Experienced tenant leaders who can advise these groups can be an hour's drive away. The physical distance between communities almost necessitates that Los Angeles tenant activism is more neighborhood based. This causes many tenants who get eviction notices to simply move; as Jones of the Inner City Law Center puts it, "Hundreds of tenants just leave their homes because they do not know what else to do."[52]

Winning stronger tenant protections and rental housing preservation laws requires strong citywide coalitions that the physical distance between neighborhoods makes harder to create. Jones, who previously worked at the Center for Community Change and ACORN (Association of Community Organizations for Reform Now) and has long experience in other cities, sees Los Angeles as having a "weak advocacy infrastructure." In contrast, landlords have powerful, well-funded organizations that do not need citywide meetings of their members to organize politically. They influence politicians the traditional way—by writing checks.

Larry Gross, the longtime executive director of the Coalition for Economic Survival (CES), sees the big challenge in Los Angeles as the fact that most politicians do not make tenant and rental housing protections a top priority. While Los Angeles is a progressive city, "We don't get a lot of the traditional liberals and celebrities on tenants' issues because many are landlords. This isn't like getting wealthy supporters to back environmental issues or to oppose nuclear power. We once did a protest against a landlord who was head of the board of the local ACLU."[53]

Gross has been among Los Angeles's leading tenant advocates for over forty years. I met him in the 1990s, when he and CES were fighting to preserve federally subsidized housing, a battle they largely won. Gross is on the front lines of virtually all the battles in Los Angeles to further protect tenants and rent-controlled housing.

In 2015, CES joined with the statewide group Tenants Together in a campaign to remove Matthew Jacobs from his role as chair of the California Housing Finance Agency (CalHFA). CalHFA "supports the needs of renters" and "programs that create safe, decent and affordable housing opportunities for low to moderate income Californians." Despite the agency's mission, Jacobs moved to eliminate affordable housing by issuing mass Ellis eviction notices for two buildings in Beverly Grove. After evicting all of the low- and moderate-income tenants, Jacobs planned to demolish the rent-controlled housing. After protests at the buildings and statewide publicity, Jacobs resigned his position at CalHFA in July 2015. The demolitions were ultimately stopped, but all of the tenants were evicted.[54]

That a Los Angeles real estate speculator engaging in Ellis Act evictions headed a state agency designed to protect affordable housing speaks to the political challenges Los Angeles tenants face. The city is a Democratic Party stronghold. But some of its politically powerful players have real estate investments that put them on the wrong side of tenant protection and rental housing preservation fights.

Condos, Demolitions, Rent Hikes

In June 2017 the Los Angeles City Council approved the Beverly Grove buildings from which Jacobs evicted the tenants for conversion into condominiums. Los Angeles has no annual numerical limit on condo conversions, nor are such conversions restricted to small buildings, as in San Francisco. Los Angeles instead ties condo conversions to vacancy rates, which does not adequately protect rental housing.

When councilmember Paul Koretz called for a condo conversion moratorium during the debate on converting Jacobs's former buildings, the planning department said it was not needed. The department also encourages demolitions of apartments if the new project increases the number of units on a given site. But unlike the housing demolished, new units are exempt from rent control under state law.

San Francisco city officials would never allow a rent-controlled building to be demolished without the landlord funding tenant relocation and subsidizing tenants' rents elsewhere during the rebuilding. Tenants would get the right to return to their former homes at their prior rent or be given new rent-controlled units at their former rent with the owner subsidizing the price difference.[55]

The Los Angeles Planning Department needs to read the *Los Angeles Times* January 2015 editorial calling for a "no net loss" policy when it comes to affordable rental housing.

Los Angeles's rent-control law gives landlords automatic 3 percent annual rent hikes even when there is no inflation. That makes no sense. The accumulation of these excessive rent hikes works against preserving the city's urban working and middle class. San Francisco used to guarantee landlords a 4 percent minimum annual rent hike. I co-authored a ballot initiative (Proposition H) whose passage in November 1992 limited increases to 60 percent of the consumer price index (the housing share of inflation). As a result, since 1993 San Francisco tenants under rent control have never had to pay even a 3 percent annual increase. In fact, only seven times in the past twenty-four years have they had to pay as much as 2 percent.

The political power of Los Angeles landlords perpetuates these unfair annual rent hikes. In San Francisco, tenants keep billions of dollars in their pockets by not paying rent hikes above the level of inflation; in Los Angeles, landlords pocket that money.

Shifting Election Dates

Landlords' ability to price out Los Angeles's working and middle class has been sustained by low turnout in local elections, which effectively disenfranchises tenants. In the March 2015 local elections, voter turnout was 9 percent.

Some councilmembers whose districts include 250,000 residents were elected by fewer than 10,000 voters. Turnout was only 20 percent for the highly contested 2013 Los Angeles mayor's race, when Garcetti was first elected, and the March 2017 election had a meager 12 percent turnout.

Who votes in these off-year, low-turnout elections? It turns out these voters are disproportionately older, whiter, and more likely to be homeowners than the electorate as a whole. This leaves councilmembers beholden to high-turnout homeowners and landlord funders, rather than to the tenants in their district.

Fortunately, in March 2015, 76 percent of voters backed a measure changing Los Angeles's election calendar to end these strictly local elections in 2020. Mayor Garcetti's second term, and those of councilmembers elected for four years in 2017, were extended from March 2021 to November 2022. Los Angeles elections will soon coincide with high-turnout state or national races.

Denny Zane, a longtime activist who co-founded Santa Monica for Renters Rights and served twelve years as Santa Monica's mayor, sees great significance for tenants in Los Angeles's new election calendar. "Spring elections ensure a municipal leadership more beholden to the older, longtime homeowners who disproportionately vote in these off-year races. By changing to November elections, Los Angeles mayors and councilmembers will be accountable to an entirely different electorate—most will serve constituencies that include far more tenants."[56]

Zane saw this shift in Santa Monica after he and other activists put a measure on the 1981 ballot shifting the city's odd-year elections to coincide with state and national contests. Prior to the change, Zane mapped turnout in the city and found the constituency voting in spring elections to be made up overwhelmingly of homeowners. In contrast, "Santa Monica got an overwhelmingly higher tenant vote in the new cycle," Zane recalled. Voter turnout in Santa Monica's recent local races—which coincide with state and national contests—was 58 percent, nearly triple that of Los Angeles's local contests.

A national study of local election turnouts shows that Zane's point applies across the nation. Citing a *Governing* magazine report on a 50 percent drop in Los Angeles and other cities' local election turnouts since the 1960s, Amaris Montes, a research and advocacy fellow with FairVote, told the *Los Angeles Times,* "This is a huge thing that's happening across the U.S." She went on to indicate that "the result is that a small electorate—usually older and whiter—is making decisions that affect a more diverse municipal population." A study of voter turnout in Seattle's local off-year elections found that 73.3 percent of registered voters over the age of sixty-five voted, as compared to 34.5 percent of registered voters aged eighteen to thirty-four. The median age of voters is fifty, compared to forty-one for the overall adult population.[57]

Politicians defer to boomer homeowners opposed to housing over pro-housing renter millennials because that is who votes in low-turnout, off-year elections. Housing and tenant advocates should make changing local elections to coincide with state and national contests a top priority. Given that the cities described in this book are heavily Democratic and favor expanding voter rights, aligning local elections to increase tenant voter turnout should draw wide support (it also saves cities from funding off-year local elections).

A NEW DIRECTION: MAYOR GARCETTI AND LA'S PRO-HOUSING COALITION

Mayor Eric Garcetti kicked off a new era in Los Angeles housing politics on October 29, 2014, when he announced that the city would build 100,000 new housing units by 2021. The mayor's leadership in winning voter approval for the $1.2 billion dollar supportive housing bond (Proposition HHH) on the November 2016 ballot and the $3.55 billion sales tax hike for homeless services (Proposition H) approved by voters in March 2017 sent a powerful message that Los Angeles was charting a new direction in housing policy. After decades in which Los Angeles did not build enough housing of any type, and particularly little affordable housing, Mayor Garcetti and a growing pro-housing coalition were setting a new agenda. A city long starved for housing funds raised nearly $5 billion in the space of less than six months.[58]

In addition to raising new revenue from voters, Garcetti also backed a "linkage fee" to raise money from development to pay for affordable housing. The city's linkage fee on residential and commercial development would "bring in an estimated $75 million to $92 million per year, enough to help pay for the construction of 1,500 new units annually for residents with lower incomes, according to the city planning department." The measure passed the council with overwhelming support at the end of 2017 and is now projected to generate $80–100 million annually in affordable housing funds. That's roughly double the amount spent on affordable housing in 2016.[59]

The linkage fee was proposed when the Los Angeles city attorney believed a court ruling barred the city from requiring private developers to include a percentage of affordable units in their projects (a policy known as inclusionary housing). In 2017 Garcetti coordinated a successful statewide effort by eleven mayors to win Governor Jerry Brown's support for a bill overturning that ruling. As a result, Los Angeles and other cities can now enact inclusionary housing laws. Los Angeles needs inclusionary housing in addition to the linkage fee for two reasons. First, inclusionary housing provides another resource to address Los Angeles's acute affordability crisis. Second, it enables working- and middle-class families to live in desirable, asset-rich neighborhoods where a lot of market-rate housing gets built.

Some housing advocates believe that imposing any fees or affordability requirements stops badly needed housing from being built. If fees and inclusionary housing requirements are too high, that can certainly occur. But for both policy and legal reasons cities typically undertake studies to assess the tipping point at which affordability requirements begin deterring new construction. In the case of Los Angeles, the city has such a massive shortage of affordable housing that the city council overwhelmingly backed the linkage fee. And given the political power of organized labor in Los Angeles, the city is not going to pass an inclusionary housing requirement that is so high that it eliminates future union jobs by killing housing developments. A linkage fee and inclusionary housing may together be too steep for some cities, but not for Los Angeles.[60]

Housing advocates appreciated Mayor Garcetti's key role in securing new funds. Anita Nelson, CEO of the SRO Housing Corporation, heads an agency in a very low-income community where the housing and homelessness crises intersect. Nelson "applauds Mayor Garcetti's leadership in addressing homelessness in Los Angeles. As an affordable housing developer in the Central City East community of downtown Los Angeles, an area more commonly known as Skid Row, we see first-hand the tremendous need for affordable housing; this is where the transformation process begins for homeless individuals. SRO Housing Corporation has been a part of the solution for over 33 years and the mayor's help in increasing resources enhances our efforts to meet our community's needs."[61]

Defeating Anti-Housing Ballot Measures

With the mayor backing efforts to expand affordable housing and a broad pro-housing coalition on the rise, Los Angeles's anti-housing, slow-growth movement returned to the ballot, where it had long had success. Backers of Proposition S, placed on the city's March 2017 ballot, hoped to tap into the same anti-traffic, anti-high-rise sentiments that had led to Proposition U's overwhelming passage thirty years earlier. Proposition S, the "Neighborhood Integrity Initiative," equated "neighborhood integrity" with severely restricting what could get built in Los Angeles. Proposition S raised millions of dollars from the Hollywood-based AIDS Healthcare Foundation, whose twenty-first-floor offices would soon be blocked by two twenty-eight-story towers.

Had developers, anti-poverty activists, labor unions, and business and housing groups not raised millions of dollars for an opposition campaign, Los Angeles's housing crisis would have worsened. But demonstrating that cities can take political action to stop the pricing out of the working and middle class, this broad coalition defeated Proposition S by a two-to-one margin.

Increasing Tenant and Rental Housing Protections

In contrast to his commitment to build more housing and reduce homelessness, Garcetti has not made tenant and rental housing protections a priority. Jerry Jones of the Inner City Law Center felt Garcetti "has not put a lot of political capital into tenants' issues." Nobody I spoke with disagreed with Jones's assessment.[62]

According to Larry Gross of CES, "No Los Angeles mayor has ever taken a strong lead on tenant issues." This has been left to the city council. Although Gross sees homelessness, new construction, and rental housing and tenant preservation as interconnected, many Los Angeles politicians "do not see the relationship between these issues. They do not see homelessness as connected to people's displacement from their homes."[63]

Garcetti began taking a more active role in promoting renter protections in 2017. In April 2017 he signed a law requiring that owners of rent-controlled buildings demolished under the Ellis Act either replace all of the rent-controlled units that were eliminated with affordable units or ensure that 20 percent of the new units were affordable—whichever number is higher. The previous law allowed the landlord to pick the lower of the two options, which meant they chose the latter option. The new measure offers the city's first major deterrent to demolitions under the state's Ellis Act (the law used to try to evict Teresa Dulalas and other San Francisco tenants as described in chapter 1). Los Angeles lost nearly 22,000 rent-stabilized housing units to the Ellis Act from 2001 to 2017, and 428 buildings and 1,824 units in 2017 alone.[64]

Garcetti reaffirmed his new focus on helping tenants in his July 1, 2017, second inaugural speech. The mayor stated, "Climbing rents threaten to make Los Angeles a city without a middle—the rich and the poor drifting apart as if split by an earthquake. . . . We want every unhoused Angeleno to have a home where they are healthy and safe and where they can pursue their dreams. Because every person living on our streets—they have dreams, too. And if that means new laws or reforming the laws that we have so that we can build the homes this city needs, let us start that work today." Garcetti also said state lawmakers should "look at revising such state laws as the Costa-Hawkins Act."[65] Costa-Hawkins prohibits rent control on vacant apartments as well as on single-family homes and condos and has caused rising unaffordability in rent-controlled cities across California.

Garcetti further promoted Costa-Hawkins repeal at the September 29, 2017, signing ceremony in San Francisco for a package of fifteen state housing bills. With Governor Brown and nearly all of the key legislators present, Garcetti called for "empowering local governments" to increase renter protections. Repealing Costa-Hawkins and the Ellis Act would do just that. Costa-Hawkins, passed in 1995, has greatly contributed to the pricing out of the working and middle class by preventing cities from limiting rent hikes on vacant apartments. Such limits would reduce California's rents over time and enhance affordability in big cities. "This is a crisis," Garcetti told the crowd. "Everything should be on the table." In April 2018 Garcetti endorsed Prop 10, a measure to repeal Costa-Hawkins on California's November 2018 ballot.[66]

The combination of a strong citywide pro-housing coalition and a mayor committed to building housing, addressing homelessness, and expanding tenant and rental housing protections would represent a dramatic political shift for Los Angeles. It will take time for the city to recover from years of failed housing policies but Los Angeles is positioning itself to remain a home for low-income people and the working and middle class. The city's tenant and affordable housing activists will not stop pursuing this goal. As Larry Gross put it, "We are chiseling down the wall inch by inch, step by step. The opposition is strong but we are making progress."[67]

3

Keeping Austin Diverse

We are sick of being on the list of the most segregated communities
in this country.

Austin City Councilmember Greg Casar

Alejandra Ramirez and her three children moved into Austin's Cross Creek
apartments in June 2014, just as the city's hot summer began. Austin averages
highs in the nineties four months a year, and the summer heat routinely
exceeds a hundred degrees. Air conditioning is a must. But Ramirez soon
discovered that her apartment's air conditioning was not working. She told
the management, who said they would fix it. They did not. This made living
in the blisteringly hot apartment "very difficult. My kids would go to a neighbor's apartment that did have air conditioning because it was too hot for
them to stay at home."[1]

Ramirez soon learned from other tenants that refusing repairs was business as usual at the Cross Creek apartments. The lack of air conditioning was
soon followed by irregular hot water; the family once went eight consecutive
days without any hot water at all. Ramirez, who worked at a nearby Jack in
the Box, thought about leaving Cross Creek but "it was too hard to find an
affordable apartment and to meet the security deposit requirements." So
instead she did something she had never done before: she joined a protest. On
June 29, 2015, the overwhelmingly Latino and non-white Cross Creek tenants protested against their landlord for not making repairs and issuing eviction notices to thirty tenants. "Joining the tenants in the protest made me
feel empowered. It was almost impossible to function without air conditioning or hot water." Ramirez also united with fellow tenants in connecting to
the renter support group BASTA (Building and Strengthening Tenant
Action) to help improve her living conditions.[2]

The story of Alejandra Ramirez and the Cross Creek Apartments is all too
common in Austin. While civic leaders bemoan the city's declining racial
diversity, Austin's Latino and African American tenants are routinely forced

to live in substandard housing. All too often their complaints about unhealthy conditions lead not to repairs but to their displacement; buildings allowed to fall into decline are then demolished and replaced with upscale dwellings. Those families able to stay in Austin are often limited to low-opportunity, segregated communities in less desirable parts of town.

This chapter discusses the pricing out of Austin's working and middle class and efforts by dedicated activists and elected officials to chart the city on a more inclusive course. Austin's housing crisis reflects the intersection of race and class, as those most likely to be priced out are racial minorities. Whether Austin increases its racial and economic diversity or continues on the path of becoming a whiter and more affluent city is the core question facing the city; the answer is a question of political will.

AUSTIN'S TWO SIDES

Austin is roughly the size of San Francisco. Its rapidly growing population adds around 17,000 residents annually and should reach one million people in 2018. Austin is viewed as a beacon of progressivism in a deeply conservative state. It voted for Clinton over Trump by a 66 to 27 percent margin in 2016, and in 2005 Austin's Travis County was the only one of Texas's 254 counties to vote against a constitutional ban on gay marriage.

Austin residents pride themselves on marching to their own beat. Since 2000, "Keep Austin Weird" has been the city's mantra. Austin's official slogan is "The Live Music Capital of the World." The South by Southwest and Austin City Limits music festivals attract thousands from across the nation, as does Austin's year-round live music scene. Quality restaurants and many start-ups and tech businesses also bring a huge number of tourists and new-comers to the city. The only complaints most visitors have about Austin are the heat and crowded music venues.

But Austin has a far less progressive side, a side its forward-thinking image and promotion of "weirdness" conceal. Austin tenants, those lacking the money to buy homes in the city, have very few rights. They likely have fewer protections than renters in any "progressive" city in the United States. Texas law preempts local rent-control laws and, arguably, just-cause eviction protections as well. Landlords can also enter a tenant's home at virtually any time. But the core problem impacting the city's Latino and African American tenants has been the city's failure to ensure that they live in safe and healthy apartments. Austin's ineffective housing code enforcement has driven tenant displacement, neighborhood gentrification, and rising racial and economic inequality.

Tenants victimized by poor living conditions in Austin are overwhelmingly racial minorities. It is a discordant element for a city housing the library of President Lyndon Johnson, who signed the nation's major civil rights laws. Austin's racial and class divisions intersect in its mistreatment of tenants. It is a part of Austin that many whites either ignore or prefer not to see. Stephanie Trinh, who represents low-income Austin tenants at Texas Rio Grande Legal Aid (TRLA) and who works with its BASTA program, told me that soon after arriving in Austin she used to ask people of color if they ever said "Keep Austin weird." She was told that "only white people say that."[3]

Far too many of Austin's Latino and African American tenants live in slum conditions. Instead of making repairs, owners demolish apartments and replace them with upscale housing. Austin's displacement and gentrification pressures are coupled with land-use policies that restrict the construction of new housing for working- and middle-class tenants. Powerful neighborhood associations deny construction of new multi-unit housing in Austin's high-opportunity communities. Austin originally enacted zoning restrictions to ensure racial segregation. Today, Austin land-use policies are not driven by racial exclusion but achieve a similar result.

In his 2017 State of the City address, Austin Mayor Steve Adler acknowledged that "longstanding families in East Austin are already being priced out of their neighborhoods. . . . If we don't change, we will only see higher rents, higher taxes, more sprawl, worse traffic and less diversity." He stated, "Too many cannot afford the places that exist" and "communities of color are feeling this impact the hardest. . . . We've got tens of thousands of people in this city living in zip codes that weren't zoned for opportunity. Most are in the Eastern Crescent of our city. This is one reason why America's favorite boomtown ends up as the most economically segregated city in the country."[4]

I spoke with some extraordinarily committed people working to implement Mayor Adler's words about protecting Austin's racial and economic diversity. As in other cities that have long pursued exclusionary housing policies, powerful interests support the status quo. But momentum for a more inclusive Austin is building, and shifting city housing policies in that direction is a winnable fight.

DEMOLITION AND DISPLACEMENT

Lakeview: Oracle Replaces Latino Families

In June 2015, a luxury developer in Austin decided to demolish the Lakeview apartment complex. Lakeview included 14 buildings and 224 units. Nearly all housed Latino families, a group whose displacement city officials claim they are eager to stop.

The Lakeview complex bordered the nationally known Lady Bird Lake. Named after former presidential first lady and Texan Lady Bird Johnson, the lake is famous for its colony of 1.5 million Mexican free-tailed bats. The bats are a major tourist attraction. Boats cruise the lake at dusk so visitors can get the best view of bats putting on their remarkable nightly air show, which lasts nearly an hour.

Robin Wilkins, a tenant at Lakeview, loved living next to the lake. "Who wouldn't like a lake at their front door? It was less than a minute's walk away. We swam there. We fished there. There were picnic tables and barbecues. Then they yanked all of that away from us to make a profit."[5]

Wilkins lived in the Lakeview complex in 1997, when she was suddenly told she had to leave the premises within seventy-two hours because her son had gotten into a fight. "The manager told me that if I got rid of my son I could stay. I didn't know my rights. My rent was paid but when I was told on Friday night that I had to turn my key in by Sunday night, I found another place."

Wilkins returned to Lakeview with her two children in 2010. She paid $635 for a two-bedroom apartment. Soon after moving in she experienced bedbugs. When she asked the manager to deal with them she was told "you brought them in there, so now you have to get rid of them." Repairs that management said it would take care of when Wilkins first saw the unit were also not made. But she didn't complain: "I wasn't educated on my rights."

Wilkins was told when moving in that the owners planned to eventually demolish the complex but that she would get "plenty of notice." Texas law makes it easy to demolish even a fully occupied, structurally sound apartment complex. It simply requires the filing of the right paperwork. Demolitions can only be stopped if a building is historic or public pressure is brought to bear on the owners.

When demolition plans were announced, neither Wilkins nor the other Lakeview tenants got the "plenty of notice" they had been promised. Instead, the demolition of an apartment complex housing almost exclusively Latino working families moved with incredible speed. On June 26, 2015, management sent a letter to all tenants stating that "the Lakeview Apartments are planned for demolition and management will not be renewing leases at the property." On August 4, a new letter said, "The official date we will be closing is Sept. 30, 2015. All residents must be out by this date. The property will no longer have water or electricity in our buildings." At the time, the owner had no demolition permit. In addition, the notice was sent to Wilkins and other tenants who had leases through December. Management felt comfortable threatening to shut off utilities if these tenants did not move, despite this being three months before the end of their leases.[6]

In California, it is a misdemeanor for a landlord to threaten a utility shut-off to force tenants to move. But in Texas, property rights are owners' rights. Tenants have almost no rights.

Robin Wilkins was told of the demolition plans two weeks after she had renewed her lease for six months. The manager then told Wilkins in early September that she had better move out before the end of the month because "it won't be livable. We're shutting off the electricity and water." Wilkins was shocked. "My heart dropped. School was starting. My kids were registered and it was the only school they knew. All of their friends were at that school."

Until the manager told her about the termination of services, Wilkins had thought, "I have a lease. I don't have to go anywhere. Then it sank in. I had to move. Every week we got a letter telling us to move." Wilkins found a social worker to help her find another place. But "nothing was available. You had 200 families from Lakeview looking for new housing and every day people were moving out. All I could do was get my name on a waiting list."

Roxana Castro, another Lakeview tenant, also had trouble relocating. When Castro arrived in Austin in 2008 she lived with her family in the Sunnymeade Apartments in East Austin. She soon had to move, and the Sunnymeade building was later demolished. She relocated to an apartment where the rent was initially $650 a month. New management arrived and raised the rent to $725 plus $140 a month for water, which was previously included in the rent. The building was also undergoing renovation, and Castro and her family decided to move before the rent was raised further. In 2013 Castro was thrilled to get a three-bedroom apartment at Lakeview for only $825. "I thought the walking trail around the lake was pretty cool. I got two dogs so I could walk them. I really liked Lakeview."[7]

Now she was forced to find an apartment on short notice again. Castro's lease expired at the end of October but "the market was saturated with all of the families looking for a place. I worked with an apartment locator who said I needed three months to find an apartment. Not even homeless shelters were taking people in." Castro's husband had just gotten a new job delivering mail for the U.S. Postal Service. He could not take a day off to help find housing because he was within his ninety-day probation period. Castro finally found a two-bedroom apartment for $993, compared to the $825 at Lakeview for a three-bedroom. But given the tight apartment market Castro "was ecstatic to get something."

Lakeview tenants who had yet to leave got further encouragement to do so when the owner stopped making basic repairs. Tenant complaints about "rats, roaches, leaks and mold" were ignored. "It seemed that management did not care that the place was becoming run-down since the apartments were going to be demolished," Castro told me. Meanwhile, 121 children attending Austin schools were being displaced. Parents now had to suddenly find new housing and new schools, all while working full-time jobs.

By the September 30 shut-off date, only around thirty tenants remained. A handful had leases through December, with the rest ending at the end of October or November. Joel Jimenez, a local construction worker, told me that when he moved to Lakeview in May he signed a six-month lease for a large one-bedroom apartment and "nobody said a word about the complex soon being demolished." Jimenez was attracted to Lakeview by the low $636 monthly rent. He was forced to move to a much smaller one-bedroom apartment where in September 2017 he was paying $800.[8]

Jimenez told me that because of the short notice for moving and the inability to quickly find comparably sized apartments, he and other tenants had to leave a lot of furniture behind. Roxana Castro felt "some residents lost everything they had." As Areli Hernandez observed in Los Angeles, urban America is becoming a place where displaced tenants who are forced to downsize have little choice but to leave their furniture and other belongings behind.

Prior to moving to Lakeview Jimenez and his family spent four years at the Solaris apartments in Austin. He left because his home was "very poorly maintained by the landlord. Water kept coming in and they refused to fix it." After talking to Jiminez I checked the Yelp reviews for that property. One said, "My mom has regrettably taken. . . residence here and seeing how these people treat their tenants absolutely disgusts me. Not only does the staff lack basic human skills but the apartments themselves should be demolished due to hazardous living conditions." Another said, "This is hands down the worst apartment complex in Austin. I haven't been here a full year and have dealt with flooded rooms, countless roaches, numerous things falling apart and a terrible office staff. . . . You're better off living out of your car."[9]

All of the Austin tenants I spoke with had suffered from bad living conditions. Tenants complaining about the lack of repairs were told "If you don't like it here, leave." Managers know that unhappy tenants have few options since the same type of habitability problems exist elsewhere. Subjecting Latino and African American tenants to slum housing is not what Austin's goal of preserving racial diversity is about. Alberto Martinez, chair of the East Cesar Chavez Neighborhood Planning Team, described what Austin landlords are doing to the Latino working class as "a cultural cleansing, which is worse than gentrification."[10]

A city cannot stop displacement if landlords can allow their properties to fall into disrepair as a prelude to demolition. Martinez saw the 308-unit Shoreline Apartments, which also bordered Lady Bird Lake and which was home to 185 residents, demolished in 2011. Its mostly Latino tenants were displaced to make room for an upscale mixed-use project. The 102-unit Vista Lago complex on Lady Bird Lake was also demolished and replaced with housing for the affluent.[11]

The Lakeview tenants' opposition to their landlord's plans was unusual. Austin's lack of code enforcement disempowers and discourages tenants from asserting even their limited legal rights. Those I spoke with believed their fellow tenants feared being evicted in retaliation for complaining to the city, and they were probably right.

Robin Wilkins was inspired when city councilmember Greg Casar and some of his colleagues attended a rally at a middle school in early September to support the tenants: "For the City Council to come support us gave us a real boost. It was uplifting for all of the tenants. I had sent emails to the media to get them to come to the rally and at the school I got connected to Ruby Roe, an activist who said she could help me find housing." In late September, Casar, a champion for Latino tenants, joined other councilmembers at the Lakeview complex to directly offer assistance to the tenants. But Casar and his colleagues were "asked to leave the premises under threat of police."[12]

Wilkins found a vacancy in late September in an apartment building where her mother lived and the manager knew her. She moved soon after. She had to pay $1,160 for her new home, $400 more per month than she had been paying at Lakeview. She is no longer across from Lady Bird Lake, and the location is not as accessible to stores and transportation. But she is still on the main street of the Riverside neighborhood, and her kids have adjusted to new schools. "I took what I could find. I got lucky. With 200 families looking for housing, finding any place to live was a struggle."

Ousted for Oracle

It was soon learned that the owner's rush to displace Lakeview tenants even before their leases expired was not about building new luxury housing. Instead, the owner built a luxury apartment complex which was then sold, along with the rest of the site, to the tech giant Oracle. Oracle then built a huge new campus, using the new upscale apartments for its employees.

In other words, Austin saw 224 affordable apartments housing mostly Latino families replaced with an office park and upscale apartments for high-paid, primarily white Oracle employees. That's not how a city improves its racial and class diversity.

While Austin could not stop the demolition, city officials could have told the owner they would not approve anything but new housing on the site. That could have saved the complex. Or the city could have publicly asked Oracle to voluntarily contribute housing assistance to the displaced Lakeview tenants.

Austin officials did neither. The city did not even ensure that the prior landlords at Lakeview made necessary repairs. Instead, city officials allowed tenants to be displaced under the false threat that their leases could be invalidated and their electricity and water could legally be turned off.

Robin Wilkins felt the city "had to know about Oracle coming to the Lakeview site" when the demolition was planned. She saw Oracle's purchase as "another slap in my face. They knocked me out of my affordable housing and now they're going to give the place I was living to their out-of-state employees. Why couldn't the second-largest corporation in the world also build housing for us?"[13]

In June 2016, sixty-nine former Lakeview tenants, who had occupied twenty-four units at the complex, filed a lawsuit against the former owner. The lawsuit revealed that less than a year after their forced displacement these tenants were paying on average $240 more per month for rent than they had paid at Lakeview, an increase of 28 percent. Some of the plaintiffs described the difficulty their children faced adjusting to new schools, a situation that could have been alleviated had the Lakeview owner allowed tenants to stay through December.[14]

Oracle, whose plans clearly drove the rapid displacement of the Lakeview tenants, refused to comment on their displacement. Oracle CEO Larry Ellison had a 2017 net worth of $63.7 billion, placing him among the ten richest people in the world. Ellison or Oracle could have easily ensured that the tenants victimized by the landlord's likely undisclosed strategy to secure a campus for the company were made whole. But they did not, and Austin city officials put no pressure on Ellison, Oracle, or the prior owner to do so. Oracle purchased forty-three acres in Austin. Ellison said in March 2018 that he expects Austin's Oracle campus to grow to about 10,000 employees in coming years.[15]

In response to the mass Lakeview evictions, Austin passed a tenant relocation ordinance on September 1, 2016. The measure required owners to give tenants facing displacement at least 120 days' notice before the filing of an application for a building or demolition permit that would force them from their homes. One hundred twenty days is certainly better than thirty. Robin Wilkins takes pride in seeing how the Lakeview struggle brought passage of the tenant relocation law: "I think it helped open people's eyes. People who run apartment complexes act like gods. Tenants are afraid to complain about problems because if they then get evicted they could have nowhere else to go."[16]

Evictions at 5020 Manor Road

Less than a year after Lakeview, the pattern of run-down housing followed by displacement and demolition or major renovation was repeated at an East Austin apartment complex at 5020 Manor Road that had recently been sold. On the same day the city passed its tenant relocation law, the new owner issued eviction notices to the entire building. Thirty Latino families faced the loss of their homes. These eviction notices were issued just as the new school year began. As with Lakeview, the landlord's timing of the evictions required working parents to find both housing and new schools for their kids.

Many of the children at 5020 Manor Road attended highly regarded Blanton Elementary School. Blanton is the type of school typically offered to children in high-opportunity neighborhoods. The low-income Latino children living at 5020 Manor Road were getting access to Blanton's quality education. It was the type of inclusion that Austin city officials publicly seek.

Blanton staff and students publicly supported the right of the children living at 5020 Manor to stay in their homes. A protest was held at the property on September 22, 2016, as the tenants and their community allies demanded more time for them to find new homes. Leandra Yanez, who had lived in the building with her three daughters for six years, stated, "My apartment had a leak that was causing mold and I had to fix it myself. My refrigerator still isn't working. And they just kept taking my rent." Tenants had complained about the prior owner's failure to make repairs; the sale of the run-down building to a speculator who then evicted all of the tenants fit an all-too-common pattern in Austin.[17]

Austin's elected officials clearly stood by the families. Mayor pro tem Kathie Tovo and councilmembers Delia Garza, Sabino "Pio" Renteria, and Greg Casar all spoke out for the tenants at a September 28 rally with tenants at the school. In a joint statement, the councilmembers said the mere thirty days' notice given by the owner was "unacceptable." The owner subsequently said he was unaware of the new tenant relocation law, which required four months' notice. Under pressure from the council, he gave the tenants more time. But by the end of September 2016, all of them had been displaced.[18]

Alberta Phillips, a columnist at the *Austin American-Statesman,* pointed out that 5020 Manor Road is "walking distance from the affluent Mueller redevelopment with its pricey homes and condos, sprawling parks and trails, trendy shops and restaurants and protected bike lanes. So the 5020 Manor Road's proximity to Mueller makes it too valuable for low-income residents who have occupied it all these years as it languished in disrepair."[19]

Phillips also noted that the Mueller redevelopment was a case in which city-owned land was transformed into upscale housing. Formerly an airport, the Mueller site could have been redeveloped to include low-income housing. Austin could also have protected the many longtime low-income African American and Latino tenants living near this upscale development, as the redevelopment made them vulnerable to future displacement. But Austin's past mayors and city managers had focused on maximizing property values. They saw no reason to offer opportunities in a redeveloped area to the non-affluent. The impact of the transformation of the site on the city's future economic and racial diversity was not part of the equation.

More than a year after the tenants vacated 5020 Manor Road, the building was still undergoing a massive renovation. Upon completion, there will be no evidence that it was ever home to working-class Latino families. Manor Road is a perfect case study of the gentrification of East Austin and the displacement of Austin's racial minorities.

Austin city government routinely allowed buildings like those at 5020 Manor Road to fall into disrepair. The city's failure to initiate legal action to force owners to make repairs has facilitated tenant displacement and the loss of affordable rental housing. In October 2013 Austin sought to encourage landlords to make repairs by putting poorly maintained buildings on a "repeat offenders" list. As Shoshana Krieger, the project director of BASTA at Texas Rio Grande Legal Aid told me, "This has become a speculator's list. Properties like 5020 Manor Road end up demolished or significantly renovated and owners then sell them for big profits. Apartments previously affordable to the working class are then replaced with upscale rental units or condos."[20]

In July 2015, a University of Texas School of Law study from the school's Entrepreneurship and Community Development Clinic under director Heather K. Way concluded that the repeat offender program "has 'major flaws' when it comes to identifying unsafe rental properties, monitoring code violations and the length of time it takes to address dangerous and hazardous conditions at repeat offender properties." Austin "is still failing to take swift and aggressive enforcement actions against rental property owners who repeatedly fail to fix dangerous building conditions."[21]

The study also found that Austin's code enforcement division "is not penalizing" owners who fail to meet required deadlines for repairs. This has created "an environment where landlords can ignore initial Notices of Violation." The city took an average of 83 days to reinspect program properties after a repair deadline and 159 days to address a code violation. These lengthy delays left "tenants exposed to dangerous living conditions for many months."

San Francisco's reinspection period after a repair deadline is either fourteen or thirty days depending on the violation. For urgent habitability violations like lack of heat and hot water, reinspections usually occur within twenty-four hours. Landlords failing to meet these deadlines are assessed reinspection fees, which become liens on their property if not paid. Austin's giving a landlord nearly three months to make repairs encourages bad living conditions for residents. According to Austin Tenants' Council Executive Director Juliana Gonzales, "It's not uncommon in Austin to see properties with repeated, serious, or longstanding code violations that threaten the health and safety of tenants, and to see those code violations go unresolved for long periods of time because there are not adequate enforcement actions Code can take."[22]

According to BASTA's Shoshana Krieger, "Historically there has never been a culture in the City's Legal Department office of suing landlords for not making repairs. Only recently has the city begun bringing habitability cases." In 2016 Austin officials conceded it had only "three inspectors to address all the inspections that are required under that repeat offender program." As of January 2016, the repeat offenders list included 38 properties, with 46 soon to be added. Another 200 were under review for inclusion. By late 2017, 166 properties were eligible, with only 78 registered. Fortunately, the city council increased funding for code enforcement in 2018, and four additional enforcement officers were added to oversee unsafe, unhealthy, and substandard properties.[23]

In 1980 when I began working with tenants in rundown SRO hotels in San Francisco's Tenderloin, I quickly learned that housing code enforcement is the foundation for preventing demolitions and tenant displacement. When owners can avoid making repairs, tenants continually leave. And when a building is allowed to fall into acute disrepair, new owners decide it is cheaper to demolish and rebuild than to make repairs. This is particularly true in Austin, where applications to demolish non-historic buildings are automatically approved. Why make repairs for existing low-income tenants when you can tear down the building and construct new housing for upscale renters?[24]

Austin's chief problem was that while the city council supported stronger code enforcement, it had only limited control over the code department's operations due to Austin's strong-city-manager form of government. Recognizing that outside groups were needed to ensure safe housing for Austin families, in late 2015 councilmember Casar and his colleagues allocated $350,000 a year for five years to launch the TRLA/BASTA Residents Advocacy Project. This was a strong move toward protecting working-class tenants of color disproportionately at risk from substandard housing. It reflected the council's commitment to a more inclusive Austin, and its acknowledgment that tenants who are organized, mobilized, and educated about their rights are the best advocates for securing city action against substandard housing.

By fall 2016 Austin's displacement of its Latino and African American population was accelerating. Reporters bemoaned "the plight of a city increasingly unable to retain a more diverse populace—ethnically, racially, socio-economically—as the wave of gentrification continues to displace a largely minority segment." Yet Austin could limit this displacement through more aggressive housing code enforcement. When eviction notices were issued to over thirty tenants at Cross Creek Apartments in June 2016, Austin got another chance to do the right thing.[25]

CROSS CREEK: AUSTIN TAKES A POSITIVE STEP

On July 1, 2014, Royce Mulholland purchased the Cross Creek apartments with the help of $2 million from the city of Austin. Austin often gives money to private owners in exchange for getting repairs made and for entering into affordability agreements. At the time Cross Creek suffered from broken passageways, damage to exterior walls, missing gutters, deteriorated stairways, broken windows, and other problems. City funding to renovate properties and ensure their long-term affordability can be a sound strategy—if the city monitors compliance with the agreement.

Mulholland got the money because city officials felt he had a positive track record following his renovation of the Palms on North Lamar apartments. The December 5, 2011, opening of that project (available on YouTube) featured testimonials from Austin's mayor, councilmembers, builders, and Mulholland himself about how the $33.5 million, 476-unit project was the "future of what affordable housing should be in Austin."[26] But Austin city officials apparently did not check Yelp reviews of the Palms before giving Mulholland more money. Here is a sample: October 10, 2013: "The complex is infested with german cockroaches, and although they offer free pest control roaches just keep coming in through the front door. I've lived here for a month and have paid to cancel my lease because this place is disgusting"; July 14, 2013: "This place is horrible . . ."; May 18, 2014: "DO NOT LIVE HERE!!! I just got my apartment and it's full of roaches." Nor did Austin's model for future affordable housing improve over time. A Yelp review from July 2015: "Every previous statement is true and then some"; May 2016: "Worst place to live. So glad I'm out and I beg anyone looking into this place to think again"; August 2017: "Unless you're homeless and have to, I would avoid this place."[27]

Although strong evidence that Mulholland's ownership did not maintain the Palms was only a click away, Austin ignored these warnings. Not surprisingly, Mulholland failed to make promised repairs at the Cross Creek apartments. By November 2014 conditions were so bad that Cross Creek was placed on the city's repeat offender list.

In June 2015 the property, which included eighteen buildings, stopped providing hot water. The city sued Mulholland on January 4, 2016, for a court order requiring that he restore hot water and make repairs. According to the city's lawsuit, "In the span of six months a city code inspector came by a total of 13 times and discovered the same problem of no hot water every time."[28] Why the city felt it needed thirteen inspections to prove the obvious is troubling, but at least the city finally broke from tradition and went to court to get building conditions improved.

Despite getting $2 million in exchange for agreeing to make repairs and keep the building's rent affordable, in June Mulholland responded to the city's legal actions by issuing eviction notices to over thirty tenants. On June 29 tenants held a rally and marched through their complex demanding their right to stay. They put up a "NOW EVICTING" sign across from the landlord's "NOW LEASING" sign.

The day after the protest the city got a court stipulation with Mulholland to restore the hot water. On July 2 Mulholland withdrew the eviction notices. The Cross Creek Tenants Association had won. The city's resort to the courts on behalf of the tenants made a huge difference. But even more important was that the Cross Creek tenants had united in a tenants' association. Its effective organizing changed the power dynamics. "Since we started organizing, the office has paid more attention to my requests," tenant Amado Ariza said. Fellow tenant Kisha Williams said, "I think they thought we would give up . . . but I'm determined to keep fighting, 'cause this isn't right."[29]

Cross Creek was one of four Austin complexes that received city funds for affordable housing despite being on the city's repeat offender list. Austin's Neighborhood Housing and Community Development (NHCD) provided millions of dollars to negligent landlords because "it was not aware there were properties it helped fund on the repeat offender list until Austin Code brought the Cross Creek situation to its attention." Oddly, NHDC officials then concluded that a building's presence on the repeat offender list "would make a compelling case for funding it even more."[30]

As a result of the October 2017 settlement of a lawsuit brought on behalf of tenants by TRLA, the long-promised repairs at Cross Creek were finally completed. But while this legal settlement and the city's affordability agreement should protect Cross Creek tenants, others Latino families in North Austin may not be so fortunate. North Austin was a community of last resort for working-class Latino families, which is why Cross Creek tenants fought so hard to stay. But as attorney Shoshana Krieger notes, "It is only a fifteen-minute drive from city hall to Cross Creek. North Austin could be an eventual stop on the city's gentrification train."[31]

As we saw in Los Angeles's Boyle Heights and Highland Park, neighborhoods that seem immune from gentrification can suddenly become at risk in response to rising housing prices in adjacent communities. This process is also occurring in Austin. If you start driving on the city's twenty-three-mile-long Lamar Boulevard south of the river, heading toward North Austin, you will pass through both longtime and newly gentrified single-family-home neighborhoods. Bouldin Creek, south of Lady Bird Lake, was a lower-middle-class single-family-home neighborhood in the 1980s that has long since been gentrified. Rosedale is another overwhelmingly white single-family-home neighborhood that has shifted from middle to upper middle class. Crestview and Brentwood are longtime primarily white working-class communities that are still somewhat affordable but in transition toward a more upscale status.

Once these neighborhoods become too expensive for the working and middle class, North Austin will become the next logical landing point for primarily young white renters needing housing. North Austin includes working-class single-family homes on many streets that intersect with Lamar Boulevard, a major artery. In addition, it is just a short drive from downtown. North Austin's geography makes it particularly vulnerable to gentrification. Its potentially more upscale future puts what has happened at the neighborhood's Trifecta Square Apartments in a more ominous context.

TENANTS NOT WINNING AT THE TRIFECTA

Eva Marroquin moved to Austin in 2004. In 2013 she found a one-bedroom home at the Trifecta Square Apartments for $750 per month. Marroquin found the fifty-two-unit garden-style apartment building in north-central Austin very convenient. When she was shown the premises she noticed that the fan over the stove was not working. The manager said that was no problem and he would fix it. Eva soon realized that the nonworking fan was the least of her problems and that management did not follow through on promises to make repairs.[32]

Hitting the trifecta at a horse race (picking the top three finishers) is a great outcome. Austin's Trifecta Square Apartments offered Eva Marroquin and her fellow tenants a much less positive experience.

Despite media coverage of Austin's failed code enforcement at Lakeview, 5020 Manor Road, the Cross Creek apartments, and other properties, when I spoke with Marroquin in September 2017 conditions at the Trifecta were as bad as ever. There was no sign the city's tenant protection efforts had improved.

Marroquin lived with rats, mold, a fly infestation, and electrical problems. "The rats are the worst. A lot of tenants left because rats were eating the food off their dinner table. My ten-year-old son is afraid to sleep alone in his bed because he is afraid of the rats." Marroquin constantly complained to the management about the rats. She was told, "If you don't like it here, move." But moving was not an option. Marroquin had signed another one-year lease in May 2017, before the rat problem worsened, and the management said that if she broke the lease they would go after her for the rent. Marroquin was left to buy wood and try to block the rats' entry point on her own.

As in most of Austin's troubled properties, the vast majority of Trifecta tenants are Latinos. Some are undocumented and do not complain to city code enforcement officials out of fear of being turned over to immigration. Austin code enforcement staff should conduct regular inspections of properties like the Trifecta instead of waiting for a complaint to trigger a visit, but the city had been informed of the Trifecta's habitability problems. Marroquin stated, "I regularly called the city and inspectors came out and issued notices of violation to the owner. But no repairs were done. I was once told that the case had been closed. I made sure it got reopened. I am very frustrated and upset that the city is not making sure the rats are eliminated and other repairs made."

In addition to the problems with rodents and repairs, when Marroquin moved to the Trifecta she was not made aware of how high the water and utility charges would be, Her rent has increased from $750 to $870 in less than four years. She pays a whopping $93 each month to the city for water and pays the owner $150 per month for other utilities. That brings her total monthly housing cost to over $1,100. Nearly all of the tenants I spoke to in Austin had very high monthly water charges on top of their rent. Tenants' actual monthly housing costs are often at least $200 higher than their stated rent figures.

When I spoke to Marroquin in September 2017 she had begun working with sixteen to eighteen other families to demand action from the city to force repairs at the Trifecta. Councilmember Greg Casar had connected her to BASTA, headed by Shoshana Krieger. Marroquin had followed all the right steps in alerting her landlord and the city that the health and safety of families with children were in jeopardy at the Trifecta, but neither had effectively responded to her requests.

The property could soon join the list of Austin's rundown buildings whose owners end up displacing tenants, demolishing or renovating their apartments, and replacing them with upscale dwellings. If Austin wants North Austin to avoid the displacement of working-class families of color and the gentrification seen in East Austin, habitability problems at buildings like the Trifecta cannot be ignored.

GREG CASAR: FIGHTING FOR RACIAL AND ECONOMIC DIVERSITY

Many Austin residents want far more done to address the city's rising inequality and racial segregation. In December 2014, backers of this goal elected to the city council a champion in Gregorio "Greg" Casar. Casar is a native Texan and the son of Mexican immigrants. He was only twenty-five when first elected to represent a district that is 70 percent non-white. Most of Casar's constituents are Latino, and he also represents the second-largest number of African Americans of any district.

Casar told me in August 2017, "I ran on a social justice platform but did not run as a planning or zoning person. I was not seen as being in a particular political camp." As he campaigned, Casar realized that the city's land-use plans "led to increased gentrification, segregation, and housing injustice." He was also concerned that the "voices of people in my community were not at the table on land-use and planning issues."[33]

Casar has worked to change this dynamic. He helped organize the first-ever tenants' associations at two mobile home parks in Austin. As with the Cross Creek tenant association mentioned above, these associations—both in Casar's district—helped stop unlawful and unfair evictions.

In 2015, councilmember Casar gave a speech promoting accessory dwelling units (ADUs) that laid out Austin's biggest challenge: reducing class- and race-based segregation. Casar saw ADUs as "allowing renters to live in high-opportunity neighborhoods," which in Austin are typically overwhelmingly white. Casar deemed expanding affordable housing in such neighborhoods as a "moral imperative. . . . We are sick of being on the list of the most segregated communities in this country."[34]

Casar emphasized that too many families of color in Austin were "zoned out" of the areas in which they preferred to live. He backed the urbanist agenda of increased walkability, civic engagement, and more livable cities, but insisted that this "needs to be for everyone. Not just those who can place a down payment on a house in order to participate in planning Austin's future." Those unable to "place a down payment" are Austin's tenants, particularly the Latino and African American renters denied access to the Austin neighborhoods that would better enrich their educational, employment, and cultural opportunities. Fifty-five percent of Austin residents are renters. They have largely been excluded from the city's broader land-use planning, which has been the province of Austin's homeowners, 66 percent of whom are white.[35]

Casar recognized that in planning and land-use debates, "It's difficult to bring in new voices. Planners need to focus on the outcomes of each proposal in order to get people engaged." In 2016, Casar sponsored a "Stay in Place" ordinance to "reduce housing restrictions for lower income and moderate-income homeowners who wish to add additional units or uses on their property so they can afford to stay on their property." It was among a package of measures he introduced to "increase economic and racial integration in 'high opportunity' areas, and slow displacement in more vulnerable neighborhoods."[36]

Austin's declining racial and economic diversity stems from its failure to aggressively combat gentrification and displacement and its perpetuation of exclusionary single-family-home zoning that excludes tenants from desirable neighborhoods. Both reflect a city whose white-homeowner-dominated neighborhood organizations have long called the shots on housing.

Now Casar and a new generation of pro-housing activists are pushing for a more inclusive, multiracial, economically diverse Austin. They are up against opposition from powerful neighborhood groups whose homeowners profit from exclusionary land-use policies that restrict housing supply and increase home prices. Most of these neighborhood groups want to keep Austin's housing and land-use policies just the way they are.

EMPOWERING HOMEOWNERS TO OPPOSE HOUSING

Austin vests its homeowner groups with unmatched urban power. It starts with giving near-veto power over rezoning and other neighborhood matters to Neighborhood Plan Contact Teams (NPCTs). According to the city's website, the "plan contact team... is a group of individuals designated to be the stewards or advocates of their adopted neighborhood plan. They work with city staff towards the implementation of the plan recommendations, review and initiate plan amendments, serve as community points of contact, and work on behalf of other neighborhood stakeholders."[37]

These city-designated teams are overwhelmingly composed of older homeowners. In fact, NPCTs are primarily made up of representatives of neighborhood homeowners' associations. These associations have used their power to stop construction of new multi-unit buildings.

On November 14, 2016, the Austin city auditor released a report that found that "planning efforts for Austin's neighborhoods are inequitable and have lacked robust and representative participation." The auditor also found that

- "Only 13 of 30 neighborhood plans were approved by more than one percent of the neighborhood's population. In one case, only 19 residents participated in crafting a plan that affected a neighborhood with nearly 13,000 residents."
- "Rental units accounted for 82 percent of the housing in one neighborhood, but only two renters were included in the plan's drafting."
- "The bylaws for 30 of the 31 contact teams the city auditor reviewed contained barriers to voter eligibility."[38]

The report confirmed that when it comes to deciding who gets to live in Austin, the city has long allowed older white homeowners to call the shots.

AURA GETS PRO-HOUSING BALL ROLLING

Susan Somers moved to Austin in 2005 to attend graduate school. She paid $475 for a one-bedroom apartment that in 2017 rented for $900. It's a good reflection of Austin's skyrocketing housing costs over the past decade.

Somers came to the housing issue as part of a broader interest in urban livability. She joined Eric Goff and other urbanists in the fall of 2013 in opposing "stealth dorm" legislation that limited the occupancy of a household to four unrelated persons (the previous limit was six). This is a common tactic to preserve single-family-home neighborhoods in college towns where many students can only make rent by living in large households. Described as a "fight between affordability and neighborhood preservation," the city council voted six to one for the latter.[39]

Goff described the campaign to stop the "stealth dorm" measure as a "test run" for AURA, Austinites for Urban Rail Action. AURA was created to address Austin's diverse livability issues. Somers joined AURA's original board in 2014 and became board president in 2015. AURA "advocates for an Austin that's inclusive, open to change, and welcoming to everyone." An inclusive Austin must be more affordable. This requires building a lot more housing than Austin has in the past.

AURA has sought to end the legacy of Austin's race-based zoning restrictions. For example, Austin has the highest minimum lot size in Texas. Its large lot sizes were approved after World War II, and many believe they were designed to prevent returning African American soldiers from using money from the GI bill to settle in Austin. Smaller lot sizes increase density, adding housing options the working and middle class, along with racial minorities, can more likely afford.

TEXAS RESTRICTS AUSTIN HOUSING OPTIONS

Texas law limits Austin's affordable housing strategies. As noted above, state law prevents cities from stopping the demolition of sound rental housing unless a historic building is involved. In addition, the state prevents cities from enacting rent control. Texas also bars cities from requiring developers of multi-unit buildings to designate a given number of those units as affordable (the practice known as inclusionary housing).

In 2016, Greg Casar backed an effort to impose linkage fees on new developments, with the money going toward affordable housing. Many cities have linkage fees, which are applied per square foot of new construction. The term refers to the link between the jobs created by commercial development and the need for more affordable housing.

Casar told me that to avoid political problems he selected a linkage fee of only $2 per square foot, an amount far less than that required in other cities. But it made no difference. The Texas Association of Builders got wind of Casar's proposal and quickly convinced the state legislature to ban Austin and other Texas cities from imposing the fees (with Austin the state capital, state legislators can easily follow local politics). The group's general counsel claimed the linkage fee ban "protects housing affordability by preventing cities from adopting fees on all new housing and construction." He said a bill designed to raise millions for affordable housing would instead "price out thousands of Texans." Although linkage fees are used in Seattle, Denver, and many other cities outside California, the sponsor of the bill wanted "to make sure that Texas does not go the way of California on this issue."[40]

Austin had viewed the linkage fees as "a pillar in a plan to raise $600 million over 10 years to help buy and preserve affordable housing for minorities." Austin Mayor Steve Adler backed the linkage fee plan. But the state legislature did not care. The Texas senate voted twenty-seven to four to bar cities from imposing linkage fees; Austin's plans for a new revenue source for affordable housing were squelched.[41]

Texas also denies Austin affordable housing funds by preventing the city from using the rising property tax revenue generated by the city's development boom. In 2018 Austin will for the first time send more property tax revenue to the state than it gets back. This state money grab frustrates Casar. He sees cranes dominating the city skyline and "buildings erected left and right," but Texas does not allow Austin to spend that increased property tax revenue on affordable housing.

AUSTIN'S POWERS

Despite state restrictions, Austin still has the power to do much more to increase racial and economic diversity. It can improve code enforcement. It can increase spending for affordable housing. The city has passed two housing bonds but the most recent one failed. When I spoke with Casar in August 2017 he foresaw the city placing a $100 million bond for new affordable housing on the November 2018 ballot; by April 2018 the worsening crisis led Casar and others to back a $300 million bond. The $250 million housing bond ultimately placed on Austin's November 2018 ballot is its biggest ever. Casar has called for a "radical increase in publicly owned and publicly funded housing, especially in Central Austin neighborhoods." He believes the city's efforts to buy public land for affordable housing "have fallen short." Austin also retains the power to grant developers density and height bonuses in exchange for providing affordable housing. This could expand housing opportunities for those otherwise priced out at no cost to the city.[42]

AURA wants Austin to implement a strategy for "abundant housing." The group believes that "when Austin has enough homes to accommodate all those who wish to live here, housing will be more affordable across the entire housing market. Abundant housing creates diverse neighborhoods of people from different economic, racial, and familial statuses, and prevents the displacement of economically disadvantaged residents."[43] AURA has a novel idea for discouraging homeowners from restricting housing in order to increase their own property values: automatic upzoning. Higher property valuations in single-family-home neighborhoods would trigger automatic increases in allowable density. Homeowners would still benefit from increased home values but not without allowing new multi-unit housing.

EVOLVE AUSTIN PARTNERS AND CODENEXT

In 2016, Austin began what AURA board member Eric Goff described as a "once-in-a-generation opportunity" to revise its land-use laws. Called CodeNEXT, this land-use code revision process will either promote housing and a more inclusive Austin or reaffirm the status quo. The outcome depends on what the city council decides in 2018. Evolve Austin Partners (EAP), a broad and diverse political coalition, is mobilizing behind the inclusive vision.

Originally created in 2014 by nonprofit groups seeking a more affordable and sustainable Austin, EAP expanded in January 2017 to meet the political challenge of securing council support for a version of CodeNEXT that would help further a more inclusive city. EAP faced strong opposition from powerful neighborhood homeowner groups that prefer to keep single-family-home zoning and have long controlled Austin's land-use politics. Thomas Visco, a young activist and AURA board member, joined his business partner Francisco Enriquez and Eric Goff in an effort to transform EAP into a political coalition that could win the battle over CodeNEXT. This required Visco to overcome a "twenty- to thirty-year discourse in Austin that developers were the problem." EAP's goal, which parallels efforts in other cities, was to shift the "underlying DNA of progressive politics in Austin to recognizing that building infill housing was the environmentalist and social justice approach."[44]

Visco met with real estate, business, affordable housing, and environmental groups and realized they all backed increased multi-family housing. But "you were asking traditional adversaries to become allies. There were a lot of tough conversations. Some of these groups had been doing things a certain way for thirty years and needed to recognize that those ways would not win this fight."

On January 30, 2017, the broadest land-use coalition in Austin's history decided to move forward. EAP included such groups as Environment Texas, the Austin Chamber of Commerce, Austin Habitat for Humanity, the Home Builders Association of Greater Austin, TexPIRG (Texas Public Interest Research Group), the Austin Technology Council, and the Austin Board of Realtors. Austin Music People, which advocates for the city's renowned music scene, also joined the effort, as did Friends of Austin Neighborhoods, a pro-housing alternative to the city's traditional associations.

I knew Luke Metzger, state director of Environment Texas, from his work in the 1990s with CALPIRG (California Public Interest Research Group). I asked him why a longtime environmental group was now engaged with hous-ing. He replied, "Environment Texas joined Evolve Austin because a new development code that permits and encourages denser housing in neighbor-hoods that can be navigated by foot, on bike, or by transit is a clear win for the environment. Failing to provide places within Austin for population growth virtually assures the continuation of the region's sprawling development pat-terns. That means more loss of open space, more carbon emissions due to longer commutes, and more contamination of our creeks and streams."[45]

Metzger is among a growing number of environmental activists who see infill housing as critical to achieving green goals. Environmental groups do not often align with homebuilders and realtors, but that's what's happening in Austin around CodeNEXT. Visco saw uniting these "strange bedfellows" as necessary for "disrupting" a city long governed by anti–rental housing neighborhood groups. The disparate groups would "sink or swim" together in seeking a more inclusive Austin.

A GENERATIONAL FIGHT

The battle over Austin's future was a "generational fight." For many millen-nials, Austin housing policies were not working. The young middle class was priced out of the city's desirable central neighborhoods. This would continue as long as neighborhood associations could maintain laws mandating large lot sizes, single-family zoning, and other strategies to exclude more affordable multi-unit housing. Many boomers personally benefited from the rising property values created by artificially restricting housing supply. Boomers might bemoan Austin's housing segregation and declining racial diversity, but these outcomes were promoted by their favored housing policies.

"CodeNEXT" was an unfortunately wonky term for a land-use revision process that could shape the future of who gets to live in Austin. Even a term like "Rezone Austin" would have given the general public a clearer sense of what was going on. Regardless of the terminology, Austin's Latino and African American tenants faced such urgent problems with unhealthy living conditions, displacement, and gentrification that they did not have the time to focus on a long-term land-use revision. EAP also had to explain to knee-jerk opponents of development that the alternative—suburban sprawl—was much worse for the environment. To raise community understanding of what the term "CodeNEXT" meant for Austin's future, EAP came up with a savvy strategy: a door-to-door housing canvass.

CANVASSING FOR HOUSING

There are hundreds of door-to-door canvassing operations in the United States; most address environmental issues. Canvassing around housing is rare. When I was promoting the creation of a national housing trust fund in 2000, my organization funded a canvass in St. Louis to pressure Missouri Senator Christopher "Kit" Bond to support the issue. The canvassing was successful on a trial basis but the national political situation soon changed so we did not proceed further. At EAP, Thomas Visco was running the CodeNEXT campaign. Visco's first job out of college had been with TexPIRG, where he had learned the nuts and bolts of canvassing. According to Visco, "The PIRGs have boiled canvassing down to a science." Now he would apply that science to securing six votes on the council for a pro-housing, inclusive version of CodeNEXT. Austin's pro-housing groups lacked the "ecosystem" necessary to move their agenda politically; Visco felt a housing canvass could change that.

The canvass began in June 2017. The standard rap used by canvassers connected current land-use policies to "massive displacement, less transit, and skyrocketing housing costs," maintaining that "the status quo has driven Austin in the wrong direction. This is the best chance we have ever had to make sure we manage growth right." Much of the rap focused on Austin's traffic gridlock. Residents were asked to sign a petition "telling the Mayor and Council to make sure we get CodeNEXT right, and pass a plan that reduces traffic gridlock in Austin."[46] The petitions can be used to mobilize signers to contact councilmembers, and collectively they create a database of between twenty and forty thousand Austin residents who support a different land-use vision for the city.

EAP was trying to build the grassroots and political infrastructure necessary to combat powerful homeowner opposition to any meaningful reforms through CodeNEXT. Given the long-entrenched power of such homeowner groups, the battle over expanding housing opportunities in Austin proved a very tough fight.

THE AUSTIN BARGAIN

CodeNEXT was intertwined with Mayor Steve Adler's call for an "Austin bargain" over new housing development. The "bargain" would protect central Austin's single-family-home neighborhoods from increased density by targeting new housing to major transit corridors. Adler's plan offered the housing boost that AURA, Evolve Austin, and other backers of increased density sought while avoiding conflict with the powerful homeowner groups insistent on protecting existing single-family-home neighborhoods. Adler thought this strategy "would mean we would begin the code revision process with agreement on as many as 95 percent of all properties in the city."[47]

But many disagree that middle-class housing opportunities should be limited to highly-trafficked streets. As the parent of two young children, Susan Somers feels traffic corridors are not that safe for kids. Councilmember Casar saw it this way: "Building more housing in transit corridors and in central Austin neighborhoods is essential for preserving racial diversity. It increases transit ridership and reduces traffic problems, all while adding a significant number of housing units. But there are a lot of high-opportunity neighborhoods that do not have transit corridors."

Casar believes land-use laws in some single-family zoned neighborhoods will "have to change." To ensure "the economic integration of Latinos and African Americans," they must obtain housing in "high-opportunity" neighborhoods. Casar understands the resistance: "It is forgivable and understandable that at a time of rapidly increasing housing costs everyday folks can give up on the idea of integration. Some figure that adding multi-unit buildings in their neighborhood will not solve the bigger diversity problem."

Mayor Adler wanted Austin to build at least 135,000 new housing units in the next decade. That is a realizable goal. Austin is a sprawling city. Density has primarily been increased in the city's downtown, which as of December 2016 had thirty-one high-rise projects either under construction, approved, or planned for completion between 2017 and 2020. But San Francisco and

Los Angeles show what happens to housing prices when cities build high-rises downtown while sharply restricting height and density in the vast swath of residential neighborhoods. Downtown housing is typically less affordable. It is also unlikely to house the Latino and African American families that Austin officials say they want to keep in the city.

These low-income and working-class families could live in thousands of new units in North Austin, which has many areas like the open space surrounding the Cross Creek Apartments. Cross Creek is among many one- to two-story apartment complexes in North Austin whose surroundings cry out for taller and denser housing. Austin could use density bonuses in these areas to expand affordable housing options. This adds racially diverse, dense, and more affordable housing to an ungentrified neighborhood along a major transit corridor. It is completely consistent with the "Austin bargain." It also creates an alternative future for North Austin that avoids its otherwise likely path toward displacement and gentrification.

Whether Austin uses density bonuses to expand working- and middle-class housing opportunities in North Austin and similar areas is a question of political will. Some are skeptical. "Mayor Adler says all the right things," Somers told me, "which allows him to get away with a lot. People do not compare what he says to what really happens."[48] Somers believes Adler wants to build more housing but lacks the political will to go against neighborhood groups. Adler faces reelection in November 2018 and has been careful about alienating homeowner groups over CodeNEXT prior to the election. EAP's broad political coalition coupled with its canvassing contacts could give the mayor the backing he needs.

ENDING RACIAL EXCLUSION

EAP's Eric Goff also sees the CodeNEXT process as forcing people to address the racial dimension of Austin's affordability crisis. It has been a "subject people want to avoid talking about," he told me.[49] Publicity surrounding the racial dimensions of exclusionary zoning may give Austin no choice but to confront its racial policies. Richard Rothstein's 2017 book, *The Color of Law: A Forgotten History of How Our Government Segregated America,* details how zoning laws were originally designed to exclude African Americans from white neighborhoods. Federal housing programs denied loans to African Americans to ensure single-family-home communities remained all white;

zoning restrictions barring apartments from these neighborhoods then completely shut the door on racial minorities. Austin's requirements for minimum lot size, restrictions on apartments, and lack of housing density are no longer intentionally race based, but their impact can be the same.[50]

Niran Babalola, head of Desegregate ATX, argues that Austin must change its segregationist land-use laws to increase affordability. "We're still segregated because it's illegal to build cheaper homes on most land. And . . . [it's] going to take more than words to fix the problem. To desegregate the city, we have to repeal our segregation laws." Desegregate ATX backs CodeNEXT and supports repealing single-family-home zoning laws to increase affordable housing available for families. Babalola offers a reminder that key land-use decisions are made locally. "We've watched prices rise and families be displaced because we've never allowed enough homes to let more people live where they want at prices they can afford. Our laws do the opposite: They're designed to stratify our neighborhoods and concentrate affluence and poverty instead of providing equal opportunity. Our affordability crisis is entirely artificial. It's literally illegal to build cheaper homes on most land in Austin."[51]

Mayor Adler recognizes the racial context of Austin's housing crisis. In a March 2017 speech to a realtors' group, Adler compared getting Austin's neighborhoods to support increased density to Lyndon Johnson's getting southerners to vote for the 1964 Civil Rights Act (the Johnson presidential library is in Austin). But if Adler thought that precedent showed that neighborhood groups' opposition to multi-unit housing could be overcome, history said otherwise. Southern senators voted against the Civil Rights Act by a twenty-one to one margin, the region's House members by ninety-seven to seven.[52]

In July 2017, Adler announced a "task force on displacement and gentrification" that would include "educators, community members" and other stakeholders. Adler said "a combination of density bonuses with affordable housing requirements, improving the middle-class job economy and creating a 'strike fund' to preserve middle-class housing are some of the policy tools the city has available to address displacement." All would help. In what may have been a positive sign that Austin will start listening more to its tenants, Adler appointed displaced Lakeview tenant Robin Wilkins to the task force.[53]

Which Way Austin?

CodeNEXT became a dividing line over Austin's future. From the very start, homeowner groups spread alarm that their exclusive single-family-home zoning was at risk. A July 2017 meeting hosted by a neighborhood group in Clarksville handed out a flyer "claiming that the proposed zoning changes would result in higher property taxes and more congestion and make the neighborhood 'the victim of gentrification.'" Yet Clarksville was once a largely African American neighborhood that is now overwhelmingly white. In July 2017 it had "few homes valued at less than half a million dollars." According to the president of the Clarksville Community Development Corporation, Mary Reed, the neighborhood was "going through its second wave of gentrification" that is forcing out middle-class families.[54]

Former city councilmember Laura Morrison and other speakers at the Clarksville meeting "denounced CodeNEXT as a threat to the character of existing single-family neighborhoods through increased density, reduced parking requirements and more mixing of commercial and residential uses." Morrison, a former president of the Austin Neighborhoods Council, announced in March 2018 that her opposition to CodeNEXT would be a central issue in her campaign against Mayor Adler in the November 2018 mayor's race: "Everywhere I go, when I talk to folks in the community now, I hear from them that they feel they're being written off," Morrison said when announcing her candidacy. "They're beginning to wonder if they're going to be part of the future of the city, and I think it's time for a change." Morrison's declaration preceded recent news reports that the opposition to CodeNEXT by neighborhood groups had "grown from compromise to scorched earth." "CodeNEXT Wrecks Austin" became a popular yard sign in the city's single-family zoned districts.[55]

Meanwhile backers of a more inclusive Austin are pushing for even more affordable housing. After a volunteer city task force recommended placing a $161 million affordable housing bond on the November 2018 ballot, councilmembers Garza, Renteria, and Casar secured a bond of $250 million. The additional funds would primarily be used for land acquisition for affordable housing. In April 2018 the three Latino councilmembers unveiled a seven-part "Housing Justice Agenda" to expand opportunities for low-income, working-class, and middle-class people to live in Austin.[56]

Which way will Austin go? The November 2018 mayoral election is likely to be seen as a bellwether on the city's openness to greater inclusion. If a status quo version of CodeNEXT passes and Morrison wins the mayor's race, Austin will see continued congestion, displacement, and economic and racial segregation. If the council enacts a pro-housing land-use revision and Mayor Adler wins, an opportunity will be created for tens of thousands more homes for the working and middle class. AURA, Evolve Austin, and others pushing for more housing would continue to face challenges in actually getting the new housing built, but the path to a more economically and racially diverse Austin would be clear. Austin is at a crossroads, with the struggle to stop the pricing out of its working and middle class remaining a winnable fight. San Francisco, Los Angeles, and Austin all failed for decades to add sufficient rental housing to meet job and population growth. In contrast, Seattle and Denver are progressive cities that have gone all out in building new housing. The next chapter explains why building significantly more new housing is essential for ensuring that working- and middle-class families can live in the new urban America.

4

Can Building Housing Lower Rents?

Seattle and Denver Say Yes

SEATTLE

In 2014 Nick Hodges and Charlotte Wheelock were living with their two kids in Albuquerque, New Mexico. Wheelock then got a good job offer in Seattle. They did not know much about the Seattle housing market but Hodges told me, "We figured there were a lot of places to live in and around Seattle so housing was not an issue." They soon learned that Seattle's housing prices were higher than they ever imagined. "We couldn't believe it was so cutthroat. We had figured on staying with friends until we found a place but as months dragged on we could not afford anywhere." Wheelock's job offer fell through and the then thirty-five-year-old Hodges had a recurrence of a health problem that prevented him from working. With Hodges unemployed, Wheelock only able to obtain temporary jobs, and the family using up its resources, they went from living in their car to spending five months in a homeless shelter. This was not the Seattle experience either had anticipated.[1]

By 2017 the family was doing well. After staying at Mary's Place, a Seattle shelter, Wheelock began performing various jobs for the nonprofit operating the facility. She was soon hired as an employment specialist and then became the housing director for Mary's Place, supervising a staff assisting homeless families in finding housing. Hodges became head of the Lowell Elementary School PTA. Lowell reflects the new Seattle: the school is across the street from million-dollar houses in the Capitol Hill neighborhood, while 20 percent of Lowell students are homeless. Seattle has seen a sharp rise in homelessness in recent years as housing prices have skyrocketed. In 2017 it had roughly 3,000 homeless people. Hodges explained one reason why: "I've met a lot of people who have been forced out of their homes by big rent increases.

Landlords see people coming to town for high-paying jobs and can charge them a lot more for rent than existing tenants can afford. Seattle has no rent control so nothing can be done. A lot of these tenants end up in homeless shelters."

Despite Wheelock's job and Hodges's disability payments, they would likely still be priced out of Seattle had they not qualified for a new Section 8 housing development owned by the Compass Housing Alliance. The family pays $1,040 per month for a two-bedroom apartment. Next door to their home is a for-profit-owned apartment building where a unit comparable to their own went for $3,200. Hodges's experience with Seattle's housing market led him to get involved with a new alliance, Housing for All. The group is dedicated to improving Seattle's response to the homelessness and housing crisis.[2]

Hodges and Wheelock's experience reflects the new, high-priced Seattle. On July 21, 2017, the *Seattle Times* asked readers, "How has Seattle's new wealth changed the city?" It was a question on many minds. Amazon's massive expansion was fueling unprecedented economic growth. Housing costs were skyrocketing. Some even feared rents and home prices could reach San Francisco levels of unaffordability. A sample of responses to the *Times* was telling: "It's not the same Seattle I was born and raised in. The grunge, artistic music scene has been nearly replaced by all things tech. Seattle's very character is not what I remember it"; "It has pushed my entire community (black and brown folks) out of the main city. It has made living a stable life inaccessible unless you work for a major company in Seattle"; "I think the growth is great for the city. . . . However, it seems like Seattle doesn't know how to handle the boom. There's nowhere to park, there's no room for the middle class and homelessness is becoming a very real problem"; "This type of economic growth doesn't provide opportunity for the middle class"; "My friends and I all live in constant terror of losing our places to live"; "It's unaffordable. We pay $2100 for a 700 sq. ft. one-bedroom apartment. This is on top of hundreds of dollars a month in parking fees (currently paying $690). My husband and I who are both over a decade into our professional careers and by most measures are considered 'upper middle class' cannot afford a home within a reasonable distance. It is heartbreaking"; "I want to pursue a career in education and nonprofit community work. I have come to terms with the fact that I can't do that work in Seattle simply because I would not be able to survive financially."[3]

This response spoke to the impact on longtime businesses:

I've lived on the top of Capitol Hill since 1989. I've had to move repeatedly over the years due to rising rents, but I've always managed to find a small apartment I could afford near 15th, our neighborhood main street, where I knew the salesclerks and shopkeepers, and felt I had made a home. Now the increased rents have forced the businesses I visited most to close. In the past few years landmarks like The Bagel Deli, On 15th Video, and the Teapot are gone, the Canterbury is now just another expensive sports bar with televisions everywhere, Chutney's has been replaced by what appears to be some kind of upscale nail salon, and Ed's Postal Plus has had to move. These were all the best businesses on 15th, some that had been here for decades.[4]

Melissa Dodge's Seattle experience shows just how much Seattle has changed. Melissa has lived in Seattle since 1969. She and her late husband Dennis came as Seattle's economy was plunging. Seattle was akin to a company town and Boeing, the city's dominant employer, was in freefall. In 1971, Seattle had a 16 percent housing vacancy rate and the nation's highest unemployment. A billboard near the airport read, "Will the last person leaving Seattle turn out the lights."

The Dodges paid $75 a month for a one-bedroom apartment in University of Washington housing. Dennis became a full-time employee of the *Daily Racing Form* in 1976 and spent the next thirty-plus years writing columns and handicapping races on tracks in Portland, Yakima, Spokane, Seattle, and Vancouver, British Columbia. Millions of dollars were wagered in reliance on Dennis Dodge's racing picks. Melissa has been a manufacturer's representative for various clothing companies. The couple took advantage of Seattle's slow housing market in 1976 to buy a 1909 three-bedroom, 3,000-square-foot two-story house north of the University District. They paid $36,000.

In 1985, the Dodge family, now with two kids, bought a home in the Laurelhurst neighborhood of North Seattle. It has beautiful views of Lake Washington and Mount Rainier. They paid $223,000. It is now assessed at $1.7 million. Houses on their dead-end street have sold for $2.2 million. For the middle-class Dodges, timing was everything: they got into the Seattle real estate game at just the right time. I asked Melissa if they could afford to buy in Laurelhurst today and she laughed. "We probably would be living in an apartment in Seattle but given how high rents now are even that would be tough." Seattle has gone from a city where a racing handicapper and manufacturer's representative could buy a house in a very desirable neighborhood to one where middle-class families like the Dodges would likely be priced out of the city.[5]

Melissa and Dennis's daughter Mary Dodge, who was thirty-eight in 2017, also had good timing with Seattle real estate. In 2012, Mary and her husband James bought a three-bedroom, one-bath home in West Seattle for $364,000, in a very different Seattle housing market than the one buyers face today. While the city's economy was not as battered as in the years following Boeing's collapse, Seattle was still recovering from the 2008 financial crisis. The national housing bubble had burst, leaving vacant, foreclosed houses across the city. Mary and her husband followed the example of her parents and got into the housing market before the boom. In 2017, the median home value in Mary's 98136 zip code was $716,900. That's nearly double what she paid only five years earlier. Mary told me that she used to think of West Seattle as the city's "best-kept secret"; it is a secret no more.

Mary is a psychotherapist and her husband James is a manager with REI. Like her parents, she has two kids. But unlike her parents, she could never afford to live in the North Seattle neighborhood where she grew up. Her 1,070-square-foot house in West Seattle cost a lot more than her parents' first house, which was 3,000 square feet, or their 2,200-square-foot Laurelhurst home. And even though they bought their home before the current boom, Mary told me that they could not have afforded it if James had not had money from his uncle's life insurance policy and Mary from her father's estate. The home-buying challenges for Seattle's middle class are far worse in 2018. Mary and James clearly could not have bought their current home at current market prices.[6]

The despair expressed by residents over the pricing out of the city's working and middle class and small businesses was new for Seattle. Longtime residents of San Francisco and New York City have talked this way since the 1980s. But Seattle was different. It was a more laid-back big city. When Seattle launched Starbucks it made sense: Seattle was known for people escaping long periods of rain by sitting down to enjoy coffee. The opening of outdoor apparel company REI in Seattle reflected the city's long months of rain and gray mists; Seattle's weather also led Eddie Bauer to launch his future clothing empire by making down jackets for the city's Boeing Aircraft workers. As for Seattle's values, its launch of grunge rock and the career of Nirvana and Kurt Cobain was associated with people who put musical integrity ahead of careerism.

Even Microsoft's opening in nearby Redmond, Washington, did not change perceptions that Seattle residents prioritized quality of life and a desire to live near nature over maximizing their income. The company's 1986 public stock offering turned thousands of Seattle residents into millionaires overnight, but Seattle's culture did not change. More than two decades after Microsoft employees hit it rich, Seattle still remained affordable to the working and middle class.

That is no longer the case. Amazon's dramatic job growth has put enormous pressure on Seattle's housing stock. Apartment rents in 2017 were 63 percent higher than in 2010, and home prices doubled from 2012 to 2017. The connection between Amazon's Seattle growth and rising housing prices is clear. In 2017 Amazon occupied 19 percent of all prime office space in the city, more than the forty next biggest employers combined. Amazon went from employing about 5,000 people in Seattle in 2010 to 40,000 in 2017; this number is projected to rise to 55,000 by 2020. Amazon occupied 8.1 million square feet of office space in 2017; that will rise to more than 12 million square feet by 2022. Amazon "has turned Seattle into the biggest company town in America."[7]

Unlike San Francisco or Los Angeles, Seattle's affordability crisis cannot be blamed on its failure to build housing to accommodate population and job growth. Seattle has steadily built more housing for decades, but the city could not have anticipated Amazon's dramatic job growth. And even if it had, in 2017 Amazon was advertising as many as 9,000 Seattle jobs a month; developers could not have built enough units in time to meet such a demand.[8] Yet Seattle's construction boom was so robust that apartment rents began declining by the end of 2017 despite Amazon's massive new job creation. If Seattle had not kept building housing, its rents and home prices may well have come close to San Francisco levels.

Seattle is not the only big city where a strong political consensus supports building housing; Denver strongly backs new housing construction as well. Both are progressive American cities where rents have been in the top ten nationally since the post-2010 boom. Both have aggressively built new housing, reducing price hikes in both cities. While neither Seattle nor Denver shows that cities can "build their way of the housing crisis," both prove that greatly expanding all types of housing is essential for increasing affordability.

Seattle's Proactive Housing Strategy

Seattle may be the nation's most proactive city for housing. Some credit is probably due San Francisco, which has become the cautionary tale of unaffordability that Seattle seeks to avoid. As *Seattle Times* columnist Mike Rosenberg put it in 2016, "Talk to just about anyone about local real estate prices and there's a good chance you'll hear this: Seattle is becoming the next San Francisco. Sure, housing prices and rents are skyrocketing here, but are we really doomed to a fate where million-dollar homes and $5,000-a-month rents will soon be the norm?"[9]

The answer is no. Seattle will never match San Francisco housing prices. Seattle's average two-bedroom apartment rent reached $2,000 for the first time in September 2017; that was below the average rent for a San Francisco studio apartment. Seattle's two-bedrooms without the amenities included in new housing went for $1,460; that likely would not even be enough to get you an SRO with bath in San Francisco. As for home prices, Seattle's median price was $635,000 at the start of 2017 and by year's end had risen to $741,000. Even with that huge jump Seattle was still far behind San Francisco's end-of-2017 median home price of $1,275,700.[10]

Seattle is much cheaper primarily because it builds a lot more housing. From 2005 to 2015 Seattle built twice the number of housing units as San Francisco, 50,000 versus 24,000. Seattle averaged 5,000 new units per year during that period, while until very recently San Francisco averaged around 1,950. Seattle's housing production was more than double San Francisco's despite Seattle having roughly 200,000 fewer people. San Francisco rents are also about double those of Seattle, and in 2015 its tenants paid 61 percent of their income in rent, compared to 38 percent in Seattle.[11]

Other than in their historic approach to housing, Seattle and San Francisco have many similarities. Both are former maritime cities offering beautiful water views, well-paid tech jobs, and a smaller scale than sprawling urban metropolises like New York, Los Angeles, or Chicago. The Seattle area is headquarters to Amazon and Microsoft while San Francisco hosts Salesforce and Twitter, with Facebook and Google based in the nearby South Bay. Seattle has a population of roughly 600,000 to San Francisco's 800,000. John Rahaim, San Francisco's planning director since the start of the tech boom, was formerly the assistant planning director for Seattle.

Seattle's Pro-Housing Path

In the 1980s, both Seattle and San Francisco voted to slow growth. In 1986, San Francisco's Proposition M capped annual downtown office construction. Seattle's 1989 Citizens' Alternative Plan initiative limited most new housing to

85 feet in height and office buildings to 450 feet. Whereas San Francisco's annual cap became one million square feet, Seattle limited growth to 500,000.[12]

Seattle took one important step in the 1980s that San Francisco did not: it passed a housing levy to help fund affordable housing. Voter approval of the 1981 measure has since been renewed every seven years, most recently with 70 percent of the vote in August 2016 at a higher amount of $290 million. The levy has added 13,000 affordable units and enabled 900 low-income families to buy homes. San Francisco did not pass its first affordable housing bond until 1996. It failed to pass another bond until 2015, when a $310 million measure was approved.

In 1990, the Washington State legislature enacted the Growth Management Act to guide planning for growth and development in the state. The act required that Seattle adopt comprehensive plans for building enough housing within its borders to address population growth. Since the 1990s Seattle has done just that.

Seattle Mayor Norman Rice set the city on the right course in 1994 when he pioneered the concept of "urban villages." These communities would get dense, commercially-oriented development. They would also support 45 percent of the city's 60,000 new housing units over the next twenty years. Seven less-dense "hub urban villages" and seventeen "residential urban villages" would accept another one-third of the expected growth. The city backed the housing plans with funding for new parks, utilities, low-income housing subsidies, new bike and pedestrian paths, expanded bus service, and an experimental van transit program.[13]

Rice's housing strategy encouraged growth inside the city, where it could best be absorbed: "Rather than allowing the nearby foothills of the Cascade Mountains to be colonized by new suburban developments, the city will try to lure growth inward by creating attractive urban living environments replete with parks, shops, and restaurants, and a convenient mass-transit system." Rice turned Seattle into "America's epicenter of urban planning."[14]

A 2014 report on the twenty-year anniversary of Rice's project found that 75 percent of the city's growth "was going to the urban villages, just where the original planners had wished." This was true even though the urban villages had comprised only about one-third of the city population when the plan went into effect.[15]

Imagine if San Francisco in 1990 had been required by the state legislature to build sufficient housing to deter suburban sprawl. The city would have much more housing and be much more affordable. Bay Area commutes would be shorter and open green space, rather than single-family homes, would fill East Bay hills. But California imposed no enforceable housing construction plans or development quotas on San Francisco. Unlike Seattle, San Francisco was free to ignore the housing needs of a growing population. It was also free to force much of its workforce to live outside the city.

Pro Density, Pro Infill Housing

To find out whether Seattle's efforts to build more housing really increased affordability, and how pro-housing forces overcame the kind of neighborhood opposition that blocked housing development in other cities, I turned to Bill Rumpf, president of Mercy Housing Northwest. I first met Rumpf in 1983 when he became housing director for Catholic Charities in San Francisco. He built one of the earliest nonprofit buildings in the Tenderloin, the Dorothy Day Apartments. He then became housing director for the San Francisco Redevelopment Agency, directing policy for the city's largest funding base for affordable housing. He then led the California Housing Partnership, which focused on state affordable housing resources. Raised in Seattle, Rumpf moved back to his hometown in 1999. He served as deputy director of housing for Seattle for a decade before taking his current job at Mercy Housing Northwest.

Rumpf knows the housing industry inside and out. He attributed Seattle's housing success to activists who long ago recognized that building infill housing is an environmental issue: "In the 1990s a growing environmental consciousness emerged in Seattle that believed that building housing where you have infrastructure is the environmental way." Rumpf believes Seattle's greater environmental orientation explains why there are far fewer appeals against new housing than in San Francisco. Rumpf was aware of only four projects in sixteen years that were subject to appeals. None of those appeals was filed against a Mercy Housing project. He cannot "recall a single project ever stopped due to neighborhood opposition." In contrast to San Francisco, Rumpf sees Seattle as "much more environment oriented. People favor green, sustainable buildings and the city is much more pro-growth."[16]

Rumpf's assessment of Seattle's environmentally-conscious, pro-growth attitudes was reflected in the election of Mayor Ed Murray in 2013. Murray was a pro-housing mayor who, like Norm Rice in the 1990s, recognized that Seattle's future affordability and livability depended on new strategies to build more homes.

The Housing Affordability and Livability Agenda

In September 2014, Murray announced the creation of the Housing Affordability and Livability Agenda (HALA) task force. The mayor and city council convened a broad section of stakeholders to develop a multi-pronged strategy for addressing housing affordability. After ten months of meetings, the task force released a report containing sixty-five recommendations. The centerpiece was the "grand bargain," a deal struck on July 13, 2015, and described in a document entitled "Statement of Intent for Basic Framework for Mandatory Inclusionary Housing and Commercial Linkage Fee." The detailed document had one underlining principle: Seattle had to be upzoned for increased height and density in exchange for increased affordability.

Upzoning meant that meeting anticipated population and job growth required changing local zoning laws to allow builders to construct more units on a site. And in exchange for giving builders more units, Seattle would require that a percentage of them be affordable. It is a common-sense strategy that expands housing opportunities for those otherwise priced out, while also stopping sprawl through infill housing. Seattle's HALA plan projected 50,000 new units over the next decade, of which 20,000 would be affordable.

Bill Rumpf was among eight signers of the document spelling out the "grand bargain." Others included Mayor Murray, councilmember Mike O'Brien, and Faith Pettis. The mayor and city council appointed Pettis in 2015 to co-chair the HALA task force. She told me in 2017 that the "grand bargain" came about "in the eleventh hour." In other words, an agreement was never assured. She also said that over the course of the HALA deliberations she was reading articles about San Francisco's unaffordability and saw the city "as a case study of where Seattle would be if we did not get a housing agreement done."[17]

Pettis saw the grand bargain as the product of an agreement between the nonprofit and for-profit sectors. Each was primarily represented by two other signers. Marty Kooistra, executive director of the Housing Development Consortium, represented affordable housing developers. Jack McCullough, an influential land-use attorney, was the representative for big private developers. "The nonprofits felt that for-profit developers were not doing their share for affordable housing. The for-profits felt that the nonprofits were not effectively using public funds. There were years of bad blood and suspicion between the two groups that had to be overcome to reach agreement."

As in Austin, addressing the pricing out of the working and middle class required uniting prior adversaries. In the case of the grand bargain, Pettis noted, "We all felt that something big was accomplished. Increasing density in urban areas addresses environmental problems, traffic problems, transit problems, and many other urban challenges. Lights were going off inside the heads of those in the room."[18]

Seattle for Everyone

The HALA report and grand bargain were major accomplishments. Nearly all of the sixty-five HALA recommendations were included in the mayor's "Action Plan to Address Seattle's Affordability Crisis." But implementation depended on public support, which would be a challenge. Seattle's neighborhood associations were accustomed to getting their way. They strongly opposed the section of HALA recommendations that promoted backyard cottages and accessory dwelling units (often known as "in-law" apartments). These provided affordable options for workers otherwise priced out of these communities, but homeowner groups did not want tenants living in their neighborhoods. An anti-HALA *Seattle Times* columnist wrote, "Neighborhoods are roiling over Murray's Housing Affordability and Livability Agenda (HALA), protesting a 'grand bargain' struck in secret among developers and housing advocates, but not with regular citizens."[19]

Neighborhood opposition to HALA led its key backers to realize they needed to organize and mobilize pro-housing forces to secure the plan's implementation. As Faith Pettis put it, "Left on its own the HALA would either die or not be implemented as the drafters intended."

This led to the formation of Seattle for Everyone (S4E). S4E expanded HALA's support base to include social justice, labor, and environmental groups and businesses in addition to the for-profit developers and nonprofit affordable housing builders whose agreement built the deal. By uniting diverse groups like Service Employees International Union 775, the Seattle Chamber of Commerce, the social justice organization OneAmerica, and the Downtown Seattle Association, S4E's membership alone spoke to the breadth of support for HALA.

Environmentalists Back HALA

As Bill Rumpf acknowledged, Seattle's pro-housing agenda is propelled by an environmental consciousness that recognizes the green benefits of infill housing. The Sierra Club's Seattle chapter and other environmental organizations offered strong support for HALA. On November 15, 2016, Jesse Piedfort, chair of the Sierra Club's Seattle Group, and Noah An from the Young Democrats at the University of Washington co-authored "Now More than Ever, Seattle Must Welcome Upzones." The authors argued that taller apartment buildings in the area around the university would be a "boon for affordable housing" and a "necessity for our climate as well." Their piece expressed the green motivation driving support for Seattle housing: "When people can afford to live in the city near job centers and transportation hubs, we avoid long commutes and suburban sprawl and opt for clean and green transit options instead."[20]

The Seattle Sierra Club is so committed to infill housing and preventing sprawl that it backed the original version of HALA, which rezoned exclusively single-family-home neighborhoods to include in-law apartments, duplexes, and triplexes. Mayor Murray quickly backed away from the recommendation after getting strong resistance from the *Seattle Times*. Yet a June 2017 poll found Seattle residents backing the upzoning of all single-family-home neighborhoods by a 48 percent to 29 percent margin. This likely reflects public recognition that with 57 percent of Seattle's buildable land zoned exclusively for single-family housing (compared to Portland's 45 percent), the city's housing demand—particularly in light of Amazon's hiring boom—requires upzoning such neighborhoods. The joint statement issued in 2015 by the Sierra Club and other environmental groups said, "It is better for society, the environment and families if people can afford to live close to where they work." Gene Duvernoy, president of the Seattle regional sustainability organization Forterra, argued that HALA reflected the importance of "concentrating growth into existing cities and towns." The grassroots green group 350 Seattle identified housing as "an urgent climate justice issue," since "when people are pushed out of the city due to rising rents (or unable to move *into* the city due to a lack of housing), they are pushed to places that are poorly served by transit, so they need to drive more."[21]

The Seattle Sierra Club's strong pro-housing position differs strikingly from the stance taken by San Francisco's Sierra Club chapter. Despite the fact that the San Francisco Bay Area suffers from suburban sprawl and two-hour driving commutes, the San Francisco Sierra Club has long opposed infill market-rate housing. As one critic who catalogued many of the opposed projects put it, "The chapter has a solid track record of opposing dense projects—time and again—that would be located along transit lines either inside or near San Francisco proper." While San Francisco workers moved to exurban East Bay cities like Brentwood, Union City, and even Tracy in search of affordable homes, the local Sierra Club remained a key ally in the city's anti-housing coalition. It has opposed nearly every market-rate project proposed for San Francisco on which the club took a stand. In 2017 it even backed a CEQA appeal for the conversion of a parking garage into a sixty-six-unit residential building (with nine affordable units).[22]

Labor Challenges Middle-Aged, White-Dominated Neighborhood Councils

Organized labor was another backer of HALA and S4E. Just as green activists saw building infill housing as promoting environmental goals, labor's pro-HALA advocates felt building housing would expand opportunities for the working and middle class.

Labor's willingness to take a high-profile role in backing HALA became clear in July 2016 when Mayor Murray signed an executive order to cut the city funding and staff support previously enjoyed by the city's district neighborhood councils. These councils had long shaped Seattle land-use policies, and not in a way that served tenants or the city's working and middle class. While 52 percent of Seattle's residents were renters, with a median age of thirty-six, the neighborhood councils were overwhelming composed of white homeowners over the age of forty. Murray stated in signing the order, "We cannot move forward if most of the people in this city—the diversity of this city—are not represented in the very neighborhood groups that this city helps fund and run." The councils were "barriers" to "immigrants and refugees, low-income residents, communities of color, renters, single parents, youth, people experiencing homelessness, LGBTQ . . . to become involved in the city's decision-making process."[23]

The mayor made his announcement after the "ongoing neighborhood backlash" against HALA's efforts to increase density in 94 percent of Seattle's single-family-home districts. But union leader and author David Rolf spoke for labor, progressives, and housing activists in backing a move that "would get city dollars and city staff out of the business of lobbying against much-needed changes to increase housing affordability. . . . While it is important that we find ways to encourage civic participation in Seattle, we should not be using taxpayer money to support neighborhood groups that have an agenda excluding renters, people of color, the young, the poor and those who need social services from their neighborhoods. Mayor Ed Murray has had the courage to finally pull the plug on public funds for these unelected and unaccountable vehicles for homeowner self-enrichment."[24]

Seattle rents rose faster than those in any other city from June 2015 to June 2016 (9.7 percent vs. San Francisco's 7.4 percent).[25] Rolf argued that slowing these hikes required "every neighborhood to have an adequate supply of emergency housing, low-income housing and workforce housing," and to "dramatically expand the supply of market-rate housing fast enough to bend the cost curve in rents and home prices." According to Rolf, the neighborhood district councils "stand in the way of both objectives. By always arguing against new development, they help slow down or prevent the growth of market-rate housing. That, in turn, causes price-spirals during periods of high demand. By always arguing against smaller units, relaxed parking requirements, accessory dwelling units and any type of affordable housing for low-income people or renters, they help create a de-facto economic apartheid that preserves housing wealth and privilege for those who already have the most." Rolf urged Seattle not to follow the lead of San Francisco, "where the power of neighborhood groups has prevented the development of new housing units for decades."[26]

In 2017 I asked Rolf why he decided to get so involved in the housing affordability debate. As the leader of SEIU 775 and an international vice president of SEIU, Rolf's chief focus is labor issues. He led Seattle to become the first city in the nation to pass a $15 minimum wage. He tells the story of the campaign in his book *The Fight for Fifteen: The Right Wage for a Working America*. "We are a large union of low-wage working people, many of whom get displaced by the lack of affordable housing," he explained. "Our workers see affordable housing as a social justice issue. When they have to commute one or two hours to work because they cannot afford to live in Seattle, that is a hidden tax on their time." Born in 1969, Rolf is a Generation Xer whose pro-housing views align him with most millennials.[27]

Arguing that opposition to housing is a "conspiracy of entrenched interests to keep poverty and privilege in place," Rolf saw HALA as a "giant leap forward." He still thinks there is "a lot more to do" to add housing to the city's core single-family-home neighborhoods: "If I were king for a day I would upzone them all." Rolf is among a number of Seattle civic leaders exploring ways for Seattle to offer rent subsidies for working-class tenants not currently eligible for such assistance, as well as strategies to raise affordable housing funds through a linkage fee or so-called mansion tax (a levy on residential properties that sell for over a certain amount).

With labor and environmentalists strongly on board, S4E's broad coalition drove HALA's implementation. By design it was not a quick process. HALA backers wanted to ensure ample community input. Anyone familiar with land-use issues knows that opponents of change often raise process issues to derail plans. Ensuring a fair public process eliminates this objection.

By September 2017 the key neighborhoods in which HALA had proposed a lot of new housing had already been upzoned. Citywide upzoning is expected in the summer or fall of 2018. Under the core principle of Mandatory Housing Affordability, or MHA (Seattle's name for the implementation of the "grand bargain"), new developments either include affordable homes on their site or make an in-lieu payment for affordable housing elsewhere in Seattle. MHA alone is expected to create nearly 6,000 affordable homes in the next ten years.[28]

Murray's termination of the city's funding of neighborhood groups opposed to housing brought him heavy criticism from the *Seattle Times* and neighborhood activists. But cities cannot bemoan the pricing out of the working and middle class while funding groups that promote that outcome. HALA laid the groundwork for Murray's goal of building 50,000 homes over the next ten years, a goal that had broad public support.

State Limits on Seattle

Constructing new housing has enabled Seattle to achieve greater affordability than San Francisco despite Washington state's denying Seattle the power to enact rent-control and just-cause eviction laws. The lack of rent control contributed to Seattle rents jumping 40 percent between 2013 and 2016 and a whopping 65 percent since 2010.[29] In 2015 Seattle councilmembers Kshama Sawant and Nick Licata led the city council to pass a resolution urging the state government to overturn its 1981 rent-control ban. In 2018 a bill to restore Seattle's ability to enact rent control was introduced in the state legislature, the first such effort since 1999. Seattle officials strongly backed it, and Democrats controlled the Washington legislature for the first time in years, but the bill failed to make it out of committee. Sawant and other city officials saw the debate spawned by the bill's introduction as a sign of progress, and a new effort in 2019 may be likely.[30]

The state also bars Seattle from imposing mandatory inclusionary housing on all developments. The mayor's MHA proposal cleverly circumvents this ban. It is also entirely voluntary. But many developers will gladly provide below-market units in exchange for a taller or denser project.

Every high-housing-cost city whose state bars inclusionary housing should implement the MHA approach. While increasing height and density can promote gentrification if done the wrong way—as in New York City under Mayors Bloomberg and de Blasio (discussed in chapter 8)—Seattle shows how upzoning can be used to preserve and expand neighborhood affordability. Seattle has upzoned the right way.

HALA increases housing density throughout most of the city. This helps prevent the economic and racial segregation that many cities now seek to avoid. HALA co-chair Faith Pettis believed that "committee members were driven to create affordable housing citywide, in all neighborhoods, not simply concentrating affordable units in less desirable areas of the city." The committee sought a housing agenda that "erased the city's clouded history of exclusionary zoning" and felt that vision could be realized through tools such as MHA.[31]

Political realities, however, stopped the HALA committee from recommending expansion of the MHA into single-family neighborhoods outside of an urban village. Instead, the committee recommended single-family neighborhoods permit a broader mix of low-density housing types, including small-lot dwellings, cottages or courtyard housing, row houses, duplexes, triplexes, and stacked flats. But neighborhood groups were up in arms over even these small-scale strategies. They unalterably opposed any new housing that added renters to their neighborhoods. To prevent this issue from jeopardizing HALA's implementation elsewhere, the committee put off this fight for another day and did not send that recommendation to the city.

Even with the restriction on expansion into single-family neighborhoods, MHA still covers roughly 37 percent of Seattle's residential districts. Over ten years it is projected to create 6,000 new units of affordable housing for households with incomes no higher than 60 percent of the area median income, which for Seattle in 2017 was $40,000 for an individual and $57,000 for a family of four.[32]

Seattle's Faster Approval Process

Central to Seattle's pro-housing orientation is a building approval process over twice as fast as San Francisco's. In Seattle, once a neighborhood design review board approves a project, the developer can apply for building permits.

The Seattle Planning Commission does not approve projects and the city council is not routinely hearing project appeals as in San Francisco. As a result, a forty-three-story apartment tower at 600 Wall Street in Seattle was approved following an eight-month approval process. According to developer Paul Menzies of the Bay Area's Walnut Creek–based Laconia Developments, this would be "impossible" in San Francisco.[33]

Impossible is right. In the heat of San Francisco's building boom in 2014 it could take twelve months for a project to even get assigned to a planner for environmental review; after that, a six-month delay remained common. San Francisco projects routinely took two to three years just to get a hearing date for approval; as discussed below, delays and opposition could then extend the approval period for years. Menzies echoed Bill Rumpf in noting "there is more of an understanding in Seattle that we have to accommodate growth." Statistics bear this out. Seattle added one housing unit for every three jobs added during the economic boom covered from 2010 to 2015; San Francisco added one housing unit for every additional twelve jobs.[34]

Maria Barrientos has owned and operated her own Seattle real estate development firm since 1999. She typically builds projects in the 75- to 150-unit range. Barrientos has been building housing in Seattle since 1989 and is one of the city's leading housing developers in a very male-dominated field. When I spoke with her in July 2017 Seattle was leading the nation in the number of cranes in the city. She felt the increased volume of work at the planning department meant that "every permit is taking four to six months longer than usual."[35]

But in talking to Barrientos I could only think of how Seattle at its slowest offered builders a faster and more predictable process than San Francisco at its fastest. Until Seattle's boom brought a slowdown, it typically took eight months from submitting a project to getting approval.; in contrast, a builder who submitted plans in San Francisco in 2014 had to wait six months for the project to be assigned to a planner, and there was a minimum two-year approval process after that. Barrientos's projects typically break ground a year after submission of the plans. That's two years faster than the standard similarly sized project in San Francisco. As Barrientos said, "The land use and building codes are pretty clear in Seattle. As long as you follow these rules, you get your permit. The city's attitude tends to veer toward working with developers and being pro-density. The code is geared toward ensuring smart growth and encouraging better design, not toward stifling production."

Builders yearn for such a process in San Francisco and in most of the surrounding Bay Area cities. As East Bay State Senator Nancy Skinner described the situation in September 2017, "Getting a permit to build housing should not be a shell game. If you meet the rules your housing should get built."[36]

But Seattle's approval process still has critics. David Neiman is an architect and small builder with two decades of experience in the Seattle housing market. Neiman was part of a Regulatory Round Table convened in 2010 that sought to streamline building approval procedures. He also sat on the HALA committee that recommended many ways to expedite the building approval process. He felt HALA "recognized there was a lot of process solely for the sake of process," and that it made critical recommendations on expediting and reforming the design review phase. Neiman feels that the sections of HALA improving the process were ultimately "watered down" and that Mayor Murray gave only "lip service" to these changes. He also felt Murray sought to avoid neighborhood opposition to meaningful changes in the approval process.[37] Others have also expressed disappointment as to how HALA played out. Some feel Murray backed down too quickly in the face of opposition to upzoning many single-family-home neighborhoods. But Seattle's next mayor can revisit this issue. (Murray did not seek reelection in 2017 after sex abuse charges were leveled against him. He resigned from office in September 2017.)

Not Becoming San Francisco

As Seattle housing prices exploded, a scary idea emerged: Was Seattle becoming as expensive as San Francisco? Dan Savage, a columnist for the Seattle weekly *The Stranger,* wrote a January 19, 2016, column titled "When It Comes to Housing, San Francisco Is Doing It Wrong, Seattle Is Doing It Right, Cont." Savage quoted a housing activist who visited San Francisco and was struck by "how little construction is going on compared to Seattle. . . . Considering the extreme housing crisis in the Bay Area, the amount of new housing is clearly inadequate." Savage cited a November 2015 story from the *Puget Sound Business Journal* that found "it's not demand that has Seattle apartment landlords worried. It's supply. More than 11,000 new units are expected to open this year in the region, and it's forecast that an equal number will open next year. For landlords this tsunami of new apartments comes at a terrible time with the market showing signs of weakness."[38]

San Francisco landlords have never had to worry about excess housing supply.

By 2015, even without rent control the Seattle neighborhoods with the most new housing saw slowing rent increases: "Rents rose 5.6 percent regionwide from March through September, and were up 8.3 percent from a year prior. But in the core of Seattle, rents went up just 3.9 percent year-over-year in September. That's down from 8.4 percent a year earlier." The report expected "rent increases to slow further as more new units open over the next years." Savage concluded, "So if you want to see rents come down, if you want apartments in the center of the city to become more affordable, then you should be delighted each time you see a new apartment building going up. The faster they build them, the more units come online, the cheaper they get."[39]

Mike Rosenberg's provocative July 2016 story in the *Seattle Times* dismissed fears that Seattle is "doomed to a fate where million-dollar homes and $5,000-a-month rents will soon be the norm." Rosenberg noted, "Seattle is roughly half as expensive as San Francisco to rent or own a home, a fact that has stayed constant through housing booms and busts of the last two decades. Almost like clockwork, every time home prices have grown a dollar in Seattle, they've risen two dollars in San Francisco."[40]

To what does Rosenberg attribute Seattle's lower costs? "The good news is Seattle has been adding homes twice as fast as construction-averse San Francisco for the last decade, which could help stave off the extreme housing shortages that have driven up costs in California." He adds, "Since 2005, San Francisco has added just 24,000 housing units, compared with about 50,000 in Seattle. . . . The political process is so heated in the City by the Bay that many projects there take years and require several alterations to even be considered, and some even require voter approval."[41] John Rahaim, who went from being a deputy planning director in Seattle to running San Francisco's planning department, observed in 2014 that San Francisco is "in a crisis partially created by many years of underbuilding." He blamed a lack of "consensus about what change is needed."[42]

Today's Tony Bennetts aren't just leaving their hearts in San Francisco; they are also leaving their wallets. San Franciscans pay over 50 percent of their incomes for housing, while Seattle homeowners and tenants pay around 30 percent. This huge affordability gap explains why many leave the Bay Area for Seattle. Seattle builds twice the number of units as San Francisco despite having 200,000 fewer people.

Upon returning to Seattle Mercy Housing's Bill Rumpf saw a crucial difference between Seattle and San Francisco in his social interactions. "San Franciscans regularly turned conversations to real estate values: how much this house had sold for and what properties were worth. I found San Franciscans far more obsessed with keeping track of their own property values than people in Seattle." Does Rumpf think that if San Francisco were to build housing at the rate of Seattle, it would increase affordability? "Absolutely. San Francisco has just choked off supply. And if Seattle built at San Francisco's rate our affordability would be horrible."[43]

Still Battling for Affordability

Despite building roughly 2,350 units a year, a remarkable number for the city's size, Seattle has not kept up with demand. The reason is Amazon. Amazon alone added 35,000 Seattle jobs from 2010 to 2017. No city could build enough housing to avoid rising rents and home prices from such massive local job growth. As a result, although Seattle opened more apartments from 2011 to 2016 than in the prior twenty-five years combined, from July 2015 to July 2016 Seattle rents rose the fastest in the nation, even faster than those in San Francisco. In 2016 Seattle ranked eighth nationally in rent prices, with San Jose and San Francisco topping the list.[44] Seattle's housing market is unquestionably better than it would be if the city had not built so much housing, but far too many Seattle residents still remain priced out.

Nick Licata has lived in Seattle since the 1970s and served on the city council from 1998 to 2015. I asked him to explain why Seattle has an affordability crisis despite the new housing. He had an obvious answer: Seattle was creating jobs faster than new housing units. Amazon's expansion alone has brought thousands of well-paid jobs to Seattle. With the average tech job now paying roughly $100,000 annually, excess housing demand continues to bid up prices. Licata told me that in 2017 the greater Seattle area ranked third in the country in the number of homeless persons, having added 1,000 in the past year alone.

Licata ran for city council in 1997 on a platform supporting rent control. He sees the Seattle city council in 2017 as "amazingly progressive when it comes to renters." Seattle is not only building housing at a record pace, it is doing what it can (given the state ban on local rent control and just-cause eviction laws) to prevent tenant displacement. Seattle "hasn't experienced anything like this before" in terms of the current affordability crisis.[45]

Soon after my conversation with Licata, Amazon announced it would be opening a second headquarters. Cities across the nation rushed to promote themselves as Amazon's ideal location. But there was less interest in Seattle. As longtime Seattle resident Nancy Anderson explained, Amazon has brought an "influx of transient, well-paid workers that has turned Seattle into a city of horrendous traffic and outrageously expensive housing that has lost its quirky, middle-class character. . . . The city is now unaffordable for young families and the flight to the suburbs is accelerating."[46]

Seattle has been remarkably proactive in building new housing to match future job and population growth. Amazon's rapid and unexpected growth does not undermine this. With 2018 projected to be another record-setting year for apartment construction, Seattle rent increases are expected to slow in future years. Although Amazon was home-grown rather than recruited, Seattle's experience nevertheless highlights how important it is that cities consider housing impacts when pursuing large employers. Cities eagerly competed to host Amazon's second headquarters without considering where the new workers would live or their impact on local housing prices. The "winner" of this competition may be in for a rude awakening.[47]

Seattle's overheated economy will not last forever. But the city's commitment to building housing to increase affordability is secure. After Mayor Murray resigned from office in the fall of 2017, interim mayor Tim Burgess moved forward with the plan to increase density in at least twenty-seven neighborhoods across the city, including most city land zoned for multi-family use. In the city's 2017 mayor's race, the two top vote getters in the November runoff were both pro-housing. The establishment supported Jenny Durkan, who was endorsed by Murray and backed his housing polices. She was opposed by progressive urbanist Cary Moon, who showed her pro-housing stance by arguing that single-family zoning was a "'socio-economic exclusion tool' like redlining was a 'racial exclusion tool.'" Durkan prevailed, confirming that the city's pro-housing future is secure.[48]

In January 2018 Seattle saw its biggest drop in rents in the past decade. The "biggest rent decreases were mostly in the popular Seattle neighborhoods that are getting the most new apartments." Rents in neighborhoods in and around downtown Seattle fell an average of $100 per month for new tenants, with a $50 decline region-wide. The decline came "as the number of new apartments opening across the area has hit record levels and has begun to significantly outpace the number of new renters." Seattle's rental price slowdown then continued into the spring, as the city saw "its smallest springtime rent increase of the decade." While rents were still 59 percent higher than in 2011, experts attributed the cooling market to the fact that "a record number of new units opened last year in Seattle." Even more are expected to open in 2018, so that the Seattle rent slowdown is now seen as "indicative of a longer-term trend."[49]

Seattle will not return to its days of easy affordability. But the city is doing what it can to stop the pricing out of the working and middle-class.[50]

Does Housing Boom Help the Middle Class?

In November 2017, the Ink! coffee shop in the Five Points neighborhood of Denver posted a sign that read, "Happily gentrifying the neighborhood since 2014." The message did not go over well. The sign went viral on social media and hit national news outlets, triggering days of grassroots protests. Its message hit Denver at a very vulnerable time. Five Points is a historically African American neighborhood that has rapidly gentrified in recent years. Its white population rose 27 percent from 2000 to 2010. Meanwhile the percentage of African Americans in Five Points fell to 22 percent in 2015, and it has likely fallen further since. In spring 2017 the median rent for a two-bedroom apartment in Five Points was the highest in the city.[51] Remarkably, only five years earlier, in 2012, the Denver City Council had determined that the Five Points neighborhood was "blighted." The community's rapid gentrification by 2017 reflects just how fast housing markets change in the new urban America.

Like Seattle, Denver promotes building housing as its key affordability strategy. "Cranes on every corner and apartments popping up is a sight that is becoming more the norm around Denver," said a 2016 report. "I've never seen anything like this. We haven't been building this many apartments since 1973," said Cary Bruteig, president of Apartment Appraisers and Consultants and Apartment Insights. "Right now renters are moving into apartments at a very fast pace but we are still building faster than that which is why [the] vacancy rate is already moving up and why rent growth is already slowing."[52] Prior to the new construction, Denver rents had risen sharply. This was caused by the post-2010 economic boom and a 13.8 percent rise in population from 2010 to 2016, a nearly 83,000-person increase.[53] Unlike Seattle, where the housing boom was outpaced by increased demand, by January 2017 Denver's building frenzy slowed apartment rent increases "to a crawl." Denver rents had their biggest drop in thirty-six years from the third to the fourth quarter of 2016, and average rents in Denver fell in the last two quarters of 2017.[54]

What explains Denver's sudden shift from rising to declining rents? More housing. According to Teo Nicolais, a Harvard real estate expert, "In 2010, only 498 new apartment units were built in the entire city. Fast forward to 2016 and we're seeing that same number being delivered every three weeks in Denver. That's the most apartments we've built during one year in Denver's entire history." Denver saw 9,692 apartments come on the market in 2016 and 13,348 in 2017, a 38 percent increase over 2016's record total. Another 10,000 to 12,000 new units are projected to open in 2018.[55]

What makes Denver's success in reducing rents less exciting is that most of the new housing was built downtown for affluent tenants. New downtown apartments had so many vacancies in 2016 that some apartments offered tenants a free month's rent and "luxury amenities"—incentives that Denver landlords had not needed to employ in recent years.[56]

Mayor Michael Hancock and the city council helped the affordability cause in 2016 by approving the city's first funding source dedicated to local affordable housing. The $150 million housing fund was expected to add 6,000 affordable units over the next decade. Hancock has been outspoken in his commitment to addressing gentrification and maintaining Denver's economic diversity. In July 2017 the mayor announced a pilot program that aims to rent 400 vacant apartments to working-class families by using a rent buy-down fund to subsidize costs. Activists in many cities have been trying to figure out how to fill vacant apartments often targeted to affluent tenants. Hancock figured out a way to do this. It's the type of creative thinking that expands housing opportunities for working- and middle-class families.[57]

An Affordability Gap

Mayor Hancock's plan to fill vacant high-end apartments with working-class families reflects a shortcoming of the Denver housing boom: it primarily reduced rents for affluent renters. According to Aaron Miripol, president and CEO of the Urban Land Conservancy (ULC), by the end of 2017 the impact of Denver's growing vacancies in new high-end rental housing had "not yet reached the middle or working class." The ULC is on the front lines of Denver's affordability crisis. The group "acquires, develops and preserves community real estate assets in urban areas for a variety of community needs such as schools, affordable housing, community centers and office space for nonprofits." In 2017 Miripol estimated a shortfall of at least 70,000 units of affordable rental and for-sale housing in metro Denver for working-class and lower-middle-income households.[58]

It's more profitable to build in high-rent neighborhoods. Denver's challenge is expanding its affordable housing supply. Inclusionary housing is not an option; Colorado state law limited Denver's former inclusionary housing law to ownership units, and that program produced so few units that the city discontinued it. Miripol and ULC's vice president of real estate, Debra Bustos, see the $150 million housing fund as a key first step for Denver in the battle to stop the pricing out of its working and middle class. It was the "first local funding source we can use," Miripol told me. His group, which has had 1,000 units of affordable rental housing built or renovated on land it purchased, strongly backed the housing fund.

The ULC joined Enterprise Community Partners, the City and County of Denver, and other investors to establish the nation's first affordable housing Transit Oriented Development (TOD) acquisition fund. The Denver TOD fund "supports the creation and preservation of over 1,000 affordable housing units through strategic property acquisition in current and future transit corridors." The ULC proposes acquiring sites around planned transit stations before the build-out of the new light rail system (Regional Transportation District's FasTracks) causes prices to jump. Taking land off the speculative market before prices spike is a tried and true strategy for preserving economic diversity and preventing gentrification. Miripol favors using a community land trust (CLT) to acquire such parcels. As discussed in chapter 1, a CLT bought Teresa Dulalas's building and saved her from eviction; CLTs can also secure still-affordable land and buildings in undeveloped areas and hold the property until the money needed to build affordable housing can be raised (a process known as land banking).[59]

In 2011, the ULC could buy land for $27 a square foot. Six years later that same land went for over $200 a square foot. The cost of transit sites near downtown Denver has skyrocketed. This is why nonprofits must purchase land before threats of gentrification and displacement drive up prices. Once these threats are at a community's door, speculators dominate the market and nonprofits get outbid. That's why Miripol's push to acquire still-affordable land around future transit stations makes so much sense.

Many cities promote transit oriented development, but transit agencies are often not in sync with urban housing needs. Denver's RTD system has never adopted a formal affordable housing plan for the sites bordering its stations, even though many new RTD stations are within Denver. Land adjacent to these stations offers an extraordinary opportunity for housing for working- and middle-class families otherwise priced out of the city. "Our local municipalities should require that at all station stops where RTD owns land in metro Denver, 25 percent should go to affordable housing," Miripol and Bustos told me.

A 2007 study found that a staggering 165,000 housing units could be built by 2030 in connection with the RTD FasTracks system. The study estimated that as many as 40 percent of these new units could be affordable to working- and middle-class families. These 66,000 affordable units would more than double metro Denver's current supply.[60]

ULC's innovative plan to get working- and middle-class housing built in Denver seems like a no-brainer. So why had it not happened? According to Miripol and Bustos, RTD is run by an elected regional board that has not made affordable housing a priority. Further, "While many metro mayors support affordable housing and Denver's Mayor Hancock has done far more than any other mayor to address this need, they have not been able to influence RTD's board to make this a priority."

Denver's downtown apartment boom initially reduced rents for the middle class and above. The city must follow this by expanding affordable housing options through transit-oriented development. This strategy is essential for preserving and expanding an economically and racially diverse Denver. Whether policymakers prioritize land acquisition and affordable housing development along transit lines is a question of political will.

．　．　．

Seattle and Denver recognize that building more housing is essential for increasing affordability. So why did San Francisco spend decades not building housing to meet population and job growth? I explain San Francisco's failure to build in the next chapter. I also describe how the city that has become the national cautionary tale for unaffordability has in recent years experienced a radical cultural shift toward building housing.

5

Will San Francisco Open Its Golden Gates to the Working and Middle Class?

When increased housing demand caused rents to skyrocket in the late 1970s, San Francisco should have built more housing. But it did not, and no political constituency seemed to care. Strange as it seems now, Mayor Feinstein was under no pressure to build homes for the young downtown workers, Central American and Southeast Asian immigrants, and gays and lesbians flocking to San Francisco. Lenders were freely handing out money for speculators to purchase existing apartments but not for new construction. Activists battling rising rents, displacement, and gentrification were focused on four strategies: limiting downtown development, making downtown pay its fair share for city services, strengthening tenant protections, and enacting rent control on vacant apartments.

Focusing on downtown made sense—as far as it went. Downtown was creating thousands of new jobs. Workers filling these positions needed places to live. Addressing what became known as the jobs/housing imbalance— cities creating more jobs than new housing units—became a top priority. But encouraging private developers to build more housing was not among activists' policy prescriptions. Instead, activists focused on extracting fees from office developers to help cover their employees' transit and housing impacts.

Nobody believed that such contributions would meaningfully narrow the growing jobs/housing imbalance, but getting office developers to pay anything for affordable nonprofit-owned housing was seen as a big victory. In the hundreds of meetings I attended in the 1980s discussing how to deal with the housing crisis, the need to build housing and expand the supply (other than the supply of 100 percent affordable nonprofit housing) never came up. It certainly never crossed my own mind as a policy solution.

As San Francisco steadily priced out its working and middle class, the city's failure to build sufficient new housing has been a constant. In 1970, when housing prices were still low, the city had 452,197 jobs and 310, 402 housing units. By 1980 employment in the city had increased 13 percent, to 510,988, but the housing supply had grown by only 2 percent, to 316,608. In the 1980s San Francisco added jobs at roughly twice the rate of new housing. By the end of that decade the city had 550,835 jobs and only 328,471 housing units. The city's growing jobs/housing imbalance was even worse for housing prices than these numbers indicate, as young workers in new downtown jobs increasingly desired to live in San Francisco.[1]

Other cities facing an emerging housing crisis took a different approach. In the late 1970s and early 1980s New York City saw a similar increase in young white-collar workers preferring to live in the city rather than commute in from the suburbs. The Big Apple's revival from its 1975 economic collapse also drove up housing prices. By the early 1980s the gentrification process was in full swing. But whereas San Francisco saw little new housing built, in 1986 New York mayor Ed Koch began a ten-year campaign that spent more than $5 billion on building low- and moderate-income housing and on rehabilitating vacant buildings. Like San Francisco, Boston, and other cities, New York City was also experiencing rising housing demand from immigration and a new generation's preference for living in the city. Koch's program eventually created more than 150,000 affordable apartments.[2] In contrast, from 1985 to 2017 San Francisco only built 57,400 units, or less than 2,000 per year.[3]

In February 2016, the California legislative analyst issued a report that directly spoke to San Francisco's experience. The report concluded that building more private housing in the state's coastal cities "would help make housing more affordable for low-income Californians." The report found that the "lack of supply drives high housing costs, that building new housing indirectly adds to the supply of housing at the lower end of the market, that new housing eases competition between middle and low-income households, and that more supply places downward pressure on prices and rents." Addressing a common argument that building market-rate housing increases displacement and gentrification, the report actually found that increased development reduced displacement. Cities with more building saw slower growth in rents for poor households.[4]

What explains San Francisco's failure to build more housing?

Mayor Dianne Feinstein's administration responded to the housing crisis in the 1980s by making it harder to build. The number of allowable units in many neighborhoods was slashed in half, a process known as downzoning. Why would the zealously pro-development Feinstein downzone neighborhoods just as new housing was urgently needed? Politics. The mayor wanted to ensure that voters in residential neighborhoods opposed citywide ballot measures restricting downtown development. By assuring residents of San Francisco's Westside that development was being channeled downtown and away from their neighborhoods, she won their political support.

Feinstein's response to the housing crisis set a pattern for San Francisco. City policies, public opposition, procedural obstacles, and pure politics have long discouraged new housing. Their cumulative impact has challenged even the best efforts of strong pro-housing mayors. As a result, in 2015 San Francisco had a workforce of 689,000 and only 382,551 housing units.[5] Failing to build housing has steadily increased the number of working- and middle-class families priced out of the city.

San Francisco's housing crisis of the 1980s did open the doors a crack for those willing to build new housing. Not surprisingly, the first group through the door was immigrant builders. Their low-budget operations, willingness to work long hours, and acceptance of smaller profit margins made building new housing potentially feasible. Irish immigrant Joe Cassidy came to embody the new generation of builders who took on what to this day remains an unenviable task: navigating the twisting, turning, and financially risky path to building middle-class housing in San Francisco. Cassidy's story, stretching over four decades, as well as those of other small builders explain San Francisco's long failure to try to build its way out of its housing crisis.

IMMIGRANT BUILDERS ARRIVE

Joe Cassidy was born in County Clare, Ireland, in 1956. Like earlier and subsequent generations of immigrants, Cassidy had little economic opportunity in his home country. He felt he had a better chance to get ahead in America and moved to San Francisco in 1976. He arrived with no money. He spent his early days sleeping on a bench in Golden Gate Park, years before that was associated with the city's homeless problem. Cassidy was prepared to start at the bottom. He worked at Red Boy Pizza for two years until 1978, when he got a job as a laborer with a contractor named Joe Imbelloni. Imbelloni Construction was typical of many San Francisco builders in the 1970s; it primarily built single-family homes. Cassidy does not recall the company building anything larger than twelve units.[6]

Cassidy worked six days a week, learning on the job how to become a builder. When his work week ended Cassidy started his second job. He left San Francisco at 6:30 p.m. on Friday and drove a truckload of furniture down to Los Angeles. He arrived in Los Angeles at 4:30 a.m., unpacked his load, and picked up a new truckload to bring back to San Francisco, arriving home by 5:30 p.m. on Saturday. He was paid $80 each way for his efforts.

Cassidy discovered he had a knack for construction. By 1980 he was a junior carpenter and was running the company's jobs. He earned his general contractor's license in 1982 and took the big step of going out on his own. He primarily built three- and four-unit projects in the Sunset and Outer Richmond neighborhoods. He also bought and sold single-family homes. Cassidy recalls that in those days "you could buy a rundown house for $20,000 to $30,000, fix it up, and make a quick $10,000 to $20,000 profit. Nobody imagined where housing prices in the city would go."

In those days, when Cassidy submitted a full set of plans to the San Francisco Planning Department he "got them back in three months." In 2017 those same projects could take two years to get back from planning.

To build housing, Cassidy needed money. To get money, he had to take out construction loans from financial institutions. Builders like Cassidy had to sign personal guarantees for loans. This meant that a failed project could cost builders their home, the college fund for their kids, and all of their remaining assets. Unfortunately for Cassidy, the start of his career as a general contractor coincided with a period of soaring interest rates (these high rates helped doom President Jimmy Carter in his 1980 bid for reelection against Ronald Reagan).

Cassidy remembers those days well. In 1981, he and fellow Irish immigrant Eamon Murphy bought a vacant lot off Ocean Avenue for $35,000. The interest rate on their loan was a whopping 19 percent. After building what Cassidy recalls as a "beautiful" house they had trouble selling it. Interest rates were 16 percent and buyers were waiting until rates went down. It took the two young builders eighteen months to find a buyer. They only made a $35,000 profit on the deal.

Cassidy recalls how that project reflected the larger problem small builders faced in the 1980s: "There was no money in the game. We were making an honest, hard living. Many builders had trouble even breaking even on projects."

Cassidy was not a nonprofit builder. Nor was he a developer who financed housing but did not get his hands dirty on the job. Cassidy sought a fair profit for himself and good wages for his crew. He went into the business of building housing for San Francisco's middle class, and his personal, profit-driven agenda coincided with the city's need for middle-class housing.

The Feinstein administration made it difficult for small builders like Cassidy by cutting in half the number of units allowed on a site in many neighborhoods. Although he ran a shoestring operation, Cassidy recalls that this downzoning "eliminated what little profit there was if you wanted to sell." And considering that small builders like Cassidy could not afford to hold on to the rental units they constructed, their inability to profit from selling those units deterred them from building additional new housing.

Cassidy faced another problem in the 1980s: the lack of demand for new homes. "You would call a realtor on Monday and ask if anyone showed up at the Sunday open house. We didn't see much interest in new housing." San Francisco buyers in the 1980s preferred restored historic Victorians to newly built homes. That is how the renovation of rundown historic residences previously housing lower-income residents fueled the upscale transformation of Noe Valley, the Castro, Haight–Ashbury, and other gentrifying neighborhoods.

San Francisco's 1979 rent-control law also encouraged people to buy and move to small, multi-unit buildings. If they purchased one of Joe Cassidy's new single-family homes, they would be solely responsible for paying the prevailing high mortgage rates. But if they bought a four-unit building and moved into a unit via eviction or vacancy, tenants in the other units could pay the mortgage. Since the rent law did not cover owner-occupied buildings of four units or fewer, these owners decontrolled the entire building. They could bring all the rents up to current market rates, using the higher rents to pay off their own mortgage. Long-term tenants suddenly faced with the loss of rent-control protections were often unable to pay market rents and had to move; such was the process of gentrifying the city's formerly working-class and affordable communities.

Cassidy's fortunes changed following the 1989 Loma Prieta earthquake. He recalled, "No real money for housing was available in San Francisco until the quake brought millions of dollars in to rebuild the damaged Marina District." He bought a site at 469 Clementina in the South of Market district, where he constructed the city's first live-work lofts.

Live-work lofts had been legalized in 1988. They were limited to former manufacturing districts in the South of Market, lower Potrero Hill, and Northeast Mission neighborhoods, where traditional housing was barred. Lofts were approved for those working in spaces who also wanted to live there as an accessory use. As legal commercial spaces, live-work lofts were exempt from many of the standard requirements imposed on housing developers. For example, loft builders did not have to make 10 percent of their units affordable. Open space and rear yard requirements were waived. The board of supervisors assumed that few children would be living in these primarily commercial lofts, so builders only had to pay half of the one-time school fees required for other new homes.

The loft law passed as San Francisco's decade-long affordability crisis was getting worse. Building traditional new housing was still not on the city's agenda. A 1987 mayor's race defined as a contest between "downtown" and "neighborhoods" paid little attention to the city's overall housing supply shortage.

If expanding new housing had been a top priority, San Francisco could have made use of a vast number of buildable sites in former industrial and manufacturing districts whose jobs were not coming back to the city. But San Francisco revered its blue-collar past. Rezoning former industrial sites for housing would acknowledge that the city's transformation into a financial and tourist center was a fait accompli. San Francisco was not ready for that. Instead, it allowed live-work lofts to be built in areas where traditional housing was still prohibited.

Joe Cassidy and his fellow Irish builders were not concerned about the limits of the loft law; they were in the business of building places for people to live, and the live-work loft law gave them a chance to do this. A slowing economy delayed most loft construction until the mid-1990s and Joe Cassidy became a pioneer in the field. Building live-work lofts would keep a growing number of Irish immigrant builders busy for years.

The Challenge of Loft Building

Cassidy completed his first lofts in the South of Market (SOMA) district in 1991–1992. SOMA was still dangerous in those days. Loft sites were adjacent to dark alleys, which potential buyers did not want to walk near at night. Few people were around and the vast emptiness of the former manufacturing sites further discouraged new residents. Cassidy's timing added to the challenging neighborhood—by the time the loft housing went up for sale in 1991–1992 the national and local economy had tanked. He sold the lofts for $130,000 per unit but the market was so weak that Cassidy sold six of the units to "Irish guys for no money down." He even gave buyers a $5,000 credit on their loans. In the midst of an acute housing crisis, Cassidy had to *pay* buyers to purchase his units.

Cassidy's next project in SOMA was at 1145 Howard, between 6th and 7th Streets. Cassidy again learned from experience that the "prices weren't there for much of SOMA." He remembered that "building in the neighborhood was still a risky investment." This time Cassidy built bigger loft units of between 1,300 and 1,500 square feet. He faced no claims that he was fostering gentrification and his project had no opposition. Cassidy's success in SOMA led other Irish builders to acquire land for live-work lofts, which by the 1990s became the dominant type of housing being built in San Francisco.

By this time Irish builders were done building in their traditional base on the city's Westside. The Feinstein downzoning was soon followed by a controversy over "Richmond Specials," projects that involved tearing down older single-family homes and replacing them with cheap-looking, small multi-unit buildings. They earned their name because they were built in the Inner Richmond on the Westside and combined a quick turnaround with a uniformly ugly stucco façade. To this day they are identifiable in the neighborhood. Cassidy stayed away from such projects.

Since Richmond residents had just gotten the Feinstein administration to limit housing development in the neighborhood, the uproar that greeted Richmond Specials was understandable. The backlash brought new leadership to the Irish-dominated Residential Builders Association (RBA). Its first order of business was disassociating its members from projects nearly everyone in the city opposed. The controversy largely ended new multi-unit housing development in the Richmond for the next thirty years.

Cassidy and other Irish builders became proficient at building SOMA lofts. Many began like Cassidy, starting with small projects, learning the business, and then becoming contractors. John O'Connor began as an electrical subcontractor. Sean Keighran was a framer. Angus McCarthy started out as a laborer. Because live-work construction operated on low profit margins, the field was pretty much limited to those with their own trucks who built housing with their own hands; the Irish builders fit the bill. Irish builders also offered employment for undocumented immigrants, which explains why the local Irish community has strongly backed at the federal level a path to citizenship for such immigrants.

I met with some of the original owners of live-work lofts in SOMA near 7th and Brannan Streets. They included a teacher, the operator of a video business, artists, and the employee of a fitness studio. All were middle class. All bought their lofts for under $200,000. That was a standard loft price at the time, and even as the dot-com boom heated up home prices lofts remained far cheaper than conventional condominiums. Sean Keighran, who has headed the RBA for over a decade, sold live-work lofts in 1998 for less than half the price of comparable housing units sold in the 1995 pre-boom economic climate.[7] Lofts were not luxury housing. Most buyers were the age of today's millennials, but in the 1990s their generation had an entry to homeownership through lofts.

By the mid-1990s building traditional housing in San Francisco was nearly dead. Builders unable to survive on the Westside due to Feinstein-era building restrictions found other neighborhoods inhospitable as well. Joe O'Donoghue, who became head of the RBA after the Richmond Specials fiasco, warned his members to "stay out of Bernal Heights" in particular. O'Donoghue felt "no one should get involved in that brouhaha," as Bernal residents had made it clear they would declare war on any proposed housing development.[8] This left live-work loft neighborhoods as the place where immigrant builders could operate.

The Rise of Live-Work Lofts

The dot-com boom spawned by the rise of nearby Silicon Valley in 1995 brought a huge amount of new money into the city. Since the city's housing supply had barely increased in the past decade this increased demand from affluent tech newcomers caused rents and evictions to rise to their highest levels ever in San Francisco.

I had built a political alliance with Cassidy, O'Donoghue, and other Irish builders, uniting tenants and builders to support stronger housing code enforcement and a better building permit process. We sponsored a successful November 1994 San Francisco charter initiative that created a new Department of Building Inspection governed by an appointed commission. I saw the builders as serving tenants' interests in two key ways: by increasing affordability through an expansion of the city's housing supply, and by building new housing that buyers could move into instead of displacing tenants through owner move-in or Ellis Act evictions.

The Backlash against Lofts

Irish builders bought every site they could for live-work lofts. Lofts became the greatest engine for building new homes in San Francisco since the city's housing crisis began, and they were the biggest source of middle-class housing in the post-1970s era. According to David Becker, a commercial real estate broker, "With prices beginning at $175,000 to $200,000, lofts [were] the cheapest nonsubsidized units on the market." He estimated that 85 percent of loft purchasers were first-time buyers, noting that it was "the only entry-level housing being produced" in San Francisco.[9]

Yet lofts became controversial. Although the planning department anticipated demand from a wide variety of small professional businesses, start-up businesses, and user groups that even included bakers, critics insisted that lofts were using a loophole to house non-artists. Lofts were blamed for the rent and eviction crisis that critics argued was turning San Francisco into a culturally hollow city.

The conflict over lofts embodied competing visions for San Francisco. Activists favored retaining the historic manufacturing sites in SOMA, lower Potrero, and the Mission in order to preserve future blue-collar jobs. Building shiny new loft units on these sites destroyed this vision. Builders and their allies felt that San Francisco did not have a future as a blue-collar town and that the departing manufacturing and light industrial jobs were not returning. Since the city desperately needed middle-class housing, they felt it made no sense to keep long-abandoned industrial land vacant when housing could be built on it. As loft projects proliferated, builders' takeover of former industrial land led critics to insist that the new housing was gentrifying working-class neighborhoods.[10]

I had a problem at the time with blaming lofts for promoting gentrification. As I wrote in the September 1999 *New Mission News,* in an article titled "Lofts and the TIC Infestation," the controversy over live-work lofts "ignores the true menace to Mission tenants: the conversion of rental housing to tenancies-in-common (TICs)." As discussed in chapter 1, TICs became the chief economic motive for Ellis Act evictions, something that is still true today. In contrast, I saw "little if any geographic connection between the construction of new lofts and owner move-in and Ellis Act evictions." The "most high-profile evictions of long-term tenants in the Mission were in buildings nowhere near lofts or any new upscale housing."

Unlike the case of the Richmond Specials, no tenants were evicted or displaced for live-work lofts, which were typically built on vacant land or long-vacant manufacturing sites. Few if any projects were adjacent to affordable or rent-controlled housing. Lofts were primarily built in locations least likely to impact nearby residential tenants.

As thousands of long-term tenants faced Ellis Act or owner move-in evictions in the 1990s, activists focused on keeping these tenants in their homes, neighborhoods, and the city they loved. They saw no benefit to live-work lofts that provided middle-class housing because the middle class had not yet been priced out of San Francisco. Activists wanted housing for low-income residents. Many associated middle-class housing, even housing for public school teachers, with a new wave of gentrification.

Instead of praising builders for addressing the growing jobs/housing imbalance, many activists accused them of profiting off the dot-com boom. This anger against builders was not targeted toward others making money from better economic times, such as owners of restaurants, upscale bars, or concert venues. Not even bankers were targeted with the venom leveled at Irish contractors whose perceived wrong was building housing.

When people are angry about evictions, rent hikes, and social dislocation in their city, they sometimes need a tangible villain. Joe Cassidy and his fellow Irish builders served that purpose. In the late 1990s they were down at the planning commission seemingly every Thursday, seeking approval for another live-work loft project. Opponents were there as well; protesting lofts was a tangible action people could take to show they did not like what was happening in San Francisco.

The Irish builders were also upset about tenant displacement in San Francisco; they couldn't understand why they were being blamed for evictions and rent hikes that were being carried out by other people. The RBA actually had a rule stipulating that any member who evicted a tenant for construction would be kicked out of the organization. But the lack of evictions for new lofts did not reduce activist opposition. Cassidy and other builders began to feel they were being "treated like criminals. . . simply because we are trying to build housing for people."[11]

In 2000, district elections brought a progressive majority to the city's board of supervisors. Most of those elected backed activists' criticism of lofts. Among the new board's first acts was to ban new live-work loft construction. The RBA had strongly backed allies of Mayor Willie Brown in the district races, and all lost. Now it was payback time for the winners. Payback meant banning future lofts.

The same supervisors who blamed live-work lofts for gentrifying SOMA later approved multiple luxury projects for that neighborhood: high-rise towers at Rincon Hill, a thirty-plus-story tourist hotel at Fifth and Mission, and exclusive condos like the fifty-eight-story Millennium Tower, said to include the priciest condos on the West Coast. These projects did far more to turn SOMA into an upscale neighborhood than live-work lofts did. But such was the politics of San Francisco that housing for the elite was approved while loft housing affordable to the middle class was stopped.

A NEW ERA OF OPPOSITION

After years in which San Francisco failed to build much housing, constructing thousands of live-work lofts triggered a neighborhood and political backlash against all new market-rate projects. Cassidy experienced this new anti-housing attitude in 2001–2002, when he proposed a fifteen-unit project for a former funeral home on 29th Street and Dolores in upscale Noe Valley. Neighbors insisted on reducing it to thirteen units even though this eliminated one of the two affordable units then required by the city's inclusionary housing law. Neighbors' preference for a smaller project with fewer affordable units was a sign of things to come.

Cassidy also found opposition to his most ambitious project ever: building on a block-long site in SOMA, on 4th Street between the freeway and AT&T Park. The city's ban on future live-work lofts did not impact projects in the pipeline, and Cassidy had secured the right to build 172 1,200-square-foot lofts. Because the site could include much more housing than approved, in 2001, Cassidy, myself, RBA head Joe O'Donoghue, and attorney Alice Barkley came up with a plan to convert the 172 units into 300 apartments. In exchange for this revised project Cassidy would have to buy a site nearby and build a fifty-six-unit apartment building there. That building would then be conveyed free and clear to the nonprofit organization I head, the Tenderloin Housing Clinic, for affordable housing for low-income former SRO residents.

Chris Daly, who was the district supervisor and among the board's progressives opposed to live-work lofts, strongly backed the idea. The project would have to comply with all of the requirements—inclusionary housing, full school fees, open space and rear yard setbacks—that critics felt should have been included for lofts.

Now you might think that other loft opponents would also be thrilled with converting the approved live-work project to traditional apartments. The new plan added 158 additional units to the city's housing supply. It also provided 56 units of very affordable housing to very low income tenants. But many regular opponents of live-work projects also opposed this project when it went before the planning commission. Calvin Welch, a nonprofit housing leader, claimed the project was "lipstick on a pig" and insisted the fifty-six affordable units would never be built.[12] Anti-development activist Sue Hestor described the revised apartment project as bailing out Cassidy for a project he could not get built. Neighbors were upset that the revised project would feature smaller, less expensive units. They told the commission that they favored the original live-work project because it would contribute more to their own property values.

Despite this opposition, the complex project was unanimously approved by the planning commission and the board of supervisors. When a hearing was held to approve the affordable building at 7th and Brannan Streets, Hestor represented a neighbor opposed to the 100 percent low-income project. Hestor said the low-income former SRO tenants who would occupy the property would include "dumpster divers" who would spread trash through the neighborhood.[13] The project was approved anyway, and the building opened as the Sister Bernie Galvin Apartments in 2006.

Overall, the approval process confirmed what many suspected: opponents of live-work lofts really opposed any new market-rate housing. It also showed again how San Francisco makes it hard to be a builder. All of these battles over projects take their toll. Even though Joe Cassidy won nearly all of these battles and stayed around much longer than most builders, he eventually gave up fighting to build in San Francisco and relocated to South San Francisco. When I asked him in 2017 whether he would consider building again in the city, he looked at me like that was the last thing he would ever do.

When seeking project approvals, San Francisco builders face delays unheard of in other big cities. Consider Sean Keighran's almost decade-long odyssey to construct two twenty-one-unit buildings on 17th Street in lower Potrero Hill.

Keighran contracted to purchase two former industrial sites in the fall of 2003. He soon learned that the district supervisor for Potrero Hill was trying to rezone his property. The rezoning allowed Anchor Steam Brewery scion Fritz Maytag to build more on his property, while slashing Keighran's housing allotment. It took a major struggle but Keighran and his builder allies ultimately defeated the rezoning by a six to five vote in December 2004.

But the next obstacle was much bigger. In March 2006, the board of supervisors issued a decision involving plans to build two four-story buildings with sixty-eight condos on the site of a vacant commercial building at 2660 Harrison. The lot was historically zoned for heavy commercial use. An appeal filed with the board challenged the planning commission's decision that an environmental impact report (EIR) was not required for the project. California's Environmental Quality Act (CEQA) requires such reports for projects that state or local agencies identify as having "significant environmental impacts." EIRs delay projects for at least a year in San Francisco and impose a major expense on developers.

The supervisors voted 8–2 to reverse the planning commission's decision. The Board said that the EIR had to "evaluate how the project would affect not just the environment but also blue-collar jobs and affordable housing in the area." This instruction was given despite CEQA not addressing job and affordable housing impacts. According to the *San Francisco Chronicle,* "The decision ended up putting on hold thousands of units scheduled to be built in the city's eastern neighborhoods, while the Planning Department analyzes how the developments will affect existing housing and the job situation in the area."[14]

Keighran's project and about 700 other future housing units on land owned by Irish builders were put on hold. The planning department interpreted its mandate to assess job impacts as applying to any site with a former industrial use. That covered most of the housing projects in the pipeline. As Gabe Metcalf of San Francisco Planning and Urban Research Association put it, "We are now living under a de facto moratorium on all housing in most of the places that would be logical to put new housing."[15]

Sue Hestor, who argued the Harrison Street appeal before the board of supervisors, agreed that a moratorium had effectively been declared. She also acknowledged that stopping market-rate housing was the goal: "We have overbuilt market-rate housing and underbuilt the housing that's needed in San Francisco. We have very, very little land here . . . so if you take up all the land that has opened up for housing, that was previously zoned industrial, and we don't look at who we are serving, there will be nowhere left to build."[16]

In other words, the problem was not that former industrial land was being used for housing; rather, it was that it was not housing low-income people. After delaying Keighran's project and more than fifty others for over a year while they studied the jobs issue, the planning department finally allowed them to proceed.

EASTERN NEIGHBORHOODS REZONING

During the 2660 Harrison delay Keighran was paying 6.5 percent interest on his $2.1 million construction loan. Like other builders, he had to personally guarantee the loan. Keighran had two daughters who would soon be going to college. Needing money for tuition, he was eager to start his project. But the city was still bogged down in the lengthy process of rezoning much of the same area that had been impacted by the 2660 Harrison appeal. Known as the Eastern Neighborhoods, the area affected by the rezoning included the Mission, Central Waterfront, East South of Market, and Showplace Square / Potrero Hill. These neighborhoods had most of the city's industrially zoned land and were now being eyed by builders for new housing.

The Eastern Neighborhoods rezoning process began in 2001 and picked up momentum in 2005. New housing remained in limbo until the rezoning was complete because developers could not know what the city would allow them to build. This city-caused halt in construction came at the worst possible time for builders, as San Francisco was still in a housing bubble and financing for housing was cheap. Once again, the city failed to treat the need to address its housing shortage as a priority.

The planning commission finally adopted the Eastern Neighborhoods rezoning on December 9, 2008, seven years after the process began. The city held up as many as 7,500 new housing units in the area. These units would finally move forward, as one critic put it, "provided of course the developers haven't either died of old age, completely lost interest, or more likely lost financing for their projects in the interim."[17]

The Eastern Neighborhoods rezoning ended just in time for Sean Keighran to face the fall 2008 national foreclosure crisis, which halted lending on most housing developments. Keighran's lender went under. The institution that took over its portfolio kept changing his loan terms. Keighran could not get all the financing and plans in place to break ground on the first of his two buildings until 2012. It finally opened in 2013. The second building opened in 2015.

Today, the 1700 block of 17th Street features two beautiful apartment buildings on what previously was vacant industrial land. A once-desolate block is filled with pedestrians. Keighran works out of the RBA offices in the commercial part of the site. He often sees a former opponent of the project sitting in the plaza drinking coffee purchased at the café space Keighran built.

THE LOSS OF SMALL BUILDERS

Keighran's twelve-year odyssey had a happy ending, but he realizes it could have gone another way. Like Joe Cassidy, Keighran is troubled when builders are treated "as worse than criminals" by opponents of projects. "You go to these hearings and people are just yelling at you. They have incredible anger. And all you are doing is trying to build homes for people."[18]

Keighran sees Irish builders and other smaller operators as becoming unable to compete financially with the real estate investment trusts and overseas money that now dominate San Francisco housing development. The city "doesn't care if they are hard on builders. With the cost of construction and constant delays, if things keep going this way I don't think it's possible for our guys to build anymore." Keighran built many projects before 17th Street but as 2018 began he had not acquired a property since. He has not joined Joe Cassidy in swearing off San Francisco, but it will take a change in policies before he again risks money as a builder in the city.

In 2018, the Terner Center for Housing Innovation at UC Berkeley released a report on the factors driving rising construction costs in San Francisco. It found that the single point on which all stakeholders agreed was that "the most significant and pointless factor driving up construction costs was the length of time it takes for a project to get through the city permitting and development processes." These delays particularly impact small builders.

The loss of small builders would drive a stake through middle-class home-ownership opportunities in most San Francisco neighborhoods. While the real estate investment trusts and offshore financiers build high-rise towers in SOMA and downtown, most of the city's residential neighborhoods only allow smaller projects. The Irish builders should be seen as the canary in the coal mine for San Francisco's ability to return the middle class to many of its neighborhoods. If small builders cannot endure the financial risks and San Francisco's excessively long development process, it is not only they who will be priced out of the city, but the future middle class.[19]

DISCRETIONARY REVIEW: PAY TO DELAY

San Francisco builders also must confront a process known as discretionary review. Here is how it works. Margaret Eve-Lynne Miyasaki lived near a proposed affordable housing project at 2060–2070 Folsom Street in the Mission district. The permanently affordable project for low-income seniors had broad community support. Under a law passed in 2016, affordable housing projects that met applicable zoning and design standards were approved "as of right." But in San Francisco, "as of right" doesn't always mean what it implies.

San Francisco allowed Miyasaki or any other member of the public to pay $578 to hold up construction of the senior housing by filing a request for discretionary review (DR). Miyasaki's request required the planning commission to hold a hearing on the 127-unit, nine-story project. DR is supposed to be limited to cases of exceptional and extraordinary circumstance. But the city attorney has ruled that the planning commission, not staff, must make this determination. This means that even the most frivolous appeals delay projects for months while they await a commission hearing.

Sam Moss, director of Mission Housing, the neighborhood's leading non-profit housing group, noted the impact of Miyasaki's appeal and similar delays: "Every time they file one of these things, it puts the entire project in jeopardy, because the funding structure nationally, at the state level and locally is just so precarious right now. When you file this you are literally filing against affordable housing for homeless families. You are saying, nope, I don't want that."[20]

In 2011 the San Francisco board of supervisors rejected legislation that would have prevented DR appeals like Miyasaki's from delaying projects. This action, on the eve of the city's tech boom, shows how San Francisco politicians still refused to treat the city's housing shortage as a crisis. It was not lost on observers that "the vast majority of DRs are filed in affluent areas such as the Castro, Noe Valley and Upper Haight, which have well-organized neighborhood groups." These former working-class turned upscale neighborhoods routinely oppose multi-unit housing. With its decision, the board of supervisors backed these affluent homeowners despite planning department findings that DR "makes the development process more lengthy and costly for all involved, and takes time away from the Commission to address larger planning issues."[21]

The board's rejection of DR reform proved to be the last vestige of San Francisco's anti-housing mentality. Mayor Ed Lee took office in January 2011 and soon became the city's first mayor to make building new housing a top priority. Lee's record shows what a city can do to slow if not stop the pricing out of the working and middle class. All it takes is political will.

ED LEE: SAN FRANCISCO'S HOUSING MAYOR

San Francisco Mayor Ed Lee was appointed to office in January 2011 and easily won election that November and reelection in 2015. After taking office, Lee focused like a laser on two priorities: jobs and housing. Critics blamed Lee's extraordinary success at sharply reducing city unemployment and boosting San Francisco as a tech hub for housing costs that have soared since the post-2011 tech boom. But Lee inherited a city of steadily decreasing affordability and did more than any prior mayor to comprehensively address the city's longstanding housing crisis.

Lee took office during a long lull in housing development in San Francisco. Lenders were still denying financing to builders in the wake of the 2008 foreclosure meltdown. In 2010, only 1,082 new housing units were completed in San Francisco, well below the roughly 1,900 built in previous years. The city added only 348 new units in 2011 and 794 in 2012, the lowest new housing totals since the 1990s. When Lee took office the city had a major pent-up demand for new housing.

In his inaugural speech, Lee made creating jobs his overwhelming priority. The city's unemployment rate was nearly 10 percent, very high by San Francisco standards. Lee talked about how jobs mean more than income; they also have a positive impact on people psychologically. Lee's focus on jobs signaled that he would also emphasize new housing development; investment in housing is among the best job creators.

New housing's role as a job creator is often overlooked. Books about the urban housing crisis focus on rising housing prices as a downside to strong job growth. But Lee's agenda reminds us that building new housing creates the blue-collar jobs that many progressive anti-housing activists claim to want to support. Not building housing creates no jobs.

Born in 1952, Lee had a view of the tech industry that is more typical of millennials than his fellow boomers. His jobs strategy involved changing the pattern whereby tech companies launched in San Francisco and then moved to the South Bay as they grew. Many relocated in order to avoid San Francisco's tax on employee stock options, which particularly impacted the tech sector. Lee encouraged the board of supervisors to eliminate the stock option tax, and even progressive supervisors backed the move. San Francisco's emergence as a tech hub followed.

From December 2011 to the end of 2012 San Francisco's economy grew faster than that of any other large city in America. The city added more than 30,000 jobs and began what would become the biggest housing development boom in its modern history. San Francisco's unemployment rate had been reduced to a remarkable 2.9 percent, significantly less than the 4 percent that a lot of us were taught in college economics classes represented full employment.

FUNDING FOR PUBLIC HOUSING

Lee's top housing priority reflected his non-politician background: he chose the politically untenable task of rebuilding the city's public housing stock. Public housing is the chief housing source for San Francisco's low-income families, and particularly for the city's low-income African American families. The city's African American population has steadily declined since its high point in 1970, and preserving public housing is a key strategy for keeping low-income African Americans in San Francisco.

Lee told me that one of his first thoughts upon becoming mayor was, "Now that I'm in charge, I can fix public housing." Lee and his five siblings lived in public housing in Seattle until he was ten. As an attorney for the Asian Law Caucus in the 1980s he represented public housing tenants dealing with habitability problems in San Francisco's Chinatown. Lee was city administrator during Gavin Newsom's mayoralty, and the mayor often called upon him to solve problems in public housing. Newsom empowered Lee and

Mohammed Nuru of the Department of Public Works to clean up the projects and make them livable.

Often described as a cautious mayor, Lee nevertheless had revolutionary ambitions for the city's public housing. He wanted to reinvent how it was managed and operated. This meant shifting control of the projects from the San Francisco Housing Authority to private nonprofit housing developers. It was a long-overdue move that no prior mayor had attempted.

Lee started his reform efforts by taking control of the Housing Authority Commission, which governed the projects. The US Department of Housing and Urban Development (HUD) had long starved public housing of the resources necessary to maintain its low-cost units. The Clinton administration tried to address the deteriorating housing stock by demolishing run-down public housing units and rebuilding on site, but the steep price of this approach, known as HOPE VI, was the net loss of 140,000 public housing units from 1995 to 2007.[22]

Lee's strategy for solving public housing's funding problem was a $1.2 billion affordable housing trust fund measure on the November 2012 ballot. If it passed, most of the money would go toward rebuilding over 6,000 public housing units and reinventing the management and ownership of public housing. I asked Lee why he thought he could get voters to direct such huge dollars to public housing, which had a bad reputation among members of the public. "I had a lot of confidence that I could sell a story about how public housing tenants had suffered in the city," Lee told me in August 2017. "I knew about HUD's broken promises and knew San Francisco could do better."[23]

Lee was right. Voters approved the public housing funding measure. Lee then began the reenvisioning process, which brought the type of diverse stakeholder engagement that the San Francisco Housing Authority had long rejected. As tenants happily moved into buildings that were indistinguishable in appearance from new condominiums, Lee's strategy for protecting the city's most economically vulnerable families was hailed as "one of the most dramatic and consequential reform efforts in the tortured, seven-decade history of public housing in the United States."[24]

Lee's next challenge was addressing the soaring housing costs triggered by the booming San Francisco economy. San Francisco was pricing out the working and middle class years before the post-2011 tech boom. Lee's challenge was two-pronged: preserve existing affordable housing and the city's long-term tenants and get San Francisco to build the new housing it had failed to construct for decades.

BUILDING MORE HOUSING

Until Ed Lee, no San Francisco mayor had prioritized building more housing. Previous mayors promoted the need for more nonprofit affordable housing, but building to meet the city's rising population was never central to any mayoral administration. Lee changed that. On February 6, 2014, Lee announced plans for San Francisco to build or renovate 30,000 housing units by 2020. That's at least 5,000 new units a year in a city that typically failed to create 2,000. Lee pledged that at least one-third of the new units would be permanently affordable to low- and moderate-income families. He also stated that affordable and middle-class housing developments would get priority in the city approval process.

Why did Lee prioritize building housing? "When I went out to job sites the CEOs warned me that their workers needed housing. I also kept hearing from workers how hard it was to find places to live in San Francisco. I realized that we had all this great talent in the city that we were going to lose if we did not build housing for them. We were not doing anything for our workers of the future."

As of March 2018, San Francisco was on target to meet Lee's 30,000-unit goal: 17,466 units had been completed, 6,460 of them affordable. That's 37 percent of the total, exceeding expectations.[25]

The mayor's target of 30,000 became a strategic tool that justified a sense of urgency to build housing. Until Lee, San Francisco had not had a pro-housing mayor like New York City's Ed Koch, who in the 1980s committed to building 150,000 new units, or Seattle's Norm Rice, whose 1990s urban village plan transformed his city from slow growth to pro-housing. Seattle mayor Ed Murray (2014–2017) built on his predecessors' pro-housing policies. Lee's all-out, top-priority campaign for building housing was a city first. San Francisco has a lot of catching up to do, however, and Lee was often blamed for the rising prices caused by his predecessors' failure to increase supply.

THE WORKING GROUP

Lee's 30,000-unit plan emerged from one of his favorite policy vehicles: the working group. Lee liked to convene a broad group of stakeholders on an issue and let their recommendations guide his policy. I have been skeptical of such processes, which often become substitutes for action or create an illusion of public input for policies that have already been decided. But Lee showed that if a working group is actually designed to bring all stakeholders behind a collective policy, it can be enormously effective. The process requires a lot of small meetings and is time consuming, but if a mayor is truly committed to getting a broad swath of stakeholders on board, there are no shortcuts. Seattle's Mayor Murray used a similar process to create his Housing Affordability and Livability Agenda, as did Los Angeles's Mayor Garcetti to win passage of a quarter-cent sales tax increase on the March 2017 ballot to raise $355 million a year for ten years for homeless services (as discussed in chapter 2).

$310 MILLION AFFORDABLE HOUSING BOND

Mayor Lee and his housing working group wanted a new affordable housing bond. At the time housing bonds in California required approval by two-thirds of voters under the infamous 1978 state ballot measure Proposition 13. This means that only 34 percent of the electorate could stop new affordable housing. San Francisco passed a $100 million affordable housing bond in 1996. But a $250 million bond on the November 2002 ballot failed, as did a $200 million affordable housing bond on the November 2004 ballot. That one got 64 percent of the vote.

In 2008, housing advocates tried to circumvent the two-thirds vote requirement through a ballot measure that funded housing through an annual budget set-aside (which is how Lee got the $1.2 billion for public housing in 2012) rather than a bond. Despite needing just over 50 percent of the vote in a November election with Democratic presidential candidate Barack Obama on the ballot, the measure failed. This history did not bode well for a November 2015 bond that would appear on the ballot in a local election in which fewer tenants vote. Lee took three steps to change past defeats to victory.

First, the mayor's working group strategy brought a much broader group of stakeholders into the process than had been involved in prior measures. Some showed their appreciation for being part of the process by donating to the campaign.

Second, the bond expanded the beneficiaries beyond the very poor. Most of the bond money targeted those with low incomes—$80 million went for public housing and $100 million for working-class residents earning less than 80 percent of the area median income. Earmarking $80 million for the middle class meant a broader share of the electorate could see itself among the bond's beneficiaries.

Third, Lee got his allies in the business and tech community to help pass the bond. Mayors must choose which "asks" to make of such supporters, and Lee requested they make passing the $310 million affordable housing bond a priority.

As a result of these strategies and the surrounding housing crisis, the bond garnered 74 percent support. Most big-city mayors talk a lot about affordable housing, but too few commit to new funding streams or to spending political capital to help those priced out of urban America; Ed Lee did.

TEACHER HOUSING

In 2016 the average salary for a San Francisco public school teacher was around $65,000. Most new teachers earned in the $50,000s. San Francisco teacher salaries rank 478th out of the state's 775 school districts, a pay so low that "some San Francisco teachers are commuting upward of three hours every day, living in in-law units with no kitchens or couch-surfing with friends." With studio apartments starting at $1,800 a month and one-bedrooms nearly double that, it is no surprise that those getting teaching jobs in San Francisco (many also paying off student loans) were priced out of housing in the city. The exclusion of teachers from housing in the city did not begin with Mayor Lee, but no previous mayor had taken action to get teachers into affordable housing.[26]

Federal and state laws prevent cities from discriminating by occupation in the allocation of public funding for affordable housing. Cities cannot even prioritize teachers as beneficiaries of privately built inclusionary housing. Until June 2017 San Francisco's inclusionary housing units were not even available to teachers, as they earned too much to qualify.

Mayor Lee and California senator Mark Leno knew something had to be done to enable San Francisco teachers to live in the city where they taught. They joined forces in 2016 to pass state legislation allowing the San Francisco Unified School District to build housing exclusively for school district employees on district-owned land. The first of what could be many projects will be built on a school district–owned site in the city's Sunset neighborhood. The city is contributing $44 million for the project, which will include

100 to 120 units; MidPen Housing is the nonprofit developer selected to construct what will likely be a four-story building with 40 percent of the units designated for classroom aides and the rest going to the city's teachers. While the paraprofessionals can live in the units indefinitely, the teacher housing is limited to seven years. The city has already found a second site for teacher housing in the Inner Sunset, with two other prospective sites under review. Meanwhile, at least one private developer has proposed partially satisfying its inclusionary housing requirements by turning a portion of its land over to the school district for teacher housing; the new state law makes this possible.[27]

San Francisco's approach to teacher housing is being replicated in other cities where teachers are being priced out. There are efforts to provide below-market housing to teachers in nearby Silicon Valley, and in Florida, Miami-Dade County plans to build an apartment building for teachers next to an elementary school. The district is also constructing a school that includes a residential floor for teachers. With the gap between Miami teacher salaries and rents only exceeded by those in New York City, Seattle, and San Francisco, it is easy to see why there are likely to be "more teachers who qualify for this program than there will be units available."[28]

THE SMALL SITES ACQUISITION PROGRAM

Lee combined his development focus with increasing protections for tenants and rental housing. He created the Small Sites Acquisition Program, which gives nonprofit groups city funds to buy buildings whose long-term tenants are facing eviction, often under the state's Ellis Act. The Ellis Act (discussed in chapter 1) preempts local eviction protections. It allows speculators who buy buildings and then claim to be "going out of the rental housing business" to evict the tenants and then sell the units off to individual buyers as tenancies in common.

Nearly two decades ago the late Ted Gullicksen of the San Francisco Tenants Union and I tried to get Willie Brown's administration to implement a small sites program, but Brown's housing chief vetoed the plan. She had inspectors assess the first property proposed for nonprofit acquisition and concluded it needed at least $500,000 in repairs. Ted and I argued that the tenants were happy to live in the units as is, especially because the alternative was potentially their eviction. Brown's housing chief insisted that buying the property was not a good use of public funds, and the idea was dropped.

When Mayor Lee heard about the small sites strategy, he loved it. The Small Sites Program was launched in July 2014. By March 2018 the program had protected 160 units in twenty-five buildings. Over $50 million in city funds had been spent to acquire the properties, and future additional purchases were anticipated. Tenants whose homes were saved by the program include Teresa Dulalas, whose fourteen-year eviction fight was discussed in chapter 1; legendary Mission District artist and Gallería de la Raza co-founder René Yañez; San Francisco historian and Critical Mass co-founder Chris Carlsson; and prominent tenant activist Benito Santiago, whose Duboce Street duplex was the first property purchased under the program. The Small Sites Program depends on nonprofit groups' willingness to own and manage small buildings. The San Francisco Community Land Trust and the Mission Economic Development Association expanded their missions to take on this role.[29]

The community land trust ownership model enables tenants to establish a cooperative and begin managing the building themselves. This model of social ownership is a perfect fit for the five- to twenty-five-unit buildings purchased by the Small Sites Program. The program has provided a major financing source for this popular housing option while achieving the core goal of protecting long-term, mostly working-class tenants facing eviction. Every high-housing-cost city should have a small sites program. It is a vital strategy for protecting tenants and preserving affordable housing.

FUNDING LEGAL DEFENSE

Convincing owners to sell to San Francisco's Small Sites Program often requires that owners who are evicting tenants change course. Many do so when a vigorous legal defense is waged on the tenants' behalf. Mayor Lee made sure that nearly all long-term San Francisco tenants facing no-fault evictions received free legal representation by more than quadrupling city funding for that purpose.

When Lee took office, the Tenderloin Housing Clinic received $125,000 to defend tenants in Ellis eviction cases. That amount did not cover legal representation for many of those in need. The inadequacy of this funding became worse as Ellis evictions rose 81 percent from 2012 to 2013. Yet in September 2013 the city agency funding THC's Ellis legal representation decided to cut our funding by 3 percent. I got the news of the funding cut the same week that hundreds turned out in North Beach to protest the Ellis eviction of an elderly Chinese American couple and their disabled daughter.

When Mayor Lee heard about the funding cut, he hit the roof. He immediately ordered that our legal representation funding be tripled to $375,000. He later increased the amount to over $700,000. Now speculators who bought buildings and assumed a quick and easy Ellis eviction faced an unexpected scenario: these cases would be litigated to the hilt, which meant that owners would have to spend tens or even hundreds of thousands of dollars to get tenants out.

In 2017, THC attorneys represented 191 tenants facing Ellis or owner move-in evictions. Attorneys prevented forty-one of these evictions and significantly delayed others. This free legal representation deters speculators anticipating a quick profit from the eviction of tenants and sale of their units. And for those already in litigation, selling to nonprofit groups through the Small Sites Program becomes a pretty attractive option. Unfair evictions will be further prevented by free legal representation after San Francisco voters approved a June 2018 "right to counsel" ballot measure. It is yet another step that cities can take to help maintain their economic diversity.

STATE LOBBYING FOR ELLIS ACT REFORM

Mayor Lee also did something else unprecedented: he went to Sacramento to directly ask state legislators to reform the Ellis Act to protect San Francisco tenants. Working with Senator Mark Leno, San Francisco sponsored a bill to require a five-year waiting period before owners could invoke the Ellis Act. The Ellis Act was passed to allow landlords to "go out of the rental housing business"; allowing speculators to buy buildings and "go out of business" the next day by issuing Ellis eviction notices twisted the law's intent. Unfortunately, state real estate interests defeated Leno's legislation. But Lee's involvement increased the chances of passage, reducing Ellis Act evictions as speculators awaited the legislative outcome.

Lee's direct contact with state legislators raises a question: Why don't big-city mayors regularly made their presence felt in state capitals in order to protect their residents from being priced out? Cities have well-connected state lobbyists, but a mayor's personal appearance sends a message about the higher level of importance connected to an appeal. I described in chapter 2 how Los Angeles mayor Eric Garcetti organized mayors from across

California to lobby Governor Jerry Brown to sign several housing bills in 2017. This group also lobbied legislators in 2018 for $1.5 billion in state funding for homeless services. In our era of limited federal funding for housing, urban mayors should see pushing for state funds as an essential part of their job.[30]

STRENGTHENING THE CITY'S RENT LAW

Mayor Lee allowed virtually every piece of legislation passed by the board of supervisors increasing tenant protections against eviction to become law. These measures range from increasing relocation payments for tenants evicted under the Ellis Act to helping to stop sham owner move-in evictions. Lee signed more measures strengthening the city's rent law than any prior mayor. But this did not stop some progressives from blaming Lee for rising evictions, rents, and home prices during his tenure. They even blamed Lee for rising Ellis evictions, despite his using all of the city government's powers to stop this state-authorized displacement strategy.

Critics felt Lee deserved blame because he encouraged tech firms to open offices and expand in San Francisco and favored building new market-rate housing. But as the 1990s dot-com boom showed, a Silicon Valley tech boom drives up San Francisco housing prices whether the companies are based in the city or not. And not building housing did not stop rents and home prices from escalating in San Francisco in the many decades in which the city earned its reputation as a city that fails to build.

David Talbot, who frequently criticized Lee's housing policies, wrote in *Season of the Witch* that former mayor Dianne Feinstein was "precisely the right leader for the time." Yet Feinstein was precisely the wrong leader for the time for anyone in San Francisco who cared about stopping tenant displacement and gentrification. Her opposition to strong rent control worsened the city's affordability crisis. Her vetoes of vacancy control legislation in the 1980s remain heavily responsible for San Francisco's current record high rents. Had such legislation been enacted, landlords would have been limited to a percentage rent hike that would be far less than the unlimited amount they now can charge after a tenant vacates a unit.[31]

One cannot underestimate how Feinstein's rejection of vacancy control allowed housing prices in California's many rent-controlled cities to spiral out of control. Had Feinstein backed vacancy control and San Francisco implemented it in the 1980s, there is no way the California legislature could have passed the 1995 Costa-Hawkins Act barring cities from enacting vacancy control. The bill ended vacancy control laws in Berkeley, Santa Monica, and West Hollywood, but those smaller cities possessed nowhere near the political clout of San Francisco. Campaigns for vacancy control dominated San Francisco politics throughout the 1980s, an issue Talbot's book ignores entirely.

San Francisco's inability to enact vacancy control eliminated a strategy that is critical to ending the pricing out of the working and middle class. That's why there is a statewide campaign in California for a November 2018 ballot initiative (Prop 10) to overturn Costa-Hawkins, which was passed when housing was much more affordable across the state.

SHORT-TERM RENTALS

Mayor Lee was less successful in regulating the billion-dollar short-term rental industry. After the industry took off with the post-2011 tech boom, cities across the nation began seeing thousands of rental units shifted from permanent housing to higher-paying tourist use. Platforms like Airbnb and HomeAway operated outside standard hotel industry restrictions. Most prominently, short-term rentals were allowed in neighborhoods whose zoning otherwise barred tourist use.

As the big city with the nation's most far-reaching tenant and affordable housing protection laws, one would expect San Francisco to have among the strongest short-term rental restrictions. But the city's 2014 measure allowed tenants to rent rooms to tourists year round as long as the tenant was on the premises. This facilitated the renting of spare rooms to tourists instead of San Francisco residents. The law's weak enforcement powers also invited speculators to illegally rent vacant apartments. Share Better SF, a coalition of tourist hotels, apartment owners, tenant groups, labor unions, and housing activists, put a more restrictive short-term rental measure on the November 2015 ballot but it failed. Supporters blamed the millions of dollars the short-term rental industry spent to defeat it.

A 2017 lawsuit settlement between the city and Airbnb then dramatically reduced short-term rental listings in San Francisco. By requiring platforms like Airbnb to remove hosts who had not registered with the city by January 2018, the settlement caused overall listings to be slashed by 6,000—4,760 from

Airbnb alone (Airbnb had 8,453 San Francisco listings in early August 2017). Although many of those delisted were infrequent hosts (Airbnb said 35 percent of its hosts had not posted a listing in at least six months), the overall 55 percent reduction in short-term rental listing returned many units to the permanent housing supply. The registration requirement also slashed listings from speculators who were illegally renting multiple units as short-term rentals. For a city that needs all the housing it can get, this was a very positive step.[32]

ISN'T SF STILL UNAFFORDABLE?

Despite Mayor Lee's efforts, San Francisco remains a very expensive city. On April 27, 2017, Kate Hartley, acting director of the mayor's Office of Housing, told the planning commission there was "virtually no housing in San Francisco available for middle-income people."

Critics of Mayor Lee point to the city's ongoing unaffordability as a sign he failed. I disagree. Mayors should be evaluated on what they have done within their power to stop the pricing out of the working and middle class. Ed Lee took office after the late 1990s dot-com boom and subsequent housing bubble drove the city to unprecedented levels of unaffordability. Faced with three decades of inadequate housing construction and the inability to control rents on vacant apartments or single family home prices, Lee did more to maintain and expand economic diversity than any prior San Francisco mayor. San Francisco is paying a steep price for decades of failed housing policies. It will take more than a single mayor to reverse this.

Progress is being made. From 2016 to 2017, evictions in San Francisco decreased 21 percent. This was the first decline in evictions since the tech boom began. In 2017–18 that downward trend continued, with evictions decreasing by 12 percent. Evictions in which the landlord seeks to remove the tenant's unit from housing use—an action that both displaces tenants and eliminates rent-controlled housing—have "gone down so low that we are no longer reporting them," said San Francisco Rent Board Director Robert Collins. Highlighting the impact of cities passing strong rental housing protection laws, Collins attributed this sharp decrease to passage of a 2016 law requiring a conditional-use authorization for the removal of any unit via demolition, conversion, or proposed merger.[33]

San Francisco median rents also fell 5.4 percent in 2017, returning to 2015 levels. This reflects the increased housing supply as new projects opened for occupancy. Median rents for vacant one-bedroom apartments still hovered around \$3,300-\$3,400 per month, but prices were no longer rising. Only the single-family-home market continues to see prices rise sharply, with the median price reaching \$1.6 million in 2018—nearly double the price only five years earlier. But such homes were out of reach for the working and middle class before Ed Lee took office.[34]

While San Francisco is certainly an expensive place to live, what is often overlooked is that all of the statistics about housing costs listed above only apply to vacant units. The statistics exclude rents paid by tenants in place, which are significantly lower than the advertised rents for vacant units. As a result of a ballot measure I co-authored in 1992, annual rent increases for existing tenants averaged less than 2 percent over the past two decades despite the city's booming economy. The housing costs we read about these days also ignore the thousands of low-income, working-, and middle-class residents living in either inclusionary affordable housing or units subsidized by a government entity.

Also excluded from published rent figures are the housing units created by Mayor Lee's \$1.2 billion affordable housing trust fund for rebuilding public housing, the \$310 million affordable housing bond, and the Small Sites Program. The affordable housing produced by the city's inclusionary housing program is also excluded from stories on current market rents. The same is true for rents paid by the thousands of very-low-income SRO residents housed via former mayor Gavin Newsom's Care Not Cash program and the city's master leasing programs for the formerly homeless (the Tenderloin Housing Clinic alone houses over 2,000).

Although many see San Francisco as a city reserved for the wealthy, the above affordable housing programs include thousands of units. The city is home to a lot more low-income, working-, and middle-class tenants than the recently published rent figures for vacant units reflect.

Whenever I talked to Lee about housing he was optimistic about San Francisco retaining its middle class. He told me in the fall of 2017 that he expected "to start seeing the impact of new construction on increased affordability in the next two years." Unfortunately, Mayor Lee did not live to see that day. San Francisco's first Chinese American mayor died suddenly of a heart attack on December 12, 2017. Stories on the mayor's legacy highlighted his role in getting the city to finally build more housing. His prediction that the upcoming wave of new construction will increase the city's affordability will likely be proven correct. Housing built with the 2012 affordable housing bond will be coming on line, and thousands of units were approved through 2017 that are not yet occupied. San Francisco's post-2011 economic resurgence has lasted longer than the 1990s dot-com boom. To meet its growing population and workforce, San Francisco must continue Lee's strategy of both building housing and protecting tenants and the city's rental housing stock. This is likely to occur, as Mayor London Breed, elected in June 2018, has publicly committed to maintaining and even expanding Lee's housing goals.

6

Millennials Battle Boomers
Over Housing

Our own kids can't find a place to live in the cities they were
raised in.

Mike Alvidrez, CEO of LA's Skid Row Housing Trust, August 2017

In 2014, twenty-eight-year-old Laura Clark (now Laura Foote) was living in
a flat in San Francisco's Noe Valley when she got a letter addressed "Dear
Fellow Homeowner." Titled "Help Protect the Victorian Feel of Your
Neighborhood," the letter was from a nearby resident. It warned that one of
Clark's neighbors wanted to build a "massive, inappropriately ultramodern,
glass/steel structure" that will "stick out like a sore thumb in our Victorian/
Edwardian/Queen Anne area."[1]

The letter's author was a boomer who lived next door to the project. He
was associated with a neighborhood group, Protect Noe's Charm. He sent
the letter to neighbors within a four-block radius of the home in question,
warning them that they would lose their "beautiful view of a sea of Victorians"
if the project were built.

The letter alarmed Clark. She did not understand why someone was trying
to stop the building of a new housing unit. Clark felt the rent was too damn
high and favored building more housing. Even though this project only
added a single unit, Clark saw similar opposition to small housing projects
happening everywhere. As she put it, "Every small project that could be doing
a little bit to help was being stopped by nonsense like this. Our housing supply was dying the death of a thousand cuts."[2]

Clark brought the letter to the home of the owners of the planned project.
She asked, "What can I do to help you?" The owners were a husband and wife
architect team who were living in a former earthquake cottage. They wanted
to build a new unit for themselves to live in upstairs and renovate and then
rent out the lower unit. This conversion of a falling-down earthquake cottage

into a modern duplex would be a non-issue in many neighborhoods—but this was Noe Valley.

Clark did not think it was fair that one neighbor felt they could control another neighbor's renovations. Since the project was consistent with existing zoning and height limitations, Clark felt there was no basis for not letting it get built. She began looking into San Francisco's housing approval process and did not like what she found. She concluded that "the city has legislated this problem of not getting housing built into existence. All we need to do to start building more housing is to change the laws."

Laura Clark grew up in a middle-class family in Washington, DC. Her parents worked for nonprofits. Clark had a "very political upbringing. I was raised in the social justice, nonprofit advocacy world. I grew up believing that social change is possible."

When Clark and her partner (now husband) moved to San Francisco, they were shocked at the city's high rents. The median rent for one-bedroom apartments citywide was $2,795, and Noe Valley one-bedrooms typically went for far more. The couple eventually found a one-bedroom fixer-upper for $3,000 in Noe Valley. Clark was "appalled at the high cost of housing in San Francisco. I felt embarrassed that we had enough money to pay such rent because I know a lot of people don't. But I felt we had no choice but to pay it." The couple "spent their own money to paint the unit and install things, all to our landlord's delight."[3]

Clark's dismay over the city's high rents was echoed in conversations she heard at a nearby café she frequented. The city seemed to be filled with newly arrived young people who were forced to pay far more for rent than they had imagined. Clark concluded that something was seriously wrong with the San Francisco housing market. She was right. Building housing can be a challenge in all cities, but in San Francisco it can be an obstacle course. Clark was not aware of San Francisco's notorious opposition to building. If she had been she might have given up before she began. Instead Clark moved full speed ahead to mobilize support for making San Francisco a far more housing-friendly city.

Clark brought three critical insights to the task:

First, she recognized that the pricing out of the working and middle class was not inevitable but was spawned by laws and policies.

Second, Clark understood the anger of millennials (those born from 1981 to 1996) over how much they had to pay to live in San Francisco. She shared that resentment. Young tech workers were being falsely blamed by many boomers (those born from 1946 to 1964) for causing the post-2011 housing price hikes. Yet it was millennials who were paying these exorbitant rents. Adding to frustration over "pissing away so much money on rent" was their inability to afford homeownership in the city. Clark felt that their only hope for ownership was for the city to begin building more housing to expand opportunities.

Third, and most important, Clark saw an opening to transform millennials' anger at housing costs into a movement to support new housing. Clark quickly noticed when talking with her fellow millennials that "they had no idea that the city had a powerful political force that opposed housing. Some literally didn't believe me. They were shocked."

After the November 2014 elections Clark joined two other millennials, Austin Hunter and Annie Fryman, to start Grow SF. Fryman met Clark while working for the architects whose building plans spawned Clark's pro-housing activism. (As of June 2017 the conversion of the cottage into a duplex was still being blocked by neighborhood opposition.) Grow SF sought to become the city's first tenant-led, grassroots, pro–housing development organization. It also aspired to be a different kind of pro-neighborhood organization, one that promoted housing for everyone. It would challenge the powerful neighborhood groups whose opposition to housing contributed to San Francisco's housing crisis. Clark believed there was a "massive, untapped base" that wanted more housing built not only in San Francisco but in other cities. She knew that attracting this "new blood" into the pro-housing movement was essential.

As Clark and her allies began speaking up for more housing at public hearings and neighborhood forums, she heard people calling her a YIMBY (Yes in My Back Yard), a counter to the frequent description of housing opponents as NIMBYs. Realizing the value of the term as an umbrella acronym embracing the many emerging pro-housing groups, Clark co-founded the SF YIMBY Party with Sonja Trauss and other activists. Trauss had quickly become the city's most visible and outspoken pro-housing activist, forming her own group, SF Bay Area Renters Federation (SFBARF).

The SF YIMBY Party would coordinate grassroots advocacy for improving housing affordability and sustainability by increasing housing and transit-oriented development. After the 2016 elections Clark turned her passion for housing advocacy and recruiting new members into a full-time job working as executive director for YIMBY Action.

Building membership was easier than she thought. "When people find us, they are thrilled. They are very relieved to find a world filled with people who agree that building new homes is necessary and probably even good." Clark explained her perspective in an October 2016 interview with the *New York Times:* "Tech is starting to recognize that this is purely a political problem and that they have to solve this by getting involved," she said. "I think they thought they could like hack their way out of this somehow, but you have to do the old-fashioned work of organizing and going door-to-door canvassing."[4]

EAST BAY FOR EVERYONE

Clark is among many millennials across the nation responding to high rents by becoming pro-housing activists. Across the bay in Oakland, Victoria Fierce co-founded East Bay Forward (since renamed East Bay for Everyone) to promote housing in Oakland, Berkeley, and other East Bay cities.

Like Clark's, Fierce's pro-housing activism was fueled by her own housing experience. Arriving in the Bay Area from Ohio in 2014, Fierce was attracted to Oakland's Rockridge neighborhood. Rockridge had a small-town feel, tree-lined streets, and a BART station that could take her right to her new job in San Francisco. She told *Oakland Magazine* in a 2017 interview, "When I first moved out here I looked at Rockridge, and thought, 'Wow, this is so great.... I wish I could afford to live here.'"[5]

But Fierce was priced out of Rockridge. She was also priced out of the nearby Temescal neighborhood, also near a BART station. She ended up living in the downtown area, among the lowest-rent districts, near an Oakland BART station. The experience of being priced out of low-density Oakland neighborhoods near transit hubs struck Fierce as very wrong. And she decided to do something about it.

East Bay for Everyone (EBE) identifies itself as "a network of citizens fighting for the future of housing, transit, tenant rights, and long-term planning in the East Bay. We believe in more housing, more renter protections, better public transit, and better infrastructure." In January 2018 Fierce and EBE went to Sacramento to support legislation to repeal the Costa-Hawkins law that bars cities from restricting rents on vacant apartments. A proud Socialist, Fierce refutes the false stereotype of pro-housing millennials as anti–rent control, anti-government libertarians. Fierce instead sees the group as a "big tent for those who support housing."[6]

EBE brings desperately needed grassroots pro-housing activism to Berkeley, a city long dominated by anti-housing neighborhood groups. EBE also provides public support for the strong pro-housing agenda of Oakland Mayor Libby Schaaf. Like other millennial-dominated pro-housing groups, EBE has directly challenged the political third rail of urban housing: zoning restrictions that create low-density, single-family-home neighborhoods that ensure high housing costs and keep out the future working and middle class.

Until EBF and this new wave of like-minded groups across the nation came along, activists and builders simply accepted single-family-home zoned neighborhoods as off limits. But millennials who pay the high costs of the housing crisis recognize that cities cannot build enough new housing to address increased population and jobs by excluding these neighborhoods. The alternative is the status quo of steadily rising inequality.

Like other pro-housing activists, Fierce sees a "huge gulf" between millennials and boomers in support for new housing. Fierce told me that "nine times out of ten I can look at someone's age and know where they stand on building housing." In May 2018 EBE had 937 members, with the "vast majority" under age thirty-five.

I confirmed Fierce's assessment of the generational divide on housing at a Berkeley City Council meeting on June 13, 2017. About fifty pro-housing activists had turned out to oppose two agenda items designed to sharply reduce housing in Berkeley. Nearly all were under forty. Every Berkeley resident that night who spoke against a housing project was a boomer. This led @CAveryLittle to tweet, "Boomer privilege on display in #berkmtg as rich old white people tell millennials to get out of the city." @MattRegan tweeted, "Generational wealth theft on full display tonight at #berkmtg. Boomers screwing millennials. This Xer says the kids are alright."

The night's agenda had a new two-story house up for approval. The project unleashed a Twitterstorm after an opponent held up a zucchini, arguing that the vegetable would not be alive if the proposed home were approved because it would cast a shadow on her garden. One Berkeley resident tweeted, "As someone w a 3 story house next door who loses sunlight in the yard around 3pm but still grew 150 lbs of tomatoes last yr I'm calling bs." Another tweeted, "Cheering on the YIMBYs at #berkmtg from my couch. Taking on neighbors who want to keep out new people because of THEIR GARDEN."

Self-interested boomer opponents of housing had long dominated the public comments at Berkeley City Council meetings. The combination of millennials attending council hearings and the use of social media to amplify pro-housing concerns has changed this dynamic. Politicians may still vote against housing but more of their constituents will hear about it.

EBE is among many millennial groups forcing cities to take a fresh look at exempting upscale neighborhoods from doing their part to increase economic and racial diversity. EBE's Oakland affordability strategy includes increasing housing in upscale but underbuilt neighborhoods like Rockridge. EBE describes Rockridge as having "been wildly successful at restricting housing growth and preserving property values"—this despite the fact that Rockridge and neighboring Temescal are major transit corridors within walking distance of BART stations. It is hard to get multi-unit projects built in either neighborhood due to homeowner opposition.

Rockridge remained affordable into the 1990s. But in April 2017 its median home price reached $1.3 million and median rents exceeded $5,000 a month. Some Rockridge residents recognize that their density and height restrictions are destroying the neighborhood's future economic and racial diversity. Dan Kalb, who represents Rockridge on the Oakland City Council, met with EBE in March 2017 and told *Oakland Magazine* after the meeting that he was "open to looking to see what we can do to get more housing near our key transit hubs."[7]

I know Kalb from his San Francisco days as a strong environmental activist. Like green activists in Seattle and other cities, Kalb believes in infill housing and smart growth (i.e., new housing that prevents urban sprawl and connects residents to public transit). I met with him at a Rockridge café in August 2017 and pointed out that across the street was a parking lot on College Avenue that seemed perfect for a new multi-unit building. Kalb agreed. He said he could see more "housing in Rockridge going down a third of a mile on either side of the BART station along College Avenue."[8]

Kalb's receptivity to EBE's ideas shows how millennials are opening new frontiers in the housing debate. By raising ideas long considered politically off limits, they are exposing the "emperor has no clothes" component of those who claim to be political progressives but who will not allow rental housing in their neighborhoods. Most importantly, millennials are providing the organizational and grassroots base necessary for these transformations to happen.[9]

CREATING A BETTER CAMBRIDGE

Cambridge, Massachusetts, is a long way from the San Francisco Bay Area but its housing affordability problems are similar. Home to Harvard and close to Boston, Cambridge's median monthly rent through June 2017 was $3,000 and the median single-family-home price was $729,000; both far exceed median housing prices in metro Boston. Since 2012 Jesse Kanson-Benanav has been steadfastly working to address this pricing out of the working and middle class, which threatens Cambridge's economic diversity.[10]

A planner and affordable housing developer, Kanson-Benanav observed neighborhood opposition to specific housing developments after moving to Cambridge in 2004. He began his pro-housing activism when he learned that a petition had been submitted to reduce allowable new housing in Cambridge's Central Square area. Massachusetts law enables as few as ten registered voters to initiate a petition for a zoning change and requires that a public hearing on the proposal be held within sixty-five days. Kanson-Benanav saw Central Square as the "lifeblood of Cambridge" and felt downzoning would choke off its vitality. He began working to defeat the proposal.[11]

"At first I felt we were at a real disadvantage, as we weren't organized," Kanson-Benanav recalled. "After I testified against the downzoning at an early hearing, people came up to me and said they were really glad that I had spoken. I realized there was a silent majority who supported housing and the challenge was mobilizing them."[12]

Jesse's comments were not popular with the Cambridge Residents Alliance (CRA), the neighborhood group backing the proposal for less housing. "The CRA filled the chambers with people, booing speakers they disagreed with and applauding their supporters," he told me. Like similar groups across the country, the CRA opposes zoning changes that would encourage new housing, claiming this "drives rents and housing prices up." Yet Cambridge housing prices have risen sharply since 2012 without such upzoning.

Some might have been intimidated by this opposition, but pro-housing advocates must have thick skin. Kanson-Benanav was encouraged by the response to his testimony and became committed to stopping the downzoning by activating the city's less visible pro-housing base. The thirty-one-year-old assembled a mailing and membership list for a new group, A Better Cambridge. He and his allies met with councilmembers, attended hearings, and served as a long-overdue counterbalance to the CRA. The council ultimately tabled the downzoning, giving A Better Cambridge and other pro-housing groups an important win.

Ever since, Kanson-Benanav has pushed to expand housing in Cambridge and the Greater Boston area. He recognizes that the housing crisis is a regional problem and is helping to build a network of YIMBY pro-housing advocates across greater Boston and to the North Shore. Kanson-Benanav sees today's exclusionary housing policies as part of "an eighty-year history of zoning restrictions being used to promote racial and economic segregation." "Zoning is a city's de facto immigration policy," Kanson-Benanav told the *Boston Globe.* "Are you open to allowing new people to live in your community, or not?" Like many green activists who have joined the pro-housing cause, he sees infill housing as the alternative to "destroying the environment" through suburban sprawl.[13]

Opposition in Cambridge to new housing development remains strong. In 2013, city council candidate Dennis Carlone, backed by the CRA, made a robo-call to Cambridge residents. In the call he claimed that "the City plans to allow the building of 16 story buildings from City Hall to Main Street." He said such proposals "are not planning" but are instead "Pearl Harbor." Equating new housing with the December 7, 1941, attack that killed over 2,000 Americans and led to the nation's entry into World War II demonstrates the fear-mongering often seen in battles against housing. Unfortunately, such scare tactics often work. Carlone won election to the council soon after these robo-calls occurred.[14]

Instead of staying on the defensive, A Better Cambridge joined pro-housing advocates in a push to rezone Central Square to increase housing. The goal was to promote housing and mixed-use developments by waiving open-space and parking requirements. The rezoning would also allow almost 58 percent more units to be built in the core business blocks of the square. To obtain this increased density developers would have to include a significant amount of housing, including affordable units, in any new building. After a long struggle, the plan won city council approval in February 2017.[15]

Kanson-Benanav sees a "heavy" generational divide around housing. "When I look on the Facebook pages of our group and the CRA, the followers are very different. Our average age is eighteen to thirty-five; theirs is forty-five and older." He sees the same millennial/boomer age gap at hearings. "CRA has a lot of older homeowners, tenured professors and the like. People with more freedom in their schedules to attend meetings. The millennials who make up A Better Cambridge do not have the luxury of taking off work to attend city events, nor as much flexibility in their schedules." Of course, the biggest difference shaping attitudes toward housing among the two generations is that millennials "did not get a chance to buy houses in Cambridge when they were affordable thirty years ago." That explains the different perspectives between the two age groups in nearly all cities.

Like Oakland's Victoria Fierce, Kanson-Benanav considers himself "strongly on the left. I am in the Bernie Sanders wing politically." But like Fierce he notes the pro-housing movement incorporates people of diverse political outlooks. At the first-ever national YIMBY conference in 2016 in Boulder, Kanson-Benanav saw "Libertarians, anarchists, and mainstream conservatives" along with progressives like himself. He sees the challenge of creating vibrant, economically diverse cities as "something all political views can buy into."

In Cambridge, opponents of new housing identify as progressive. Yet they insist, as city councilor Jan Devereux put it, that the housing crisis is "not merely a supply problem" but "stems from a complex interplay of forces largely beyond our direct local control."[16] That's a great excuse for local inaction. It says that Cambridge and other cities are powerless to expand housing for the working and middle class, which is false. It's like those blaming "deeper forces" for the gentrification of Los Angeles's Highland Park (detailed in chapter 2) rather than examining the local policies that caused that outcome.

A Better Cambridge members Eugenia Schraa and Bret Matthew responded to Devereux's claims by citing actions the city could take to increase housing affordability. Cambridge squanders buildable land on excessive parking requirements and raises housing costs by limiting building heights and density. The city talks about enhancing "livability" but "livability means nothing to those who can't find an affordable unit in which to live." Seattle environmentalists recognized that increasing density is the only route to a more environmentally sustainable city. Yet some "progressive" Cambridge councilors reject more density, thereby promoting suburban sprawl.[17]

Kanson-Benanav earns a middle-class salary, but even when combined with his wife's earnings the couple cannot afford to buy a house in Cambridge. Cambridge has seen the percentage of its working- and middle-class residents decline as they are priced out of the city. He notes, "There are a lot of young people who've come to Cambridge and want to stay here but can't afford to."

Cambridge is limited in preventing rising rents and tenant displacement because Massachusetts bans local rent-control and just-cause eviction laws. Even Kanson-Benanav and his wife could be forced to leave Cambridge should they get a steep rent hike. The unavailability of these key tenant protections makes it even more imperative that Cambridge build more housing to increase affordability.

Laura Loe is a longtime LGBTQ, environmental, and immigrant rights community activist who in 2015 had a political epiphany: "I realized that land use determines so much of generational wealth and is the root cause of inequality. I had never before thought of it as an equity issue." Loe's environmental consciousness has made her a longtime supporter of urban density and infill housing. Since 2016 she has prioritized expanding Seattle's support for new housing.[18]

Like all good organizers, Loe builds support without disparaging opponents. Her October 31, 2016 *Urbanist* article, "How to Talk to Your NIMBY Parents," captures the generational divide around housing and suggests how pro-housing advocates should bridge it. Loe writes, "I didn't try to convince my mom that she was wrong. Progressives of her generation are proud of their strides towards a more just and inclusive world. They self-identify as liberal and donate their time or money to worthy causes. They are even ready to admit they don't have all the answers. But when their little corner of the world and their routines are threatened, an irrationality comes out that needs to be treated with caution."[19]

Loe's mother had just helped gather signatures for a ballot measure restricting new building heights in Santa Monica, California, to thirty-two feet (three to four stories). Carrying out her view that YIMBYs "can't fight back if we don't know what motivates" their opponents, Loe asked her mother, "Did she want my brother and his family to be able to afford to live nearby? Did she want people to be able to walk to the grocery store or walk to and from their jobs? What were the arguments that mobilized her to show up to fight a low-income housing project for victims of domestic abuse?"

Among Loe's list of "7 Practical Steps for Talking to Your NIMBY Parents" is "connect the struggle for walkable, affordable cities to struggles your parents advocated for when they were your age." That seems particularly savvy when trying to sway boomers whose environmental activism still looms large in their lives. Another is "don't use data if there is an anecdote that tells the same story (unless your parent is a wonky engineer and gets fired up about data)." Housing policy discussion can be far too wonky. Stories about working- and middle-class people priced out of cities will sway boomers more than the latest housing construction data.

Like many pro-housing activists, Loe's politics are on the left. She spent twenty years in the Green Party and was a big supporter of Bernie Sanders's

2016 presidential bid. She was elected to the Sierra Club's Seattle Group in 2016 and soon chaired its housing working group. A frequent writer on housing, Loe's persuasive abilities impressed her adversaries so much that a neighborhood activist labeled her Seattle's "Worst Urban Propagandist"—such was the effectiveness of her columns in swaying readers to the pro-housing cause.

Loe was prominently featured in the national *Sierra Magazine* in a September/October 2017 story on pro-housing urban millennials. Asked how to convert a NIMBY to a YIMBY, Loe pointed to Seattle's Equity and Environment Agenda as an example of how to invite both sides to the conversation. The initiative sought to bring together historically white-led groups and communities of color and led them through a process to develop a set of commitments around equitable development and density. For Loe, "This isn't about *my* backyard. It's about all of our backyards, and how we are going to sacrifice and be innovative together."[20]

HOUSING BOOSTS RETAIL IN SAN DIEGO

Maya Rosas grew up in rent-controlled housing in Santa Monica before moving to San Diego in 2011. Her work as a city planner with Circulate San Diego, a transit advocacy group, led her to recognize that the city could build a lot more housing along its transit corridors. Rosas also saw the city's rising rents as connected to its lack of housing. She is another millennial building public support for more housing.

Rosas "absolutely" sees a generational divide around housing. In 2016 she was elected to serve on the Uptown Planners, a board of volunteers that advises the San Diego Planning Department on development-related matters. As "probably the only person of child-bearing age" in the group (she was twenty-seven), Rosas became the committee's leading advocate for raising building heights in the twelve-block commercial core of the Hillcrest neighborhood. Rosas argued that more housing was needed. She considered the city's 2 percent vacancy rate a "crisis."[21]

Rosas also noted that Hillcrest had many vacant storefronts while other hip neighborhoods like North Park and Little Italy were thriving. The latter are bike-friendly neighborhoods whose ample new development draws the young millennial retail crowd that Hillcrest lacks. The Hillcrest Business Association believes that the "lack of new housing [is the] main reason why retail is dying in Hillcrest."[22]

But the older residents on the Uptown Planners were not swayed. They opposed increased heights regardless of the retail benefits, arguing that "the newcomers will add more traffic, more demand for park and outdoor space, and more stress on infrastructure in an area where the infrastructure barely supports the existing population and the people who come to shop, dine, and visit."[23]

This opposition to newcomers combined with high housing costs explains why San Diego County had one of the smaller millennial population increases in the nation from 2005 to 2015. This was no surprise to Rosas. "San Diego has no entry-level housing for millennials to rent. Where are they supposed to live?"

At a 2016 hearing on Uptown's Community Plan Update, "A number of millennial residents spoke in favor of the plan, saying they wanted to live, work, shop, walk, bike and play in the same neighborhood." The city council adopted the plan in November 2016, agreeing with millennials and others "that density and increased heights were necessary to bring affordable housing to the Uptown communities." In 2018 the group YIMBY Democrats of San Diego County formed to increase support for housing and transit issues within the party. Rosas noted, "There's plenty of Democrats who are rightfully opposed to sprawl development. The point of this club is to foster conversations within the left, to see if this new YIMBY perspective that more housing is good and that we especially need infill housing near transit can take hold."[24]

BOULDER: FROM HIPPIE HAVEN TO MILLION-DOLLAR HOMES

Known in the 1970s as a hippie capital, Boulder, Colorado, is very different today. Its median family income in 2016 was $106,908 and the median single-family home price in March 2018 was $693,000.[25] As the working and middle class are priced out due to dramatically rising housing costs, Boulder residents face a choice: restrict development and become a city whose longtime residents are all millionaires or increase housing density and preserve the city's economic diversity.

Zane Selvans has fought for a more inclusive Boulder since arriving in 2002 to attend graduate school at the University of Colorado. He had lived in shared housing before and wanted to do the same in Boulder. He was lucky; he joined a shared housing cooperative that was legally grandfathered in before Boulder barred more than three unrelated people from living in the same household.

Selvans soon realized that "thousands of people were living illegally in five- to six-bedroom houses. People were afraid to register to vote out of fear that that would reveal they were living in an illegal household." Even as late as 2014 one of the leading anti-housing neighborhood activists was a Democratic Party member using voter registration information to target "illegal" households—he was displacing primarily Democratic voters.[26]

Realizing that Boulder needed increased housing advocacy, Selvans, who was thirty-seven at the time, founded Better Boulder in 2013. The group's website explains its mission: "Some have argued that the way to achieve community goals is to oppose growth, and try to preserve Boulder as it once was. Better Boulder disagrees. We aim to shape our city's future by updating policies and encouraging infill development and smart growth."

A self-described "raging left enviro progressive," Selvans was drawn to housing activism because "urban housing causes far less greenhouse gas emissions than car-reliant suburban and exurban communities." He soon recognized that decisions to restrict housing also impact race and class, with some housing opponents "willfully ignorant" of these social justice implications.

Selvans sees a "very strong age divide" in Boulder's views toward housing. Much of this generational divide is correlated to homeownership. Like other expensive cities, Boulder is filled with older middle-class homeowners who were able to buy twenty or thirty years ago, when prices were still affordable. Many of these homeowners now oppose the increased density necessary to allow the future working and middle class to live in the city.

Boulder has a 20 percent inclusionary housing requirement. This means that for every ten units built, two will be affordable to working- or middle-class families otherwise priced out of the city. But Selvans notes that it is not a major factor in reducing Boulder's inequality because so little housing gets built.

"NEIGHBORHOOD INPUT"

In February 2015, Selvans wrote an article for the Boulder *Daily Camera* ("These People Are in Your Neighborhood") that addressed the power dynamics of homeowner opposition to new housing. Selvans stated:

Boulder's vocal neighborhood associations tend to represent the interests of somewhat older, wealthier owners of single-family homes who have been well served by Boulder's status quo, and who already enjoy access to our civic processes. However, renters—many younger, or of modest means—make up more than half of Boulder, and plenty of people who own their homes live in condos or townhouses. Unfortunately, our neighborhood organizations aren't always welcoming to these other kinds of neighbors, and attempts to gather input from neighborhood residents can be ad hoc and subject to powerful confirmation biases. If we want an open and inclusive society, we need to create civic forums that are inviting and accessible to everyone.[27]

Boulder's neighborhood associations sound like those in Seattle, which led Mayor Ed Murray to stop city funding of these groups in 2015. Selvans warned that if Boulder's new city-funded "neighborhood liaison" position focuses outreach on the "already well-organized associations," there will be more "neighborhood-driven projects" of large, single-family homes that "provide little broader community benefit."

Instead, Selvans maintained, "We should figure out who isn't at the table, and actively recruit them to the conversation." This means seeking input "from renters, from multi-family homeowners' associations, those living in permanently affordable housing, the Latino community that makes up 9 percent of our city, seniors on fixed incomes, and even the 30,000 CU students. We need more of the kind of neighborhood engagement that . . . brings out voices we wouldn't otherwise hear."[28]

Selvans acknowledged that a more democratic input process "has created tension with some homeowners who are accustomed to being overrepresented, but renters aren't that scary. We share many of the city's progressive, environmentalist values. We're neighbors too, and we deserve just as much of a say in our city's future as anyone lucky enough to have bought their house before the turn of the century."[29]

Selvans gets to the core of neighborhood activism's shift from its progressive roots to promoting exclusionary land-use policies: It's about power. Neighborhood associations often emerged to oppose attacks on middle- and working-class communities posed by urban renewal. They fought to control what happened in their community and largely won. But the risk to these neighborhoods' ability to remain economically and racially diverse no longer comes from bulldozers. Instead it comes from a changing housing market that denies entry to the non-affluent. Neighborhood opposition to new housing has made existing homes much more expensive and turned once afford-able communities into luxury neighborhoods.

Boulder has many powerful neighborhood groups intent on stopping housing. The Boulder Neighborhood Alliance is "a group of citizens commit-ted to neighborhood preservation, measured growth, and protecting the integrity of neighborhood zoning." Its website in July 2017 identified the threats to Boulder: "Cooperative housing. Gentle infill. Housing crisis. YIMBY! . . . It seems like Boulder is under constant assault by a variety of interest groups who are bent on turning Boulder into the next Portland or San Francisco." But not building enough housing risks turning Boulder into San Francisco when it comes to housing unaffordability and pricing out the middle class. And Boulder is far more expensive than Portland.[30]

The group Livable Boulder reflects the siege mentality among homeowner groups. In July 2017 its website included a link to a Boulder *Daily Camera* opinion piece denouncing the city council for allowing housing cooperatives in every zoning district, which it deemed an "anti-neighborhood position." The opinion piece also praised a 2015 letter to the *Daily Camera* that warned, "You can't build your way to affordable housing—as has been demonstrated in San Francisco and Aspen. Boulder has fallen behind the wisdom of Palo Alto and other cities, which now understands this fallacy well." Perhaps only in Boulder is San Francisco a cautionary tale for building *too much* housing. Those frustrated by Palo Alto's refusal to build housing might find it curious that the city's promotion of sprawl is being touted in Boulder as "wisdom."[31]

In November 2017, *National Geographic* identified Boulder as "The Happiest Place in the United States." Its story focused on eighty-eight-year-old "citizen activist" Ruth Wright, who has spent a career "questioning the unquestioned virtue of development." She represented Boulder in the state legislature for fourteen years. According to the story, Boulder wouldn't be so happy a place if in 1971 Wright had not "championed a ballot measure limit-ing building heights to five stories." Two nights prior to her interview Wright had testified before the Boulder City Council in favor of extending a mora-torium on new buildings over forty feet for another fifteen months. The council backed the measure by a vote of eight to one.[32]

As in Palo Alto, which in March 2018 had a $3.2 million median home price and which built only forty-four housing units from 2014 to 2016, Boulder's opposition to new housing keeps longtime residents happy while excluding the working and middle class. Boulder's skyrocketing housing prices are not mentioned in the *National Geographic* article, as many boomers do not pay them and millennials struggling to do so are not so "happy."[33]

Despite the obstacles Selvans is optimistic about Boulder's future. He believes that "to be progressive is to believe in the possibility of positive change." Like Seattle's Laura Loe and other YIMBYs, he sees increasing density in cities as requiring "new political alignments." A longtime leftist, he finds himself joining builders and developers in trying to expand Boulder's housing supply.

Selvans believes the city can build hundreds of thousands of new housing units. While Boulder's charter does impose a fifty-five-foot height limit, Paris's six-story limit has not prevented it from building ample housing—and from being among the most visually inspiring cities in the world. Selvans and other YIMBYs are true believers in the possibility of positive change. As he puts it, "It's time for boomers to accept that cities are evolving; to join with millennials to build the future instead of hunkering down in the past."[34]

PORTLAND FOR EVERYONE

Until the past decade, Portland, Oregon, was prized for its affordability, but those days are gone. The city's working and middle class face skyrocketing rents and home prices and are increasingly priced out. Portland is among many cities where increasing affordability requires changing land-use laws in order to boost infill housing. Fortunately, Portland for Everyone (P4E), a strong and diverse coalition of housing and environmental groups, is working to overcome homeowner association opposition to building new multi-unit housing in traditional single-family-home neighborhoods.

P4E believes the city "should provide for abundant, diverse, and affordable housing to meet the needs of all family sizes in every neighborhood—from smaller apartment buildings and accessory dwelling units in established neighborhoods to downtown skyscrapers to single-family housing." Taking on the core challenge of increasing infill housing in cities across the nation, P4E insists that "it makes no sense when a standard 50 × 100′ lot within easy walking distance of downtown can't be used for anything more than a single-family house."[35]

P4E's sponsoring organization is 1000 Friends of Oregon. Founded in 1975, its mission is "to enhance our quality of life by building livable urban and rural communities, protecting family farms and forests, and conserving natural areas."[36] The group is the state's leading watchdog for ensuring urban growth has the least possible impact on the natural environment. The extremely broad-based support of 1000 Friends of Oregon is reflected in the diversity of P4E's coalition, which includes housing, transit, urban design, bike advocacy, and other urbanist and livability groups.

Portland has a generational divide around housing. P4E coordinator Madeline Kovacs told me that while there are some boomers on the pro-housing side, they tend to be affordable housing professionals. She finds few young people and virtually no renters who are against infill housing. She does find "second-generation boomer environmentalists who think we can just stop growth by not building housing." Portland's affordable and infill housing movement may be the most green-driven in the nation. This is critical in overcoming opponents' environmental arguments for keeping neighborhoods restricted to single-family homes.[37]

Like many millennials, Kovacs came to the housing issue through a deep commitment to fighting climate change. She spent a decade as a youth climate activist and was a key figure in building the youth climate change movement. Many of P4E's coalition members are environmental groups that recognize that infill housing reduces suburban sprawl and the greenhouse gases produced by long car commutes. As Kovacs sees it, one reason for the generational divide around infill housing is that "young people growing up around climate change connect the dots between transit and land-use policies."

Portland's green-driven affordable housing movement is exemplified by the environmental justice group Organizing People, Activating Leaders (OPAL). OPAL's strategies connect the housing, racial justice, and environmental crises. OPAL took on the powerful Oregon real estate industry by organizing a statewide coalition of racial and social justice advocates to repeal the state's inclusionary housing ban, which passed in 1999. Cities' inability to require on-site affordable units in market-rate projects denies working- and middle-class families access to high-opportunity neighborhoods and reinforces housing segregation. In February 2016, OPAL demonstrated the power that grassroots activism has to help stop the pricing out of working people when its efforts led the Oregon legislature to repeal the inclusionary ban for Portland. OPAL followed this huge victory with a local campaign to enact inclusionary zoning in Portland. OPAL's Vivian Satterfield played a key role in shaping the inclusionary housing proposal, which passed in December 2016. As a result, new buildings of twenty units or more will have to include affordable units for those earning 60 percent to 80 percent of the area's median income.[38]

In December 2016 Portland voters also passed a $258 million "Yes for Homes" bond measure that will build or preserve 1,300 affordable housing units for low-income people. It was Portland's first affordable housing bond. OPAL supported the measure as part of its ongoing effort to ensure that Portland's new housing developments benefit racial minorities and the working and middle class.

As in many cities, Portland's unaffordability crisis disproportionately falls on residents of color. As described in a 2015 report, "ReBuilding Community," "a largely unregulated housing market, lack of rent controls, limited public investment in affordable housing, urban renewal policies that fail to protect communities of color, all lend to decreased housing choice and forced displacement. Displacement and gentrification are neither an accident nor the outcome of 'inevitable economic market forces,' but rather the outcome of years of intentional public and private investments, the commoditization of housing, market forces, structural oppression, and overt and institutional racism."[39]

PORTLAND AT A CROSSROADS

Portland's inclusionary housing victory occurred as the city was undergoing a state-mandated process for redrawing its comprehensive land-use plan, which is updated every twenty years. Because Portland housing prices have jumped dramatically since the last plan revision, the outcome of this process in 2018 is critical. Decisions on expanding housing will determine whether middle-class residents are part of Portland's long-term future.

P4E has focused on two key areas. The first is the Residential Infill Project, which addresses "the feasibility and appropriateness of more duplexes, triplexes and accessory dwelling units (ADUs) to provide more housing options in single-dwelling zones." In arguing for more housing options, P4E notes that "45 percent of the city's total land area is zoned for single-family homes and only 10 percent for multi-family housing—most of which would arrive in the form of larger apartment buildings. A choice between downtown highrises, five-story apartment buildings located on certain corridors and traditional (and larger) single-family homes misses the needs of many Portlanders. It is time to bring our zoning code more into line with the needs of our families—today and tomorrow."[40]

P4E also echoes other urbanists in noting that promoting economic and racial diversity requires more than building housing on transit corridors. Housing in such areas is politically popular because it avoids neighborhood opposition. But P4E believes people of all income levels deserve neighborhoods where one can "walk to school, neighborhood stores or a park." It is calling for duplexes, triplexes, and cottages and ADUs in neighborhoods currently zoned for single-family homes. This will allow "teachers, first responders and other middle-class people to live in the neighborhoods they serve."

P4E's second focus is on the Better Housing by Design (BHD) project, which seeks to expand housing opportunities in the city's medium- to high-density residential zones. P4E has urged the city to revise the BHD to increase housing "abutting high frequency transit and existing commercial hubs." The coalition also called for upzoning key corridors and recommended several measures that would make building housing more cost effective. P4E believes the BHD should be driven by the overarching question "Will this plan meaningfully expand housing options and increase affordability for Portlanders in most neighborhoods?" Overall, P4E seeks to add more types of housing to more neighborhoods. It is a commonsense goal for a city whose outdated zoning restrictions price out the working and middle class.[41]

NEIGHBORHOOD OPPOSITION

Despite P4E's comprehensive, thoughtful approach, opponents see a nefarious agenda. The group DontRezoneUs.org argues on its website, "You love your neighborhood the way it is . . . right? If you don't ACT NOW, together with your neighbors, it could radically change forever. And NOT for the better." The group's website depicts its overwhelmingly boomer membership marching at the Multnomah Parade. The group carried signs reading, "Save Our Neighborhood! Stop Rezoning."[42]

The group was particularly fearful of tenants living in their neighborhoods. "The proposed zoning changes include allowing multiplexes and apartments in Single-Family Residential zones throughout the city. . . . Our neighborhood falls within these new proposed zones!" Ignoring the fact that Portland renters needed more housing, the group saw the land-use plan as a developers' scam: "They say it's to make housing affordable, but the result will be that rich developers win, our neighborhoods lose and the resulting housing won't be affordable at all. And our neighborhood character will be destroyed in the process."

The group further claims that P4E's "proposed zoning provides additional incentive for developers to tear down our neighborhood and build multi-family housing! And, to make it even worse, parking for these high-density residences WILL NOT be required and many trees will be purged from our greenscape (they will not have any protections)." The neighborhood association saw multi-unit housing for tenants as having a "serious, negative long-term impact on our wonderful neighborhood."[43]

A group called Stop Demolishing Portland also opposes P4E's plans to expand multi-unit housing. Its opposition to "higher density construction in our vintage low and medium density neighborhoods" is connected to a more progressive agenda backing "subsidized and/or public housing, inclusionary zoning, affordable housing, and stopping gentrification." But no public or subsidized housing has any chance of being built in Portland's single-family-home neighborhoods. The group's pro-affordability message is really about ensuring that new housing is not built in their backyard.[44]

The website for United Neighborhoods for Reform describes 1000 Friends of Oregon and P4E as a "developers' lobby" that has been "thoroughly co-opted." It claims that "building more has led to a housing crisis, and in some areas near-complete displacement." Arguing that building housing, rather than not building, worsens the housing crisis is a common position of neighborhood groups in high-housing-cost cities.[45]

So who will prevail in this battle over Portland's future? When we spoke in June 2018, P4E's Madeline Kovacs was hopeful that the Portland City Council would do the right thing. The council "wants to house everyone," she said, and it recognizes the need for a more "flexible" approach. She noted that commissioner Chloe Eudaly, elected in 2016 on a campaign focused on addressing the housing crisis, has brought to the council a strong voice for housing that could advance P4E's goals.

The council is expected to vote on the new land-use plan in the fall of 2018.

BOOMERS BLAME MILLENNIALS FOR HOUSING CRISIS

Many boomer homeowners strongly oppose millennial-backed pro-housing groups. They do not appreciate young people influencing what gets built in their neighborhoods, and many existing homeowners oppose new multi-unit housing almost anywhere in their city. To counteract the rising influence of pro-housing millennials, many boomers have challenged their right to live in high-housing-cost cities and the "housing for everyone" agenda that many in the younger generation support.

Consider a 2017 news story, "Millennials Tell Boomers 'Yes in My Backyard,'" by reporter Lilia Luciano of Sacramento's ABC-TV affiliate. Two longtime Bay Area activists, Becky O'Malley and Calvin Welch, spoke for boomers. Both were outspoken opponents of building the new market-rate housing that millennials typically support. Berkeley's O'Malley has long criticized the city as too "pro-development." She used the money she and her husband made in the computer industry to fund a newspaper, the *Berkeley Daily Planet*, to promote her views.

O'Malley can sound like she supports new middle-class housing: "What's needed in cities like Berkeley is more homes for people at the low end of the pay scale, coupled with better pay, so that workers like teachers, firefighters and UC Berkeley service employees don't need to commute such long distances to find housing," she wrote in 2017. "What's not needed is more luxury condos in hyper-urban areas like those under construction in downtown Berkeley." But O'Malley routinely opposed new multi-unit housing in Berkeley. She told reporter Luciano that what she sees at public meetings in Berkeley are "a bunch of entitled young white people. The people that I know that are my children, grandchildren live where they can afford to live and don't whine about it."[46]

O'Malley said millennials would not be "whining" over Berkeley's high housing costs if the tech industry left the Bay Area for "Idaho or Oregon." There are "plenty of places that need those jobs."[47] Of course, opening tech campuses out of state would not address Berkeley's need to build housing for those already working in the Bay Area. Nor would it change Berkeley's exclusionary zoning and density policies, which have priced out public school teachers and service workers—jobs that must be performed in Berkeley.

O'Malley's comment reminded me of a meeting I had with housing activists in 2000 in Washington, DC, when we were urging HUD officials to support a national housing trust fund. One official said there was not really an affordable housing crisis because there was plenty of affordable and available housing in Nebraska and that people could just move there. When we responded that people could not move to Nebraska without jobs there, he insisted that did not change the fact that Nebraska had affordable housing available.

Calvin Welch, for decades San Francisco's leading spokesperson for non-profit housing groups, also used the ABC-TV interview to brush aside young people's housing concerns. Boomer Welch told Luciano that it was no big deal for millennials to live in crowded housing. After all, he "lived with six other students when [he] attended San Francisco State." Looking at Luciano, Welch said that the problem was that "your generation doesn't want to do that anymore." Luciano reminded Welch that she was a thirty-two-year-old working woman who needed a place she could live with a child.[48]

In 1973, Welch and his wife and another couple purchased a duplex on Ashbury Street in the Haight-Ashbury for $31,000. Forty-four years later, the market value of Welch's duplex was over $2 million. Welch bought his duplex for the equivalent of $176,000 in 2017 dollars, a tiny fraction of what any house costs in San Francisco today. Welch would be priced out of today's Haight-Ashbury. Yet he believes that millennials like Luciano do not need more housing

Welch saw new market-rate housing as bringing more moderate voters into San Francisco. He preferred keeping them out. As he put it, "Who lives here is who votes here, and that's what it's about." Yet only a rich person can afford to buy a Victorian home or flats in Welch's Haight-Ashbury. Welch is so hostile to new market-rate housing that he described the city's 2016 plan to provide a density bonus to builders adding affordable units as "ethnic cleansing."[49]

THE TRUTH ABOUT "LUXURY" HOUSING

Some boomers challenge millennials' support for new housing by denying it helps the middle class. That's why O'Malley, Welch, and their allies characterize market-rate housing as "luxury" homes for "the elite." This puts a progressive and populist spin on neighborhood groups' opposition to development. But if new housing were the affordability culprit, urban America would not have seen home values jump from 2007–2014 when very little housing was built. What really creates "luxury" housing is scarcity; this occurs when neighborhood groups prevent new housing from being built in the community. Skyrocketing single-family-home prices in Calvin Welch's Haight-Ashbury show this. The neighborhood has seen little new housing built for decades—but instead of the lack of supply causing prices to fall, the shortage turned all existing homes into luxury dwellings.

In June 2017 the Washington, DC–based Urban Institute released a study of San Francisco's affordable housing crisis. It defined "luxury housing" as units that sold for at least $1 million. The study found that the vast majority of luxury sales in San Francisco came from existing housing stock: "In 2016, at the height of the million-dollar home market of the past eight years, only 10 percent of home sales worth a million dollars or more were located in new complexes."[50]

The report concluded, "So what is driving the rapid rise in high-priced housing? The primary factor is that the demand for housing in the region has outstripped new supply. Between 2010 and 2015, as million-dollar homes became commonplace, the region added six times as many jobs as it did housing units, despite Census data indicating that people typically lived just two or three to a unit." In other words, housing prices have skyrocketed because far too little housing has been built to keep up with demand.[51]

Where is the "luxury" housing in San Francisco? In the Haight-Ashbury, Noe Valley, Bernal Heights, the Richmond, and other neighborhoods whose anti-housing policies artificially restrict supply. Nearly all of their houses are sold at "luxury" prices. San Francisco's largest luxury housing market is older houses in the city's historic neighborhoods. The same is true for Berkeley. The city's failure to build in most neighborhoods has left fewer existing Berkeley single-family homes selling for under $1 million. In May 2017 a two-bedroom, 811-square-foot house on Berkeley's traffic-heavy corner of Hearst and San Pablo sold for $970,000. Houses in political veteran Loni Hancock's Le Conte neighborhood that sold in the 1970s for $25,000 now go for $1.2 million.[52]

To be clear, new luxury housing is routinely built in San Francisco, New York, Los Angeles, and other cities. But other than in New York City, these multi-million dollar luxury towers are usually constructed in or adjacent to downtown. They are built outside the primarily single-family-home neighborhoods where pro-housing activists seek more density. In San Francisco, some activists routinely oppose smaller, more affordable market-rate projects in residential neighborhoods on the grounds they are "luxury" housing. Yet two of the city's biggest luxury housing developments, the Rincon and Millennium Towers, located near downtown, were backed by the board's progressive supervisors. Both were conceived as housing for the rich. Yet activists and neighborhood groups quick to label all market-rate housing "luxury" did not oppose these towers.

As Jesse Kanson-Benanav of A Better Cambridge put it in an August 15, 2017, tweet, it is hard to overlook "the irony of $1M homeowners arguing w/

renters that barely afford #CambMA saying our approach to hsng focuses too much on 'luxury housing.'" Stopping housing has not prevented rich people from coming to San Francisco; to the contrary, it helps ensure that in many neighborhoods *only* the rich, or their children, can afford to come.

THE NEW SERFS

Despite the acute housing crisis suffered by millennials, boomer-dominated neighborhood associations continue to oppose new housing in many communities. In the spring of 2017 the Bay Area Council released a nine-county poll on attitudes toward new housing. The poll found "seventy percent of millennials were in favor of building more housing in their own neighborhood, while only 57 percent of residents age 40 to 64 supported additional homes near them." Newer residents were also much more likely to support housing than those who had lived in the region for twenty years or more.[53]

The poll erred by including forty-year-olds as boomers when they had to be at least fifty-one to qualify when the survey was taken. But if only those between fifty-one and sixty-four had been polled the opposition to housing would likely have been even higher. This over-fifty demographic dominates public hearings against new housing in San Francisco. Boomers are the most common media spokespersons in anti-housing fights.

This generational divide makes sense. Many boomers bought homes or rented apartments decades ago when prices were still affordable. They could buy homes with far less income than millennials, many of whom are forced to live with their parents, earn today. Homeowners in once affordable but now upscale neighborhoods see no benefit to them in new housing. But they do see the downsides: construction noise, more competition for street parking, and an increased housing supply that could reduce their own home values.

In contrast, middle-class millennials are paying the price—literally—of a limited housing supply. They are often priced out of the urban neighborhoods where they most want to live. Some define this generation as the "new serfs," condemned to a lifetime of paying exorbitant rent.[54]

A national study found that from 1983 to 2013 housing wealth increased "almost exclusively among the wealthiest, older Americans." Wealth is limited to property owners, as tenants accrue no equity no matter how much rent they pay or for how long. Joseph Gyourko, co-author of the study, noted, "The [chief beneficiary of] binding restrictions on the supply of new housing is the owners at the time the restrictions were imposed." This study concluded before home prices across major cities soared, making today's boomer homeowners even more property rich. Meanwhile, millennials are priced out.[55]

BLAMING MILLENNIAL TECH WORKERS FOR THE CRISIS

Starting in 2011, millennials began arriving in San Francisco to work for Twitter, Zynga, Zendesk, and other rapidly growing tech firms. They faced a rude surprise: the city's already high rents were skyrocketing. Given the influx of new residents, after the city failed for years to build much housing, this outcome was foreseeable, but it still shocked new arrivals. As Laura Clark described above, millennials' anger that their rent was "too damn high" led many to become pro-housing activists.

But instead of identifying young tech workers as the victims of a housing shortage and working with them on solutions, many boomers blamed them for the crisis. Millennial tech workers were charged with threatening the city's "soul." Many boomers and their allies demonized millennials as corrupting San Francisco's way of life rather than seeing them as potential allies in the struggle for increased tenant protections and affordable housing.

How do you undermine sympathy for the demographic group paying the ridiculously high rents everyone was complaining about? By promoting anecdotes attacking millennials. Stories abounded of tech workers unable to afford housing because they were spending lavishly on avocado toast. Or of them stealing Mission-district soccer fields from Latino youth; the latter incident turned confusion over the city's park scheduling procedures into a culture war.[56]

Activists showed their dislike for tech workers by blocking Google buses that picked up workers and drove them to Silicon Valley. These oversized vehicles blocked cars from passing on narrow Noe Valley and Mission District streets and often illegally occupied public bus zones. This justifiably angered many. But activists were primarily motivated by their opposition to tech workers' living in San Francisco. As a December 20, 2013, report noted, "Today's protests centered on low-income tenants evicted from their homes as a result of the area's housing situation, a situation some blame on the high-income individuals employed by tech companies—who have been bidding up housing prices in the area."[57]

The media was drawn to the Google bus issue as it provided great visuals and a cultural conflict. But young tech workers were not the ones issuing Ellis

Act evictions and pursuing no-fault evictions against low-income tenants. The often-repeated claim that millennial tech workers were the market for former rental units now being sold as tenancies in common was also false; in fact, builders I knew complained that tech workers did not want to buy because they were not sure how long they would be in the city. It was actually wealthy, older speculators who were evicting long-term tenants during the tech boom. Yet this group, made up primarily of boomers, got far less blame than young tech workers for the worsening housing crisis.

Few media stories connected the need for Google buses to South Bay cities' failure to build housing along with tech campuses. City councils in Sunnyvale, Cupertino, and elsewhere that approved massive tech campuses without requiring housing for the new workers were the real villains. But activists and supportive media ignored the role of these cities in San Francisco's housing crisis. They instead demonized tech workers who were simply trying to find housing in a desirable city relatively close to their job.

Once the idea that tech workers were endangering San Francisco values was established, the media piled on. *The Guardian* asked in February 2014, "Is San Francisco Losing Its Soul"? In November 2015 *Salon* proclaimed, "San Francisco Sells Its Soul: Money Rules the City Now, Bohemia Be Damned." An October 2015 *New York Times* article, "Seattle, in Midst of Tech Boom, Tries to Keep Its Soul" suggested that San Francisco's battle for its soul had already been lost. *The Daily Beast* chimed in with an October 2015 piece, "San Francisco's Alarming Tech Bro Boom: What Is the Price of Change?"[58]

The "tech is costing San Francisco its soul" stories required the media to invent a fictional affordable San Francisco that preceded the post-2011 tech boom. Reporters eager to capture what was happening now were not interested in learning that San Francisco no-fault evictions were far higher during the late 1990s dot-com boom, when the media also declared that the city's soul was being lost. The *New York Times* had warned as far back as 1981 that unless San Francisco built more housing its middle class would soon be priced out ("Changing San Francisco Is Foreseen as a Haven for Wealthy and Childless").[59] The fact that San Francisco's historic affordability had been lost decades before the new tech boom was ignored in favor of the false but far more dramatic story of tech companies destroying the city's character.

Alexandra Pelosi's October 2015 HBO special *San Francisco 2.0* took false media accounts of pre–tech boom San Francisco to the extreme. Pelosi blamed tech for killing the city's "spirit of anti-materialism" without saying when this era of "anti-materialism" *ever* existed in San Francisco. It certainly was not present in the 1960s and 1970s, when the redevelopment agency demolished thousands of affordable housing units in the South of Market area and the Fillmore, displacing countless low-income tenants in a process described for the latter neighborhood as "Negro removal." Nor was it in evidence in the 1980s, when San Francisco's steady gentrification and speculator evictions hit full steam. The 1980s downtown high-rise boom, often described as the city's "Manhattanization," was anything but anti-materialistic; likewise the 1990s dot-com boom. Pelosi, like others, mistakenly saw the new tech boom as a break from San Francisco's past. Instead it was a continuation.[60]

A MILLENNIAL-BOOMER ALLIANCE

Imagine if most boomers had responded to San Francisco's rising economy in 2011 by saying, "We've spent too many decades failing to build enough housing. Now our own children and a younger generation of teachers, nurses, firefighters, and other working- and middle-class families have been priced out. We need to stop our exclusionary policies and open our neighborhoods to a lot more housing. And we ought to do so fast."

One influential San Francisco boomer did respond this way: Mayor Ed Lee. Lee understood that for San Francisco to build enough housing he needed to get millennials on board. After appointing thirty-year-old Katy Tang to fill a vacant supervisor's seat to represent the Sunset District on the Westside, Lee worked with Tang to get housing built in that underdeveloped part of San Francisco.

Most tourists to San Francisco never see Tang's district. It is often said that it does not look like the popular perception of San Francisco. In contrast to the city's famous hills, it is largely flat. It is primarily a neighborhood of two-story buildings that includes far less ground-floor retail than the Mission, North Beach, and other communities that are tourist destinations. Housing advocates have long dreamed of increasing height and density in the Sunset and other parts of western San Francisco. But Westside residents vote in large numbers. Their fierce opposition has prevented new housing in an area that could easily accommodate new units.

Katy Tang brought a millennials' sensibility about housing to her job as supervisor. She was troubled that San Francisco was rapidly losing its middle-income households and felt that unless the city built more housing for this population it would no longer have a middle class. She also recognized that views toward new housing among her heavily Chinese American constituency were changing. Parents feared their kids would not be able to afford to live in San Francisco and recognized that only by building more housing could their multi-generational families remain together in the city.

In 2017, millennial Tang and boomer Lee forged an alliance to overcome the third rail of city housing politics by creating HOME-SF. HOME-SF would bring new housing to neighborhoods that had not seen much development, such as Tang's Sunset District. The strategic genius of the HOME-SF plan was threefold. First, it was not expressly targeted at the Sunset but instead applied to multiple neighborhoods. Second, it focused on building in transit and commercial corridors, which is where urban planners and environmentalists favor new housing. Third, and perhaps most important, HOME-SF was expressly billed as helping teachers, nurses, firefighters, police officers, janitors, and construction workers stay in San Francisco. Lee and Tang recognized that broadening the beneficiaries of affordable housing programs would get moderate Westside voters on board. These are lessons pro-housing activists in all cities can apply.

In 2016, an effort by the San Francisco Planning Department to pass legislation almost identical to HOME-SF had failed miserably. Using the wonkish name Affordable Housing Density Bonus Program, planners assumed there would be broad support for a program that granted builders two extra stories in exchange for 33 percent affordable units. But anti-housing neighborhood groups and affordable housing organizations opposed to market-rate housing killed the legislation.

In 2017, Tang revived the proposal under the more populist sounding HOME-SF and provided the political leadership needed for its passage. Tang did so in the face of enormous pressure from her district. In 2016 she had joined the planning department in convening a community meeting in the Sunset to discuss the density bonus plan. The crowd of roughly 250 mostly older, white homeowners—which one observer described as "the old Sunset," as Asian Americans now comprise 40 percent of the neighborhood—was incensed over the legislation. People had heard the government was planning to seize Sunset homes as part of a new urban renewal plan. Facing a "tsunami of anger," it would have been easy for Tang to back away from the measure. But she did not. Instead, she defused the fear. Tang never wavered in her support of the measure.[61]

HOME-SF also passed in 2017 because Laura Clark's SF YIMBY, the San Francisco Housing Action Coalition, and Sonia Trauss's SF Bay Area Renters

Federation added the grassroots support that had been lacking in 2016. Millennials mobilized behind HOME-SF more than they had for any prior city measure, and it paid off. Instead of anti-housing neighborhood groups dominating hearings, those groups were matched by millennials testifying about their affordability woes.

The politics around creating density bonuses in San Francisco had swung so dramatically from 2016 to 2017 that the final board vote on HOME-SF was unanimous. Every supervisor wanted to be on record as supporting more housing for the working and middle class.

Thanks to the Lee-Tang boomer-millennial alliance, over the next two decades HOME-SF will create 16,000 new housing units, 5,000 (30 percent) of which will be permanently affordable. Those benefiting will be middle-income working-class families making $60,000 to $150,000 a year for a family of four. These are households for which no public housing programs or subsidies currently exist, and which are generally unable to afford the high cost of housing in San Francisco.

In order to create units large enough for families with children, 40 percent of HOME-SF's new units must include two or more bedrooms. The program also prohibits any displacement of existing tenants.

At the signing ceremony for HOME-SF, Tang stated, "San Francisco prides itself on being an inclusive city. But we haven't been inclusive in our housing policies. HOME-SF restores this policy of inclusion that San Francisco needs."[62]

HOME-SF alone will not end the pricing out of the working and middle class from San Francisco. No single law or policy can make up for decades of inadequate new housing. But measures like HOME-SF are part of the solution. Reversing decades of rising inequality in urban America requires comprehensive policy changes that expand housing supply, improve tenant protections, and preserve rental and affordable housing from demolition, conversion, or other loss.

San Francisco has far greater protections for tenants and rental housing than most cities but has done far worse at building housing. That's what makes HOME-SF particularly significant. It signals that "the times they are a-changin'" as far as housing in San Francisco is concerned.

As millennials promote housing policies offering opportunities for the middle class to live in the new urban America, support for new housing grows. But boomer-dominated homeowner associations in many cities still retain enormous power to stop housing.

The story of how boomers promote local land-use policies that raise their own property values while putting the future economic diversity of urban America at risk will leave some uncomfortable. But if we are serious about stopping the pricing out of the working and middle class from progressive cities, the truth about who has caused and benefited from this exclusion must be understood. The next chapter, on neighborhood opposition to housing, further exposes this generational dynamic.

7

Get Off My Lawn!

How Neighborhood Groups Stop Housing

"SAVE ELIZABETH STREET GARDEN"

In New York City I regularly visit the Nolita (North of Little Italy) neighborhood east of SOHO. Nolita has steadily become more upscale over the past decade. Elizabeth Street, the heart of Nolita, is now filled with chic clothing stores, hipster cafés, and destination restaurants. Nolita has reached a level of affluence where affordable housing is unlikely to even be proposed. It was not always this way.

In 1983, a large vacant site on Elizabeth Street was earmarked for affordable housing. It remained a derelict 20,000-square-foot lot until 1991. That is when the city, awaiting development of the site, leased the space to the adjacent Elizabeth Street Gallery. It charged the gallery only $4,000 a month. This generated revenue while the affordable housing was pending, but it left New York City taxpayers providing a bargain rent to a business using the space as overflow for its indoor trade selling garden statues to the wealthy.

In 2012, district councilmember Margaret Chin began the process of turning the space into 70 to 100 units of affordable senior housing. Chin got a commitment from the city to build the senior housing as part of an agreement addressing Lower East Side development. Chin asked the administration of Mayor Michael Bloomberg to select a city-owned site in her district for affordable housing. Bloomberg's people chose the Elizabeth Street site.[1]

The site, long closed to the public, seemed it would make a wonderful place for seniors to live. As Chin explained, "New York City has over 200,000 seniors on housing waiting lists. We have over 5,000 in my district alone. Every day seniors come to my office needing housing, particularly with elevators. Seniors who have spent their entire lives in the area should be able to age in the neighborhood they built."[2]

But neighbors were not happy about Chin's taking the initiative to house seniors; they preferred the site remain open space. From the very start they strongly opposed the site's use for addressing the city's acute housing shortage for low-income seniors. Chin told me that at the very first informational meeting held by the city and the local community board, "Opponents had mobilized people to attend. They had already created a video with music to oppose housing on the site. I definitely did not anticipate such opposition."[3]

Nolita had changed dramatically between 1983 and 2012. It was now the type of upscale neighborhood where affordable housing is neither contemplated nor built. Nolita residents and businesses used their ample skills and connections to wage an all-out campaign to stop senior housing on the site. The once derelict lot became an "oasis," and the battle to "Save Elizabeth Garden" began.

Nolita is a politically progressive voting district. Its residents support social and economic justice. Yet the community became engaged in a struggle to stop the only chance working- and middle-class seniors had to live in the neighborhood. Nobody disputed that these future residents could only afford to live in Nolita through government-funded affordable housing, which Nolita's politically savvy residents were hell-bent to stop.

To convince the city to forgo building housing on the site, Nolita activists transformed and renamed the privately leased area as the "Elizabeth Street Garden." The space was opened to the public in 2013 as part of the neighborhood strategy to prevent the planned housing.

I was there in September 2015 when residents were gearing up for a hearing about the property's future. I had been visiting the area for years, and the space now looked completely different. Instead of statues randomly filling the area, professional gardeners and landscapers had designed the space and maintained it. Seating was available and the former overflow site for statues had been rebranded as an urban "oasis," one that opponents of the proposed affordable housing would fight hard to preserve.

New York is a very racially diverse city but that was not on display during my multiple visits to the site. Instead, nearly everyone I saw in the so-called garden was white. The only people of color were nannies with babies in strollers. Most visitors appeared to be European tourists. A table had been set up to distribute literature and a petition against the housing. I asked the woman in charge some questions about their opposition.

The woman assured me that she was in favor of senior housing but that this was the "wrong" neighborhood. She said that there were no nearby supermarkets that low-income seniors could afford. She pointed out a flyer stating, "Community Board 2 has identified a site that can provide five times as much housing in a preferable location." I later learned that this alternative site, at Hudson Square, had never been evaluated for affordable housing. In fact, that site was itself slated to become a park.

One reason low-income housing is not proposed for affluent neighborhoods is that upscale residents have the resources and political connections to stop it. The Elizabeth Street Garden advocates were no exception. They created a professional-looking opposition campaign featuring a sophisticated website, a YouTube video, and social media outreach. Housing opponents even launched a Change.org petition to urge support for keeping the garden and to "find a different site" for the affordable housing.[4]

Given the wealth of many of the housing opponents, one wonders why they didn't just buy a site in Nolita with private funds and create their own green space. Savvy, well-connected neighbors crusading to save the garden included actor Gabriel Byrne, who lived in a $3.4 million condo nearby. Byrne appeared in a six-minute video testifying to the garden's importance in community life. Kent Barwick, the president emeritus of the Municipal Arts Society, who helped save Grand Central Terminal, became chair of the 400-member Friends of the Elizabeth Street Garden.[5]

Over 140 opponents turned out for a hearing on the Elizabeth Street project in 2014, and an equally large turnout spoke against the project for nearly four hours on September 17, 2015. Opponents knew that the rising cost of land in Manhattan made it hard for affordable housing developers to buy sites. That made the campaign to deny housing on city-owned Elizabeth Street particularly troubling. Also disturbing was how the larger size of the anti-housing crowd contributed to opponents' narrative that "the community's will" must be respected. In their view, the "process" could only be respected if plans to use the site for safe and affordable housing to low-income seniors were derailed.

Bobbie Sackman, then-director of public policy for a pro-seniors advocacy group, LiveOn NY, reminded the crowd that there was a desperate shortage of affordable housing in New York City for low-income seniors. She stated, "One in three New Yorkers over the age of sixty-five live[s] in poverty and two in every three people over seventy pay more than 30 percent of their income in rent, [30 percent being] the affordable housing level. There are literally tens of thousands of seniors on waiting lists for affordable housing in NYC—and there are actually waiting lists to get on a waiting list. Elizabeth Street has the potential for seventy-five to a hundred apartments for seniors. Upwards of a hundred or more [seniors] can be safely housed at an affordable level."[6]

Councilmember Chin reminded the crowd what happened when a life-long Little Italy resident faced eviction from her apartment above the nearby Italian American Museum because of rising rent. "When the time came to move out it was impossible to find an affordable apartment for her in the neighborhood that she loved," Chin said.[7]

But opponents were not swayed. In an August 3, 2017, article, Jeannine Kiely, president of Friends of Elizabeth Street Garden, claimed, "Chin has dug in her heels to develop the garden, pushing a secret deal she made without any public review or discussion. . . . Chin stubbornly refuses to consider alternatives even though CB2 [Community Board 2] held four public hearings where overwhelming support was expressed for saving the garden. She continues to ignore her constituents who have written nearly 5,700 letters in support of saving the garden."[8]

The attacks on Chin's motives and integrity were combined with a further rebranding of the city-owned space. Originally acquired for affordable housing, it was now a "neighborhood melting pot," a popular image in a city of immigrants. Backers claimed "senior citizens, families, children, young adults, new residents, and old-timers flock to this magnificent green oasis, consistently ranked as one of the top 10 most beautiful parks in the City." Opponents continued to push an alternative site far from Nolita, not appreciating Chin's point that both city-owned sites should become affordable housing.[9]

I again visited the site in March 2017. Posters covering the garden fence urged people to call Mayor Bill de Blasio and tell him to save the garden. But de Blasio stood by Chin, who narrowly won reelection in November 2017, largely because of her support for senior housing on Elizabeth Street. The *Villager* newspaper cited Chin's support for the housing as evidence of her "disconnect" with the community; it also claimed she was "stubbornly deaf" to the community's concerns. The paper endorsed challenger Christopher Marte, who "stands strongly with the thousands of supporters of the Elizabeth St. Garden and backs the CB2 alternative plan for the senior housing that the mayor and Chin want to bury the garden under."[10]

Chin's willingness to risk her reelection by supporting senior housing against neighborhood opposition is the exception. Even more unusual is Chin's willingness to take on opponents as wealthy and politically connected as the crowd that rallied around Elizabeth Street. But Chin's deep roots in housing steeled her resolve. Prior to being elected to the council, Chin worked for Asian Americans for Equality, which developed low-income housing. She understood what new affordable housing meant for low-income seniors; she recognized that many faced leaving their longtime communities because they could not obtain the accessible housing that the new Nolita project would offer.

Thanks to Chin's courage, seniors will finally get their long overdue homes in Nolita. Named "Haven Green" for its energy efficiency, the 123-unit project to be developed in a joint effort between Pennrose and Habitat for Humanity will house seniors with annual incomes between $20,040 and $40,080, as well as formerly homeless seniors. Chin made sure that the housing on the site will include 5,000 square feet of open space, a compromise unappreciated by opponents.[11]

Chin felt her reelection ensured "I'll be around to make sure the housing gets built." She has often said that elected officials "sometimes had to make tough decisions," and going up against the Nolita residents certainly fits that category. "I've been fighting for seniors and their families to be able to remain in the neighborhood they helped build," she said in a *New York Times* interview in 2015. "Not building on that site is wrong. That site has not been fully utilized for years."[12]

NEIGHBORHOOD ANTI-HOUSING ACTIVISM

The battle over the Elizabeth Street site is not unique. As discussed in connection to Los Angeles and Seattle, neighborhood opposition to housing occurs across urban America. It is even common in progressive cities whose officials promote the economic and social diversity that new housing can bring. Residents oppose new housing when it is 100 percent affordable, as in Nolita, or when it is market rate with inclusionary housing units set aside for the working and middle class. Proposed projects are like the bowls of porridge in the classic tale of Goldilocks and the three bears: they are never the right size or serve the appropriate population to pass neighborhood muster.

Most proposed sites for senior or affordable housing lack the beauty of the Elizabeth Street Garden yet still draw opposition. For example, the most-challenged senior housing development in Berkeley's history was proposed for an empty lot on Sacramento Street featuring a graffiti-laden abandoned storefront. The site was particularly desirable for seniors as it was served by three bus lines, was within walking distance of BART, and was close to shopping, services, and even a library branch. Most saw the structure as a community blight and the proposed forty-unit senior project as a positive upgrade. But that's not how nearby neighborhood groups saw it. After the nonprofit developer submitted plans in 2001, neighborhood opponents put the project through eight public meetings, six design overhauls, and a lawsuit. The delays raised project costs by $3 million, and seniors did not get their homes until 2006.[13]

Since 100 percent affordable and inclusionary housing offer the only entry points for the non-rich to live in many urban neighborhoods, resident opposition to new housing promotes urban inequality. Its exclusionary impacts price low- and middle-class people out of neighborhoods with more desirable schools, shopping, playgrounds, and transit. It also denies the non-rich the chance to live in cities with better job and education prospects. Meanwhile, opposing new housing raises the cost of existing homes by artificially restricting supply.

The impact of resident opposition on the pricing out of the working and middle class from urban America has not gotten sufficient attention. This is likely because neighborhood activism has progressive roots. The neighborhood activism movement emerged in the 1970s to stop threats to middle-class neighborhoods from urban renewal plans. It produced a set of progressive values that emphasized maintaining and expanding open space, preserving neighborhood scale, and preventing the massive demolitions and displacement that characterized an era of misdirected urban redevelopment.

These are important values. My own political education was infused with these views. But neighborhood battles against redevelopment agencies no longer explain urban America's unaffordability, displacement, and gentrification crisis. This crisis now requires progressive activists to back housing opportunities for the working and middle class in their neighborhoods. Just saying no to new housing is not a strategy for increasing middle-class inclusion or racial diversity. It instead furthers exclusion. It does nothing to stop the pricing out of all but the rich.

As Richard Rothstein details in *The Color of Law: A Forgotten History of How Our Government Segregated America,* zoning laws were originally designed to exclude African Americans from white neighborhoods. Segregation was advanced by denying federal housing loans to African Americans seeking to buy houses in white single-family-home communities.

It was also boosted by zoning these neighborhoods to prevent the building of new apartments where minority tenants might live. Today's restrictions on apartments and increased density are seen as class rather than race based, but the impact is often the same.[14]

Giving homeowners near-veto power over what gets built in their community is still seen by many as progressive. But neighborhood preservation commonly justifies racial and class exclusion. There are countless examples in the United States of neighborhoods opposing federally funded housing because it would bring racial minorities to all-white neighborhoods; Yonkers, New York, famously fought such housing for twenty-seven years on the grounds of preserving the neighborhood's white character.[15] A neighborhood preservation movement that once successfully prevented the demolition and displacement of affordable homes through urban renewal now practices its own politics of exclusion by blocking new housing.

Some label neighbors who oppose new building projects NIMBYs. In response, some pro-housing activists call themselves YIMBYs. But the negative NIMBY labeling is not productive; it puts residents on the defensive and minimizes what they see as their legitimate right to challenge what they believe is a flawed project. "NIMBY" also wrongly implies that community members only oppose housing in their own "backyards." In my experience, many oppose new market-rate housing in most if not all neighborhoods.

Since the 1970s the neighborhood preservation movement has enshrined single-family-home zoning, residency and density limits, excessive lot size minimums, costly parking requirements, and multiple project appeal rights. All contribute to the failure of cities to build sufficient housing to meet population and job growth, and to the worsening urban affordability crisis. Cities cannot preserve the urban working and middle class without revising some or all of these policies.

Nor can cities allow affluent communities to routinely stop more affordable housing in their neighborhood. I have previously discussed successful efforts to build affordable units in the wealthy neighborhoods of Venice and Nolita, but San Francisco shows how these victories are the exception.

FOREST HILL: NO SENIOR RENTERS ALLOWED

In the fall of 2016, a low-income housing development was proposed for San Francisco's upscale Forest Hill neighborhood. Backed by Christian Church

Homes of Northern California, the 150-unit housing development for low-income seniors would be built on the current site of the Forest Hill Christian Church. Efforts to build affordable housing in affluent neighborhoods are rare in San Francisco. Despite San Francisco's progressive reputation, developers know better than to get into a battle with such communities. This project only emerged because the church owned land which it now sought to use to address the city's housing crisis.

On November 14, 2016 a community meeting was held to solicit neighborhood input on the project. To nobody's surprise, most Forest Hill residents in attendance were opposed. Neighbors claimed the project:

- had insufficient parking;
- would cause environmental damage;
- could house sex offenders;
- posed a threat to the safety of kids in the area, particularly young girls;
- was a good idea proposed for the wrong block and neighborhood;
- was poorly designed;
- would bring people with mental illness and drug addictions into the community;
- would prevent kids from being able to play outside.

These and other objections were then topped off by the response from Norman Yee, who represents Forest Hill on the board of supervisors. Yee regularly bemoaned the city's housing crisis and was identified in San Francisco politics as one of the board's progressives. He had recently voted for the city to declare a housing emergency. Yet neighborhood opposition to the senior housing in Forest Hill gave Yee a different perspective. He said that "given the lack of community support," he was "unable to support . . . this project in its current form." Yee showed how even self-identified progressive politicians can oppose affordable housing under the mantle of doing what's best for a neighborhood.[16]

The proposed Forest Hill project, an affordable senior housing project on a major thoroughfare in a neighborhood lacking economic diversity, made perfect sense. As *San Francisco Chronicle* reporter J.K. Dineen explained, "Paradoxically, it's more expensive to build in those poorer downtown districts than in places like Forest Hill, where height limits and more expansive parcels mean projects can use cheaper, wood-frame construction. Sites near downtown tend to be small and pencil out economically only if the structures are tall, which requires costly concrete or steel-frame construction." The logic of building affordable senior housing notwithstanding, the combination of supervisor and neighborhood opposition led the city to withdraw funding for the project in March 2018.[17]

San Francisco is only forty-nine square miles in size. Is there room for more housing? Attorney Joseph Bravo did not think so. Bravo had lived in San Francisco's Forest Hill neighborhood for twenty-one years when the 150-unit affordable senior housing project was proposed. "The more you build, the more you're going to attract more people; it's that simple. Why is nobody looking around and saying this city may perhaps have limits? That you can't just keep building more? Why is [it] nobody's thinking about that?"[18]

Many share Bravo's view that the city cannot accommodate more people without sacrificing quality of life. Yet San Francisco's planning department believes the city can readily fit in another 140,000 units without radical zoning changes. The city's vast Westside is ripe for building housing. One architect has suggested that San Francisco's Sunset district could become the next Paris by raising current allowable heights to match the French city's six-story limit.[19]

As San Francisco's population heads toward 900,000 and its jobs continue to increase, the city will need tens of thousands of new units. Where will the immigrants and other newcomers fueling innovation, creativity, and economic growth in the city live? There is no political support in San Francisco for restricting immigrants or refugees because "the city has limits," yet neighborhood groups continually make that argument to justify opposing housing.

Forest Hill is an exception: most affluent neighborhoods never have to mobilize to stop affordable housing projects because developers and city officials avoid such fights. At the height of San Francisco's housing crisis in 2014 the city spent $9.9 million to prevent housing from being built on the long-closed Francisco Reservoir on upscale Russian Hill. The site was perfect for new middle-class housing but nearby wealthy residents feared that dwellings would block their views and increase traffic. So neighbors raised private donations to help cover the cost of building a park on the site and used their political influence to convince the city to acquire the reservoir from the

California Public Utilities Commission. That's how potential housing for sixty middle-class families became open space. Meanwhile, longtime Russian Hill residents bemoan that "families like we were" are priced out of the neighborhood.

Today's fierce opposition to new housing for low-income, working-class, and middle-class residents is less racially based than driven by a demand that communities be "protected" from multi-unit developments. This is what often now defines "neighborhood preservation." Neighborhoods have erected economic barriers to racial diversity that replace those previously built intentionally around race.

NOE VALLEY: NO NEW MIDDLE-CLASS RESIDENTS ALLOWED

San Francisco's Noe Valley is an example of how "preserving neighborhood character" can translate into excluding future middle-class residents. Noe Valley is filled with Victorian homes and flats. It is a tight-knit community west of the Mission district. Noe Valley has no signs at its borders barring new middle-class residents, but it might as well. Home prices and rents are through the roof. Only the upper middle class and above can afford to buy or rent there.

It wasn't always so. I lived in Noe Valley from December 1983 to May 1989 and loved the neighborhood. My wife and I were very involved in the community. She was the Noe Valley area coordinator for Art Agnos's 1987 campaign for mayor (he won). My older daughter's birth was covered with a story and photo in the *Noe Valley Voice*.

Today, Noe Valley looks a lot like it did when we lived there over thirty years ago. Fewer houses are run-down and new upscale homes and small condominiums have been built, but the neighborhood is largely unchanged. Noe Valley has not been the site of the big new market-rate housing developments that critics believe foster gentrification.

Noe Valley residents typically are among the city leaders in filing appeals with the planning commission to stop neighbors from engaging in room additions, kitchen remodels, and similar projects. Builders shy away from the area, knowing it means years of battling neighbors. Noe Valley is the anti-housing activists' ideal: a neighborhood where almost no new market-rate multi-unit housing gets built.

Having artificially limited its housing supply, Noe Valley is now a super-expensive neighborhood. The average sales price for a Noe Valley home in 2016–2017 was over $2.5 million. Condos and TICs went for an average of over $1.3 million. Nearly all homes sold for over the asking price, and most were sold within a month of going on the market. In February 2018, the average sales price of a Noe Valley single-family home was $3.5 million.[20]

Tech workers have flocked to the neighborhood for its easy access to highways leading to Silicon Valley; Google buses pick up Noe Valley residents in the morning and return them at night. It's nearly an hour-long commute to Silicon Valley but the South Bay's failure to build housing for its workers has led many to live in Noe Valley. The huge demand for homes in the neighborhood has been great for Noe Valley homeowners and landlords, whose property values have skyrocketed, but it's a different story for middle-class families seeking to move to the area. They have been completely priced out.

The city's inclusionary housing law ensures that 20 percent of new market-rate housing is affordable to the working or middle class, and such multi-unit housing is likely the only way such families could be "priced in" to Noe Valley. But Noe Valley activists oppose such projects. In 2016, they helped defeat legislation that would have allowed developers to exceed current height restrictions in Noe Valley and other parts of the city by two stories. In exchange, the legislation—known as the Affordable Housing Density Bonus program—would have required that 30 percent of the units in new buildings be affordable for low- and moderate-income residents. Backers of the legislation argued that market-rate housing with the required affordable units is the *only* way the millennial generation's middle class will ever be able to afford to live in Noe Valley (unless their parents buy them a place). Yet when faced with a choice between offering homes for the middle class and denying them access, neighborhood activists chose the latter.

Laura Fingal-Surma, who heads a pro-housing group called Progress Noe Valley, recalls the density plan being discussed on the popular neighborhood website Nextdoor. Noe Valley residents opposed to housing "were horrified at the thought of the Walgreens parking lot at Castro and Jersey being replaced by a potential six-story building." But as Fingal-Surma points out, "Can you imagine if we were talking about the reverse—bulldozing five stories of housing and the commercial space below to make room for a surface parking lot in the middle of a vibrant urban neighborhood?"[21]

The problem is that Noe Valley residents, along with activists from other neighborhoods opposing the density bonus law, are trapped in the framework of past urban renewal fights. A historic preservationist (not affiliated with Noe Valley) supported this view while giving a talk on the city's LGBTQ historical sites. He said "the housing density proposal 'evokes' for him the redevelopment plans city leaders instituted in the 1950s that devastated minority neighborhoods like the Fillmore." He also claimed the density bonus measure would also lead to the "annihilation of legacy LGBTQ businesses and historic sites."[22]

Recent San Francisco history actually has few if any examples of new housing demolishing "historic" small buildings and legacy businesses. But opponents of the density bonus plan routinely cited widely discredited redevelopment agency actions from the 1960s and 1970s to justify denying homeownership opportunities for today's working and middle class. As inclusionary housing expert Rick Jacobus describes it, "Many activists are so wedded to 1970s neighborhood preservation narratives that they fail to recognize that the challenge to the community's economic diversity has changed."[23]

When I lived in Noe Valley in the 1980s, many saw the city's economic growth and rising rents and home prices as putting the neighborhood's small-town, village-like character at risk. My longtime friend Miriam Blaustein, who moved into her Noe Valley apartment in 1959, was among the activists troubled by the more upscale new businesses moving to 24th Street, the neighborhood's commercial corridor.

Blaustein, who died in 2005 at age 91, was the type of neighborhood champion every community needs. She was a leader of the area's chief neighborhood group, the Friends of Noe Valley. Active in the San Francisco Gray Panthers, she co-authored the *Cheap and Nutritious (and Delicious) Cookbook* to foster healthy eating for tenants living in SRO hotels without kitchens. Blaustein constantly pushed the city to enforce laws banning the conversion of housing to offices and retail uses along 24th Street. She also fought to restrict chain stores. Many of us saw her as the conscience of Noe Valley as she joined Jean Amos, Claire Pilcher, and other neighborhood women in creating a wonderful neighborhood.

But the strategies that "preserved" Noe Valley and other urban neighborhoods in the 1980s and 1990s now run counter to the community's longtime goal of protecting economic diversity. The middle-class families that once could buy houses and rent apartments in Noe Valley have been priced out. Fighting to preserve Noe Valley's status quo means maintaining it as a neighborhood where future residents must be rich. That's the exact opposite of what Blaustein and her allies wanted. In fact, if the neighborhood had been like that decades earlier, Blaustein and others who made Noe Valley a desirable community would have been unable to afford to live there.

The rise of urban housing prices beyond the reach of the working and middle class is why the neighborhood preservation agenda of the 1960s and 1970s does not speak to the chief challenges now facing cities. Today, preserving the neighborhood status quo does not protect economic diversity; it promotes exclusion. Activists seeking to "protect neighborhood character" should instead be aggressively pushing for new housing. That's the only way that middle-class people—which is what most longtime activists were when they came to the neighborhood—have a future in the community.

Todd David, a housing activist who has lived in Noe Valley for twenty years, thinks the neighborhood's attitudes are changing. "Many younger families and young people in Noe Valley support upzoning and increasing density in our neighborhood," he told me. "They realize that 'community character' advocacy has not evolved with the times and now excludes middle-income people."[24]

BERNAL HEIGHTS FOLLOWS NOE'S PATH

Bernal Heights, Noe Valley's neighbor to the southeast, is also a politically progressive urban neighborhood whose staunch anti-housing activism has enriched longtime owners while excluding non-affluent future residents.

Bernal Heights is San Francisco's most progressive voting neighborhood. It also has a long history of opposing new housing. Buck Bagot has been active in Bernal Heights since moving there in 1976. Soon after arriving, Bagot helped organize a campaign called "Save Elsie Street" to prevent the construction of eleven market-rate housing units. The neighborhood stopped the project, paving the way for Bernal to create design review boards that had to approve future developments. Bernal's fierce opposition to housing led even the combative Joe O'Donoghue of the Residential Builders Association to tell his members that the neighborhood should be off limits.

While Noe Valley was gentrifying in the 1980s, Bernal Heights was affordable until after the 1990s dot-com boom. Bernal activists relied on the traditional "progressive" neighborhood preservation strategy of restricting development and maintaining neighborhood scale. Thanks to their efforts, Bernal became such a desirable community that its real estate prices skyrocketed when its proximity to the freeway to Silicon Valley companies made it a go-to neighborhood in the post-dot-com and tech boom eras. In the summer of 2017, the median single-family home price in Bernal Heights was $1.46 million.[25]

Bernal is a longtime working-class neighborhood whose anti-development politics have priced out future working and middle-class residents. Its public and subsidized housing ensures it will never be as upscale as Noe Valley, but that very low-income housing does not help working- and middle-class residents who are not eligible for such units.

Bagot was the founding director of the Bernal Heights Neighborhood Center and was instrumental in the creation of the nonprofit Bernal Heights Housing Development Corporation. He says of his neighbors, "They are good-hearted people. They've just never seen a market-rate development that they like." Bernal's absence of new middle-class housing replicates the pricing out that happened in Noe Valley. Bernal's neighborhood activism created a great community for existing residents—and the rich people who will be the only ones able to purchase homes or rent there in the future.[26]

THE BERKELEY ROOTS OF NEIGHBORHOOD PRESERVATION

In 1973, voters in Berkeley passed the nation's first neighborhood preservation ordinance (NPO). The measure provided that for two years Berkeley "could not issue a permit for building or demolition without a public hearing before the board of adjustments, with possible appeal to the City Council." The NPO restricted development in some parts of the city and prevented the demolition of existing housing unless affordable replacement housing was included in any new development. The measure also was decades ahead of its time in requiring developers to provide 25 percent affordable units in any development over four units (a financial burden on builders that ensured little housing was added in Berkeley for decades). Berkeley became the first city to legally mandate that neighborhood residents control development in their community.

In 2017, Tamara Nicoloff, the daughter of Martha Nicoloff, co-author of the measure, explained why her mother drafted the initiative: "She had been frustrated by several big housing developments being built next to small houses. She told me that community members were upset that neighbors were not notified before big six-story, densely populated buildings were built beside them. The ordinance was designed to give the immediate community a chance to have a say before the buildings were approved for construction."[27]

Neighborhood activist Loni Hancock's strong support for the NPO propelled her to a political career that spanned more than forty years. After being elected to the Berkeley City Council in 1971 she went on to serve as mayor, state assemblyperson, and state senator. Hancock became engaged in Berkeley politics through her local Le Conte Neighborhood Association. Like other neighborhood organizations that emerged across the United States in the late 1960s and early 1970s, the Le Conte group formed to find "solutions to the problems of what the city had labeled 'a declining neighborhood.'"[28]

In a 1978 interview, Hancock recalled that "the people in the neighborhood are anxious whenever a house goes on the market, fearing that it will be bought by a real estate developer who will put up an apartment building." The NPO was "intended to put each ticky-tack apartment building into the political limelight, and give neighborhoods a chance to protest development that had been routinely OK'd in the past by administrators." The NPO created a committee appointed by each council member that would "review, rewrite, and update the city's Master Plan and zoning ordinances." Hancock recalled that "it was hoped that this would include a great deal of downzoning."[29]

The NPO succeeded all too well. In the short run it built support for Hancock and Berkeley's left opposition to the city's traditional Democratic Party. In the long term it stopped construction of new apartments so effectively that Berkeley had an epic housing shortage by the early 1980s. For decades UC Berkeley students had to struggle for off-campus housing in which to live.

The 1970s middle-class Berkeley homeowners opposing "six-story, densely populated buildings"—otherwise known as apartments—and "ticky-tack" buildings—the apartments where the city's low-income residents could afford to live—did not see themselves as elitist or exclusionary. Their support for civil rights, peace and justice, and the farmworkers' movement put them on the political left of the time. But the housing needs of those who could not afford to buy in Berkeley were not in their consciousness. Where did they think Berkeley's low-wage workers would live if not in "ticky-tack" apartments? Berkeley had a design review board, so the "ticky-tack" denigration likely spoke to the multi-unit building type more than its architecture. In hindsight, the roots of Berkeley's housing shortage can be found in the NPO, though few recognized it at the time.

Hancock's own position on housing development shifted dramatically during her career. She and her second husband, longtime Berkeley mayor and former assembly member Tom Bates, became very pro-housing. Bates even ushered in a dramatic increase in downtown housing development during his fourteen years as mayor (2002–2016). But many Berkeleyans who identify as progressive still raise the flag of "neighborhood preservation" to stop even small housing projects in their neighborhoods.

Consider the saga of a three-unit housing project proposed for 1310 Haskell Street in South Berkeley. In March 2016 the Berkeley Zoning Adjustment Board approved replacing a single-family home on the site with three new detached two-story homes. Since the lot was zoned for up to four three-story units, the developer addressed neighborhood concerns by building a smaller project than the zoning allowed.

But neighbors turned out in force at a Berkeley City Council meeting to oppose the project. Many held signs saying "Protect Open Space" and "Protect Our Community." The council denied the proposal in July 2016. A pro-housing group, SF Bay Area Renters Federation (SFBARF), sued the city over the denial. The suit argued that state law prevents cities from denying a housing development that meets zoning and planning guidelines unless it has a "specific adverse impact on public health or safety." Berkeley officials had identified no such issues. Berkeley settled the lawsuit by rescinding the council's vote.

But this did not end the matter. When the council reheard the case on February 28, 2017, it was like something out of the movie *Groundhog Day:* neighbors again turned out in opposition and the council again denied the project. The five-to-two rejection came against the advice of the city attorney, who on Berkeley's behalf had just rescinded the council's prior denial. The council's second vote caused Berkeley to squander even more taxpayer dollars in what would ultimately be a failed effort to stop three units from being built during a housing crisis.

Such is the power of neighborhood residents to stop development. As Brian Hanlon of the California Renters Legal Advocacy and Education Fund, which funded the civil suit, put it, "You have massive organizing at the local level to obstruct three homes. That some people think this is a social justice effort is completely asinine. These types of actions over and over again are why we have a housing shortage." In May 2017 Hanlon's group filed a new suit to overturn the city council's denial. The court again ruled against the city and again returned the case to the council for yet another hearing.[30]

Berkeley officials finally got the point. On September 4, 2017, the city council approved the Haskell Street project, along with authorizing payment of the plaintiff's attorneys' fees. The amount awarded was $44,000. The city's anti-housing forces then suffered a far bigger setback when Berkeley's own state senator Nancy Skinner sponsored and won enactment of a bill (SB 167) imposing fines of $10,000 per housing unit when projects are wrongfully denied or have their density reduced. This would have required Berkeley to pay $30,000 for rejecting Haskell Street's three units, on top of the $44,000 in attorneys' fees. Skinner stated, "We all know homelessness, displacement, continuously rising costs hurts Californians. What's the cause? The housing shortage."[31]

I've known Nancy Skinner since we both attended UC Berkeley in the 1970s. She has long been among Berkeley's leading progressives on environmental and tenant issues. Skinner has also become one of the Bay Area's strongest backers of infill housing development. Skinner believes that once a city enacts zoning rules—and Berkeley updates its zoning laws more often than most cities—a builder should have the right to assume that a project that complies with the zoning will be approved. Otherwise, as Skinner put it during the September 29 signing ceremony for her bill and fourteen other housing measures, it becomes a "shell game."

Berkeley is among many cities in which builders and their supporters face well-organized homeowner opposition at public hearings. Their anger and self-righteousness can create an extremely emotional and volatile climate that many politicians prefer either to defer to or avoid. As angry a crowd as I have ever seen attended a building approval hearing in Minneapolis where homeowners vigorously opposed new rental housing—in a majority-renter neighborhood. It was captured on video and is discussed below.

BATTLING AGAINST APARTMENTS IN MINNEAPOLIS

Minneapolis's Lowry Hill East community is in a council district that is 80 percent tenants. Yet like many neighborhood associations in big cities, the Lowry Hill East Neighborhood Association (LHENA) is a homeowner-dominated group that mobilizes against new rental housing. A stark example of LHENA's fights against new apartments in the neighborhood was captured on video in 2016. The video shows how such neighborhood groups use their power to deny housing to the working and middle class. It also shows how these groups target the elected officials who courageously back new rental housing, in this case a visionary Minneapolis councilmember named Lisa Bender.

Lisa Bender was elected in 2013 to represent the council district covering Lowry Hill East. She told me her victory was "unexpected" since she was challenging a first-term incumbent. Bender's win was particularly significant for two reasons. First, she openly called for increasing housing and public transportation, while her opponent was not supportive of new infill housing in the district. Second, Bender was a thirty-five-year-old millennial running against a boomer in her sixties, so the generational divide around housing became part of the race.

Bender won with 63 percent of the vote. She carried every precinct and was one of seven new councilmembers elected in 2013. All were millennials. Three were people of color. The turnover of more than half the seats on the thirteen-member council reflected voter support for a new direction in housing policy. Bender and others promote housing for everyone, not just those who can afford to buy homes. In Bender's case it is clearly a popular message in her district: she faced no serious challenger in winning her 2017 reelection, becoming the first councilmember from her district to do so in twenty years. Bender's election propelled her to the position of city council president, where she is joined by a pro-housing majority.

Bender is an urban planner by trade. She founded the Minnesota Bicycle Coalition and is among many millennial urban politicians whose support for bike lanes, less parking, and improved transit is connected to a land-use vision that recognizes that adding housing is essential to stop the pricing out of the working and middle class. Minneapolis rents have sharply risen in recent years but they have yet to reach the extreme heights of other progressive big cities. If Bender's policies prevail, she believes that will never happen. "We are making sure that in ten years we do not become a housing-crisis city like San Francisco or Seattle."[32]

Bender told me she is "significantly more supportive of growth" than the old guard that she defeated in 2013. She is part of a primarily younger generation of Minneapolis residents who believe new housing "eases pressure on a tight housing market." Bender and her peers also recognize that single-family zoning is an obstacle to inclusion and increased affordability.[33]

Minneapolis is barred by state law from enacting rent-control and just-cause eviction laws, which makes enacting inclusionary affordable housing laws a vital local strategy. Bender introduced an inclusionary ordinance in 2015 and again in February 2018; the more progressive council elected in 2017 makes a version of inclusionary housing likely to pass. In the debate over whether all development projects above a certain size should be required to include affordable units or whether this should only be triggered if projects get special benefits (such as increased density or height), Bender favors "a policy that applies to the most developments possible and that require[s] a certain percentage of units to be affordable."[34]

Bender feels the city "should spend every available penny buying buildings and land banking sites."[35] San Francisco's Small Sites Acquisition Program has shown the value of the former strategy, while land banking—which occurs when cities must acquire housing sites before obtaining all of the money necessary for construction—is essential in this era of uneven funding for affordable housing. Bender also backs increasing density through building multi-unit housing as a critical strategy for a more inclusive Minneapolis.

Bender's support for new apartments has made her a target of groups dominated by longtime homeowners, like LHENA and the Minneapolis Residents for Responsible Development Coalition. Bender and her husband once sat on the board of LHENA but this has not stopped her from questioning whether the homeowner-dominated group actually represents the views of the majority-renter neighborhood.

"Stopping Benderfication"

Homeowner resistance to Bender's inclusive, pro-housing agenda was captured in a ten minute video, "LHENA Goes to City Hall (extended)." The video was created by Wedge LIVE!, a site started by a resident of the Wedge neighborhood of Lowry Hill East named John Edwards. Edwards was handed a flier in 2014 urging residents of the area to oppose a proposed apartment building. The flier asked people to come to a public meeting regarding the project, and Edwards did. After he "listened to homeowners carping about their renting neighbors," he concluded, "If you're not careful, the loudest people will get what they want." Edwards's videos have since become a mainstay of city politics.[36]

Thanks to Edwards, some very disturbing testimony from an April 21, 2016, Zoning and Planning Committee hearing on neighbors' opposition to a ten-unit building at 2008 Bryant in Minneapolis is available for all to experience. The video captures the hostility, anger, and outright despair felt by homeowners and neighborhood associations over the prospect of renters moving to their block. The video convinced me that pro-housing activists should regularly distribute ten-minute clips of public opposition to apartments in every city; showing "LHENA Goes to City Hall" is a great way to expose the anti-rental housing agenda behind homeowner demands for "neighborhood preservation."

LHENA was founded over two decades ago and is part of Minneapolis's long tradition of neighborhood associations. In 1975, neighborhood groups won a major victory when new "anti-apartment zoning" regulations were approved. The regulations prohibited new apartment buildings in four South Minneapolis neighborhoods. Bender's district is not among those that barred apartments and is overwhelmingly made up of renters, but this has not stopped LHENA from opposing new rental housing.

The April 2016 hearing emphasized personal attacks on Bender. Speakers described the new housing as part of the "Benderfication" of the neighborhood, a perspective at odds with Bender's leadership in city efforts to fight gentrification. They also accused her of allowing their neighborhood to be taken over by the building of "Bender boxes."[37] This is the modern equivalent of the Berkeley activists in the 1970s decrying rental housing as "ticky-tack apartments."

I could not believe the vitriol against tenants when I saw the video. Speakers insisted that rental housing for working- and middle-class residents "creates a lot more trash," and asked the zoning committee who would be picking up the "couches and mattresses" that would be dumped in front of their homes across the street. Neighborhood homeowners seemed to think that those unable to buy homes were ignorant of how to properly dispose of rubbish.

Although the homeowners who testified lived in a majority-renter neighborhood that they claimed they wanted to preserve, speakers maintained that "people who own their own homes" create safe communities. One speaker said that "after the building opens we expect we'll be frequently calling the 311 app [for city services] on our phones." People talked about "saving the children" as if renters were a threat to homeowners' kids, or as if the renters had no kids of their own. The zoning board was urged to "stop being anti-family," which was equated with approving rental housing.

The hearing got worse and worse. A real estate agent claimed, "I don't have a problem with density" but then complained, "They are taking away parking and adding more people." A white former school board member denounced the project as "white housing in a white part of town and we don't need any more of that," yet stopping the project would do nothing to increase racial diversity.

A key motive for the personal attacks on Bender became clear when she was falsely charged with seeking to defund neighborhood associations for being unrepresentative of the majority-renter community. To her opponents, this was part of Bender's plan to "destroy" the neighborhood.

The ten-unit project was ultimately approved. Bender attributes opponents' vehemence to their support for a rival candidate in 2013 and their hope to unseat her in 2017. She saw LHENA as having fought against increased density in the neighborhood for years and as not having adjusted to a world in which new housing is essential to meet the city's rising population.

PAST VS. FUTURE

Lisa Bender had the political courage to back new housing despite the intimidation tactics of neighborhood associations long accustomed to getting their way. Like Venice councilmember Mike Bonin and New York City councilmember Margaret Chin, supportive local representatives can make all the difference in whether or not housing moves forward.

Bender's generation is planning Minneapolis's future. As in other cities, new groups like MSPyimby have emerged to challenge homeowner-controlled neighborhood associations that have long promoted housing policies that exclude the new middle class. Another pro-housing group in the city is Neighbors for More Neighbors. Its message about housing echoes what is increasingly being heard across the nation: "Single-family zoning is the biggest roadblock when it comes to providing access to jobs, schools, public transit, or even quiet and clean air. A large chunk (greater than 60 percent) of Minneapolis is zoned this way.... Advocates of this have spent the past few decades working to keep more people out of their neighborhoods, causing displacement and gentrification."[38]

LINKING DENSITY TO AFFORDABILITY

Proposals for inclusionary housing and citywide fourplexes also raise questions of how Minneapolis can tie increased density to greater affordability. Russ Adams, the executive director of the Minneapolis-based Alliance for

Metropolitan Stability, sees density as "helping achieve affordability, but only if discretionary upzoning policies are tied to robust affordability requirements." Having been in his position since 1995, Adams and his group have become more engaged with housing as prices have soared in the past five years. He is part of the Make Homes Happen campaign that seeks to secure a $50 million per year commitment in Minneapolis "to build more affordable homes, preserve existing homes, and protect tenants' rights."[39]

When I spoke with Adams in April 2018 he noted that local groups primarily concerned with affordability have had tensions with pro-density forces opposed to attaching affordability requirements to city policies encouraging more housing. This tension is not confined to Minneapolis and is something that groups must address. Seattle for Everyone (chapter 4) offers a case study in how aligning these forces can increase both density and affordability by building political support against those opposed to new housing in their neighborhoods. In 2017 Adams's organization pulled transit, housing, and environmental advocates together and joined a pro-density group of local neighbors to get the city council to rezone a former Ford auto plant in St. Paul. The council approved a maximum density of up to 4,000 units on 130 acres, with a 20 percent affordable-housing requirement (800 affordable apartments, half of them affordable at 30 percent of the area's median income). Adams points to the Ford plant outcome as a model for addressing Minneapolis's affordability crisis and sees forging such coalitions as requiring "persistent conversations and trust."[40]

Adams thinks fourplex policies should include 25 percent affordability (one in four units) to expand housing options for those being priced out of the city. With hundreds of city-owned sites available for thousands of new units in the Minneapolis area, an intentional zoning policy, targeted for people of color, offers great hope for a more affordable city. As Adams told me, "Now that the outside world has discovered Minneapolis real estate, it is imperative that we challenge and require the private sector to be part of the solution."[41]

In city after city, groups trying to stop the pricing out of low-income residents and the working and middle class confront entrenched homeowner-dominated neighborhood associations insistent on keeping the status quo. The outcome of these struggles will determine who gets to live in the nation's progressive big cities and who is excluded.

8

New York City, Oakland, and San Francisco's Mission District

The Fight to Preserve Racial Diversity

The pricing out of the working and middle class also impacts racial diversity. Rising housing costs disproportionately displace Latinos and African Americans, turning multiracial neighborhoods into upscale, primarily white communities. Cities can slow if not stop this process—if they have the political will to do so. Here is how New York City, Oakland, and San Francisco's Mission District are meeting—and failing to meet—this challenge.

NEW YORK CITY

De Blasio Promotes Gentrification in Crown Heights

At his January 27, 2013, mayoral campaign kickoff in Brooklyn, Bill de Blasio declared, "Here we are after twelve long years and here's the truth, our city isn't living up to its potential, not by a long shot. This mayor's policies have been very good for some in our city, but so many middle-class New Yorkers have been ignored and priced out." He then uttered the phrase that became his campaign theme: "This is a place that in too many ways has become a tale of two cities, a place where City Hall has too often catered to the interests of the elite rather than the needs of everyday New Yorkers."[1]

Vaughn Armour was excited by de Blasio's "tale of two cities" message. Armour had lived in the Brooklyn neighborhood of Crown Heights since 2000. At the time of the 2013 election he was very concerned about Brooklyn's upscale transformation. Armour believed in what de Blasio was saying and thought he "would be the housing mayor of New York City."[2] He and other African Americans in Crown Heights became active volunteers on de Blasio's winning 2013 campaign.

Armour's concern about the future affordability of Crown Heights was understandable. In 2010, Crown Heights was roughly 75 percent African American and 20 percent white. Many of the latter were Lubavitch Hasidic Jews. By the 2013 mayor's race, however, Armour was already seeing the neighborhood change: "African-Americans and other people of color were moving out of the neighborhood." Crown Heights' gentrification process has since accelerated. As nearby Brooklyn neighborhoods such as Prospect Park, Fort Greene, Park Slope, Williamsburg, Bushwick, and even Bedford-Stuyvesant price out the working and middle class, many have turned to more affordable Crown Heights. This encourages speculators and drives up prices. Armour pays $783 for a rent-controlled apartment while comparable newly renovated ones in the same building go for $1,921.

Donna Mossman, a founding member of the Crown Heights Tenant Union (CHTU) tells a similar story. A thirty-nine-year Crown Heights resident, Mossman has seen "rapid change" in the community over the past five years. "When I moved to Crown Heights it was a beautiful neighborhood. We are a transit hub. We are walking distance to Prospect Park. Yet nobody wanted to live here except mostly people of color. Now we have owners coming in and out flipping buildings and the market rent for an apartment like mine is $3,100. The majority of tenants moving in are not people of color."[3]

The owners of Armour's and Mossman's buildings followed a similar strategy: First, convert vacant units from one-bedroom apartments to two bedrooms by eliminating living rooms. The unit size remains the same but now the apartment is marketed at the much higher two-bedroom rate. Second, make sure renovations and the accompanying construction noise are prolonged. This encourages long-term tenants to take a financial buyout so they can move to a quieter property. One reason Mossman started the CHTU was because so many tenants were getting buyout offers; she wanted to make sure tenants knew they could reject such an offer without jeopardizing their tenancies.

Legendary television director Norman Lear came to Mossman's building in 2016 to meet with tenants and film how the ongoing construction was affecting them. The resulting film, "A House Divided: Inequality in Housing in New York City," is part of Lear's *America Divided* series, which was first released on the Epix.com television network in the lead-up to the 2016 election (it is available via streaming). Lear brought national attention to Crown Heights' gentrification. The series also gave newly elected Mayor Bill de Blasio a golden opportunity to use Crown Heights as a model for the city's new direction on housing. Few neighborhoods offered de Blasio a better chance to show that the right policies could slow if not stop the displacement of African Americans from a community where they had historically been the majority.

Consider the history of Crown Heights. Built by slaves, Crown Heights was the home of Ebbets Field and the Brooklyn Dodgers baseball team. In 1947, the Dodgers' Jackie Robinson broke the color barrier for major league baseball and African Americans flocked to Ebbets Field to see Robinson play. Crown Heights became increasingly African American through the 1950s. Racist federal housing policies denied loans to white buyers in Crown Heights and other Brooklyn neighborhoods, encouraging white flight to the suburbs. Nevertheless, in his book *Modern Coliseum* Benjamin Lisle notes that Crown Heights was "relatively prosperous through the mid-1950's." Its increasing African American population, however, troubled Dodgers owner Walter O'Malley. O'Malley felt the area had become unsafe for his "mother-in-law and wife to go to Ebbets Field unescorted." Lisle found no evidence of increased threats to white women from the area's African American residents. Yet O'Malley used the "changing social scene" in Crown Heights to justify moving the Dodgers to Los Angeles. After fleeing African Americans in Crown Heights, O'Malley displaced and demolished the Latino community of Chavez Ravine to build his new stadium for the Dodgers.[4]

The Bloomberg administration openly backed the gentrification of Crown Heights. Amanda Burden, the city's planning director, told the *New York Times* in 2012, "We are making so many more areas of the city livable. Now, young people are moving to neighborhoods like Crown Heights that 10 years ago wouldn't have been part of the lexicon." Burden's words explain why Crown Heights' African American community enthusiastically embraced candidate de Blasio's pledge to reverse Bloomberg's approach. Facing increasing threats of displacement and gentrification, they needed a mayor on their side. Fortunately, Mayor de Blasio had a block-sized, city-owned parcel at the Bedford Union Armory that could be used for affordable senior and family housing, and perhaps a new school. It was a potential game-changer for Crown Heights. The Armory could offer affordable housing to those displaced from Crown Heights and send a message to speculators that their efforts to transform the neighborhood would have to overcome the mayor's opposition.[5]

But de Blasio had other ideas. His plan transferred control of the Armory to a private developer, BFC Partners, who would then build fifty-six condominiums. The condos were projected to sell for at least $1 million each and would subsidize a new recreation center at the site. Instead of rectifying Walter O'Malley's betrayal of Crown Heights, de Blasio was repeating it. As Celia Weaver of New York Communities for Change (NYCC) tweeted on July 19, 2017, "deblasio is going to end the tale of two cities by entirely displacing one of the cities."

BFC: Bad for Crown Heights

Mayor de Blasio's 2017 plan for the reuse of the Bedford Union Armory (BUA) left Vaughn Armour, Donna Mossman, NYCC, the CHTU, and most Crown Heights residents shocked and confused. Instead of building affordable housing on a city-owned site, de Blasio favored luxury condos. Of the 330 rental units slated for the site, only a paltry 18 would be affordable to those living at the neighborhood median income of $40,000.

"The recreation center is driving the strategy for the BUA site," Weaver told me.[6] Yet Armour and others felt Crown Heights "needs housing more than a gym. Our kids can't sleep in a gym." CHTU's Mossman pointed out that "Park Slope, which de Blasio represented on the council, has a recreation center independent of any housing. So why does the mayor say that Crown Heights cannot have a center unless it is paid for by luxury housing?"

Few residents saw luxury condos as appropriate for a city-owned site. As Beverly Newsome, president of the Ebbets Field Tenants Association (representing tenants in the apartment complex built on the site of the former Dodgers ballpark) put it, "Why should we have luxury condominiums in an environment that screams for affordable housing?" Mossman said that while de Blasio claimed the project responded to the community's needs, "Who in the community asked for fifty-six million-dollar condos?"[7]

The de Blasio administration favored this upscale BUA plan "because it reflects the mayor's housing policy in general: to foster mixed-income projects in which developers include affordable units and other community benefits in exchange for being allowed to build more market-rate apartments than they could without government's say-so." But de Blasio was misapplying this strategy to a city-owned site in a neighborhood where speculators were driving up land prices. The city could not be outbid for the land. The BUA site should have been used for a 100 percent affordable project, like the one proposed at the city-owned Elizabeth Street site in Nolita.[8]

In addition, de Blasio's BUA plan was not even consistent with his housing policy because the market-rate units would subsidize a recreation center, not more affordable housing. Armour and others felt low-income Crown Heights residents would be displaced prior to the recreation center even becoming a reality and so were not excited by its future opening; nor were they impressed by its being used as an excuse for new luxury housing.

African Americans were key to Mayor de Blasio's election in 2013. NYCC strongly backed him in that race. Normally, when a mayor gets major pushback from a previously loyal constituency, he or she sits down to hear the neighborhood's concerns. De Blasio at first seemed to be moving in that direction, stating, "I understand the frustrations of the community. The neighborhood has changed a lot and there's a lot of fear of displacement. . . . We have to do a better job of explaining what the benefits are for the community."[9]

That last comment did not sit well with Vaughn Armour and others in Crown Heights. "It was condescending and insulting," Armour told me. "The mayor is saying 'Crown Heights residents need to be educated on what's best for them.'" The coalition opposing the BUA plan jumped on the mayor's statement to invite him to a town hall meeting where he could try to sell the project. After all, if de Blasio thought Crown Heights residents needed to be "educated" about the project, then he should come to the community and explain his position. As Esteban Girón, a CHTU leader, put it, "Since he thinks he knows more about our homes than we do, we invited him here today to explain what's so great about luxury housing on public land."[10]

De Blasio passed on the meeting, instead attending an event in Harlem. But the town hall meeting packed with residents proceeded in his absence. A stand-in for the mayor appeared on stage wearing a paper de Blasio mask and answered questions from the audience. State senator Jesse Hamilton spoke against the project: "Where are our progressive elected officials? They're only progressive when it's pertaining to them. The issue is, people are being pushed out. And what are we doing about it?"

That's not a question progressives or African American and Latino tenants expected to be asking about Bill de Blasio when he was elected in 2013. As Ebbets Field tenant leader Newsome put it, "The mayor who came to Ebbets Field in 2015, is not the mayor we're looking at today. That mayor was concerned about affordable housing, that mayor had serious ideas about how to create affordable housing, how to maintain affordable housing."[11]

Armour saw a "twenty-five-year plan" behind the mayor's proposal to use city-owned property for luxury housing. "They want to kill the history of

Crown Heights. White folks moved out of here years ago, and now they want to come back. So we are seeing speculators buy up houses and apartments, gutting and renovating, and then selling to people coming into the neighborhood." He saw nearby downtown Brooklyn as a cautionary tale for Crown Heights: "It's like the Land of Oz. So many skyscrapers have gone up so fast it's scaring people. And very little built there is affordable."

Mossman sees all of the public improvements going on in Crown Heights as well as the upscale new housing being built "every two or three blocks" and asks, "Why was the city not paying attention to us before? Why do we only get neighborhood improvements after people are being displaced from the community?" Mossman met then-mayoral candidate de Blasio when he visited Crown Heights during his 2013 campaign. He made a big impression on Mossman and she looked forward to electing someone she thought would be a pro-housing mayor. She has been deeply disappointed.

Adding to community suspicions about the mayor's agenda was the opening of three new homeless shelters in the neighborhood as he was pushing his Bedford Armory plan. None of the shelters was accompanied by investment in more affordable housing to keep African Americans and the working and middle class in Crown Heights.

As CHTU's Mossman puts it, "Over 1,600 units and 5,000 tenants have been displaced from Ebbets Field in recent years. Crown Heights has become one of the eviction capitals of the nation. Yet the mayor opened 'transitional' homeless shelters without providing housing in the neighborhood where they can transition." As Vaughn Armour and Marcus Moore described it, de Blasio's funding shelters instead of housing "shows that he is more committed to maintaining the Tale of Two Cities than he is in solving it."[12]

A Housing Policy Failure

Mayor de Blasio's position on the BUA plan was bad policy and worse politics. Cities seeking to preserve economic and racial diversity must use city-owned land for affordable housing. Rising land costs in transforming neighborhoods enable upscale developers to outbid affordable housing groups for sites. Building on city-owned sites saves the cost of purchasing the land.

The BUA presented Mayor de Blasio with a rare opportunity to transform a block-sized parcel in the rapidly gentrifying Crown Heights neighborhood into desperately needed affordable housing. But instead of using the BUA to maximize low-income and working-class housing opportunities in a changing community, de Blasio opted for luxury condos that would accelerate Crown Heights' upscale transformation. And when the community that had supported his election challenged him, he refused to engage. No wonder Crown Heights residents felt disrespected. Vaughn Armour, who was sixty-seven when I spoke with him in 2017, felt the BUA site would be perfect for affordable senior housing. The site could also enable African American and other working and middle-class families to stay in Crown Heights instead of being priced out.

De Blasio's Misguided Housing Plan

De Blasio announced his highly awaited housing plan with media events in Brooklyn and the Bronx on May 5, 2014. He pledged $41 billion to create 200,000 affordable units in the next ten years, 120,000 through preservation and 80,000 through new construction. A *New York Times* editorial praised the mayor's ambition, describing the plan as "Mr. de Blasio's moon shot." But more than three years later the *Times* saw its impact as "subtle. The vast majority of these affordable units are existing apartments, not new construction—a strategy born of design and necessity."[13]

Fierce opposition from Latino and African American residents meant than only two of the mayor's fifteen proposed major neighborhood rezonings were completed when de Blasio faced voters in November 2017. This was a telling commentary on how the two ethnic groups most at risk from displacement and gentrification evaluated the mayor's housing agenda. Residents in the New York neighborhoods that had thus far avoided gentrification saw de Blasio's rezoning strategy as furthering that outcome. Councilmember Rafael L. Espinal Jr., who represented a rezoned part of very low-income East New York, told the *Times,* "So far, in the rezoned area, there has been zero units built to date. If you were to speak to some residents, they would say they have seen an uptick in the number of speculators knocking on their doors, trying to buy their properties."[14] The Reverend David K. Brawley of the St. Paul Community Baptist Church in East New York was among the leaders of a 5,000-person protest by Latino and African American religious congregations against the mayor's affordable housing plan in October 2017.

When de Blasio took office, New York City developers were not required to include affordable housing units in their projects. Such inclusionary housing laws allow cities to create units for the working and middle class without spending public funds. They also allow these income groups to live in high-opportunity neighborhoods they otherwise could not afford. A progressive city like New York should already have had an inclusionary housing law; it was an obvious first step for the city's self-identified progressive mayor. But de Blasio's misleadingly labeled "Mandatory Inclusionary Housing" plan only applied to projects benefiting from zoning changes or increased height and density. Housing built consistent with current land-use rules was not covered. And considering that over 35 percent of the city had been recently rezoned, a lot of housing was left uncovered by de Blasio's "mandatory" plan.

De Blasio's plan also excluded developments in upscale, recently rezoned neighborhoods from inclusionary requirements. This reduced middle-class housing options in neighborhoods that had been rezoned under Bloomberg. Cities committed to economic diversity cannot restrict neighborhoods from being open to the non-rich. This restriction of inclusionary housing seemed to undermine de Blasio's claim that his housing plan "will be a central pillar in the battle against inequality."[15]

What happened to the candidate de Blasio, who vowed to help the middle class? According to the *New York Times,* "Despite Mr. de Blasio's pledge to 'drive a hard bargain' with developers, his plan contained few ideas that would rattle the real-estate industry. That was both a concession to the city's dependence on developers to increase its housing stock for a growing population of mixed incomes, and a reflection of the more pragmatic, less fiery approach Mr. de Blasio has adopted since taking office in January." The president of the Real Estate Board of New York praised de Blasio's plan for providing "a realistic road map for solutions."[16]

Continuing Bloomberg's Strategy

NYCC's Celia Weaver is among many who recognized that de Blasio was "elected with a lot of real estate money."[17] Alessandro Busà describes in *The Creative Destruction of New York City* how the media covering the 2013 campaign was so intent on portraying de Blasio as a radical, "Che de Blasio," that they downplayed his real estate support. Had the media paid closer attention they would have realized how de Blasio's proposed housing policies resembled rather than challenged those of outgoing Mayor Bloomberg—the politician whose policies de Blasio's "tale of two cities" campaign theme would supposedly reverse.

After taking office de Blasio appointed Alicia Glen, an executive of the Goldman Sachs investment banking firm and a former city official, as deputy mayor for housing and economic development. This sent a strong message that the new mayor's housing policies would not break from those of his predecessor.

Bloomberg's core housing strategy was to upzone neighborhoods in order to permit high-rise development. In 2005 alone, New York City upzoned 45 blocks on Manhattan's far West Side and 170 blocks in Brooklyn's Williamsburg and Greenpoint communities. Under Bloomberg the historic working-class and industrial neighborhood of Hell's Kitchen was renamed Hudson Yards and rezoned for office, hotel, and residential towers. High-rise waterfront condos for the rich were built in Williamsburg as the Bloomberg administration greenlighted the demolition of over a hundred buildings that housed artists and working- and middle-class residents.

Julian Brash, author of *Bloomberg's New York: Class and Governance in the Luxury City*, recounts testimony at a September 2004 planning commission hearing denouncing Bloomberg's plan for Hudson Yards: "I love my neighborhood. . . . When I moved [here] 21 years ago . . . I found wonderful and affordable family-owned businesses: barber shops, a shoe-repair, butcher shops, a farmers' market, fish markets, spice shops, family-owned pharmacies, bodegas, bakeries and restaurants of all types. The family pharmacies are history now, and all the remaining family businesses here are already threatened, being replaced by banks, phone stores, or yet another Starbucks."

An actor testified that "an apartment that we used to rent for $450 so that we could afford to be a playwright and an actor are now renting in our building for $2000 a month. Where are our young people going to live?" Brash felt that "at stake here were not just questions of policy and economic interest but fundamental questions of urban meaning and belonging." As one resident put it, "What kind of city do we really want? That is what we really have to analyze."[18]

This was the tale of two cities that Crown Heights' Armour and Mossman expected de Blasio to reverse. Bloomberg did not ignore the city's affordable housing crisis. During his tenure from 2002 to 2013 the city invested more than $5.3 billion of city money, and leveraged three times that from other sources, to preserve or build 165,000 affordable housing units. But Bloomberg sharply decreased working- and middle-class housing opportunities in New York City, leaving fewer neighborhoods affordable to the non-rich.[19]

Upzoning: A Double-Edged Sword

The Bloomberg administration gave upzoning a bad name. A strategy that Seattle (HALA) and San Francisco (HOME-SF) are using to increase affordability was used in New York City for the upscale transformation of affordable neighborhoods. Luxury high-rise development does not increase economic and racial diversity even if some affordable units are included. These below-market units neither reduce the gentrifying impacts of luxury towers nor protect nearby small businesses from displacement.

Upzoning is best applied in already gentrified neighborhoods. It opens up middle-class housing opportunities in these otherwise off-limits communities without any risk of displacing low-income residents. But de Blasio extended the Bloomberg upzoning strategy to low-income, non-gentrified neighborhoods like East Harlem, Washington Heights, and East New York. This would promote displacement and gentrification rather than prevent it. The below-market units triggered by the density and height bonuses in de Blasio's upzoning plan did not even serve the community's existing residents. Most residents of these low-income communities earned too little to qualify for this "affordable" housing. No wonder Crown Heights and East New York, both with large African American communities, rejected de Blasio's housing vision for their neighborhoods, as did the Latino majority in East Harlem.[20]

Busà described how the Bloomberg and de Blasio administrations promised communities that "the magic wand of rezoning would bring 'unprecedented' affordable housing and services to their neighborhoods." But instead it served as a "Trojan horse for unaffordable developments, gentrification and displacement." Both mayors typically targeted upzoning to low-income neighborhoods while affluent areas were downzoned. This misuse of upzoning helped gentrify affordable communities while failing to expand middle-class housing options in neighborhoods that otherwise excluded the non-affluent.[21]

De Blasio's team claimed that upzoning was targeted at low-income neighborhoods already heading toward gentrification. They defended the strategy as reducing future displacement. But low-income residents of areas like East New York—where nobody believed gentrification was imminent—were not about to make that leap of faith. The mayor was asking them to jump-start a process that had already caused displacement and the upscale transformation of other neighborhoods. East New York residents knew what had happened when the Bloomberg administration upzoned Brooklyn's similarly very low-income Coney Island neighborhood in 2009. Instead of protecting residents from future displacement, upzoning "sparked the frenzy of land speculation that has ravaged the amusement district and most of the historical landmarks" in the years that followed.[22]

Given the amount of attention devoted to New York City's gentrification, it is easy to overlook its many low-income, non-white neighborhoods that have not yet been gentrified. Urban scholar Richard Florida found that from 1990 to 2010–2014, neighborhoods like Washington Heights / Inwood— targeted for upzoning by de Blasio—saw rents go up only 29 percent. Rents for South Crown Heights rose only 18 percent. When de Blasio took office many African American and Latinos lived in neighborhoods not at imminent risk of gentrification—but they would be threatened under the mayor's upzoning plans.[23]

De Blasio Defends His Record

During his easy campaign for reelection in 2017, Mayor De Blasio said he "kept our promises to New Yorkers" for affordable housing.[24] He claimed the city had financed the construction or protection of nearly 78,000 homes since 2014, the most the city had ever constructed or renovated in three years' time. According to de Blasio, "We build for everyone, because we want to remain a city for everyone." But others felt that "the core components [of de Blasio's housing plan] benefit higher income bands, new arrivals, and industries like finance and real estate." If protests against de Blasio's proposed upzoning by many African American and Latino residents and community groups in Crown Heights, East New York, and East Harlem were any indication, the people who would be most impacted did not see the mayor's strategy as creating housing for all.[25]

Winning the Battle for Crown Heights

For residents of Crown Heights, the luxury housing proposed for the city-owned property at the Bedford Union Armory represented a line drawn in the sand. The mayor used all of his political savvy and connections to win support for his plans for the BUA. This included the age-old strategy of offering nonprofit groups free space in the new development; in this case, the West Indian American Day Carnival Association, which puts on the popular annual Labor Day Carnival in Brooklyn.

Politico reported on August 10, 2017, that "the mayor and his team are quietly helping Councilwoman Laurie Cumbo," who the community saw as backing a project that her Crown Heights constituents opposed. The article described the city council race as a "referendum on one of his administration's embattled redevelopment proposals." While Cumbo had bowed to community pressure and announced her opposition to the project in May, opponents did not trust her. "If she really did not want the project she would already have killed the deal," Armour told me.[26]

"I think the mayor is putting all of his weight into the Laurie Cumbo race knowing this is a lightning rod project in the neighborhood and that they've seen the community rising up against it," Jonathan Westin of NYCC told *Politico*. The article notes that de Blasio called on other councilmembers, unions, and donors to carry Cumbo to victory. Cumbo did prevail, helped by a mailing from Brooklyn congressmember Hakeem Jeffries telling voters that Cumbo had "killed the deal" at the BUA.

Despite Cumbo's victory, de Blasio's luxury housing plan for the BUA was doomed. Influential Brooklyn borough president Eric Adams announced that he "couldn't get behind a project that did not include full city ownership over the property." Adams wanted to see more permanent affordable housing and units set aside for formerly homeless families. The city council ultimately approved a project in late November 2017 that eliminated all of the luxury condos. Instead of 330 rental units, half at market rate, it approved 400 apartments; 152 will go to families of four making around $57,000 a year and 98 to families earning $29,000 to $48,000. Ten percent of the apartments will be set aside for people moving out of homeless shelters. The city put in $50 million in subsidies to make the project happen. Monthly costs for the project's recreation center were also restricted.[27]

Project opponents were furious that the BUA deal was not "killed." They felt the "affordable" units were too expensive for at-risk Crown Heights families. They also correctly insisted that city-owned land in a rapidly gentrifying neighborhood should have become 100 percent affordable housing. "Plainly and simply: this is planned gentrification, driven by the gentrification mayor and rubber-stamped by Laurie Cumbo," said Jonathan Westin.[28]

Mayor de Blasio's insistence on using city-owned property at the BUA for market-rate housing was a troubling introduction to his second term. Using city-owned land to maximize affordable housing in at-risk neighborhoods is a bedrock strategy for slowing if not stopping the pricing out of the urban working and middle class; Crown Heights residents were simply asking their mayor to practice the polices he had preached when running for mayor. As disappointed as Vaughn Armour, Donna Mossman, and community residents were over the outcome of the BUA fight, they waged one of the most successful housing struggles in New York City during the Bloomberg / de Blasio era. It should inspire other African American and Latino neighborhoods still battling de Blasio's plans for upscale development in their communities.

OAKLAND

A Struggle to Preserve Racial Diversity

Harold Dawson was born in 1980. He has lived in Oakland, California, since he was three. He grew up in a house owned by his grandfather in the neighborhood of North Oakland. Like many African Americans who came to Oakland during or soon after World War II, Harold's grandfathers were connected to the armed forces. One was an army man. The other worked as a butcher on the army base located on the Oakland waterfront just south of the eastern entrance to the San Francisco–Oakland Bay Bridge. Harold's mother was a warehouse foreperson at the army base, one of many African Americans living in Oakland who found jobs there.

The Oakland base closed in 1999 as part of a nationwide base closure effort. Some of its African American workers left for jobs with the army in the rural town of Manteca. Others left for work elsewhere. "My first awareness that Oakland was changing was when the army base moved," Harold told me. "A lot of African American families were displaced. It got worse when Granny Goose, Mother's Cookies, and Coca-Cola all closed their plants. Oakland was losing its industrial jobs."[29]

Harold and many African Americans used to frequent a mall at MacArthur and Broadway that was known as the MB mall. That mall closed, as did Oakland's Eastmont mall. Both closures eliminated not just shopping opportunities but African American jobs and places that created social connections among residents.

In 2006 or 2007 Harold moved to a one-bedroom apartment in West Oakland for $800 per month. That was roughly what it would have cost for an SRO hotel unit in San Francisco's Tenderloin neighborhood. Oakland was still a far cheaper alternative to the City. Harold then moved to a North Oakland duplex owned by his other grandfather, who had bought it with money from the GI bill.

Harold saw North Oakland's demographics change even before the post-2011 tech boom. "It used to be a dominant African American community. Now the black population was primarily elderly and new buyers were white or Asian." North Oakland was a center of Oakland's post-2008 foreclosure crisis. New buyers purchased homes at bargain prices and few were African American.

Harold was forced to sell his grandfather's duplex in 2015 in one of those inter-family disputes that often occur when houses become a major financial asset. He could no longer afford North Oakland rents and moved to a four-bedroom house in the Seminary neighborhood of East Oakland. His rent was $2,825 per month. East Oakland also saw a foreclosure wave. One of Harold's neighbors purchased his house in 2009 for only $90,000. Today, even a run-down East Oakland house goes for over $400,000.

Harold grew up in Oakland and raised his daughters there. He very much wants to stay in the city. "I love Oakland. My heart is in Oakland. This is where I want to live," he told me. But Oakland's now-expensive housing market has caused Harold to think the once unthinkable: moving to a more affordable city. Harold's brother left Oakland and moved to Stockton in the Central Valley. In exchange for a ninety-minute commute to his East Oakland job with Federal Express, he bought a beautiful old corner house on a large lot for only $210,000. It got Harold thinking about his own future. At Harold's ten-year Oakland Tech high school reunion, it seemed that most of the classmates he knew no longer lived in Oakland; they had either relocated to the more affordable East Bay cities of Pittsburg or Antioch or left the Bay Area.

Harold's high East Oakland rent might have already led him to buy outside the city if his elderly grandmother and uncle did not still live in a house they own in Oakland. If plans go as Harold expects, he would eventually get an ownership interest in that Temescal neighborhood house and move there. He would then be set in Oakland for life. Otherwise, Harold will likely join the ranks of other middle-class African Americans priced out of the city they grew up in and still love.

Oakland's African American Decline

The departure of Harold Dawson's Oakland Tech classmates from the city reflects a larger trend. From 2000 to 2010, Oakland's African American population decreased by 24 percent—a loss of 33,502 residents (and a loss of 54,003 residents—a 33.6 percent decline—since 1990). This decline surpassed

San Francisco's during the same time period. During the same decade Oakland's Latino, white, and Asian populations increased by 13 percent, 7.8 percent, and 7.8 percent, respectively.[30] Harold's East Oakland neighborhood is now primarily Latino. Rising Latino numbers in many cities have helped them retain their multicultural identity despite the departure of African Americans.

Many northern cities have seen their African American populations decline. The reversal of the Great Migration that saw earlier generations of African Americans head north to escape harsh Jim Crow laws "began as a trickle in the 1970s, increased in the 1990s, and turned into a virtual evacuation from many northern areas in the first decade of the 2000s." Oakland's loss of African American residents is primarily associated with its exploding housing prices. As of April 2014, median rents in Oakland were 24 percent higher than the monthly average over the previous four years. From November 2013 to November 2014, rents on vacant apartments in Oakland jumped 9.1 percent, more than in any other city in the nation (San Francisco rents rose 7.4 percent during that time).[31]

Few northern cities are as closely identified with the African American community as Oakland. The Black Panthers began in Oakland. Generations of young progressive African American politicians got their start there, including former congressman and later mayor Ron Dellums and his congressional successor, Barbara Lee. African Americans have long held top positions in Oakland city government and in the city's civic institutions and labor unions.

This history explains why, in response to Oakland's declining African American population, the city council in 2014 contracted with PolicyLink to survey national best practices to slow or stop this displacement. After extensive meetings with stakeholders, the council adopted "A Roadmap toward Equity" in September 2015. Backed by new mayor Libby Schaaf and shaped by the PolicyLink study, the "Roadmap" framework provided many policy options that have since been implemented by the city council. All aim toward "building an equitable and inclusive community."[32]

Roadmap toward Equity

The Oakland City Council sought to protect 17,000 households from displacement and build 17,000 new homes by 2022. In July 2017 the city released its first-year progress report on the implementation of the roadmap. The good news was that Oakland was meeting its new construction goals, having built 2,781 units. The bad news was that only 170 of those were affordable. That's just 6 percent. And of the 1,348 homes approved by the city and awaiting construction or still in the entitlement process, only 7 percent were slated to be affordable. That's far below Oakland's 28 percent affordability target.[33]

The report acknowledged that 2016–2017 was very difficult for Oakland. The December 2, 2016, Ghost Ship fire triggered a steady loss of illegal artist live-work housing due to city and landlord crackdowns. Homelessness almost doubled. It also became far more visible, with encampments under freeway overpasses a common scene. A major apartment fire on San Pablo Avenue displaced tenants and left four residents dead. Suspicious fires targeted new housing developments. And Oakland rents continued to rise, increasing pressure on the city to protect tenants and add and preserve affordable housing.

The first year of the roadmap to equity did see positives. In July 2016 the council passed a tenant protection ordinance backed by Causa Justa/Just Cause and other tenant groups. In October 2016 it approved a development fee that will bring millions of dollars into the city's housing trust fund, and a month later Oakland voters strengthened the city's just-cause eviction ordinance. Alameda County voters also passed a $540 million housing bond in November 2016, which is projected to create 3,000 affordable homes in Oakland. Oakland will get an additional $100 million for affordable housing as part of a $600 million infrastructure bond Oakland voters passed in November 2016, and city officials are working to secure millions of affordable housing dollars from the state's cap and trade program.

None of the new funding approved in 2016 was reflected in the low affordability numbers of the first-year progress report. Those numbers should start to rise by 2018.

Obstacles to Success

Oakland's implementation of its roadmap to equity faced three critical obstacles.

No Inclusionary Law. First, unlike neighboring Berkeley and San Francisco, Oakland had no inclusionary housing law for new rental housing. This alone could have added roughly 200 affordable units to the city's first-year total. Why did Oakland lack such a law? Councilmember Dan Kalb and others blame the Oakland city attorney for opining that the city was barred from enacting such a law by a California Court of Appeal decision known as the *Palmer* case. Yet that ruling did not stop Berkeley from collecting in-lieu fees for affordable housing and San Francisco from requiring inclusionary units on site. Kalb led efforts at the council to pass a linkage fee on development, but whereas a 100-unit building with a 10 percent affordable housing requirement creates ten affordable units, the linkage fee adds only three to five. For a city steadily pricing out the working and middle class, the linkage fee is not enough. Mayor Schaaf was among eleven California big-city mayors who got Governor Jerry Brown to sign a bill in 2017 expressly overruling *Palmer,* eliminating any legal obstacle to inclusionary housing.

Some believe Oakland's housing market is not robust enough for inclusionary housing and that such a requirement would discourage new construction. They point to rising construction costs, increased land prices, high sewage fees, the new linkage fee, and difficulty in obtaining affordable financing and feel that adding inclusionary units to all of that is a deal breaker. However, the same concerns were raised by opponents of San Francisco's original 10 percent inclusionary law, and they have been repeated whenever San Francisco has sought to increase this percentage. Oakland and other cities are required to do economic studies to justify their inclusionary requirements. These determine at what percentage an inclusionary requirement deters construction, how large projects must be to trigger inclusionary housing, and address other issues surrounding inclusionary laws. In light of Oakland's red-hot housing market and the high number of residential projects that will otherwise have no on-site affordable units, these economic feasibility studies in support of an inclusionary law should move forward.

Oakland tenant and progressive groups often oppose new market-rate housing and have not prioritized enacting an inclusionary housing law. They see the 80 to 90 percent of non-price-restricted units as promoting gentrification even if 10 to 20 percent are required to be affordable. But market-rate housing is being routinely approved and built in Oakland anyway—only without any accompanying affordable units.

"Money Costs More in Oakland." The second challenge to Oakland's creating greater equity and inclusion is the city's uneven history of housing development. As Robert Ogilvie, director of Oakland SPUR (San Francisco Bay Area Planning and Urban Research Association), put it, "Money costs more in Oakland. There is a history of developers losing their shirts on big projects and that makes it harder to attract financing even in today's booming

economy." Ogilvie noted that "entire years have gone by in Oakland with virtually no market-rate housing getting built. In 2012–13 only about fifty market-rate units were constructed." Developers believe that "what pencils out in Oakland is smaller market-rate projects"—which makes the 2,781 units built in the first year of the roadmap a larger accomplishment than the numbers may indicate.[34]

Many approved Oakland projects fail to get financing. Despite the current boom, lenders lack sufficient confidence in Oakland's rental market to lend at affordable rates. Things aren't as bad as when lenders redlined homes in Oakland's African American neighborhoods but financing is surprisingly difficult to obtain given that rents in the city have steadily risen in recent years. Some Oakland projects remain unbuilt because speculators who own the land never intended to build. Heather Hood of Enterprise Community Partners, who is co-chair of the city's Housing Impact Cabinet and a co-author of the one-year progress report on the implementation of the roadmap, described why: "Speculators sometimes buy land, get projects entitled, and profit by selling the package to another developer instead of building. It's like a game of Monopoly. That game is about making profits, not making a great city."[35]

Exclusionary Zoning. The third obstacle to implementing Oakland's roadmap is exclusionary zoning. Single-family-home zoning and restrictive height limits hamper housing development throughout the city. Longtime Oakland journalist Robert Gammon castigated Oakland's housing restrictions in a May 2017 article, "The Real Cause of Gentrification." Describing how Oakland zoning restrictions emerged in the early 1900s to keep out African Americans and Asians, Gammon noted how even major Oakland thoroughfares like College, Claremont, Broadway, and Telegraph still largely prohibit new buildings over four stories. All are on transit corridors or near BART stations. All could offer expanded housing options for African Americans and the working and middle class—if Oakland would allow it.[36]

Gammon argued that "when cities like Oakland prohibit new apartments and condos in wealthy neighborhoods, low-income areas pay the price." That's because limiting housing in the face of rising population growth shifts buyers to neighborhoods they can afford, accelerating their gentrification. That's how West Oakland went from being what was considered a sketchy neighborhood to pricing out the working and middle class. The same process gentrified Los Angeles's Highland Park and threatens to do the same in Boyle Heights.

Oakland appears to be meeting its housing production goals through high-rise development near downtown, but those units are primarily upscale housing. High-rise towers are unlikely to attract many African American or other working- or middle-class families with children. Most would prefer living in the same high-opportunity Oakland neighborhoods where more affluent families reside—yet the city's exclusionary zoning keeps them out.

It's hard to see Oakland fulfilling its equity and inclusion goals without the broad-based coalitions that moved Portland and Seattle in this direction. I spoke with many longtime Oaklanders who felt homeowner groups would never agree to loosen exclusionary zoning and height restrictions. But organizing, outreach, and new political alliances can change this dynamic. Oakland homeowners who support racial and economic diversity and oppose exclusionary zoning need to become more politically engaged. Whether the strategy is enacting a density bonus measure like San Francisco's HOME-SF or a carefully tuned upzoning of transit corridors, Oakland cannot stop the pricing out of African Americans and the working and middle class without opening more quality neighborhoods to tenants.

Preserving Existing Housing

Oakland has passed many laws designed to stop displacement and preserve rent-controlled housing. But city enforcement remains uneven. For example, in December 2016 the Oakland City Council imposed emergency regulations to help preserve the city's SROs. But a December 2017 report by the Anti-Eviction Mapping Project found that thanks to a lack of enforcement, Oakland may have lost as much as a third of its residential SROs since the moratorium's enactment.[37]

Oakland should also protect tenants and rent-controlled housing by launching a small sites acquisition program like San Francisco's. Councilmember Kalb told me that Mayor Schaaf supports buying existing buildings to protect tenants, and the East Bay Asian Local Development Corporation has moved toward prioritizing the acquisition and rehabilitation of such housing. But as is often the crucial difference between Oakland and San Francisco, the East Bay city apparently lacks the money to put a program like small sites in place.

I asked a lot of people involved with Oakland civic affairs whether they thought the city would succeed in reducing inequality and expanding economic diversity. Heather Hood spoke for many on Oakland's future as a home for the working and middle class: "Facing the challenge of keeping Oakland a place for people of all cultural backgrounds and income levels is like hiking up a hill that gets steeper and steeper with slippery sections. So everyone has to find the energy and stamina needed to face that hill. Oakland needs to dig deep into its soul and never stop focusing on remaining an inspiring, inclusive city."[38]

SAN FRANCISCO

Saving the Latino Mission District

As in New York City and Oakland, San Francisco's rising housing costs have disproportionately impacted African Americans and Latinos. The city's Mission District is ground zero in the city's struggle to preserve its Latino working and middle class. Few know the neighborhood better than Pete Gallegos. He has been there each step of the way as the Mission transformed from a community of pan dulce (Mexican sweet bread) to one of drip coffee and croissants. Gallegos was among the young Latinos who shaped the Mission's cultural imprint from the 1960s through the 1980s; he still works to preserve a primarily Latino Mission for future generations.

Pete Gallegos and his family arrived in the Mission District from northern New Mexico in 1955. The youngest of five children, he was four years old at the time and only spoke Spanish. His family rented various flats throughout the Mission, from Folsom Street, to 26th Street, to 24th Street, to Bryant Street. His father worked as a laborer for the San Francisco Housing Authority. When Gallegos was sixteen the family bought a house on Florida Street for under $20,000. Family members still own and live in the house today.

Gallegos's parents became very engaged with building Latino power in the community. They volunteered with the Mexican American Political Association. "In those days," Gallegos recalled, "it seemed like every Latino family had a bust of President John F. Kennedy in their house right next to La Virgen de Guadalupe." Gallegos attributes his lifetime of community involvement to his parents' example.[39]

His father also inspired in him a strong work ethic. After working a full-time job, Gallegos's father and the family would go to orchards on weekends and pick fruit. As a teenager Gallegos actually enjoyed picking the fresh peaches and apricots, and the kids were adding to the family income.

In the 1960s Gallegos was attracted to the era's social movements. He and his friends would go to the Safeway at 24th and Potrero, which was being boycotted by the United Farm Workers for selling non-union grapes. "We would go into the Safeway to protest and squeeze some tomatoes on the way out," he remembered with fondness. The site of that Safeway became the Betel Apartments, a fifty-unit project for low-income families that was Mission Housing's first development. Pete Gallegos later chaired Mission Housing's board of directors.

After graduating from Balboa High School, in 1970 Gallegos entered City College of San Francisco, where he connected with the La Raza Unida organization, part of a movement centered on Chicano nationalism. This led him to become a volunteer tutor at La Raza en Action. La Raza's office was at 3174 24th Street, in the heart of the Mission, so Gallegos was now living and working in the community.

In those days you could rent a flat in the Mission for $100 per month. Split three ways, it was $33 per month per person. "We all thought San Francisco would remain a working-class city," Gallegos recalled. "We saw the city as unique, and as a blue-collar town." The income levels of San Franciscans in 1970 were not that different from those in the 1950s and 1960s, though the Mission had become far more Latino dominated. It still had a lot of Irish guys, who Latinos referred to as ICBM's. This was during the Cold War, when people knew that acronym to mean intercontinental ballistic missiles. Mission Latinos used the term for "Irish Catholic Boys from the Mission." While the Latinos and the Irish had different backgrounds, class was a common denominator.

La Raza's Growth

Gallegos arrived at La Raza as Latino power was growing across the nation. The center of the Mission's Latino political activities was 24th Street. The La Raza Information Center opened next door to a grassroots organization set up to defend seven young Latinos charged with killing a police officer. The "Free Los Siete" campaign spread through the Mission, and the La Raza Information Center started making posters and then silkscreen prints to promote the effort. Eighteen months after the shooting all of the defendants were acquitted, setting off a parade down Mission Street.

This was Pete Gallegos's world. La Raza director Al Borvice, who later formed a nonprofit housing development group in the Mission, had the idea for making posters as a permanent part of the group's program. This ultimately became the nationally known La Raza Graphics Center (previously La Raza Silkscreen Center). Its political posters on issues ranging from the Mission to international campaigns hang in museums today. Gallegos learned the art of fundraising at La Raza, bringing in the foundation dollars that helped build the organization.

BART Helps Transform the Mission

The Mission had a heavily Latino flavor in those days. It was a safe, affordable working-class neighborhood. Looking back now, Gallegos sees the first sign of change in the decision in the 1960s to open two BART stations in the Mission, one at 16th Street and the other at 24th. Most San Francisco residential neighborhoods are not near a BART line but the Mission got two stations. Many Mission merchants opposed BART because the construction ripped up the street around their businesses for over two years. A mural painted by Michael V. Rios above the 24th and Mission station shows working-class residents subsidizing a transit system designed to bring suburban professionals to San Francisco's downtown.

Gallegos feels that BART's opening in 1973 is when the "ball started to roll" toward a more upscale Mission neighborhood. Prior to the arrival of BART, he felt the Mission was "still relatively intact." The change to the Mission after BART was initially slow, but the pace picked up in the late 1970s as downtown development increased housing demand in the neighborhood. Mission residents got to downtown jobs far faster on BART than MUNI, and for the same monthly price. BART still gets Mission residents downtown faster than residents using public transit from other neighborhoods.

BART also made it easy to get in and out of San Francisco. If you lived in the Mission and wanted to go to Berkeley or Oakland, you could simply walk to BART. Residents of most other San Francisco neighborhoods had to take a car or bus or ride a bike to a BART stop, extending their trip. By improving transit options, BART made Mission District housing much more valuable.

BART's facilitating the Mission's gentrification now seems obvious. But as discussed in chapter 2 in connection with Boyle Heights, transit access to low-income communities of color is a double-edged sword. In the 1970s and 1980s, Mission Latinos faced a number of pressing problems. In the July 1976 Mission-based *El Tecolote* newspaper, editor Juan Gonzales cited the

Mission's 16 percent unemployment rate (the citywide rate was 11 percent), the fact that 22 percent of its residents lived below the federal poverty line, and that only 12 percent of Latinos over age twenty-five had a college degree as among the "social inequalities in the Mission." BART's arrival made none of these problems worse. And as long as housing was still cheap, little attention was paid to BART's role in driving up Mission housing costs.[40]

Redevelopment and the Rise of Mission Nonprofits

Pete Gallegos worked for over a decade at La Raza Graphics and from 1985 to 1992 with Roberto Hernandez, founder of the Mission Economic Cultural Association, on Carnaval SF. Carnaval SF is an annual spectacle of cultural events culminating in a boisterous parade down Mission Street. It now attracts over 400,000 people to the Mission. Gallegos helped organize other Mission street fairs and parades as well.

The Mission became home to a dramatically rising number of nonprofit organizations in the 1970s and 1980s. Some were formed by activists involved in the 1965–1967 campaign to stop the San Francisco Redevelopment Agency from bringing "urban renewal" to the Mission. Led by the Mission Community Organization, the Mission's effort to stop the agency from coming to the neighborhood was ultimately successful. But the threat of redevelopment, along with the neighborhood's experience with BART, led Gallegos and his colleagues to distrust the city's plans for the Mission. They felt that "government was the enemy." Gallegos became a top-notch fundraiser for La Raza Graphics because the group refused city money.

Gallegos sees the rise of Mission nonprofits as restricting community advocacy against city hall's plans for the neighborhood. He feels that nonprofit demands on the city for action were especially lacking when the dot-com boom that began in 1995 caused rents and evictions to skyrocket. "We have a lot of self-proclaimed Mission 'revolutionaries' living on the city's dole," he told me. "They're more focused on the next neighborhood funding cycle than on protecting the Mission's affordability."

Many nonprofit workers did fight for the Mission's affordability. Groups like the Mission Anti-Displacement Coalition were filled with employees of neighborhood nonprofits. But some Mission service providers avoided challenging city policies, either out of fear of losing funding or because they saw providing services to Mission residents, not community advocacy, as their primary goal. How much these key nonprofit leaders could have accomplished to reduce the displacement and rising housing prices caused by the dot-com boom cannot be known.

The Dot-Com Boom

Gallegos's concerns about the Mission's direction heightened when the post-1995 dot-com boom forever transformed the neighborhood. The *New York Times* wrote in a January 21, 1999, story titled "In Old Mission District, Changing Grit to Gold," "The entire Mission District, port of entry for San Francisco's Hispanic immigrants for more than 50 years, is changing by the day. New people, people who have money, are moving in altering life for everyone. . . . For all its grit, the Mission has played an important role in a city where prices were already extraordinarily high and low-income housing especially scarce." It was long "the one neighborhood where new immigrants knew they could find a home. Now there is a fear that as San Francisco becomes more affluent, the ingredients that make the Mission District unique will be lost."[41]

Here's how Pete Gallegos describes the Mission's transformation, two decades after the dot-com boom was followed by a housing bubble and a post-2011 tech boom that has made the Mission even less affordable for its traditional Latino population:

> Through the 1980s and 1990s, there were seven or eight bakeries (panaderias) on 24th Street alone that served Mexican pastries. On Sundays the churches were filled and it was part of the experience for families to buy pan dulce at the bakeries. Going to the bakery for pan dulce on these Sundays brought the Latino community together and helped explain why so many bakeries selling similar pan dulce could stay in business.
>
> But today there are only a few bakeries left. As the neighborhood changed, fewer residents went to church. Newcomers to the Mission prefer croissants and scones to pan dulce. A lot of the small businesses serving Latino residents were supported by a population that no longer dominates the Mission, and many have not survived.

Gallegos's view that the dot-com boom had a unique impact on the Mission is widely shared. For the first time people were moving to the Mission who worked outside the city, many of them in Silicon Valley. Just as BART facilitated commutes from the Mission to downtown offices and the East Bay, the Mission's three freeway access points to the South Bay made it a particularly desirable place for tech workers to live.

The Bay Area–wide negative impacts caused by the failure of Silicon Valley and the South Bay to build housing for their workforce deserves its own book. This failure has had enormous implications for the Mission. An environmental impact report for Apple's $5 billion, 14,000-worker campus in Cupertino, which opened in the spring of 2017, found that more Apple workers lived in San Francisco, an hour away, than in Cupertino. Yet Cupertino residents strongly opposed plans for a 600-unit housing development less than two miles from Apple that was proposed soon after Apple announced its campus.

The refusal of South Bay cities adding thousands of jobs to provide housing for workers has driven up demand for Mission housing for two decades. In 2017 San Francisco groups like the San Francisco Housing Action Coalition began joining the fight to get Cupertino and other South Bay cities to build housing. This campaign is long overdue. The Mission's affordability has worsened due to the lack of a regional approach to Bay Area housing, and there is little evidence that Palo Alto, Cupertino, and other South Bay cities will begin addressing their staggering jobs/housing imbalance without more pressure.

Gallegos sees a big difference between people moving to the Mission because of easier commutes or access to quality flats and those who wanted to be part of its historic Latino culture. He bemoans that these newcomers have "no community consciousness." I asked him about all the white activists who lived in the Mission, and whether this also inflated housing costs and changed the neighborhood. He replied that "it's never been about race. It's about your mentality. People coming now don't care about the community. We have fewer people in the Mission who feel they should be taking care of each other."

Gallegos has three adult children. None can afford to live in the Mission. "I think it's terrible that kids growing up in the Mission can no longer afford to live there. They can't experience what I experienced. The friends they grew up with have left the city. I have relationships that go back to kindergarten, to fifth grade. My kids don't have that connectivity anymore."

Despite the Mission's upscale transformation over the past two decades, Gallegos remains positive about the neighborhood's future as the cultural hub for the city's Latinos. "I'm actually optimistic. I'm seeing new energy by a younger Latino population. The housing crisis has pushed them to get involved. They are more inquisitive than we were about what is really going on in the city and neighborhood. I feel there are more people sitting at the table now. Latinos have deep roots in the community and the Mission will always be a Latino-dominated neighborhood. But we will never go back to the days when working-class Latino families could arrive in San Francisco and easily find housing in the Mission. Those days are gone."

One reason for Gallegos's optimism is that a lot of Latino families kept their houses in the Mission, as his did. His nieces live there today. He's also happy to see dramatically increased affordable housing activity in the Mission. This follows a fourteen-year period (2003–2017) during which the city denied funding to Mission Housing, the neighborhood's largest affordable housing provider.

The Failure to Build Affordable Housing

Mission Housing was defunded by the city of San Francisco following an internal staff crisis in 2003. Formed in 1971 after the neighborhood's defeat of urban renewal, Mission Housing was long the city's largest nonprofit housing developer. But the firing of a popular executive director, followed by the mass resignations of an unusually talented staff, led city officials to defund the organization. No group stepped up in its place.

Gallegos sees the long period in which the Mission was not building affordable housing as the "most stupid" thing to have happened in his long history in the neighborhood. "Activists fell asleep," he said, "and by the time they woke up real estate prices in the Mission were way too high."

One cannot understand the pricing out of the Mission's middle and working class without acknowledging this failure. After the dot-com boom ended, real estate speculators were not bidding up prices for buildable sites in the Mission. The city's Eastern Neighborhoods rezoning process (which included the northeast Mission) began in 2003 and pretty much killed the private market. This created a unique opening for nonprofit groups to pick up land relatively cheap. But no nonprofit was purchasing land in the Mission.

I discuss in my book on San Francisco's Tenderloin neighborhood how nonprofit housing groups used the 2003–2012 period to aggressively acquire sites for affordable housing; it helped insulate the Tenderloin from gentrification after the post-2011 tech boom. But because the city defunded Mission Housing and the community did not get the funds redirected to another nonprofit housing group, potential affordable units were not built. Sam Moss, current executive director of Mission Housing, estimates that from 500 to 750 affordable units for families of two to six people were forever lost to the neighborhood. Based on past housing patterns, Latino families would likely have gotten most of those units.[42]

Gallegos estimates that thousands of affordable housing units could have been built. Even using Moss's lower estimate, 2,000 to 3,000 people lost a chance to live in the Mission. But the damage goes beyond that. Most neighborhoods have key sites whose use impacts adjacent properties and perhaps the entire block. Strategic acquisition of these sites by affordable housing developers can make a huge difference. Had the Mission continued to add affordable housing in the fourteen years it failed to do so, over a dozen critical sites would likely be affordable housing today rather than market rate. Failure to buy such sites has altered the feel of the neighborhood.

In a 2005 article for BeyondChron, "New Affordable Housing Engine Needed in Mission," I raised the concern that "nonprofit housing groups have secured few parcels for affordable housing. Considering that land in high-priced San Francisco will not simply lay fallow, failure to build affordable housing in the Mission has facilitated upscale development. . . . The sad fact is that for all the great activists and anti-gentrification groups in the Mission, the lack of an affordable housing engine is killing the neighborhood's economically diverse future."[43]

I described the neighborhood's failure to acquire affordable housing sites as "an absolute tragedy." It also made no sense. Mission activists have opposed market-rate housing on the grounds that all available housing sites should be for 100 percent affordable projects. Yet a decade passed without any affordable sites being acquired. This was true even though the economic climate invited opportunities for nonprofits to land bank sites. The deluge of market-rate projects proposed for the Mission starting in 2012 was a product of private developers' having available sites in the neighborhood all to themselves. They had bought the then lower-priced land while nonprofits remained on the sidelines.

Gallegos still gets angry thinking about the Mission's failure to buy affordable housing sites before the market exploded after 2011. He blames a larger problem that he first noticed in response to the dot-com boom: "community organizations turning on each other." He feels Mission activists "were too busy fighting each other. They did not pay attention to the need to fund affordable housing in Mission Housing's absence." I know many involved with the Mission Housing fight, and they regret that the conflict cost the Mission neighborhood desperately needed affordable housing.

Gallegos also blames "the City and all those well-paid planners who ignored the impact that transforming a working-class neighborhood would have on its low-income working-class residents. What was supposed to happen to them when all the dust settled? Transportation needs were planned for, market-rate and luxury housing was approved, but what about the people, well they forgot about them! Or was that part of the plan?"

The Mission's Latino Decline

One's perception of when the Mission first became "gentrified" may depend on when you first connected to the neighborhood. Pete Gallegos felt the Mission was "still relatively intact" through the 1980s. It had lower rents than nearby neighborhoods and a strong Latino majority. I agree with him.

My office represented a lot of Latino tenants in the era before the dot-com boom. Most were having to put up with acute habitability problems such as mold, faulty plumbing, leaky roofs, and lack of heat. I was in so many run-down buildings in the Mission that I assumed they comprised much of the neighborhood housing stock. The many Latino families in the Mission living in squalor and without heat was a chief focus of a campaign I led in November 1994 for a new agency to run San Francisco's housing and building code enforcement. Prior to our initiative winning, the city did not even have a Spanish-speaking housing inspector.

In 1994, the sharp rise in owner move-in and Ellis Act evictions and the upscale transformation of the Mission were still in the future—a future that nobody foresaw.

For two decades after the start of the city's housing crisis in the late 1970's, Mission activists successfully resisted gentrification and the pricing out of working- and middle-class Latinos. This was an extraordinary achievement. Tenant groups like St. Peter's Housing Committee and the San Francisco Tenants Union, the many Latino arts and cultural organizations like the Mission Cultural Center, Precita Eyes Muralists, and Pete Gallegos's La Raza Graphics Center, affordable housing groups like Mission Housing and Al Borvice's Housing Development and Neighborhood Preservation Corporation, neighborhood newspapers like Victor Miller's *New Mission News* and *El Tecolote,* and too many other organizations and activists to name deserve credit for this success.

I first connected to the Mission in 1979 when I walked a precinct in the neighborhood for that November's Proposition R rent-control campaign. Even back then most activists I knew saw the neighborhood as ground zero in the fight against gentrification. And for longer than most expected, anti-gentrification activists won that fight. As other once-affordable neighborhoods became upscale, the Mission resistance held off the trend.

Then came the late 1990s dot-com boom. The Silicon Valley–based tech explosion came without warning. It was a tidal wave for which the Mission was not prepared. Citywide, the number of owner move-in evictions hit a record high of 1,301 in 1997, more than three times as many as in any single year from 1990 to 1995. The 1998 total of 983 OMI evictions doubled that of any year during that earlier six-year period. The Mission had twice as many OMI evictions from 1990 through July 1998 as any other neighborhood.

The dot-com boom's rising housing prices and the displacement of families through OMI and other no-fault evictions reduced the percentage of Latinos in the Mission from 60 percent in 2000 to 48 percent in 2015. Latino families were moving to cheaper housing in the Tenderloin by the start of the new century, and Latino households increased in the Bayview, Mission Terrace, Excelsior, and Lakeshore neighborhoods.[44]

Like Pete Gallegos, many saw an ominous trend in the pricing out of Latinos from the Mission. These fears were confirmed when in 2015 the budget and legislative analyst for the board of supervisors found that if current trends continued, the Mission's Latino population would fall to 31 percent in 2025.[45]

Preserving a Latino Mission

The end of the dot-com boom in 2000 did not slow the Mission's red-hot market. Instead, a housing bubble followed. It did not burst until the national financial crisis in the fall of 2008. This ushered in a few years of calm in the rental housing market, while halting new housing as builders could not obtain financing.

The years of quiet preceding the post-2011 tech storm led the media to describe this later boom as if the first had not occurred. Here is a sampling of article titles: "The Tech Boom Turned This Working-Class San Francisco Neighborhood into a Hipster Haven"; "Tech Boom Forces a Ruthless Gentrification in San Francisco"; and "Vexed in the City: Tech's Fraught Transformation of San Francisco 2014." These and dozens more described a supposedly "working-class" Mission neighborhood now being gentrified by tech.[46]

The 2011 tech boom drove up rents and single-family home prices in the Mission and everywhere else in San Francisco. But the working and middle class had been priced out of vacant rental units and home purchases in the Mission prior to the boom.

The city's post-2011 economic resurgence impacted the Mission differently than other neighborhoods. First, the Mission saw a wave of new market-rate housing developments, largely due to the backlog from so little new housing having been built over the prior decade. Activists who saw new market-rate housing as a cause of displacement raised alarms about the impact of these projects; this is a key reason—along with the conversion of former used appliance stores into upscale restaurants along Valencia Street—that the media so often used the Mission as a backdrop for its "tech is transforming San Francisco" narrative.

Second, the Mission was less gentrified than nearby neighborhoods. Despite the steady erosion of its Latino working class culture, as described by Pete Gallegos, at the start of the 2012 tech boom the Mission still had many long-term tenants paying below-market rates. It still had many working and middle-class Latino homeowners. It still had all of the nonprofit affordable housing built before the funding stream was stopped. It still had its SRO hotels.

This meant that the Mission's affordability and Latino character were at risk from the new boom in a way that differed from such long gentrified communities as Noe Valley, the Castro, or Haight-Ashbury. Tenants in these neighborhoods were personally at risk of Ellis or OMI evictions, but their neighborhoods had already been transformed. Due to decades of powerful grassroots activism, this was not the case for the Mission.

Third, the Mission was the only San Francisco neighborhood with a non-white majority at risk of displacement from the post-2011 boom. Pete Gallegos and others fought for decades to preserve the Mission's Latino culture, and this goal lies at the heart of the battles to save the Mission. That the Mission's Latino majority could be lost due to the rising housing prices caused by the post-2011 tech boom raised the stakes for activists fighting to preserve the Mission's racial diversity.

The strategies needed to maintain the Mission for its Latino residents are clear. And they are equally applicable to communities across the country trying to preserve racial and class diversity amid rising urban inequality.

Maximizing Affordable Housing

The core strategy for preserving the Mission's Latino population is maximizing its affordable housing. In the Mission, this happens in four ways.

Building Nonprofit Housing. The best and most popular strategy is through nonprofit housing development. If the federal government since the Reagan years had not abandoned its commitment to funding affordable housing for all who need it, nonprofit development alone could protect the Mission's Latino population. But those days are long gone. Now nonprofit groups must leverage federal dollars with state, local, and private sources and build as many projects in the Mission as the funding stream allows. Mission Housing's funding was restored in 2016 under Mayor Ed Lee. The group has returned to its historic role of building affordable housing in the Mission. Other nonprofit housing groups are also building in the community. The Mission now has the type of aggressive nonprofit housing site acquisition program that every neighborhood facing the pricing out of its working and middle class needs. This is an essential element of a more comprehensive plan to prevent displacement and promote economic and racial diversity.

Buying Small Sites. San Francisco's Small Sites Acquisition Program funds the nonprofit purchase of at-risk small buildings. This program was used to buy Teresa Dulalas's building and to acquire many buildings in the Mission. One of the properties purchased by the program housed legendary Mission artist René Yañez, whose Ellis eviction case was fought for years by my colleague at the Tenderloin Housing Clinic, Raquel Fox. Fox kept Yañez in his home long enough for its sale to a nonprofit to finally occur.

The small sites program should also be part of every big city's strategic toolbox for promoting racial diversity. Unlike new nonprofit housing, where placements are via lottery, the small sites program allows public funds to be targeted toward specific beneficiaries. It also adds affordable units to the city's supply upon purchase, while new construction takes years. The program is no substitute for larger nonprofit projects but is an important component in the fight to deter speculator-driven evictions and stop the pricing out of the working and middle class.

Demanding More from Developers. Mission activists also maximize affordable housing opportunities for low-income, working- and middle-class Latinos by aggressively opposing new market-rate projects until the developer offers the best possible housing deal. Many builders resent this strategy, seeing it as a "shakedown" that forces them to offer more than the city's inclusionary law requires in exchange for their projects not being further delayed. But as discussed regarding the aggressive tactics used by anti-gentrification activists in Los Angeles's Boyle Heights (chapter 2), Mission activists' "by all means necessary" approach has worked. Activists have frequently increased affordable housing in the Mission by threatening to delay projects through the city's many forums for doing so. The most high-profile example was likely the campaign against a massive 335-unit housing development that opponents labeled "the beast on Bryant."

After multiple protests and four lengthy planning commission hearings, the Bryant Street project was approved in 2016. This only occurred after the developer (the Podell Company) conveyed a portion of the site to the city for below-market-rate housing. This tripled the amount of affordable housing that would have been created under the city's inclusionary law. It also meant that the city now owned another 100 percent affordable housing site in the Mission even if the market-rate project was never built. While some opponents of the project remained unhappy and appealed the project to the board of supervisors—one activist described the housing as promoting "cultural genocide"—the board ruled eleven to zero to uphold the approval. Meanwhile, some developers were angry that Podell had to give away a portion of its site to secure approval; they felt that it showed the city's development rules could be changed on a project-by-project basis.[47]

While a confrontational approach has brought benefits in the Mission, building a positive community-developer relationship can achieve equally big results. I was involved in a project on the border of the Tenderloin and the Mid-Market neighborhood in the fall of 2016 where a very positive community-developer relationship was forged. Developer Joy Ou of Group I went out of her way to pursue a course of action that was similar to that on Bryant. She agreed to our request that she acquire a site for nonprofit-owned housing rather than include affordable units in her project. This did not occur because the community threatened to oppose or delay Ou's project; SRO tenants in the Tenderloin had already given it their support. It happened because their positive working relationship encouraged the developer to pursue the tenants' preferred approach. Ou succeeded in purchasing a parking lot a few blocks from her site and then donated the land to the city for affordable housing.

In 2015, Mission activists further challenged developers by pushing legislation for a moratorium on new market-rate housing in the neighborhood. While its passage by the board of supervisors was doubtful, as the legislation was pending Mayor Lee announced that $50 million of the $310 million affordable housing bond on the November 2015 ballot would fund a Mission

Action Plan for affordable housing. While the Mission would have gotten money from the bond without this set-aside, the threat of a moratorium garnered a whopping $50 million for the neighborhood. Promoting a moratorium also brought increased attention to the Mission's lack of affordable housing sites caused by the defunding of Mission Housing and the failure of other nonprofit groups to fill the gap. To address the Mission's crisis, Mayor Lee announced in July 2015 that the city was spending $18.5 million to purchase an already approved seventy-two-unit market-rate project in the heart of the Mission at the corner of 16th Street and South Van Ness. A site approved for market-rate condos would now be affordable family housing.[48]

The Mission moratorium went on the November 2015 ballot and lost, 57 to 43 percent. But as much as it angered opponents, the idea brought attention to the Mission's crisis and resulted in additional affordable housing. It was another example of the confrontational approach of Mission activists bringing additional housing dollars to the community.

Supporting Market-Rate Housing. The fourth strategy the Mission needs to expand housing for the Latino working and middle class is to build new market-rate housing. Most Mission activists oppose this strategy, believing it increases gentrification. Pete Gallegos is among them.

Pete Gallegos supported the Mission moratorium ballot measure. He thinks market-rate housing only brings in more wealthy people and that the inclusionary units "still mean that 75 percent of the new residents are rich." I disagree with Gallegos on this. If stopping market-rate housing prevented displacement, rising rents, and increased home prices, we should have seen Mission housing prices stabilize if not plunge from 2001 to 2012, when little housing was built. But that did not happen. The only reason there was less displacement in the years preceding the post-2011 tech boom is that the city's economy was in decline; the unemployment rate was nearly 11 percent when Mayor Ed Lee took office in January 2011, meaning there was much less demand for housing.

A May 2014 study by UC Berkeley's Urban Displacement project found that "despite high demand for the area, the Mission District has failed to see significant increases in its housing stock, thereby exacerbating pressures on existing housing." In other words, *not* building housing in the face of rising demand raises the prices for vacant apartments and homes for sale. The study also found that roughly one-third of the Mission's rental housing stock rose to market rate from 2000 to 2010 due to the city's inability—a result of the state's Costa-Hawkins Act—to restrict rent hikes on vacant apartments.[49]

Affluent people move to the Mission regardless of whether newly built housing is available. They outbid the working and middle class for available housing. Preventing development in the Mission restricts the neighborhood's population but does not stop the steady decline in the number of its Latino residents.

San Francisco's inclusionary housing law requires that for every three market-rate units in a Mission project there must be one affordable unit. While designating 25 percent of units as affordable is not good enough for some, that's still 25 percent more units than the Latino working and middle class would get if those inclusionary homes were not built.

As of August 1, 2017, there were roughly 900 nonprofit-owned affordable units and between 250 and 350 affordable inclusionary units in the Mission's pipeline. As fewer and fewer buildable sites remain, the two-decade-old debate over market-rate housing's impact in the Mission is becoming less relevant.

In March 2017 the San Francisco Planning Commission adopted the Mission Action Plan. It is designed to "retain low to moderate income residents and community-serving businesses (including Production, Distribution and Repair), artists, and nonprofits in order to strengthen and preserve the socio-economic diversity of the Mission neighborhood." Even before the plan's adoption, census figures showed that the steady annual declines in the Mission's Latino population from 2000 to 2011 began to reverse in 2012. By 2016 there were over 1,500 more Latinos in the Mission than in 2011. The nonprofit affordable housing that is in the pipeline should continue this trend.[50]

Pressure from Mission activists has gotten San Francisco's political leadership fully on board with taking actions to preserve its racial and economic diversity. But the larger challenge for the Mission and other urban neighborhoods remains the same: securing vastly more state and federal affordable housing funds so that far more truly affordable housing units can be built. Cities must pass local funding measures and states with an acute housing crisis, like California, must do much more (California has a $4 billion affordable housing bond on the November 2018 ballot that is expected to pass). Affordable housing is historically a federal concern, and efforts to preserve racially diverse neighborhoods like the Mission would be greatly boosted by a sharp increase in federal funding for affordable housing.[51]

Conclusion

Ten Steps to Preserve Cities'
Economic and Racial Diversity

Should Teresa Dulalas be able to live in San Francisco? Should mariachis whose culture defines Boyle Heights have the right to remain in their Los Angeles neighborhood? What about low-income Latino and African American tenants living in Austin and New York City—should the city protect and expand their housing opportunities? Most people in these high-cost, politically progressive cities would overwhelmingly answer yes to these questions, as there is broad public support for greater economic and racial diversity. But urban housing strategies too often price out the very working- and middle-class residents whose departure is then bemoaned. Urban America must change course. Cities must replace misguided policies that reduce racial and economic diversity with those that promote far greater equity and inclusiveness.

Here are ten steps toward achieving this goal.

1. Build More Housing

Cities must build significantly more housing of all types and in all neighborhoods. From 2010 to 2017 the greater San Francisco Bay Area added 546,000 new jobs but only 76,000 new housing units. Where did civic leaders think these hundreds of thousands of additional people would live? California, which has the nation's worst statewide housing crisis, needs to build 180,000 units a year just to keep up with population growth. Yet in no year from 2007 to 2017 did the state build even 100,000 units.[1]

Building all types of housing means constructing accessory dwelling units (ADUs), duplexes and fourplexes (often described as "missing middle" housing), teacher housing, and Micro-PAD and modular housing in addition to traditional structures. Building in all neighborhoods means ending exclusionary zoning laws that further class and racial segregation by preventing rental housing in homeowner communities. It also requires increasing density in traditional neighborhoods and building larger projects along transit corridors. Building more housing also requires cities to expedite the building approval process and to stop empowering individuals to file frivolous appeals that delay projects.

2. Link New Housing to Affordability

Cities must use market-rate housing developments to expand affordable housing. Inclusionary housing is the best approach. Where state law bars this strategy cities should impose a development linkage fee to raise funds for affordable housing. In neighborhoods where it's necessary to increase affordability, cities should offer height and density bonuses to developers in exchange for affordable units. Done correctly, as in Seattle's HALA program, such upzoning expands working- and middle-class housing opportunities without triggering gentrification. Done incorrectly, as in New York City under Mayors Bloomberg and de Blasio, this strategy accelerates the upscale transformation of once-affordable neighborhoods.

3. Use Public Land for Affordable Housing

High-rent cities must, whenever feasible, use publicly owned land for affordable housing. In our present era of rising urban land prices, affordable housing developers have trouble competing for buildable sites with private developers. City-owned land eliminates this competition and must be prioritized for affordable housing.

4. Enable Nonprofits to Purchase Small Sites

Cities should fund the nonprofit purchase of four- to twenty-unit buildings in neighborhoods facing displacement and gentrification. These acquisitions bring economic and racial diversity to neighborhoods where even the middle class has been priced out. They also bring affordable housing to communities where sites for new construction are not available. San Francisco's Small Sites Acquisition Program turns many of the properties into nonprofit community land trusts, a popular option for giving residents ownership rights.

5. Seek Local and State Funding for Affordable Housing

Since 2015, many cities have passed local affordable housing funding measures. In light of the federal government's nearly five-decade failure to fully fund affordable housing for those who need it, all cities must use this approach. Activists and their political allies must also push states to increase affordable housing funding.

6. Enact Strong Tenant Protections

Proponents of building more housing often ignore that preserving the urban working and middle class in high-housing-cost cities also requires strong tenant protections. Cities that can legally enact rent-control and just-cause eviction laws must do so. Cities where state law bars such measures can impose rent-control and just-cause protections as a condition of granting density or height bonuses to developers. Statewide rent-control bans were passed in a much more affordable housing environment. Such laws deny cities like Austin, Boston, Portland, and Seattle a tool that localities need to address their affordability crises, as does California's ban on laws that limit rent increases on vacant apartments (the Costa-Hawkins Act, which voters will have a chance to repeal in November 2018). State preemption can boost affordability when used to prevent local exclusionary zoning laws, but denying cities the ability to restrict rent hikes only makes housing more expensive.

7. Preserve Rental Housing

Cities must restrict demolitions, unit mergers, condominium and SRO hotel tourist conversions, and other strategies that deplete the rental housing supply for the working and middle class. It costs hundreds of thousands of public dollars to build a single affordable rental unit. It makes no sense for cities to then readily allow the loss of existing units. SRO preservation is particularly vital because such housing is less vulnerable to gentrification because the rooms lack private kitchens and most lack private bathrooms. They are a vital low-income and working-class housing option in high-cost cities.

8. Effectively Enforce Housing Codes

Cities must ensure that working and low-income tenants live in safe and healthy housing. City inaction on housing code enforcement facilitates displacement and gentrification. It forces tenants to vacate their affordable but unhealthy units and paves the way for renovations that bring in far more affluent tenants. Since the cost to a city of code enforcement can be recovered from landlords through fines and fees, inadequate enforcement is less a financial issue than one of misguided policy.

9. End Exclusionary Zoning

Cities that support racial and economic diversity must walk the talk by ending exclusionary zoning laws that promote inequality. These include single-family-home zoning, restrictive height and density limits, large minimum lot sizes, and overly stringent occupancy restrictions. Such measures are the pillars of a "neighborhood preservation" agenda that has transformed affordable communities into luxury neighborhoods. In 2018, the California legislature introduced a far-ranging bill (SB 827) that overcame local exclusionary laws by increasing heights and density on or near transit corridors. Although the bill failed to get out of committee, many opponents support ending restrictive zoning that prevents cities from increasing their housing supply. A more politically acceptable version of the bill is likely to return in 2019. It could become a model for other state governments whose housing goals are blocked by local defenders of exclusionary zoning.

10. Organize, Educate, and Get Political

These nine strategies for preserving the urban working and middle class require that backers organize, educate, and get political. Forging inclusive, environmentally sustainable housing policies is the obvious choice for cities, yet this agenda faces powerful opposition. Overcoming it may require activists to realign traditional urban political dynamics to create a new pro-housing electoral coalition. Activists must expand their political comfort zones to build the alliances necessary to preserve racial and economic diversity. A good example is green groups and builders, who do not usually find themselves on the same side. But in cities seeking greater inclusion and diversity they are working together to support infill housing.

Getting political requires activists to ask local candidates for their specific plans for creating a more inclusive city. Saying they support "more affordable housing" is not sufficient. Voters cannot stop the pricing out of the working and middle class without electing politicians publicly committed to providing housing in all neighborhoods.

EXTERNAL LIMITATIONS

Cities' power to promote economic and racial diversity is not unlimited; external factors play a role. From state laws barring local rent control or inclusionary housing to the anti-housing policies of adjacent localities, urban housing prices can be impacted by factors beyond cities' control. For example, when Silicon Valley cities approve tech campuses for thousands of new workers without requiring new housing, it drives up housing prices not simply in Cupertino, Palo Alto, San Jose and the South Bay but in Oakland, San Francisco, and other cities within an hour's drive. Other external factors causing city housing prices to rise include state tax policies like California's Proposition 13, a federal tax code that encourages real estate speculation, foreign buyers shifting assets to urban real estate, rising construction costs, and new transit lines that increase pressures for gentrification.

I do not want to minimize the impact of these external factors, but they do not justify city policies that increase rather than slow the pricing out of the working and middle class. As with those arguing that cities' exclusion of the non-affluent is "inevitable," focusing on external factors allows people opposing new housing to downplay their city's responsibility for declining economic and racial diversity.

Cities decide what gets built in their neighborhoods. Cities determine what buildings get preserved or demolished. Cities control neighborhood zoning laws and decide whether or not to keep exclusionary measures like single-family-home zoning and excessive minimum lot sizes. Cities implement housing code enforcement. Cities decide whether to fund affordable housing, either through direct spending or bonds.

Cities also decide how much housing they will build and what type of housing. Cities largely control the nature of their building approval process. State laws like California's Environmental Quality Act impact the latter, but cities that want to build more housing are not blocked by state or federal restrictions from doing so.

Cities also determine the jobs/housing balance within their borders. When San Francisco launched a downtown high-rise boom in the 1980s it was foreseeable that housing demand would skyrocket; yet the city did not build much housing as prices sharply rose. Cities are always making decisions about whether to seek and approve new large employers, as creating jobs is a top priority. But when new jobs are added without new housing, city policy is to blame for the resulting rise in housing prices. A city cannot always anticipate future job growth—as Amazon's staggering hiring boom in Seattle shows—but cities routinely recruit large employers without addressing the housing impact.

IT'S NOT TOO LATE

When I told people I was writing a book on preserving the urban working and middle class, some asked, "Isn't it too late for that?" It *is* too late for cities to return to the fondly remembered days when the working and middle class could easily rent and often buy in quality neighborhoods in what are now high-housing-cost cities. It is not too late, however, for cities to far better protect existing working- and middle-class residents. Nor is it too late to greatly expand housing opportunities for both income groups in cities where they are being steadily priced out. We know cities can do both—if they adopt laws and policies to accomplish these goals.

The stakes have never been higher. Big cities are where the better-paying jobs are. Big cities offer higher quality schools and far broader cultural opportunities. Working- and middle-class people fight so hard to live in big cities for the same reason wealthy residents choose such areas: they offer a great place to live. And the alternatives are not so great. A 2017 study found that smaller cities have such vulnerable economies that they can be "dangerous places for working people." Those forced out of big cities have far fewer economic opportunities elsewhere.[2]

I interviewed a lot of people who strongly believe that pro-housing policies can create a more inclusive urban America. I did not hear the fatalism and hopelessness or predictions of a dystopic urban future that opponents of new housing often espouse. Much of this reflects the generational divide around housing. Despite being victimized by steep rents and priced out of homeownership, millennials expressed more hope for the future of big cities than boomer homeowners. Part of this is the greater optimism of those just beginning their adult lives. But it also reflects the fact that boomers' longtime strategy of not building housing offers little hope for ever reversing the pricing out of the working and middle class.

The next few years will reveal whether urban America's high-housing-cost cities adopt the millennial-driven push for greater inclusion or continue on an exclusionary path. I'm betting on the former.

NOTES

PREFACE

1. Johana Bhuiyan, "Mark Zuckerberg's Personal Charity Is Part of a Push to Steer $500 Million to Affordable Housing," *Los Angeles Times,* January 24, 2019.

2. Habitat for Humanity, "Raising Our Voices: Habitat for Humanity Launches Cost of Home Campaign to Improve Home Affordability for 10 Million People in the United States," June 12, 2019, www.habitat.org/newsroom/2019/raising-our-voices-habitat-humanity-launches-cost-home-campaign-improve-home.

3. Habitat for Humanity Advocacy, www.habitat.org/about/advocacy.

4. Interview with Matthew Dunbar, July 2019.

5. People's Action, https://peoplesaction.org/2019/09/breaking-peoples-action-unveils-plan-to-win-a-national-homes-guarantee/, September 5, 2019. A young generation of climate change activists in groups like the Sunrise Movement also recognize that "climate + affordable housing crises are inherently linked" (https://twitter.com/sunrisemvmt, November 18, 2019).

6. Yimbytown 2020: Fair & Sustainable Cities, https://yimby.town.

7. Graham MacDonald, "Luxury Housing Is Not to Blame for San Francisco's Affordable Housing Crisis," Urban Institute, June 1, 2017, www.urban.org/urbanwire/luxury-housing-not-blame-san-franciscos-affordable-housing-crisis.

INTRODUCTION

1. Conversation with Heather Baker, June 9, 2017.

2. Gustav Niebuhr, "Religion Leaders Call Housing a Sacred Right," *New York Times,* September 10, 1999, A21; Clinton administration credit conveyed in letter from HUD Secretary Andrew Cuomo to Randy Shaw, February 10, 2000.

3. I am relying on the Pew Research Center for generational years defining millennials; see https://theoutline.com/post/3569/what-years-are-millennials?zd=

1&zi=hrgrpymf. Other sources see millennials as starting in 1977 rather than Pew's 1981; see http://genhq.com/generational_birth_years/.

1. BATTLING DISPLACEMENT IN THE NEW SAN FRANCISCO

1. Anthony Busa, *The Creative Destruction of New York City: Engineering the City for the Elite* (New York: Oxford University Press, 2017), pp. xiv, xv.

2. Conversation with Paul Boschetti, summer 2017.

3. From the original version of the San Francisco Rent Stabilization and Arbitration Ordinance, chapter 37 of the San Francisco Administrative Code.

4. Feinstein's most significant impact on the city's current housing prices were her two vetoes of vacancy-control legislation restricting how much landlords could raise rents on vacant apartments. The battle over vacancy control dominated city politics through the 1980s. In 1995, the California legislature passed the Costa-Hawkins law, barring cities from enacting vacancy control and paving the way for the skyrocketing rent hikes of recent years. It is unlikely Costa-Hawkins could have passed if a major city like San Francisco had had vacancy control.

5. 2000 U.S. Census, www.bayareacensus.ca.gov/counties/SanFrancisco County.htm.

6. Owner move-in (OMI) evictions allow the owner or a member of the owner's family to evict a tenant in order to occupy a unit as their principal residence. During the dot-com boom such evictions were increasingly used to displace long-term tenants paying below-market rents. OMI evictions are a major source of sham evictions in San Francisco, as many owners fail to move in and instead re-rent the units at current market rates.

7. Conversation with Teresa Dulalas, June 27, 2017.

8. The Ellis Act has wrongly displaced thousands of California tenants. The law was passed in response to landlord claims that compliance with just-cause eviction laws constituted involuntary servitude under the Thirteenth Amendment—though owners could end their "slavery" by selling their property. California's Democratic-controlled legislature passed the Ellis Act in 1986. Sponsor Jim Ellis predicted the law would be seldom used because few owners would want to keep a vacant building. But anti–rent control judges grossly expanded the Ellis Act to allow rental units to be sold as tenancies in common (TICs). TICs differ from condominiums in that owners own a percentage of the building rather than individual units. Since the Ellis Act prohibited overriding local condo conversion restrictions, the legislature clearly wanted to protect rental housing. Had TICs been common at the time, they too would have been expressly regulated.

9. www.beyondchron.org/tenants-and-supporters-rally-against-ellis-act-evictions/.

10. Jeremy Mykaels, "My Fight Against the Ellis Act to Save My Home," *San Francisco Bay Times,* http://sfbaytimes.com/my-fight-against-the-ellis-act-to-save-my-home/.

11. www.beyondchron.org/soma-family-battles-4th-ellis-eviction-attempt/.

12. Obituary for Lola McKay, *San Francisco Chronicle,* March 22, 2000, www
.sfgate.com/news.article/Lola-McKay-2767601.php.

13. Ibid.

14. Liz Rodda, "I Can't Leave Here," *POOR Magazine,* November 12, 2002,
www.poormagazine.org/node/1001.

15. Michael Steinberg, "Her Own Personal Mansion," *POOR Magazine,* June
24, 2002, www.poormagazine.org/node/842.

16. Rodda, "I Can't Leave Here."

17. Regan Brooks, "Out of Luck," *SF Weekly,* January 13–19, 1989, p. 16.

18. "Jeremy Mykaels vs. 460 Noe Group LLC," Eviction Free San Francisco,
www.facebook.com/events/530577640342147.

19. Liz Mak, "From AIDS to Housing Crises, They've Seen It All: Castro's
Long-Time Residents Fight to Stay," KALW, February 3, 2014, http://kalw.org
/post/aids-housing-crises-they-ve-seen-it-all-castro-s-long-time-residents-fight-
stay#stream/0.

20. Mykaels, "My Fight Against the Ellis Act."

21. Ibid.

22. Ken Hu, "Eviction Threat Drives Man to Suicide, His Mother to Despair,"
Sing Tao Daily, December 3, 2009, www.tenantstogether.org/updates/eviction-
threat-drives-man-suicide-his-mother-despair.

23. Conversation with Xi'an Chandra Redack, April 16, 2017.

24. I got the rent control exemption used by Imhoff changed by the new San
Francisco Rent Board appointed by Feinstein's successor, Art Agnos. But the story
of 250 Taylor shows how city policies can either stop or promote displacement and
gentrification. Feinstein favored encouraging investment in buildings even if tenants were displaced and rent control protections lost.

25. "Rent Trend Data in San Francisco, California," Rent Jungle, www.rentjungle
.com/average-rent-in-san-francisco-rent-trends/.

2. A HOLLYWOOD ENDING FOR LOS ANGELES
HOUSING WOES?

1. Conversation with Areli Hernandez, September 18, 2017.

2. Conversation with Maru Galvan, September 14, 2017.

3. Kenneth Reich, "The Bloody March That Shook L.A.," *Los Angeles Times,*
June 23, 1997, http://latimesblogs.latimes.com/thedailymirror/2009/05/crowd-
battles-lapd-as-war-protest-turns-violent-.html.

4. Times Editorial Board, "L.A. Has a Serious Housing Crisis and It's Time for
City Officials to Do Something about It," *Los Angeles Times,* January 11, 2015.

5. Los Angeles Department of City Planning, "Housing Element 2013–2021,"
https://planning.lacity.org/HousingInitiatives/HousingElement/Text/Housing
Element_20140321_HR.pdf.

6. See www.jchs.harvard.edu/sites/jchs.harvard.edu/files/harvard_jchs_state_ of_the_nations_housing_2017_chap6.pdf; Dennis Romero, "If Rent Hikes Continue, Nearly 2,000 Angelenos Will Be Put on the Streets," *LA Weekly*, www .laweekly.com/news/if-los-angeles-rents-continue-to-rise-nearly-2000-will-be-homeless-report-says-8491973; Dennis Romero, "In L.A.'s Minority Communities, Rent Costs an Average 60% of Income," *LA Weekly*, March 30, 2017, www.laweekly .com/news/in-los-angeles-renting-in-minority-neighborhoods-requires-a-greater-slice-of-income-8075145.

7. Times Editorial Board, "L.A. Has a Serious Housing Crisis."

8. Ross's door-to-door strategies laid the groundwork for the similar approach used by Barack Obama's 2008 presidential campaign. I describe this in *Beyond the Fields: Cesar Chavez, the UFW, and the Struggle for Justice in the 21st Century* (Berkeley: University of California Press, 2008).

9. See www.laalmanac.com/population/po24la.php; http://maps.latimes.com /neighborhoods/neighborhood/boyle-heights/; https://planning.lacity.org /complan/CPA_DemographicProfile/2014_BOYLE_HTS.pdf.

10. Research has established "an association between gentrification and new transit development." But as Richard Florida has found, "A lack of transit access can severely impede economic opportunities." This is particularly true when public transit is needed for low-income residents to access jobs, schools, and cultural opportunities. New transit also creates alternatives for working people facing nightmarish daily commutes on clogged freeways. Anti-gentrification activists can protect at-risk neighborhoods without trying to stop new transit. See Richard Florida, "Mass Transit Doesn't Cause Gentrification," CityLab, July 23, 2015, www.citylab.com /transportation/2015/07/no-mass-transit-does-not-cause-gentrification/398957/; and Yunie Chang, "Gentrification, Public Transit, and Infrastructure in LA," *Cornell Policy Review*, December 12, 2016, www.cornellpolicyreview.com/gentrification-public-transit-and-infrastructure-in-la/.

11. Bianca Barragan, "Will Boyle Heights Be LA's Gentrification Hot Spot of 2015?" Curbed LA, January 2, 2015, https://la.curbed.com/2015/1/2/10006018/is-boyle-heights-going-to-be-2015s-gentrification-hot-spot-1; Bianca Barragan, "Boyle Heights Freaks Out about Being Sold as the Next DTLA," Curbed LA, May 28, 2014, https://la.curbed.com/2014/5/28/10094384/boyle-heights-freaks-out-at-being-sold-as-the-next-downtown.

12. Sahra Sulaiman, "Parcel Containing Businesses on Mariachi Plaza up for Sale," LA.Streetsblog.org, August 8, 2017, http://la.streetsblog.org/2017/08/08 /parcel-containing-businesses-on-mariachi-plaza-up-for-sale/.

13. Benjamin Gross, "Boyle Heights Is Winning Its War against Gentrification," Curbed LA, January 26, 2015, https://la.curbed.com/2015/1/26/9999040/boyle-heights-is-winning-its-war-against-gentrification.

14. https://la.curbed.com/2017/8/8/16115606/mariachi-plaza-stores-for-sale-development.

15. Conversation with Margarita Perea, September 28, 2017.

16. Ruben Vives, "As Rents Soar in L.A., Even Boyle Heights' Mariachis Sing the Blues," *Los Angeles Times,* September 9, 2017.

17. Ibid.

18. Conversation with Francisco Gonzalez, September 26, 2017.

19. Jason McGahan, "Facing Eviction, Boyle Heights Mariachis Are Going to Court," *LA Weekly,* September 13, 2017, www.laweekly.com/news/boyle-heights-mariachis-facing-eviction-go-to-court-8643684.

20. The Tenderloin's strategies to stop gentrification are the subject of my book *The Tenderloin: Sex, Crime, and Resistance in the Heart of San Francisco* (San Francisco: Urban Reality Press, 2015).

21. Hillel Aron, "Boyle Heights Activists Demand That All Art Galleries Get the Hell Out of Their Neighborhood," *LA Weekly,* July 14, 2016, www.laweekly.com/news/boyle-heights-activists-demand-that-all-art-galleries-get-the-hell-out-of-their-neighborhood-7134859; Bianca Barragan, "Boyle Heights Activists Want to Banish All Art Galleries," Curbed LA, July 14, 2016, https://la.curbed.com/2016/7/14/12191266/boyle-heights-art-galleries-gentrification; http://defendboyleheights.blogspot.com/2016/12/boycott-art-galleries-in-boyle-heights.html.

22. Ruben Vives, "A Community in Flux: Will Boyle Heights Be Ruined by One Coffee Shop?" *Los Angeles Times,* July 18, 2017.

23. Ruben Vives, "Race-Based Attacks on Boyle Heights Businesses Prompt this L.A. Councilman to Take Sides," *Los Angeles Times,* July 29, 2017; Doug Smith, "Change of Heart on Housing Plan," *Los Angeles Times,* March 7, 2018, www.pressreader.com/usa/los-angeles-times/20180307/281702615222628.

24. Danielle Gersh, "Is Boyle Heights Coffee Shop Vandalism an Anti-Gentrification Message?" CBSlocal.com, July 19, 2017, http://losangeles.cbslocal.com/2017/07/19/boyle-heights-vandalism-gentrification/.

25. Times Editorial Board, "Boyle Heights Anti-Gentrification Activists Hurt Their Cause by Making It about Race, Rather than Economics," *Los Angeles Times,* July 20, 2017; Jason McGahan, "Who's Winning and Losing in the Boyle Heights Gentrification War," *LA Weekly,* July 18, 2017, www.laweekly.com/news/boyle-heights-gentrification-war-shows-no-signs-of-stopping-8438794.

26. www.crmvet.org/docs/60s_crm_public-opinion.pdf.

27. Randy Shaw, *The Activist's Handbook: Winning Social Change in the 21st Century* (Berkeley: University of California Press, 2015), p. 209.

28. Jacob Woocher, "5 Lessons Learned from the Mariachis' Victory over B.J. Turner," KNOCK, February 16, 2018, https://knock-la.com/5-lessons-learned-from-the-mariachis-victory-over-bj-turner-438d6581db58.

29. Bianca Barragan, "Housing Developers Eyeing Boyle Heights Lot across from Mariachi Plaza," Curbed LA, November 16, 2016, https://la.curbed.com/2016/11/29/13780622/housing-developers-eyeing-boyle-heights-lot-across-from-mariachi-plaza.

30. James Poniewozik, "In 'Vida,' Home Is Where the Gentrification Is," *New York Times,* May 2, 2018.

31. "About Highland Park," KCET.org, www.kcet.org/shows/departures /projects/highland-park.

32. *Marketplace*, "York and Fig: At the Intersection of Change," https://features .marketplace.org/yorkandfig/.

33. Shivani Vora, "Low Rents Fuel a Change of Pace," *New York Times*, January 21, 2018.

34. Mike Davis, *City of Quartz: Excavating the Future in Los Angeles* (New York: Vintage, 1992), pp. 153, 156.

35. https://la.curbed.com/2016/3/22/11284584/los-angeles-starter-homes; Mark Vallianatos, "Undo L.A.'s Racist Zoning Legacy," *Los Angeles Times*, April 2, 2018.

36. Laura Kusisto, "Venice Beach Is a Hot Place to Live, So Why Is Its Housing Supply Shrinking?" *Wall Street Journal*, July 16, 2017, www.wsj.com/articles/venice-beach-is-a-hot-place-to-live-so-why-is-its-housing-supply-shrinking-1500206400; Hillel Aron, "Can Mayor Garcetti Convince Neighborhood Groups to Stop Opposing Homeless Housing?" *LA Weekly*, April 27, 2017, www.laweekly.com/news /la-mayor-eric-garcetti-is-trying-to-generate-support-for-permanent-supportive-housing-for-the-homeless-8165892.

37. Conversation with Becky Dennison, August 1, 2017. To learn more about Venice's recent history and residents' approach to homelessness, I strongly recommend Andrew Deener's *Venice: A Contested Bohemia in Los Angeles* (Chicago: University of Chicago Press, 2012).

38. Gale Holland, "Venice Residents Fight over Homeless Housing Project— and Character of the Neighborhood," *Los Angeles Times*, March 11, 2017.

39. Gale Holland, "Fears Mount over a Homeless Plan That Residents Say Will 'End Venice as We Know It,'" *Los Angeles Times*, October 18, 2016.

40. www.scpr.org/programs/airtalk/2017/06/14/57343/not-everyone-s-happy-about-la-s-1-billion-plan-to/.

41. Aron, "Can Mayor Garcetti Convince Neighborhood Groups?"

42. Times Editorial Board, "The Desperate Fight for Homeless Housing," *Los Angeles Times*, February 27, 2018.

43. Aron, "Can Mayor Garcetti Convince Neighborhood Groups?"

44. Doug Smith, "Council Panel Deals Setback to Proposed Homeless Housing Project in Boyle Heights," *Los Angeles Times*, August 16, 2017; Emily Alpert Reyes, "L.A. Lawmakers Pledge 222 Units for Homeless Residents in Each District," *Los Angeles Times*, March 20, 2018, www.latimes.com/local/lanow/la-me-ln-homeless-pledge-20180320-story.html.

45. Davis, *City of Quartz*, p. 159.

46. Better Institutions, "Keep Los Angeles Affordable by Repealing Proposition U," May 16, 2016, www.betterinstitutions.com/blog/2016/5/16/keep-los-angeles-affordable-repeal-proposition-u; Andrew H. Whittemore, "Zoning Los Angeles: A Brief History of Four Regimes," *Journal of Planning Perspectives* 27, no. 3 (2012): 403.

47. Davis, *City of Quartz*, pp. 193–194.

48. Friends of Westwood v. City of Los Angeles, 191 Cal. App. 3d 259; 235 Cal. Rptr. 788, March 27, 1987, http://resources.ca.gov/ceqa/cases/1987/fow_032787.html.

49. "Measure S: 8 Things to Know about LA's Anti-Development Ballot Measure," Curbed LA, March 7, 2017, https://la.curbed.com/2017/2/23/14607558/ballot-measure-s-2017-los-angeles-development; Times Editorial Board, "Los Angeles' Homelessness Crisis Is a National Disgrace," *Los Angeles Times,* February 25, 2018, www.latimes.com/opinion/editorials/la-ed-homeless-crisis-overview-20180225-htmlstory.html.

50. See https://en.wikipedia.org/wiki/Neighborhood_councils_of_Los_Angeles.

51. Paavo Monkkonen, "Understanding and Challenging Opposition to Housing Construction in California's Urban Areas," UC Center Sacramento White Paper, December 1, 2016; Juliet Musso, Christopher Weare, Mark Elliot, Alicia Kitsuse, and Ellen Shiau, "Toward Community Engagement in City Governance: Evaluating Neighborhood Council Reform in Los Angeles," School of Policy, Planning and Development, University of Southern California, 2007.

52. Conversation with Jerry Jones, July 5, 2017.

53. Conversation with Larry Gross, July 5, 2017.

54. Tenants Together, "Tenant Advocates Demand Removal of CalHFA Chair over Ellis Evictions," BeyondChron, June 4, 2015, www.beyondchron.org/tenant-advocates-demand-removal-of-calhfa-chair-over-ellis-act-evictions/.

55. I worked out such an agreement in 2005 to protect tenants and 360 rent-controlled units at the Trinity Plaza Apartments in San Francisco. It became the city standard. San Francisco imposes a deed restriction requiring rent control on the number of new units equal to the number destroyed; the landlord must agree to the restriction as a condition of demolition.

56. Conversation with Denny Zane, June 24, 2017.

57. Emily Alpert Reyes, Alice Walton, and Peter Jamison, "L.A. Election Demonstrates the Power of the Few," *Los Angeles Times,* March 4, 2015; Portland State University, "Who Votes for Mayor? Seattle," www.whovotesformayor.org/cities/5755a108db1eab405dd5f187#takeaways.

58. Tim Logan and Tiffany Hsue, "Garcetti: Build 100K new homes in Los Angeles by 2021," *Los Angeles Times,* October 29, 2014, www.latimes.com/business/realestate/la-fi-garcetti-build-100k-new-units-20141029-story.html.

59. Jenna Chandler, "'Linkage Fee' to Spur Affordable Housing Production Clears City Committee," Curbed LA, August 22, 2017, https://la.curbed.com/2017/8/22/16186528/linkage-fee-plum-vote-developer-fees-affordable-housing.

60. Opponents of such fees include many associated with "market urbanism"; see http://market urbanism.com.

61. Email from Anita Nelson, July 17, 2017.

62. Conversation with Jerry Jones, July 5, 2017.

63. Conversation with Larry Gross, July 5, 2017.

64. See the website of the Coalition for Economic Survival, www.cesinaction .org, and the San Francisco–based Anti-Eviction Mapping Project, February 2018, www.antievictionmappingproject.net/losangeles.html.

65. Dakota Smith, David Zahniser, and Emily Alpert Reyes, "Garcetti Takes Oath for Second Term as L.A. Mayor," *Los Angeles Times,* July 1, 2017.

66. Ibid.

67. Conversation with Larry Gross, July 5, 2017.

3. KEEPING AUSTIN DIVERSE

Epigraph: Jennifer Curington, "Restrictions on Accessory Dwelling Units, or ADUs, May Decrease under City Proposal," *Community Impact Newspaper,* November 17, 2015, https://communityimpact.com/austin/city-county/2015/11/17 /restrictions-on-accessory-dwelling-units-may-decrease/.

1. Conversation with Alejandra Ramirez, September 28, 2017.

2. Ibid.

3. Conversation with Stephanie Trinh, September 20, 2017.

4. www.mayoradler.com/2017-state-of-the-city-address-the-spirit-of-austin/.

5. Conversation with Robin Wilkins, September 23, 2017.

6. Tony Cantu, "Lakeview Residents Not Ready to Leave," *Austin Chronicle,* October 2, 2015, www.austinchronicle.com/news/2015–10–02/lakeview-residents-not-ready-to-leave/.

7. Conversation with Roxana Castro, September 23, 2017.

8. Conversation with Joel Jimenez, September 25, 2017.

9. www.yelp.com/biz/solaris-austin.

10. Tony Cantu, "Displaced Austin Tenants Formerly at Lakeview Apartments Sue Landlord after Mass Evictions," *Austin Chronicle,* June 28, 2016, https://patch .com/texas/downtownaustin/displaced-austin-tenants-formerly-living-lakeview-aparements-suing-landlord.

11. Ibid.

12. Ibid.

13. Conversation with Robin Wilkins, September 23, 2017.

14. Cantu, "Displaced Austin Tenants Formerly at Lakeview Apartments Sue Landlord."

15. Laura Lorek, "Oracle's Founder Larry Ellison Says Austin Campus Is Going to Grow to 10,000 Employees," Silicon Hills, March 22, 2018, www.siliconhillsnews .com/2018/03/22/oracles-founder-larry-ellison-says-austin-campus-going-grow-10000-employees/.

16. Conversation with Robin Wilkins, September 23, 2017.

17. Tony Cantu, "East Austin Apartment Tenants Protest Forced Move-Out by New Property Owner," Patch.com, September 23, 2016, https://patch.com/texas/ eastaustin/east-austin-apartment-tenants-protest-forced-move-out-new-property-owner.

18. KXAN staff, "East Austin Apartment Complex Gets Notice to Move Out," September 28, 2016, http://kxan.com/2016/09/28/east-austin-apartment-complex-gets-notice-to-move-out/.

19. Alberta Phillips, "More Evictions for Austin's Low-Income Families from Once-Affordable Homes," *Austin American-Statesman,* October 3, 2016.

20. Conversation with Shoshana Krieger, September 13, 2017.

21. Robert Maxwell, "Report: Austin Code Gives Problem Landlords Too Many 'Chances,'" KXAN.com, July 25, 2015, http://kxan.com/investigative-story/report-austin-code-gives-problem-landlords-too-many-chances/. The full report is at https://lintvkxan.files.wordpress.com/2015/07/rop-report-june-30–2015-final.pdf.

22. Joseph Caterine, "Cross Creek Evictions Retracted," *Austin Chronicle,* July 8, 2016.

23. Calily Bien and Kylie McGivern, "Austin Apartment in 'Hot Water' after Numerous Code Violations," KXAN.com, January 4, 2016, http://kxan.com/2016/01/04/lack-of-hot-water-forces-city-of-austin-to-seek-injunction-against-apartment-complex/.

24. I was so fed up with San Francisco's housing code enforcement system that in 1994 I authored a ballot initiative that called for the firing of the top five enforcement officials and created an entirely new department. It passed that November and San Francisco has since been a national model for housing code enforcement.

25. Cantu, "East Austin Apartment Tenants Protest."

26. "The Palms on Lamar Grand Opening—December 5, 2011 Austin, TX," www.youtube.com/watch?v = FI8Oe84UF_c.

27. Yelp reviews for the Palms on North Lamar, www.yelp.com/biz/palms-on-north-lamar-austin.

28. Kylie McGivern and Joe Ellis, "Millions of Taxpayer Dollars Subsidizing Problematic Apartments," KXAN.com, August 10, 2016, www.kxan.com/news/investigations/rundown-apartments-still-receiving-money-from-austin-to-provide-housing/1156461991.

29. Caterine, "Cross Creek Evictions Retracted."

30. McGivern and Ellis, "Millions of Taxpayer Dollars Subsidizing Problematic Apartments."

31. Conversation with Shoshana Krieger, October 12, 2017.

32. Conversation with Eva Marroquin, September 21, 2017.

33. All conversations with Greg Casar occurred on August 8, 2017.

34. Curington, "Restrictions on Accessory Dwelling Units, or ADUs, May Decrease."

35. Mose Buchele, "Data Shows Big Differences between Austin Renters and Homeowners," KUT.org, August 15, 2016, http://kut.org/post/data-shows-big-differences-between-austin-renters-and-homeowners. In 2014, University of Texas professor Eric Tang issued a report that found that among the fastest-growing U.S. cities between 2000 and 2010, only Austin saw a decline in its black population. Tang followed this up with "Those Who Left" (http://liberalarts.utexas.edu/iupra/_files/pdf/those-who-left-austin.pdf), a study that found that the majority of people left Austin

because of unaffordable housing. Corrie MaClaggan, "Austin's Black Population Leaving City, Report Says," *New York Times,* July 17, 2014; Audrey McGlinchey, "Residents of East Austin, Once a Bustling Black Enclave, Make a Suburban Exodus," NPR, July 12, 2017, www.npr.org/2017/07/12/536478223/once-a-bustling-black-enclave-east-austin-residents-make-a-suburban-exodus?utm_campaign=storyshare&utm_source = twitter.com&utm_medium = social.

36. www.austintexas.gov/edims/document.cfm?id = 260401.

37. Jack Craver, "Arguments Continue over Neighborhood Plan Contact Teams," *Austin Monitor,* January 23, 2017, www.austinmonitor.com/stories/2017/01/arguments-continue-neighborhood-plan-contact-teams/.

38. Nolan Hicks, "Audit Lists Shortcomings with Insular Neighborhood Plan Groups," *Austin American-Statesman,* November 15, 2016.

39. Sarah Coppola, "Austin Council OKs 'Stealth-Dorm' Limit on Initial Vote," *Austin American-Statesman,* February 14, 2014.

40. Jo Clifton, "Linkage Fees Challenged at Legislature," *Austin Monitor,* April 11, 2017, www.austinmonitor.com/stories/2017/04/linkage-fees-challenged-at-legislature/.

41. Bob Sechler, "Over Austin's Objections, Texas Senate Votes to Ban 'Linkage Fees,'"*Austin American-Statesman,* May 18, 2017, www.mystatesman.com/business/over-austin-objections-texas-senate-votes-ban-linkage-fees/DABQNqYerzTqIMZNtCJdJI/.

42. Conversation with Greg Casar, August 8, 2017; Jack Craver, "Garza, Renteria, Casar Unveil Housing Justice Agenda," *Austin Monitor,* April 4, 2018, www.austinmonitor.com/stories/2018/04/garza-renteria-casar-unveil-housing-justice-agenda/.

43. www.aura-atx.org/.

44. All comments by Thomas Visco are from our conversation on August 2, 2017.

45. Email from Luke Metzger, July 27, 2017.

46. Email from Thomas Visco, August 2, 2017.

47. Christopher Neely, "Austin Mayor Steve Adler's State of the City Address Dominated by Affordability and Growth Management," January 28, 2017, *Community Impact Newspaper,* https://communityimpact.com/austin/central-austin/city-county/2017/01/28/austin-mayor-steve-adler-state-of-the-city-address-dominated-by-affordability-and-growth-management/.

48. Conversation with Susan Somers, July 12, 2017.

49. Conversation with Eric Goff, July 21, 2017.

50. Richard Rothstein, *The Color of Law: A Forgotten History of How Our Government Segregated America* (New York: Liveright, 2017).

51. "Group Says Austin Perpetuates Segregation with Zoning Laws," June 13, 2016, KLBJ radio, www.newsradioklbj.com/news/austin-local-news/group-says-austin-perpetuates-affordability-crisis-zoning-laws; Niran Babalola, "Two Views: CodeNext Will Test Austin's Talk about Community Inclusion," *Austin American-Statesman,* December 13, 2017, www.mystatesman.com/news/opinion/two-views-

codenext-will-test-austin-talk-about-community-inclusion/Robp7Jk42m4sh7
T8Nmos6I/.

52. March 9, 2017, tweet from Christopher Neely @TopherJNeely. Neely was a city hall reporter for *Community Impact Newspaper.*

53. Chad Swiatecki, "UT Study, Proposed Task Force Would Tackle Residential Displacement," *Austin Monitor,* July 21, 2017, www.austinmonitor.com/stories/2017/07 /ut-study-proposed-task-force-tackle-residential-displacement/.

54. Jack Craver, "Clarksville Meeting Displays Fear of CodeNEXT and Density," *Austin Monitor,* July 28, 2017, www.austinmonitor.com/stories/2017/07 /clarksville-meeting-displays-fear-codenext-density/.

55. Elizabeth Findell, "Laura Morrison Launches Her Campaign for Mayor," *Austin Statesman,* March 27, 2018, www.statesman.com/news/local-govt--politics /laura-morrison-launches-her-campaign-for-mayor/It8xwdKj3WE8Ph1h80FSxM/; Philip Jankowski, "CodeNext Foes Are Done with Compromise. They're Going for the Kill," *Austin American-Statesman,* March 9, 2018, www.mystatesman.com /news/local/codenext-foes-are-done-with-compromise-they-going-for-the-kill /D1iIDoxm7ZhUnNaIiAB7DK/.

56. Craver, "Garza, Renteria, Casar Unveil Housing Justice Agenda."

4. CAN BUILDING HOUSING LOWER RENTS?

1. Conversation with Nick Hodges, October 18, 2017.
2. www.housingforallseattle.org/.
3. Staff, "Readers Speak Out: 'Seattle Doesn't Know How to Handle the Boom,'" *Seattle Times,* July 21, 2017, www.seattletimes.com/pacific-nw-magazine /readers-speak-out-seattle-doesnt-know-how-to-handle-the-boom/.
4. Ibid.
5. Conversation with Melissa Dodge, October 11, 2017.
6. Conversation with Mary Dodge, October 10, 2017.
7. Mike Rosenberg, "Thanks to Amazon, Seattle Is Now America's Biggest Company Town," *Seattle Times,* September 27, 2017.
8. Daphne Howland, "Amazon's Hiring in Seattle Declines by 60%," Retail Dive, December 13, 2017, www.retaildive.com/news/amazons-hiring-in-seattle-declines-by-60/512951/.
9. Mike Rosenberg, "Will Seattle Really Become the Next San Francisco?" *Seattle Times,* July 28, 2016.
10. Mike Rosenberg, "Seattle Rent Hikes Slow amid Apartment Boom, but Average Two-Bedroom Tops $2,000," *Seattle Times,* September 25, 2017; tweet by Mike Rosenberg, December 31, 2017; SF median figures come from Zillow, San Francisco Market Overview, https://www.zillow.com/san-francisco-ca/home-values/.
11. Rosenberg, "Will Seattle Really Become the Next San Francisco?"
12. www.historylink.org/File/3539.

13. www.csmonitor.com/1994/0502/02071.html.

14. www.governing.com/columns/assessments/gov-seattle-comprehensive-plan
.html; http://crosscut.com/2015/01/seattle-comprehensive-ed-murray-peter-
steinbrueck/.

15. www.csmonitor.com/1994/0502/02071.html.

16. Conversation with Bill Rumpf, June 1, 2017.

17. Conversation with Faith Pettis, September 5, 2017.

18. Ibid.

19. Jonathan Martin, "Get Ready for a Neighborhood Rebellion," *Seattle Times,*
July 21, 2016, www.seattletimes.com/opinion/get-ready-for-a-neighborhood-
rebellion-against-mayor-murray/.

20. Noah An and Jesse Piedfort, "Guest Editorial: Now More than Ever, Seattle
Must Welcome Upzones," *The Stranger,* November 15, 2016, www.thestranger.com
/slog/2016/11/15/24690297/guest-editorial-now-more-than-ever-seattle-must-
welcome-upzones.

21. "HALA's Grand Bargain Is Key to an Equitable and Sustainable Seattle,"
Guest Opinion, *Seattle Times,* August 3, 2015, www.seattlemet.com/articles
/2015/8/3/hala-s-grand-bargain-is-key-to-an-equitable-and-sustainable-seattle/;
Heidi Groover, "Poll Finds Nearly Half of Seattleites Support Changing Single
Family Zoning," *The Stranger,* June 21, 2017, www.thestranger.com/slog/2017
/06/21/25230243/poll-finds-nearly-half-of-seattleites-support-changing-single-
family-zoning; http://350seattle.org/housing/.

22. Scott Beyer, "San Francisco's Sierra Club Is a Bastion of Faux Environmen-
talism," Forbes.com, May 31, 2017, www.forbes.com/sites/scottbeyer/2017/05/31
/san-franciscos-sierra-club-is-a-bastion-of-faux-environmentalism/#394f8c3e7c34.

23. Heidi Groover, "The Mayor Is Blowing Up the City's Old Neighborhood
Council System—and That's Good News for Renters," *The Stranger,* July 14, 2016,
www.thestranger.com/slog/2016/07/14/24342645/the-mayor-is-blowing-up-the-citys-
old-neighborhood-council-systemand-thats-good-news-for-renters; Jonathan Martin, "Get Ready for a Neighborhood Rebellion."

24. David Rolf, "Seattle's Neighborhood Councils Have Raised Selfishness to
an Art Form," *Seattle Times,* July 25, 2016.

25. Mike Rosenberg, "Seattle Rents Now Growing Faster Than in Any Other
U.S. City," *Seattle Times,* July 21, 2016.

26. Rolf, "Seattle's Neighborhood Councils."

27. Conversation with David Rolf, August 17, 2017.

28. James Brasuell, "Mandatory Housing Affordability Details Released in
Seattle," Planetizen, November 12, 2017, www.planetizen.com/news/2017/11/95759-
mandatory-housing-affordability-details-released-seattle.

29. Mike Rosenberg, "After Brief Slowdown, Seattle-Area Rents Surge Back Up
Again; When Will It End?" *Seattle Times,* March 27, 2017, www.seattletimes.com
/business/real-estate/after-brief-slowdown-seattle-area-rents-surge-back-up-again-
when-will-it-end/.

30. Hayat Norimine, "State Will Uphold Its Ban on Rent Control," SeattleMet, February 5, 2018, www.seattlemet.com/articles/2018/2/5/state-will-uphold-its-ban-on-rent-control.

31. Conversation with Faith Pettis, September 5, 2017.

32. www.seattle.gov/Documents/Departments/Housing/PropertyManagers/IncomeRentLimits/Income-Rent-Limits_Rental-Housing-HOME.pdf

33. Blanca Torres, "Housing's Tale of Two Cities: Seattle Builds, S.F. Lags," *San Francisco Business Times*, April 28, 2017, pp. 22–23.

34. Ibid.

35. Conversation with Maria Barrientos, July 26, 2017.

36. Nancy Skinner speech in San Francisco, September 29, 2017.

37. Conversation with David Neiman, July 6, 2017.

38. Dan Savage, "When It Comes to Housing, San Francisco Is Doing It Wrong, Seattle Is Doing It Right, Cont.," *The Stranger*, January 19, 2016, www.thestranger.com/blogs/slog/2016/01/19/23446347/when-it-comes-to-housing-san-francisco-is-doing-it-wrong-seattle-is-doing-it-right-cont.

39. Ibid.

40. Rosenberg, "Will Seattle Really Become the Next San Francisco?"

41. Ibid.

42. Blanca Torres, "If Seattle Can Build Enough, Why Can't We," *San Francisco Business Times*, June 30, 2014.

43. Conversation with Bill Rumpf, June 1, 2017.

44. Rosenberg, "Will Seattle Really Become the Next San Francisco?"

45. Conversation with Nick Licata, August 9, 2017.

46. Letter to Editor by Nancy Anderson, *New York Times*, October 1, 2017.

47. Rosenberg, "Seattle Rent Hikes Slow amid Apartment Boom." Amazon's job postings had sharply declined by the end of 2017, which might finally give breathing room to the housing market.

48. Tweet from @DBeekman, September 29, 2017.

49. Mike Rosenberg, "As New Apartments Flood the Market, Seattle Area Sees Smallest Spring Rent Hikes in a Decade," *Seattle Times*, April 10, 2018, www.seattletimes.com/business/real-estate/smallest-springtime-rent-increase-of-the-decade-for-seattle-area-as-new-apartments-flood-the-market/.

50. Mike Rosenberg, "Seattle-Area Rents Drop Significantly for First Time this Decade as New Apartments Sit Empty," *Seattle Times*, January 12, 2018, www.seattletimes.com/business/real-estate/seattle-area-rents-drop-significantly-for-first-time-this-decade-as-new-apartments-sit-empty/.

51. Joe Rubino, "Gentrification Moves Fast: A Hard Look at Economic Displacement in Denver's Most Historic Black Neighborhood," *Denver Post*, December 15, 2017, www.denverpost.com/2017/12/15/denver-five-points-gentrification/.

52. Macradee Aegerter, "Denver's Hot Rental Apartment Market Could Finally Be Cooling a Bit," KDVR.com, October 1, 2016, http://kdvr.com/2016/10/01/denvers-hot-rental-apartment-market-could-finally-be-cooling-a-bit/.

53. Sally Mamdooh, "There's a New Plan to Lower Rents in the Denver Metro Area," TheDenverChannel.com, May 21, 2016, www.thedenverchannel.com /money/consumer/theres-a-new-plan-to-lower-rents-in-the-denver-metro-area; Jon Murray, "Denver Grows by Another 18,582 People as City's Boom Accelerates," *Denver Post,* March 24, 2016.

54. Christopher Dean, "Denver Rents Decrease, Vacancies Increase as Denver Adds 13,000 New Apartment Homes," Apartment Association of Metro Denver, January 19, 2018, www.aamdhq.org/news/denver-rents-decrease-vacancies-increase-as-denver-adds-13000-new-apartment-homes; Megan Arellano, "Average Denver Rents Fell $21 for Largest Ever Decrease in Survey," Denverite, January 16, 2017, www.denverite.com/denver-rents-fall-21-in-fourth-quarter-2016–27431.

55. Aldo Svaldi, "Metro Denver's Housing Market Developing a Split Personality, Sending Rents Down and Home Prices Up," *Denver Post,* January 15, 2017; Dean, "Denver Rents Decrease, Vacancies Increase."

56. Mamdooh, "There's a New Plan to Lower Rents"; Aegerter, "Denver's Hot Rental Apartment Market."

57. Allisa Walker, "How Denver Pushed Rents Down Citywide," Curbed, January 25, 2017, www.curbed.com/2017/1/25/14342828/denver-rents-affordable-housing-apartments; Jon Murray, "Denver Council Approves Creation of City's First Affordable-Housing Fund," *Denver Post,* September 19, 2016; Jaclyn Allen, "Denver Mayor Announces Housing Experiment That Could Bring Affordability Back to City," TheDenverChannel.com, July 11, 2017, www.thedenverchannel.com /news/local-news/mayor-announces-rent-buy-down-program.

58. All quotes are from my conversation with Aaron Miripol and Debra Bustos, August 22, 2017.

59. Urban Land Conservancy website, www.urbanlandc.org/denver-transit-oriented-development-fund/.

60. Reconnecting America's Center for Transit-Oriented Development, "Realizing the Potential: Expanding Housing Opportunities Near Transit," April 2007, www.enterprisecommunity.org/resources/realizing-potential-expanding-housing-opportunities-near-transit-13902.

5. WILL SAN FRANCISCO OPEN ITS GOLDEN GATES TO THE WORKING AND MIDDLE CLASS?

1. San Francisco Rent Board, "Affordable Housing Data Book," http://sfrb.org /sites/default/files/FileCenter/Documents/1868-housing.pdf; see under "Job and Housing Growth, 1970–2000."

2. www.nytimes.com/2013/02/03/nyregion/so-how-did-mayor-koch-do.html.

3. Joshua Switzky, "Informational Overview of San Francisco Job-Housing Imbalance," Memo to the Planning Commission, February 22, 2017.

4. Some cite a later UC Berkeley study finding that building affordable housing is the best strategy to combat gentrification, but that conclusion does not detract

from the legislative analyst report. See Miriam Zuk and Karen Chapple, "Housing Production, Filtering and Displacement: Untangling the Relationships," Institute of Government Studies, University of California, Berkeley, May 2016, www.urbandisplacement.org/sites/default/files/images/udp_research_brief_052316.pdf.

5. Switzky, "Informational Overview"; San Francisco Planning Department, "2015 San Francisco Housing Inventory," http://default.sfplanning.org/publications_reports/2015_Housing_Inventory_Final_Web.pdf.

6. Conversation with Joe Cassidy, June 21, 2017.

7. Conversation with Sean Keighran, May 21, 2017.

8. Conversation with Joe O'Donoghue, December 5, 2016.

9. John McCloud, "Live-Work Law for Artists Roils San Franciscans," *New York Times,* April 27, 1997.

10. San Francisco Department of City Planning, "Citywide Live/Work Zoning Legislation: Summary Report," January 1988, https://archive.org/details/citywidelivework19sanf.

11. Conversation with Joe Cassidy, June 21, 2017.

12. I heard Welch state this in planning commission testimony, June 27, 2002.

13. Randy Shaw, "Planning Commission Says Yes to Unique Affordable Housing Project," BeyondChron, February 4, 2005, www.beyondchron.org/planning-commission-says-yes-to-unique-affordable-housing-project/.

14. Marisa Lagos, "Mission Condo Project Opens a Can of Worms: Supes' Decision to Halt Construction Has Broader Effect," *San Francisco Chronicle,* April 12, 2006.

15. Ibid.

16. Ibid.

17. "About the Eastern Neighborhoods," http://sf-planning.org/about-eastern-neighborhoods; Matt Regan, "San Francisco Eastern Neighborhoods Plan Passes—Finally," Bay Area Council, www.bayareacouncil.org/transportation_land_use/san-francisco-eastern-neighborhoods-plan-passes-finally/.

18. Conversation with Sean Keighran, May 21, 2017.

19. Carolina Reid and Hayley Raetz, "Perspectives: Practitioners Weigh In on Drivers of Rising Housing Construction Costs in San Francisco," Terner Center for Housing Innovation, January 23, 2018, http://ternercenter.berkeley.edu/uploads/San_Francisco_Construction_Cost_Brief_-_Terner_Center_January_2018.pdf.

20. Laura Wenus, "SF Planning Rules Swirl with Sewage to Clog Affordable Housing Pipeline," *Mission Local,* February 20, 2017, https://missionlocal.org/2017/02/sf-planning-rules-swirl-with-sewage-to-clog-affordable-housing-pipeline/.

21. San Francisco Planning Department, "Discretionary Review (DR) Reform Effort," http://sf-planning.org/discretionary-review-dr-reform-effort; C. W. Nevius, "Discretionary Review: SF Should Raise Standard," *San Francisco Chronicle,* February 3, 2011.

22. Council of Large Public Housing Authorities, "Facts about Public Housing," www.clpha.org/facts_about_public_housing.

23. Conversation with Ed Lee, August 15, 2017.

24. Heather Knight and Joaquin Palomino, "Teachers Priced Out," *San Francisco Chronicle,* May 13, 2016.

25. Roland Li, "Housing Champion Award: Mayor Ed Lee," *San Francisco Business Times,* March 22, 2018, www.bizjournals.com/sanfrancisco/news/2018/03/22/housing-champion-award-mayor-ed-lee-sf.html.

26. David Talbot, *Season of the Witch: Enchantment, Terror, and Deliverance in the City of Love* (New York: Free Press, 2012), p. 336.

27. Knight and Palomino, "Teachers Priced Out."

28. Douglas Hanks, "Teachers Can't Afford Miami Rents. The County Has a Plan: Let Them Live at School," *Miami Herald,* March 27, 2018, www.tampabay.com/news/education/Teachers-can-t-afford-Miami-rents-The-county-has-a-plan-Let-them-live-at-school-_166766798; Katie Marzullo, "Silicon Valley Seeks Solutions for Affordable Teacher Housing," ABC7 News, January 25, 2018, http://abc7news.com/education/silicon-valley-seeks-solutions-for-affordable-teacher-housing-/2990354/.

29. Joshua Sabatini, "Small Sites Program a Major Asset to SF Housing," *San Francisco Examiner,* March 25, 2018, www.sfexaminer.com/small-sites-program-major-asset-sf-housing/.

30. Liam Dillon, "California Mayors Push State for Funding to Address Homelessness," *Los Angeles Times,* February 21, 2018, www.latimes.com/politics/essential/la-pol-ca-essential-politics-updates-california-mayors-push-state-for-1519244314-htmlstory.html.

31. Joshua Sabatini, "Mayor Lee's Promised Airbnb Regulation Working Group Never Set Up," *San Francisco Examiner,* March 2, 2017, www.sfexaminer.com/mayor-lees-promised-airbnb-regulation-working-group-never-set/.

32. Carolyn Said, "Airbnb Listings in San Francisco Plunge by Half," *San Francisco Chronicle,* January 18, 2018.

33. Laura Waxmann, "Reported Evictions in SF Decline for Second-Straight Year," *San Francisco Examiner,* March 23, 2018, www.sfexaminer.com/reported-evictions-sf-decline-second-straight-year/.

34. Edwin M. Lee, "Finding a Winning Formula for Housing," Medium, May 3, 2017, https://medium.com/@mayoredlee/finding-a-winning-formula-for-housing-bbef489caca3; Adam Brinklow, "San Francisco's Median House Price Climbs to $1.61 Million," Curbed SF, April 5, 2018, https://sf.curbed.com/2018/4/5/17201888/san-francisco-median-home-house-price-average-2018; Adam Brinklow, "San Francisco Rents Freeze in First Month of 2018," Curbed SF, February 2, 2018, https://sf.curbed.com/2018/2/2/16965618/san-francisco-rents-january-2018.

6. MILLENNIALS BATTLE BOOMERS OVER HOUSING

Epigraph: Dennis Romero, "If Rent Hikes Continue, Nearly 2,000 Angelenos Will Be Put on the Streets," *LA Weekly,* August 3, 2017, www.laweekly.com/news

/if-los-angeles-rents-continue-to-rise-nearly-2000-will-be-homeless-report-says-8491973.

1. Email with attachments provided to me by Ann Fryman, June 22, 2017.

2. Conversation with Laura Clark, June 12, 2017.

3. "The San Francisco Rent Explosion," Priceonomics, July 18, 2013, https://priceonomics.com/the-san-francisco-rent-explosion/.

4. Mike McPhate, "California Today: Silicon Valley, Housing Villain, Tries to Make Amends," *New York Times,* October 6, 2016.

5. Robert Gammon, "The Real Cause of Gentrification," *Oakland Magazine,* May 2017.

6. https://eastbayforeveryone.org; conversation with Victoria Fierce, June 20, 2017.

7. Gammon, "The Real Cause of Gentrification."

8. Conversation with Dan Kalb, August 4, 2017.

9. Gammon, "The Real Cause of Gentrification"; conversation with Dan Kalb, August 4, 2017.

10. www.zillow.com/cambridge-ma/home-values/.

11. Cambridge Residents Alliance, "Sign the Petition to Keep Cambridge Livable!" www.cambridgeresidentsalliance.org/residents_petition; www.mass.gov/hed/docs/dhcd/cd/zoning/adoptingamending.pdf.

12. Conversation with Jesse Kanson-Benanav, June 21, 2017.

13. Tim Logan, "Five Things You Should Know about Jesse Kanson-Benanav," *Boston Globe,* June 24, 2016, www.bostonglobe.com/business/2016/06/24/jesse-kanson-benanav-community-organizing-with-focus-housing/EnfbCiNBM-mM6582JO40PZJ/story.html.

14. David Scharfenberg, "Boston Needs an Honest Commitment to Racial Integration," *Boston Globe,* December 26, 2017; Saul Tannenbaum, "How Many People Will Central Square Development Kill," Cambridge Community Television, November 3, 2013; www.cctvcambridge.org/CentralSquarePearlHarbor.

15. Monica Jiminez, "Councilors Attack Delays to Central Square Revitalization," Wicked Local Cambridge, January 11, 2017, http://cambridge.wickedlocal.com/news/20170111/councilors-attack-delays-to-central-square-revitalization; James Sanna, "Cambridge City Council OKs Central Square Rezoning. So, What Will It Do?" Wicked Local Cambridge, February 28, 2017, http://cambridge.wickedlocal.com/news/20170228/cambridge-city-council-oks-central-square-rezoning-so-what-will-it-do.

16. Eugenia Schraa and Bret Matthew, "In Development, 'Livability' Means Nothing to Those Unable to Afford Cambridge Living," Cambridge Day, September 16, 2017, www.cambridgeday.com/2017/09/16/in-development-livability-means-nothing-to-those-unable-to-afford-cambridge-living/.

17. Ibid.

18. Conversation with Laura Loe, June 26, 2017.

19. Laura Loe, "How to Talk to Your NIMBY Parents," *The Urbanist*, October 31, 2016, www.theurbanist.org/2016/10/31/how-to-talk-to-your-nimby-parents/.

20. Jonathan Hahn, "Pro-Housing Urban Millennials Say 'Yes in My Backyard,'" *Sierra Magazine,* August 23, 2017, www.sierraclub.org/sierra/2017–5-september-october/grapple/pro-housing-urban-millennials-say-yes-my-backyard. The article appears in the September/October 2017 paper edition with the headline "Getting to YIMBY."

21. Conversation with Maya Rosas, June 28, 2017.

22. June 13, 2017, tweets from Maya Rosas and Ben Nicholls of @FabHillcrest.

23. Marty Graham, "Hillcrest's Uptown Planners Wonder WTF," *San Diego Reader,* June 30, 2016, www.sandiegoreader.com/news/2016/jun/30/stringers-hillcrest-planners-wonder-wtf/#.

24. Andrew Keatts and Scott Lewis, "Politics Report: San Diego's Blue Wave May Not Be Big," Voice of San Diego, February 18, 2018, www.voiceofsandiego.org /topics/news/politics-report-san-diegos-blue-wave-may-not-be-big/; Phillip Molnar, "Millennials Aren't Settling in San Diego. Here's Why," *San Diego Union-Tribune,* November 15, 2016, www.sandiegouniontribune.com/business/real-estate/sd-fi-millennial-growth-20161114-story.html; Ken Williams, "Uptown CPU Is Approved; Gateway Plan Added," *San Diego Uptown News,* November 18, 2016, http://sduptownnews.com/uptown-cpu-approved-gateway-plan-added/.

25. www.deptofnumbers.com/income/colorado/boulder; www.zillow.com /boulder-co/home-values/.

26. Conversation with Zane Selvans, July 7, 2017.

27. "Zane Selvans: These People Are in Your Neighborhood," *Daily Camera,* February 4, 2015, www.dailycamera.com/columnists/ci_27460205/zane-selvans-these-people-are-your-neighborhood.

28. Ibid.

29. Ibid.

30. Website of Boulder Neighborhood Alliance, http://boulderna.org/.

31. Bill Karelis: When a City Dashes Forward," *Daily Camera,* June 3, 2017, www.dailycamera.com/guest-opinions/ci_31033449/bill-karelis-when-city-dashes-forward.

32. "Where Is the Happiest Place in the United States?" *National Geographic,* November 2017, pp. 57–59.

33. https://caanet.org/palo-alto-weigh-possible-rent-control-study/; www .zillow.com/palo-alto-ca/home-values/.

34. Conversation with Zane Selvans, July 7, 2017.

35. http://portlandforeveryone.org/.

36. www.friends.org.

37. Conversation with Madeline Kovacs, July 27, 2017.

38. Some believe that Portland's inclusionary law has reduced housing in Portland, since developers followed the law's local enactment by reducing projects to under twenty units so that the affordability requirements were not triggered. But as of this writing, too little time has passed to fairly assess the law's long-term impact.

39. ReDefine, Center for Community Change and the Urban League, "ReBuilding Community: A Disparate Impacts Analysis and Cross-Cultural Agenda to

Prevent Displacement and Gentrification," p.1, https://static1.squarespace.com
/static/5501f6d4e4b0ee23fb3097ff/t/5935cb971e5b6c0cd0c97458/1496697798853
/Rebuilding+Community+-+Low+Res.pdf.

40. https://portlandforeveryone.org/what-we-believe/; P4E policy letter
emailed to me by Madeline Kovacs, August 3, 2017.

41. https://www.portlandoregon.gov/bps/71903; http://portlandforeveryone
.org/wp-content/uploads/2018/04/P4E-BHD-DD-Letter.pdf.

42. www.dontrezoneus.org/.

43. Ibid.

44. www.stopdemolishingportland.org/.

45. http://unitedneighborhoodsforreform.blogspot.com/.

46. http://berkeleydailyplanet.com/issue/2017-03-24/article/45583?headline
= State-Senator-Skinner-targets-Berkeley-s-zoning-laws—Becky-O-Malley.

47. www.abc10.com/news/millennials-tell-boomers-yes-in-my-backyard
/440668204.

48. Ibid.

49. Joe Rivano Barros, "SF Delays Controversial Housing Law amidst Opposition, Cry of Ethnic Cleansing," *Mission Local,* January 29, 2016, https://mission
local.org/2016/01/sf-delays-controversial-housing-law-amidst-opposition-cries-of-ethnic-
cleansing/.

50. Graham MacDonald, "Luxury Housing Is Not to Blame for San
Francisco's Affordable Housing Crisis," Urban Institute, June 1, 2017, www.urban
.org/urban-wire/luxury-housing-not-blame-san-franciscos-affordable-housing-
crisis.

51. Ibid.

52. www.redfin.com/CA/Berkeley/1253-Hearst-Ave-94702/home/1460574.

53. www.bizjournals.com/sanfrancisco/news/2017/04/02/bay-area-housing-
millennials-nimby-development.html?ana = e_ae_set2&s = article_du&ed =
2017-04-03.

54. Joel Kotkin, "The High Cost of a Home Is Turning American Millennials
into the New Serfs," *The Daily Beast,* February 4, 2017, www.thedailybeast.com
/articles/2017/02/04/the-high-cost-of-a-home-is-turning-american-millennials-into-
the-new-serfs.

55. Dan Kopf, "US Housing Wealth Is Growing for the Oldest and Wealthiest
Americans, at the Expense of Everybody Else," *Quartz,* May 1, 2017, https://
qz.com/972873/us-housing-wealth-is-growing-for-the-oldest-and-wealthiest-
americans-at-the-expense-of-everybody-else/?utm_content = buffer04756&utm_
medium = social&utm_source = twitter.com&utm_campaign = buffer.

56. Carolyn Tyler, "SF Rec & Park Changes Reservation System after Soccer
Field Dustup," October 16, 2014, ABC7 News, http://abc7news.com/society
/sf-changes-reservation-system-after-soccer-field-dustup/353985/.

57. Sean Hollister, "Protesters Block Silicon Valley Shuttles, Smash Google Bus
Window," *The Verge,* December 20, 2013, www.theverge.com/2013/12/20/5231758
/protesters-target-silicon-valley-shuttles-smash-google-bus-window.

58. www.theguardian.com/world/2014/feb/23/is-san-francisco-losing-its-soul; www.salon.com/2015/11/05/san_francisco_sells_its_soul_money_rules_the_city_now_bohemia_be_damned_partner/; www.nytimes.com/2015/10/09/technology /seattle-in-midst-of-tech-boom-tries-to-keep-its-soul.html; www.thedailybeast .com/san-franciscos-alarming-tech-bro-boom-what-is-the-price-of-change.

59. Wayne King, "Changing San Francisco Is Foreseen as a Haven for Wealthy and Childless," *New York Times,* June 9, 1981, www.nytimes.com/1981/06/09/us /changing-san-francisco-is-foreseen-as-a-haven-for-wealthy-and-childless.html.

60. Randy Shaw, "HBO's Dishonest San Francisco 2.0," BeyondChron, September 28, 2015, www.beyondchron.org/hbos-dishonest-account-of-san-francisco/.

61. Conversation with Joel Engardo, June 29, 2017.

62. Email from Katy Tang, June 13, 2017.

7. GET OFF MY LAWN!

1. Danielle Tcholakian, "Here's What You Need to Know about Fight over Elizabeth Street Garden," dnainfo.com, September 18, 2016, www.dnainfo.com /new-york/20160918/nolita/heres-what-you-need-know-about-fight-over-elizabeth-street-garden.

2. Conversation with Margaret Chin, September 25, 2017.

3. Ibid.

4. http://elizabethstreetgarden.org/.

5. Sheila Anne Feeney, "Elizabeth Street Garden Supporters Battle to Save Manhattan Oasis," amny.com, www.amny.com/news/elizabeth-street-garden-supporters-including-actor-gabriel-byrne-fight-to-save-manhattan-oasis-1.10853096.

6. Testimony of Bobbie Sackman, September 17, 2015, Lower Manhattan Development Corporation Public Forum.

7. Danielle Tcholakian, "Local Seniors Want Affordable Housing over Elizabeth Street Garden," dnainfo.com, September 23, 2015, www.dnainfo.com/new-york/20150923/nolita/local-seniors-want-affordable-housing-over-elizabeth-street-garden.

8. Jeannine Kiely, "Why Destroy the Elizabeth Street Garden When a Vacant Lot Will Provide More Housing?" *WestView News,* August 3, 2017, http://westviewnews .org/2017/08/destroy-elizabeth-street-garden-vacant-lot-will-provide-housing/.

9. Kiely, "Why Destroy the Elizabeth Street Garden"; conversation with Margaret Chin, September 25, 2017.

10. "Christopher Marte for Council in District 1," *The Villager,* September 8, 2017, http://thevillager.com/2017/09/08/christopher-marte-for-city-council-in-district-1/.

11. Devin Gannon, "City Will Replace Nolita's Elizabeth Street Garden with 121 Affordable Apartments for Seniors," December 8, 2017, 6sqft, www.6sqft.com /city-will-replace-nolitas-elizabeth-street-gardens-with-121-affordable-apartments-for-seniors/.

12. David W. Dunlap, "Tumult in a Manhattan Oasis over an Affordable Housing Plan," *New York Times,* September 23, 2015.

13. "CEQA: A Good Law in Need of Reform: NIMBY Group Use CEQA Lawsuit to Stop Affordable Housing Project for Seniors," http://ceqaworkinggroup .com/wp-content/uploads/2013/02/CEQA-Misuse-Sacramento-Senior-Homes.pdf.

14. Richard Rothstein, *The Color of Law: A Forgotten History of How Our Government Segregated America* (New York: Liveright 2017).

15. Lisa Belkin, "The Painful Lessons of the Yonkers Housing Crisis," *New York Times,* August 14, 2015, www.nytimes.com/2015/08/15/opinion/the-painful-lessons-of-the-yonkers-housing-crisis.html?_r = 0.

16. J. K. Dineen, "In a Wealthy SF Neighborhood, Residents Fight Low-Income Housing," *San Francisco Chronicle,* November 16, 2016.

17. Ibid.

18. Adam Brinklow, "Forest Hill Resident Explains Why Neighborhood Doesn't Want New Senior Housing," Curbed SF, November 16, 2016, http:// sf.curbed.com/2016/11/18/13681294/forest-hill-sf-senior-housing-joe-bravo.

19. "What if We Turned the Sunset into Paris," June 11, 2017, Joel Engardio Blog, www.engardio.com/blog/2017/6/8/what-if-we-turned-the-sunset-into-paris.

20. Corrie M. Anders, "The Cost of Living in Noe," *Noe Valley Voice,* September 2017, p. 19; Randy Shaw, "Should Cities Tax Huge Homeowner Profits from Stopping Housing?" BeyondChron, April 10, 2018, www.beyondchron.org/cities-tax-huge-profits-stopping-housing/.

21. Email from Laura Fingal-Surma, July 27, 2017.

22. Mattnew S. Bajko, "Political Notebook: Battle Brewing over SF Housing Density Proposal," *Bay Area Reporter,* January 21, 2016, http://ebar.com/news /article.php?sec = news&article = 71233.

23. In 2017 the San Francisco Board of Supervisors reversed course and enacted the density bonus proposal, renamed Homes SF. Conversation with Rick Jacobus, April 21, 2017.

24. Todd David email, July 31, 2017.

25. Todd Lappin, "Median Home Price Hits $1.46 Million in Summer 2017 Bernal Heights Real Estate Report," Bernalwood.com, August 10, 2017, https:// bernalwood.com/2017/08/10/median-home-price-hits-1–46-million-in-summer-2017-bernal-heights-real-estate-report/.

26. Conversation with Buck Bagot, August 11, 2017.

27. Tamara Nicoloff, "Opinion: Reflections on Growing Up with a Political Mom in Berkeley," Berkeleyside, April 21, 2017, www.berkeleyside.com/2017/04/21 /opinion-reflections-growing-political-mom-berkeley/.

28. Harriet Nathan and Stanley Scott, eds., "Experiment and Change in Berkeley: Essays on City Politics 1950–1975," Institute of Governmental Studies, University of California, Berkeley, 1978.

29. Ibid., p. 390.

30. Lance Knobel, "Legal Action Likely after Berkeley City Council Rejects Housing Project on Haskell Street," Berkeleyside, March 1, 2017, www.berkeleyside

.com/2017/03/01/legal-action-likely-berkeley-city-council-rejects-housing-project-haskell-street/; Tracey Taylor, "Berkeley's Bid to Stop New Housing Being Built Overruled by Judge," Berkeleyside, July 25, 2017, www.berkeleyside.com/2017/07/25 /berkeleys-bid-stop-new-housing-built-overruled-judge/.

31. Katy Murphy, Jeff Collins, and Casey Tolan, "Gov. Brown Signs Bills to Spur More Affordable Housing, Curb Costs," *Orange County Register,* September 29, 2017, www.ocregister.com/2017/09/29/brown-signs-bills-seeking-to-address-california-housing-crisis/.

32. Conversation with Lisa Bender, August 2, 2017.

33. Peter Callaghan, "Growing Pains: As Minneapolis Pushes for Greater Housing Density, More Neighborhoods Push Back," *MinnPost,* November 18, 2016, www.minnpost.com/politics-policy/2016/11/growing-pains-minneapolis-pushes-greater-housing-density-more-neighborhoods-.

34. Peter Callaghan, "Inclusionary Zoning: Will Minneapolis See It This Year?" *MinnPost,* February 19, 2018, www.minnpost.com/politics-policy/2018/02 /inclusionary-zoning-will-minneapolis-see-it-year.

35. Conversation with Lisa Bender, August 2, 2017.

36. www.citypages.com/news/wedge-live-pokes-at-minneapolis-politics-one-video-at-a-time/410496945.

37. All quotes from John Edwards's video are from www.youtube.com /channel/UCiKFyG2M8e62HOrDDJ7HYbw.

38. https://streets.mn/2016/03/14/map-monday-minneapolis-residential-zoning/; https://medium.com/neighbors-for-more-neighbors/how-can-minneapolis-improve-its-housing-policy-ee142eae962a; Adam Belz, "Minneapolis Housing-Density Backers Come Together Ready for Action," *Star Tribune,* March 14, 2018, www.startribune.com/the-pro-density-movement-in-minneapolis-seeks-to-find-its-voice/476884973/.

39. Conversation with Russ Adams, April 13, 2018; www.facebook.com /MakeHomesHappenMPLS/.

40. Email from Russ Adams, April 24, 2018.

41. Conversation with Russ Adams, April 13, 2018.

8. NEW YORK CITY, OAKLAND, AND
SAN FRANCISCO'S MISSION DISTRICT

1. Hunter Walker, "Bill de Blasio Tells 'A Tale of Two Cities' at His Mayoral Campaign Kickoff," January 27, 2013, Observer.com, http://observer.com/2013/01 /bill-de-blasio-tells-a-tale-of-two-cities-at-his-mayoral-campaign-kickoff/.

2. Conversation with Vaughn Armour, August 16, 2017.

3. Conversation with Donna Mossman, August 23, 2017.

4. Benjamin D. Lisle, *Modern Coliseum: Stadiums and American Culture* (Philadelphia: University of Pennsylvania Press, 2017), pp. 35–38.

5. Julie Satow, "Amanda Burden Wants to Remake New York. She Has 19 Months Left," *New York Times*, May 18, 2012, www.nytimes.com/2012/05/20/nyregion /amanda-burden-planning-commissioner-is-remaking-new-york-city.html.

6. Conversation with Celia Weaver, July 22, 2017.

7. Phoebe Taylor Vuolo, "Rowdy Bedford Union Armory Meeting Decries de Blasio, Cumbo," KingsCountyPolitics.com, August 4, 2017, www.kingscountypolitics .com/rowdy-bedford-union-armory-meeting-decries-de-blasio-cumbo/; conversation with Vaughn Armour, August 16, 2017.

8. Will Bredderman, "Mayor Eyes Rescue of Crown Heights Armory Redevelopment," *Crain's*, July 12, 2017, www.crainsnewyork.com/article/20170712 /REAL_ESTATE/170719951/mayor-eyes-rescue-of-crown-heights-armory-redevelopment.

9. Ibid.

10. Conversation with Vaughn Armour, August 16, 2017; Vuolo, "Rowdy Bedford Union Armory Meeting."

11. Vuolo, "Rowdy Bedford Union Armory Meeting."

12. Marcus Moore and Vaughn Armour, "Mayor de Blasio Is Out of Touch with Crown Heights' Reality," KingsCountyPolitics.com, July 27, 2017, www .kingscountypolitics.com/mayor-de-blasio-touch-crown-heights-reality/.

13. "Mr. de Blasio's Moon Shot," Opinion, *New York Times*, May 6, 2014; J. David Goodman, "De Blasio Expands Affordable Housing, but Results Aren't Always Visible," *New York Times*, October 5, 2017.

14. Goodman, "De Blasio Expands Affordable Housing."

15. Mireya Navarro and Michael M. Grynbaum, "De Blasio Sets a 10-Year Plan for Housing, Putting the Focus on Affordability," *New York Times*, May 5, 2014, www.nytimes.com/2014/05/06/nyregion/de-blasio-affordable-housing-plan .html?hpw&rref = nyregion.

16. Ibid.

17. Conversation with Celia Weaver, July 22, 2017.

18. Julian Brash, *Bloomberg's New York: Class and Governance in the Luxury City* (Athens: University of Georgia Press, 2011), pp. 250–251.

19. Ibid., p. 2.

20. Abigail Savitch-Lew, "East Harlem Committee Rejects Current de Blasio Rezoning Plan," CityLimits.org, June 17, 2017, http://citylimits.org/2017/06/17 /east-harlem-committee-rejects-current-de-blasio-rezoning-plan/.

21. Alessandro Busà, *The Creative Destruction of New York City: Engineering the City for the Elite* (New York: Oxford University Press, 2017), pp. 92, 115.

22. Ibid., p. 160.

23. Richard Florida, *The New Urban Crisis: How Our Cities Are Increasing Inequality, Deepening Segregation, and Failing the Middle Class—and What We Can Do about It* (New York: Basic Books, 2017), p. 71.

24. "Mayor de Blasio to Complete Affordable Housing Plan 2 Years Ahead of Schedule, Accelerate Pace and Expand Goals," October 24, 2017, www1.nyc.gov /office-of-the-mayor/news/682–17/mayor-de-blasio-complete-affordable-housing-

plan-2-years-ahead-schedule-accelerate-pace-and#/0; Bill de Blasio, "Building a More Affordable City: Mayor de Blasio Says His Housing Push Is Helping Many Lower-Income New Yorkers Live in Gotham," *New York Daily News,* July 13, 2017, www.nydailynews.com/opinion/building-affordable-city-article-1.3321762.

25. Busà, *Creative Destruction,* p. 226, citing Gregory Jost, "Housing Plan Misses the Big Question of How We Got into this Mess in the First Place," City Limits, January 19, 2016, https://citylimits.org/2016/01/19/cityviewshousing-plan-misses-the-big-question-of-how-we-got-into-this-mess-in-the-first-place/. For an analysis of the income levels benefiting from the 78,000 units funded in de Blasio's first term, see New York Communities for Change, "Increasing Real Affordability in New York City: An Action Plan for Mayor de Blasio's Second Term," September 14, 2017, www.nycommunities.org/increasing-real-affordability-new-york-city-action-plan-mayor-de-blasio%E2%80%99s-second-term.

26. Sally Goldenberg, "De Blasio Team Supports Council Incumbent in Race Defined by His Development Agenda," *Politico,* August 10, 2017, www.politico.com/states/new-york/city-hall/story/2017/08/10/de-blasio-team-supports-city-council-incumbent-in-race-defined-by-his-development-agenda-113880.

27. Rachel Holliday Smith, "Bedford-Union Armory Plan Rejected by Borough President," DNAinfo.com, September 5, 2017, www.dnainfo.com/new-york/20170905/crown-heights/bedford-union-armory-crown-heights-eric-adams-recommendation.

28. Erin Durkin, "City Council Strikes Deal to Approve Brooklyn's Bedford Union Armory Project," *New York Daily News,* November 21, 2017, www.nydailynews.com/news/politics/city-council-strikes-deal-approve-bedford-union-armory-project-article-1.3648721.

29. Conversation with Harold Dawson, August 24, 2017.

30. Kalima Rose and Margaretta Lin, "A Roadmap toward Equity: Housing Solutions for Oakland, California," PolicyLink, 2015, www.policylink.org/sites/default/files/pl-report-oak-housing-070715.pdf.

31. William Frey quoted in Greg Troppo and Paul Overberg, "After Nearly 100 Years, Great Migration Begins Reversal," *USA Today,* February 2, 2015, www.usatoday.com/story/news/nation/2015/02/02/census-great-migration-reversal/21818127/; Rose and Lin, "A Roadmap toward Equity."

32. Rose and Lin, "A Roadmap toward Equity."

33. "Oakland at Home Update," July 2017, https://files.acrobat.com/a/preview/c3218e79-b4b8-43db-b29b-321928ec0899.

34. Conversation with Robert Ogilvie, August 25, 2017.

35. Conversation with Heather Hood, August 25, 2017.

36. Robert Gammon, "The Real Cause of Gentrification," May 2017, www.oaklandmagazine.com/May-2017/The-Real-Cause-of-Gentrification/.

37. Anti-Eviction Mapping Project, "Precarious Housing: The Loss of SRO Hotels in Oakland," December 28, 2017, www.antievictionmap.com/#/precarious-housing/; Darwin BondGraham, "New Oakland Law Fails to Protect Low-Income Residents," *East Bay Express,* November 16, 2017.

38. Conversation with Heather Hood, August 25, 2017.

39. Conversation with Pete Gallegos, July 20, 2017.

40. Cary Cordova, *The Heart of the Mission: Latino Art and Politics in San Francisco* (Philadelphia: University of Pennsylvania Press, 2017), p. 123.

41. Evelyn Nieves, "In Old Mission District, Changing Grit to Gold," *New York Times,* January 21, 1999.

42. For a full account of the strategies used by San Francisco's Tenderloin neighborhood to avoid gentrification, see my book *The Tenderloin: Sex, Crime, and Resistance in the Heart of San Francisco* (San Francisco: Urban Reality Press, 2015).

43. Randy Shaw, "New Affordable Housing Engine Needed in Mission," BeyondChron, October 7, 2005.

44. San Francisco Rent Board statistics, *San Francisco Examiner,* October 25, 1998.

45. Rebecca Bowe, "S.F. Study Documents Sharp Decline in Mission's Latino Population," KQED, October 28, 2015, https://ww2.kqed.org/news/2015/10/28/s-f-study-documents-sharp-decline-in-missions-latino-population/.

46. www.businessinsider.com/mission-district-tech-takeover-2016–6; www.newsweek.com/2014/04/25/tech-boom-forces-ruthless-gentrification-san-francisco-248135.html; www.cnet.com/news/san-francisco-tech-industry-backlash-internet/.

47. Adam Brinklow, "Beast on Bryant Opponents Lose Two Appeals, Threaten Lawsuit," Curbed SF, September 15, 2016, https://sf.curbed.com/2016/9/15/12931964/beast-on-bryant-loses-appeals-lawsuit.

48. http://medasf.org/programs/community-real-estate/mission-action-plan-2020/.

49. Department of City and Regional Planning, University of California, Berkeley, "Residential Displacement in the Bay Area: A Regional Perspective," May 2014, www.urbandisplacement.org/sites/default/files/images/studio_report_2014.pdf.

50. Data on Latinos in the Mission comes from the 2000, 2010 Census and the American Community Surveys of the Census (years 2009–2016). It is based on Census Tracts 177, 201, 202, 207–10, 228.01–228.03, 229/03. Also see http://default.sfplanning.org/Citywide/Mission2020/MAP2020_Plan_Final.pdf.

51. Mission Action Plan 2020, http://sf-planning.org/mission-action-plan-2020.

CONCLUSION

1. Sarah Karlinsky, Sarah Jo Szamelan, and Kristy Wong, "Room for More: SPUR's Housing Agenda for San Jose," August 2017, www.spur.org/sites/default/files/publications_pdfs/SPUR_Room_for_More.pdf; Ben Christopher and Matt Levin, "Californians: Here's Why Your Housing Costs Are So High," CALmatters, August 21, 2017, https://calmatters.org/articles/housing-costs-high-california/.

2. Eduardo Porter, "Why Big Cities Thrive, and Smaller Ones Are Being Left Behind," *New York Times,* October 10, 2017, www.nytimes.com/2017/10/10/business/economy/big-cities.html?_r = 0).

INDEX

350 Seattle, 113

600 Wall Street (Seattle, WA), 118

1000 Friends of Oregon, 172–173, 176

A Better Cambridge, 163–165, 179

ABC-TV, 177–178

Accessory dwelling units. *See* ADUs

ACLU (American Civil Liberties Union), 67

ACORN (Association of Community Organizations for Reform Now), 66

ACT UP (AIDS Coalition to Unleash Power), 51

The Activist's Handbook, 51

Adams, Eric, 220

Adams, Russ, 207–208

Adler, Steve, 11, 76, 94, 98–101

ADUs (accessory dwelling units), 90, 112, 115, 174–175, 243; in Seattle, 112

Affordability, 3, 8, 10, 23, 35, 81, 111, 122, 224

Affordable housing, 4, 5, 10, 49, 155, 176, 191–192, 194, 234, 238; bond funding for, 145, 147, 148, 240–242; city funding for, 87, 243–244, 246; as condition of development, 44, 111; developers, 235; opposition to, 138

Affordable housing bond measure (San Francisco, 2015), 240–241

Affordable Housing Density Bonus Program (San Francisco), 184, 197

Affordable housing trust fund ballot measure (San Francisco, 2012), 145

African Americans, 2, 37, 51, 59, 209–215, 218–219, 221–223, 226–227, 243; displaced by gentrification and redevelopment, 3, 9–10, 13, 24–25, 41, 83, 85, 101, 123, 144; and goal of racial diversity, 90–91, 98–99; and segregation, 99–100, 192–93; and substandard housing, 74–76, 80, 97

Agnos, Art, 196

AIDS, 6, 21, 26, 27, 34, 51

AIDS Healthcare Foundation, 72

Airbnb, 153–154

Alameda County, CA, 224

Alamo Square (San Francisco, CA), 31

Albuquerque, NM, 103

Alliance for Metropolitan Stability (Minneapolis, MN), 207–208

Alvidrez, Mike, 157

Amazon, 104, 107, 108, 113, 121–122, 248; effects of company growth on Seattle area, 104; employees, 107; office occupancy in Seattle, 107; search for second headquarters, 122

America Divided (TV series), 210

Amos, Jean, 198

An, Noah, 113

Anarchists, 165

Anderson, Nancy, 122

Anderson, Tyler, 47, 52

Anti-Eviction Mapping Project (San Francisco, CA), 227

Anti-gentrification, 236–237, 239

Antioch, CA, 222

Apartment Appraisers and Consultants (Denver, CO), 123
Apartment Association of Greater Los Angeles, 65
Apartment Insights (Denver, CO), 123
Apple, 233
Ariza, Amado, 87
Armour, Vaughan, 209–210, 212–215, 217, 221
Art galleries, 49, 50
Artists, 11, 28, 29, 32–33, 50, 58, 150, 217, 239; housing for, 1–3, 32, 224
Arts and Crafts architecture, 54
"Artwashing," 49
Asian Americans for Equality, 191
Asian Law Caucus, 144
Aspen, CO, 171
@CAveryLittle (Twitter user), 161
@MattRegan (Twitter user), 161
AT&T Park (San Francisco, CA), 137
The Atlantic, 11
Austin, TX, 2, 3, 5, 7, 9, 11, 74–102, 243, 245; "bargain" on new housing, 98, 99; housing code enforcement/violations in, 76, 80, 84–85, 86–89, 94
Austin American-Statesman, 83
Austin Board of Realtors, 96
Austin Chamber of Commerce, 95
Austin City Council, 80, 83, 85, 95
Austin City Limits (music festival), 75
Austin Habitat for Humanity, 96
Austin Music People, 96
Austin Neighborhood Housing and Community Development, 87
Austin Neighborhoods Council, 101
Austin Technology Council, 96
Austin Tenants' Council, 84
Austinites for Urban Rail Action (AURA), 92, 93, 94, 95, 98, 102
Avicolli Mecca, Tommi, 32

Babalola, Niran, 100
Bagot, Buck, 199, 200
Baby boomers. *See* Boomers
Baker, Heather, 1
Balboa High School (San Francisco, CA), 229
Ballot measures, 5, 155, 171

Barclay, Felisa, 22
Barclay, Joseph, 22
Barclay, Lolita, 20
Barclay, Luciano, 22
Barclay, Uldarico, 19
Barger, Kathryn, 60
Barkley, Alice, 137
Barrientos, Maria, 118
BART (Bay Area Rapid Transit), 160, 162, 192, 226, 230–232; effects of construction on San Francisco Mission District, 230–232
Barwick, Kent, 189
BASTA (Building and Strengthening Tenant Action), 74–75, 84, 85, 89
Bates, Tom, 202
Bay Area Council, 180
Bay Area Rapid Transit. *See* BART
Bayview (San Francisco, CA), 237
Becker, David, 135
Bedford-Stuyvesant (New York, NY), 210
Bedford Union Armory (BUA), 10, 211–215, 219–220
Bender, Lisa, 203–207
Bennett, Tony, 120Berkeley, CA, 3, 5, 9, 62, 153, 160, 177, 179, 191–192, 200–203, 206, 224, 230; city council, 161, 200–202; home prices, 179; master plan, 201; neighborhood preservation ordinance, 200–201; zoning adjustment board, 202
Berkeley Daily Planet, 177
Bernal Heights (San Francisco, CA), 13, 134, 179, 199–200; housing prices, 200; opposition to housing, 134
Bernal Heights Housing Development Corporation, 200
Bernal Heights Neighborhood Center, 200
Better Boulder, 169
Better Housing by Design (BHD, Portland), 175
Beverly Grove (Los Angeles, CA), 67
Beverly Hills, CA, 39
BeyondChron, 235
BFC Partners, 211
Bike-friendly neighborhoods, 167
Black Panthers, 3, 223
Blanton Elementary School (Austin, TX), 82

Blaustein, Miriam, 198, 199
Bloomberg, Michael, 117, 187, 211, 216–218, 221, 244
Bloomberg's New York: Class and Governance in the Luxury City, 217
Bond, Christopher "Kit," 97
Bonds, for affordable housing, 109, 147–148, 155, 242; Alameda County (2016), 224; Austin, 94, 101; Portland (2016), 174; San Francisco (2015), 240–241
Bonin, Mike, 59, 60, 62, 207
Boomers, 4, 8, 70, 96, 144, 204; boomer-millennial conflict, 4, 8, 157–186, 248–249
Borvice, Al, 229, 236
Boschetti, Paul, 13Boston, MA, 128, 162, 164, 245; median home prices in, 163
Boston Globe, 164
Boulder, CO, 3, 5, 9, 165, 168–172
Boulder Daily Camera, 169, 170
Boulder Neighborhood Alliance, 171Bouldin Creek (Austin, TX), 88
Boyle Heights (Los Angeles, CA), 2, 6, 7, 41–55, 61, 64–65, 88, 226, 230, 240, 243
Boyle Heights Alliance Against Artwashing and Displacement, 49
Brash, Julian, 217
Bravo, Joseph, 195
Brawley, Reverend David K., 215
Breed, London, 156
Brentwood (Austin, TX), 88
Brentwood, CA, 114
Bronx, NY, 215
Brooklyn, NY, 209–211, 214–215, 217–218, 220
Brooklyn Dodgers, 211
Brooklyn Labor Day Carnival, 219Brown, Jerry, 71, 73, 152, 225
Brown, Willie, 23, 29, 137, 149
Bruteig, Cary, 123
Builders, 8, 196, 246; Irish, in San Francisco, 129, 132–136, 139, 141–142
Building approval process, 8, 62, 244, 247; in San Francisco, 117–119, 135, 240; in Seattle, 117–119
Building inspections, 18, 84–85, 87, 89, 135
Burden, Amanda, 211
Burgess, Tim, 122

Burton, John, 24
Busà, Allesandro, 216, 218
Bushwick (New York, NY), 210
Bustos, Debra, 126
Byrne, Gabriel, 189

Cabande, Angelica, 18
Cady, Benjamin, 31
California, 78, 93, 94, 225, 246; affordable housing bond (2018), 242; legislative analyst's report on housing (2016), 128
California Apartment Association, 65, 66
California Court of Appeal, 225
California Environmental Quality Act. *See* CEQA
California Housing Finance Agency (CalHFA), 67
California Housing Partnership, 110
California Renters Legal Advocacy and Education Fund, 202
California State University, Northridge, 37
CalPIRG, 96
Cambridge, MA, 3, 5, 9, 162–165
Cambridge City Council, 165
Cambridge Residents Alliance (CRA), 163, 164Canoga Park, CA, 37
Canvassing, for housing, 97, 99
Cap and trade, and money for affordable housing (California), 224
Capitol Hill (Seattle, WA), 103
Care Not Cash (San Francisco, CA), 155
Carlone, Dennis, 164
Carlsson, Chris, 150
Carnaval SF, 231
Carter, Jimmy, 130
Casar, Greg, 7, 74, 80, 83, 85, 89–91, 93–94, 98, 101
Cassidy, Joe, 129, 130–133, 136–138, 141
Castro, Roxana, 78, 79
Castro District (San Francisco, CA), 13, 17, 26–28, 34, 131, 143, 238
Catholic Charities (San Francisco, CA), 110
Causa Justa/Just Cause, 224
Center for Community Change, 66
Central Austin, 94
Central Square (Cambridge, MA), 163–164
Central Valley, CA, 222

Century City, CA, 40
CEQA (California Environmental Quality Act), 63, 64, 114, 139, 247
Chan, Alda, 19, 20
Chan, Joe Nim, 19
Change.org, 189
Chavez, Cesar, 50
Chavez Ravine (Los Angeles, CA), 211
Cheap and Nutritious (and Delicious) Cookbook, 198
Chelsea (New York, NY), 2
Cheng, Hung, 17, 18
Cheng, Judy, 17, 18
Chicago, IL, 108
Chin, Margaret, 187–188, 190, 207
Chinatown (San Francisco, CA), 29–30, 144
Chinese Americans, 29, 151, 155, 184
Chiu, David, 31, 61
Christian Church Homes of Northern California, 193–194
Chu, Daniel, 30
Circulate San Diego, 167
Citizens' Alternative Plan (Seattle, WA), 108
City College of San Francisco, 229
City funding: for affordable housing, 87, 243–244, 246; for renovation, 86
City Lights Bookstore, 29
City of Quartz (Davis), 55
City-owned property. *See* Publicly owned property
Civic Center (San Francisco, CA), 6
Civil Rights Act (1964), 100
Clark, Laura, 157–160, 181, 184
Clarksville (Austin, TX), 101
Clarksville Community Development Corporation, 101
Climate change: and commuting, 5, 96; and in-fill housing, 112–113
Clinton, Bill, 5, 6, 145
Clinton, Hillary, 75
Coalition for Economic Survival (CES), 67, 72
Code enforcement. *See* Housing code enforcement/violations
CodeNEXT (Austin, TX), 7, 95–101
Cohen, Mickey, 42

Collier, Steve, 20, 27–28, 30, 32
Collins, Robert, 154
The Color of Law: A Forgotten History of How Our Government Segregated America (Rothstein), 99, 192
Community Board 2 (New York, NY), 189, 190
Community land trusts, 23, 125, 244–245; cooperative ownership model, 150
Community of Friends (Los Angeles, CA), 53
Community Tenants' Association (San Francisco, CA), 29, 30
Commuting: as contributor to climate change, 5, 96; in Los Angeles, 53, 62, 65; in New York, 126; in San Francisco, 109–110, 148; in Seattle, 113
Compass Housing Alliance (Seattle, WA), 104
Condominiums, 27, 134, 226, 241; affordable, 33, 35; conversion to, 67–68; Costa-Hawkins and, 73; luxury, 2, 10, 83, 137, 177, 197, 212–213, 217, 220; moratorium on, 68; recommended restrictions on, 245
Coney Island, 219
Construction costs, 141, 194, 225, 247
Construction lending, 127, 130–131, 140–141, 143, 237, 245; associated risks, 130, 133
Cooperative housing, 150, 169, 171. *See also* Community land trusts
Costa-Hawkins Act (California), 46, 73, 153, 160, 242, 245; 2018 repeal effort, 245; Proposition 10 and, 73, 153
Coyle, W. B., 29
The Creative Destruction of New York City (Busà), 216
Crestview (Austin, TX), 88
Cross Creek Tenants Association, 87
Croucher, June, 25, 26
Crown Heights (New York, NY), 9–10, 58, 209–215, 217–220; demographics (2010), 210; evictions, 214; rents, 210
Crown Heights Tenant Union (CHTU, Brooklyn, New York), 210, 212, 213, 214
Cumbo, Laurie, 220

Cupertino, CA, 182, 233, 247
Curbed LA, 44, 45

Dabbs-Mann, Gloria, 59
Daily Beast, 182
Daily Racing Form, 105
Daly, Chris, 138
David, Todd, 199
Davis, Mike, 55, 62–63
Dawson, Harold, 221, 222, 223
de Blasio, Bill, 10, 117, 190, 209–221, 244
Defend Boyle Heights, 49, 50, 52
Dellums, Ron, 223
Democratic Party, 67, 70, 169, 201
Democratic Socialists of America, LA, 52
Demolition, 7, 14, 17, 32, 35, 67–68, 72,
    75–82, 84–85, 90, 93, 154, 183, 185, 192,
    198, 200, 217, 245
Dennison, Becky, 58–59, 61–62
Density, 93, 96, 98, 100–101, 162, 168, 193,
    199, 205–206, 244; density bonuses,
    99–100, 178, 185
Denver, CO: housing boom in, 8, 123–126;
    linkage fees in, 93
Denver City Council, 123
Department of Neighborhood Empower-
    ment (Los Angeles, CA), 64
Desegrate ATX (Austin, TX), 100
Design review boards, 199, 201
Devereux, Jan, 165
Dierkes-Carlisle, Jean, 28
Dineen, J. K., 194
Disabled tenants, 24, 27, 28
Discretionary review, 142–143
Displacement, 6–7, 11, 15, 17, 20, 22, 24, 33,
    35, 42, 50, 64–65, 75–77, 83–84. 95, 121,
    127–128, 152, 174, 176, 192, 203, 214,
    218, 237–238, 244, 246
Diversity, 9–10, 58, 74–102, 162, 175, 214,
    218, 221, 227, 235, 238–239, 246; eco-
    nomic, 35, 124, 126, 154, 163–165, 194,
    198–199, 216, 218, 227, 235, 243–249;
    racial, 126, 196, 207, 209–249; as
    strategy for preserving, 6
Dodge, Dennis, 105–106
Dodge, Mary, 106
Dodge, Melissa, 105–106
DontRezoneUs.org, 175–176

Dot-com boom (1990s), 15, 24, 40, 134,
    136, 152, 154, 156, 182–183, 199–200,
    231–235, 237
Downtown Seattle Association, 112
Downzoning, 63, 129, 131, 133–134, 163,
    201, 218. *See also* Zoning
Dulalas, Daynelita, 22
Dulalas, Marti, 22
Dulalas, Teresa, 6, 16–23, 25, 28, 32, 46, 72,
    125, 150, 239, 243
Durkan, Jenny, 122
Duvernoy, Gene, 113

Eagle Rock, CA, 40
EAP (Austin, TX), 97, 98, 99
Earth First!, 51
Earthquake cottage, 157
East Austin, TX, 76, 82–83
East Bay (California), 9, 110, 114, 160,
    222
East Bay Asian Local Development Cor-
    poration, 227
East Bay for Everyone, 160–162
East Bay Forward, 160
East Cesar Chavez Neighborhood Plan-
    ning Team, 80
East Harlem, NY, 218
East New York, NY, 215, 218
East Oakland, CA, 222–223
Eastern Neighborhoods rezoning (San
    Francisco, CA), 140–141, 234
Eastmont Mall, 221
Ebbets Field, 211, 213, 214
Ebbets Field Tenants Association, 212
Echo Park (Los Angeles, CA), 44, 64
Economic diversity, 35, 124, 126, 154,
    163–165, 194, 198–199, 216, 218, 227, 235,
    243–249
Edwards, John, 205
El Tecolote (newspaper), 230, 236
Elizabeth Street Garden, 187–189, 191
Ellis Act (California), 5, 19–32, 67, 72–73,
    135, 136, 149–152, 181–182, 236, 238–239;
    reform efforts, 151
Ellison, Larry, 82
Enriquez, Francisco, 95
Enterprise Community Partners, 125, 226
Environment Texas, 95–96

Environmentalists, 116, 170, 172, 173, 208, 246; and support for infill housing, 96, 112–113, 162, 164, 165–166; and support for affordable housing, 173
Equity and Environment Agenda (Seattle, WA), 167
Espinal Jr., Rafael L., 215
Eudaly, Chloe, 176
Eviction, 3, 16–17, 20–21, 23–25, 29, 33, 34, 52, 82, 87, 134, 154, 183, 231, 214; no-fault, 6, 15, 31–32, 182, 237; OMI, 15, 26, 28, 135–136, 151–152, 236–238
Eviction Free San Francisco, 27
Evolve Austin Partners, 95–96, 98, 102
Excelsior (San Francisco, CA), 237
Exclusionary zoning, 42, 76, 78, 91, 99, 117, 177, 226–227, 244–246. See also Zoning

Facebook, 108, 164
FairVote, 69
Fastracks (Denver light rail), 125
Federal government: funding for housing, 4–5, 9, 99, 152, 239, 242, 245; housing loans, 192; housing programs, 99; subsidized housing, 67; tax code, 247
Federation of Hillside and Canyon Associations, 63
Feinstein, Dianne, 14, 33, 35, 127, 129, 131, 133, 152
Ferlinghetti, Lawrence, 29
Fierce, Victoria, 160, 161
The Fight for Fifteen: The Right Wage for a Working America (Rolf), 115
Filipinos, 16–18, 20
Fillmore (San Francisco, CA), 13–14, 24, 183, 198
Financial crisis (2008), 15, 141, 106, 143, 222, 237
Fingal-Surma, Laura, 197
Five Points (Denver, CO), 123
Flipping properties, 22, 54, 210
Florida, Richard, 219
Florio, Anthony, 34
Ford Motor Company, 208
Foreclosure, 38, 222
Foreign real estate investment, 141, 247

Forest Hill (San Francisco, CA), 9, 193–195
Forest Hill Christian Church, 194
Forterra, 113
Fox, Raquel, 18–20, 23–24, 239
Francisco Reservoir (San Francisco, CA), 195
Friends of Austin Neighborhoods, 96
Friends of Noe Valley, 198
Friends of the Elizabeth Street Garden, 189, 190
Fryman, Annie, 159

Gallegos, Pete, 228–238, 241
Gallería de la Raza, 150
Galvan, Maru, 39, 40
Galvin, Bernie, 5, 138
Gammon, Robert, 226
Garcetti, Eric, 7, 41–42, 60–62, 69–73, 147, 151
Garcia, Amparo, 20
Garcia, Hector, 20
Garcia, Romulo, 20
Garza, Delia, 83, 101
Gehry, Frank, 57
Generation X, 9, 115, 161
Generational divide, 248
Gentrification, 4, 7, 10, 26, 35, 42, 50, 54, 65, 76, 80, 101, 124, 128, 152, 174, 176, 183, 192, 196, 218, 225–226, 230, 244–247. See also Anti-gentrification
Ghost Ship fire (Oakland, CA), 1–3, 6, 224
GI Bill of Rights, 93, 221
Gill, Gregory, 26–28
Girón, Esteban, 213
Glen, Alicia, 217
Glide Memorial Church, 33
Goff, Eric, 92, 95, 99
Golden Gate Park, 130
Golden Properties, 21
Goldman Sachs, 217
Gonzales, Juan, 230
Gonzales, Juliana, 84
Gonzalez, Francisco, 47–50, 52
Google, 56–57, 108, 181–182, 197
Governing (magazine), 69
Grand Central Terminal, 189

Green Party, 166
Greenpoint (New York, NY), 217
Gross, Larry, 67, 72–73
Groundhog Day (movie), 202
Group I, 240
Grow SF, 159
Growth Management Act (Washington, 1990), 109
Grynberg, Noah, 52
Gullicksen, Ted, 23, 25–26, 149
Gyourko, Joseph, 180

Habitat for Humanity, 96, 191
Haight-Ashbury (San Francisco, CA), 13, 17, 34, 131, 178–179, 238
HALA (Seattle, WA). *See* Housing Affordability and Livability Agenda
Hamilton, Jesse, 213
Hancock, Loni, 179, 201
Hancock, Michael, 124, 126
Hanlon, Brian, 202
Harlem (New York, NY), 213; East Harlem, NY, 218
Harris-Dawson, Marqueece, 60
Hartley, Kate, 154
Harvard Joint Center for Housing Studies, 41
Hayes Valley (San Francisco, CA), 13
Height limits, 157–158, 171–172, 194, 197, 226
Hell's Kitchen (New York, NY), 217
Hernandez, Areli, 37–40, 79
Hernandez, Roberto, 231
Hestor, Sue, 138, 140
Hickey, John, 24
Highland Park (Los Angeles, CA), 2, 6–7, 41–42, 50, 53–55, 64–65, 88, 165, 226
Hillcrest Business Association, 167
Hodges, Nick, 103, 104
Hollywood, CA, 39–40
Hollywood Community Housing Corporation, 58
HomeAway, 153
Homebuilders Association of Greater Austin, 96
Homeless shelters, 59, 79, 203, 214, 220
Homelessness, 7, 14, 36, 41, 56, 203, 224; in Seattle, 103–104, 121; in Los Angeles, 40

Homeowner groups, 7, 42, 55–56, 62–63, 65, 92, 100, 185, 227
Homeowners, 69–70, 91, 205, 206; and opposition to housing, 60, 95, 98, 169, 172, 177, 203
Homeownership, 159, 169, 198
HOME-SF, 184–185, 218, 227
Hood, Heather, 226–227
HOPE VI, 145
Hotel Mariachi: Urban Space and Cultural Heritage in Los Angeles (Kurland), 47
A House Divided: Inequality in Housing in New York City (film), 210
House meetings, 58–59
Housing: for artists, 1–3, 32, 224; canvassing for, 97, 99; cooperative, 171; failure to build, 3, 36, 39, 107, 126, 128–129, 137, 193, 233–235, 241, 249; federal funding for, 4–5, 9, 67, 99, 152, 239, 242, 245; homeowner opposition to, 60, 95, 98, 169, 172, 177, 203; infill, 5, 95–96, 110, 113, 162, 166, 172, 174, 203, 246; minimum lot size requirements for, 93, 96, 100, 246–247; modular, 243; neighborhood opposition to, 60–61, 110, 159, 170–171, 175, 186, 190–191, 194–195, 197, 202; public, 94, 144–145, 155, 176, 185, 200; subsidized, 41, 43, 45, 109, 115, 200; supportive, 51, 57–62; for teachers, 148–149, 243; waiting lists for, 49, 187, 190. *See also* Affordable housing
Housing Affordability and Livability Agenda (HALA; Seattle, WA), 8, 111, 112, 113–117, 119, 147, 218, 244; neighborhood opposition to, 112
Housing approval process. *See* Building approval process
Housing bubble (2000s), 140, 232, 237
Housing code enforcement/violations, 5, 18, 76, 80, 84–85, 86–89, 94, 134, 236, 246–247
Housing Development and Neighborhood Preservation Corporation, 236
Housing Development Consortium (Seattle, WA), 111
Housing for All (Seattle, WA), 104
Housing Rights Committee of San Francisco, 27, 31–32

Housing safety, 2, 5, 7. *See also* Housing
code enforcement/violations
Housing-to-jobs ratio. *See* Jobs/housing
imbalance
Housing units built: in Denver, 124, 126;
in New York, 128, 217; in San Fran-
cisco, 108, 128, 143; in Seattle, 108, 121
HUD (Department of Housing and
Urban Development), 145, 177
Hudson Square (New York, NY), 189
Hudson Yards, 217
Huizar, José, 51, 53, 61
Hung, Tammy, 30
Hunter, Austin, 159

Iantorno, Sergio, 21, 23
Idaho, 177
Imbelloni Construction, 130
Imhoff, Robert, 33
Immigrants/immigration, 17, 20, 33–34,
39, 40, 114, 128, 164, 195, 232; from
Central America, 14, 127; from Ireland,
8, 13, 129–130, 134, 229; from Southeast
Asia, 14, 127
Inclusionary housing, 35, 71, 93, 125–126,
137–138, 145 148–149, 173, 174, 191–192,
197–198, 204–205, 207, 224–225, 242,
244, 247; in Seattle, 116
Inclusionary housing requirements, 169,
239–240; in Berkeley, CA, 200; in San
Francisco, 242; in New York, NY,
215–216
Indiana, 26–27
Inequality, 2–3, 7, 36, 76, 92, 166, 185, 192,
227, 231, 238, 246
Infill housing, 5, 95–96, 162, 166, 172, 174,
203, 246; as environmental issue, 110;
and Sierra Club, 113
Inglewood, CA, 37
Inner City Law Center (Los Angeles, CA),
66, 72
Insecure (HBO series), 37
Integration, 91, 98
Interest rates, 130, 131, 226
Interim control ordinances, 63
International Hotel (San Francisco,
CA), 16
Irish builders, 129, 132–136, 139, 141–142

Jacobs, Matthew, 67–68
Jacobus, Rick, 198
Jarvis, Howard, 55
Jeffries, Hakeem, 220
Jim Crow laws, 223
Jimenez, Joel, 79
Jobs/housing imbalance, 122, 127–129, 136,
233, 247–248; in San Francisco, 118; in
San Francisco Bay Area region, 243; in
Seattle, 118
Johnson, Lady Bird, 77
Johnson, Lyndon, 76, 100
Jones, Jerry, 66, 72
Just-cause evictions, 5, 22, 32, 75, 165, 204,
224, 245

Kalb, Dan, 162, 224, 227
Kanson-Benanay, Jesse, 163–165, 179
Keep Austin Weird, 75–76
Keighran, Sean, 134, 139–141
Kennedy, John F., 228
Kiely, Jeannine, 190
Koch, Ed, 128, 146
Kooistra, Marty, 111
Koretz, Paul, 68
Kovacs, Madeline, 173, 176
Krieger, Shoshana, 84–85, 87–89
Kurtland, Catherine, 47
KXTV (Sacramento TV station), 177

La Raza en Action, 229
La Raza Graphics Center, 230–231, 236
La Raza Information Center, 229
La Raza Unida, 229
La Virgen de Guadalupe, 228
LA Weekly, 60
Labor unions, 71, 114, 116, 223
Laconia Developments, 118
Lady Bird Lake (Austin, TX), 77, 80, 88
Lakeshore (San Francisco, CA), 237
Lakeview (Austin, TX), 77–79
Lancaster, CA, 37–38
Land banking, 101, 125, 205, 235, 239
Land use, 76, 91 95–97, 100, 166, 186, 204,
246. *See also* Zoning
Landmark Realty, 33
Latinos, 13, 45, 50, 53, 97–99, 101, 170, 181,
213, 215, 218–219, 221, 223; displaced by

gentrification and redevelopment, 2–3, 40–43, 50, 77–91, 209, 211; and goal of racial diversity, 10; mariachi culture, 45–47, 52; in San Francisco Mission District, 228–242; and substandard housing, 74–76; as voting bloc, 42

Laurelhurst (Seattle, WA), 105, 106

Le Conte Neighborhood Association, 201

Lear, Norman, 210

Lee, Barbara, 223

Lee, Ed, 8, 23, 32, 143–144, 146–155, 183–185, 239–241

Legal assistance/representation for tenants, 6, 150–151; ballot measure guaranteeing (San Francisco), 151

Leno, Mark, 148, 151

Leung, Wing Hoo, 29, 30

LGBTQs (lesbian, gay, bisexual, and transgender people), 2–3, 13, 26–27, 33, 114, 127, 166, 198

Libertarians, 165

Licata, Nick, 116, 121

Linkage fees, 70–71, 93–94, 115, 225, 244

Lisle, Benjamin, 211

Little Italy (New York, NY), 190

Little Italy (San Diego, CA), 167

Livable Boulder, 171

LiveOn NY, 189

Live-work housing, 1, 31, 224; backlash against, 135–137; building requirements vs. other housing types, 132; as entry-level housing, 134–135; loopholes in artist requirements, 135; in San Francisco, 132–138

Loe, Laura, 166–167, 172

Long Beach, CA, 38

Los Angeles, CA, 2, 5–7, 36–73, 79, 88–89, 102–103, 130, 147, 151, 165, 179, 191, 211, 226, 240, 243; Arts District, 43; city attorney, 71; city council, 42, 62, 66, 71; county board of supervisors, 60; downtown area, 40, 48; planning department, 68; police department, 40

Los Angeles Center for Community Law and Action (LACCLA), 47, 52

Los Angeles Community Action Network (LACAN), 58

Los Angeles Tenants Union, 52

Los Angeles Times, 40–42, 51, 59, 61, 64, 68–69

Lower East Side (New York, NY), 2, 187

Low-income housing, 10, 115, 189, 191, 200, 232

Lowry Hill East Neighborhood Association (LHENA), 203, 205, 206, 207

Luciano, Lilia, 177–178

Lummis, Charles, 54

Luxury housing, 2, 10, 178, 212–213, 215, 218, 220, 236

MacArthur Park (Los Angeles, CA), 38

Macchiarini, Peter, 29

Make Homes Happen, 208

Mandatory Housing Affordability (MHA) (Seattle, WA), 116, 117

Manhattan (NY), 189

Manilatown (San Francisco, CA) 16

Mansion tax, 115

Manteca, CA, 221

Mar Vista (Los Angeles, CA), 40

Mariachi Crossing, 47

Mariachi Plaza (Los Angeles, CA), 6, 43–48, 53

Mariachis, 45–47, 52

Marina District (San Francisco, CA), 132

Marketplace (radio program), 54

Market-rate housing, 9, 71, 115, 177–179, 184, 196, 213, 225–226, 236, 238, 241, 244; opposition to, 137, 138, 235, 239

Marroquin, Eva, 88, 89

Marte, Christopher, 190

Martinez, Alberto, 80

Mary's Place (Seattle, WA), 103

Massachusetts, 165

Master leasing of hotels, 155

Matthew, Bret, 165

Maytag, Fritz, 139

McCarthy, Angus, 134

McCullough, Jack, 111

McKay, Lola, 24

Mecca, Tommi Avicolli, 27

Menzies, Paul, 118

Mercy Housing Northwest, 110, 121

Metcalf, Gabe, 139

Metro Rail (Los Angeles, CA), 43–45, 48, 53

Metzger, Luke, 96
Mexican American Political Association, 228
Mexico City, 46
Miami-Dade County, FL, 41, 149
MicroPAD housing, 243
Microsoft, 106–108
Mid-Market (San Francisco, CA), 31, 240
MidPen Housing, 149
Milk, Harvey, 14, 26
Millennials, 4, 8, 9, 70, 96, 144, 197, 204; boomer-millennial conflict, 4, 8, 157–186, 248–249
Millennium Tower (San Francisco, CA), 137
Miller, Victor, 236
Mills College, 1
Minimum lot size requirements for housing, 93, 96, 100, 246–247
Minimum wage, 41, 115
Minneapolis, MN, 5, 9, 203–208
Minneapolis Residents for Responsible Development Coalition, 205
Minnesota Bicycle Coalition, 204
Miripol, Aaron, 124–126
Misadventures of Awkward Black Girl, 37
Mission Action Plan, 242
Mission Anti-Displacement Coalition, 231
Mission Community Organization, 231
Mission Cultural Center, 236
Mission District (San Francisco, CA), 3, 10, 13, 132, 135–136, 142, 150, 196, 181, 183, 209, 228–242
Mission Economic Cultural Association, 231
Mission Economic Development Association, 150
Mission Housing, 142, 229, 234–236, 239, 241
Mission Terrace (San Francisco, CA), 237
Miyasaki, Margaret Eve-Lynne, 142
Modern Coliseum (Lisle), 211
Modular housing, 243
Mold, 83, 89. See also Housing code enforcement/violations
Monkkonen, Paavo, 64
Montez, Amaris, 69
Moon, Cary, 122

Moore, John, 59
Moore, Marcus, 214
Morrison, Laura, 101
Moscone, George, 14
Moss, Sam, 142, 234
Mossman, Donna, 210, 212, 214, 217, 221
Mother's Cookies (Oakland, CA), 221
MSPyimby, 207
Mueller (Austin, TX), 83
Mulholland, Royce, 86–87
Multnomah Parade, 175
MUNI (San Francisco, CA), 230
Municipal Arts Society (NY), 189
Murphy, Eamon, 130
Murray, Ed, 110–114, 116, 119, 122, 146–147, 170
Muscle Beach (Venice, CA), 56
Mykaels, Jeremy, 21, 26–28

National Geographic, 171–172
National housing trust fund, 177
National Low Income Housing Coalition (NLIHC), 4
Native Americans, 59
Nebraska, 177
Neighborhood groups, 61, 63, 76, 91, 96, 99–101, 143, 157, 163, 170, 176, 178, 180, 184, 187, 189, 195, 203, 205–208; in Los Angeles, 64; in San Francisco, 115; in Seattle, 112
Neighborhood opposition to housing, 60–61, 110, 159, 170–171, 175, 186, 190–191, 194–195, 197, 202
Neighborhood Plan Contact Teams (NPCTs), 91, 92
Neighborhood preservation, 4, 6, 9, 72, 193, 196, 198–200, 202, 206, 246
Neighbors for More Neighbors, 207
Neiman, David, 119
Nelson, Anita, 71
New Mexico, 228
New Mission News, 135, 236
New York, NY, 2, 4–5, 11–12, 40, 42, 106–108, 117, 128, 146, 149, 179, 187–191, 207, 209–221, 228, 243–244; 1970s economic collapse, 128
New York Communities for Change (NYCC), 212–213, 216, 220

New York Times, 5, 14, 24, 53, 55, 160, 182, 191, 211, 215, 232
Newsom, Gavin, 144, 155
Newsome, Beverly, 212, 213
Nextdoor, 197
Nicolais, Teo, 124
Nicoloff, Martha 200
Nicoloff, Tamara, 200
NIMBY, 60, 166, 167, 193
Nob Hill (San Francisco, CA), 13
Noe Valley (San Francisco, CA), 13, 17, 24, 31, 34, 131, 137, 143, 157–158, 179, 181, 196–200, 238
Noe Valley Voice (newspaper), 196
No-fault eviction, 6, 15, 31–32, 182, 237
Nolita (New York, NY), 9, 58, 187–191, 193, 212
Nonprofit housing, 45, 49, 61, 142, 145, 187, 234, 238–240, 242
Nonprofit organization, 23, 231, 235, 242, 244
North Austin, TX, 87–90, 99
North Beach (San Francisco, CA), 2, 13, 28–31, 151, 183
North-Central Austin, TX, 88
North Hollywood, CA, 38
North Park (San Diego, CA), 167
North Seattle, WA, 105–106
North Shore (MA), 164
Not Yet New York, 63
Nuru, Mohammed, 145

O'Brien, Mike, 111
O'Connor, John, 134
O'Donoghue, Joe, 134, 137, 199
O'Malley, Becky, 177–178
O'Malley, Walter, 211–212
Oakland, CA, 1–3, 10, 12, 159–162, 165, 209, 221–228, 230, 247; city attorney, 224; city council, 162, 223–224, 227; decline in African American population, 222–223; housing goals, (2017), 223–224; infrastructure bond (2016), 224; median rents, 223; north Oakland, 221, 222; west Oakland, 221, 226
Oakland Magazine, 160, 162
Oakland SPUR, 225
Oakland Tech High School, 222

Obama, Barack, 147
Ogilvie, Robert, 225, 226
Ohio, 160
OMI evictions, 15, 26, 28, 135–136, 151–152, 236–238; in San Francisco (1990s), 237
OneAmerica, 112
Opposition to housing, 7–9, 57, 91, 96, 100, 115, 140–142, 157–158, 184, 188–189, 239–240; homeowner opposition, 60, 95, 98, 169, 172, 177, 203; neighborhood opposition, 60–61, 110, 159, 170–171, 175, 186, 190–191, 194–195, 197, 202
Oracle Corporation, 77, 81–82
Orange County, CA, 38
Oregon, 177
Organizing People, Activating Leaders (OPAL), 173
Ou, Joy, 240
Outer Richmond (San Francisco, CA), 130
Owner move-in evictions. See OMI evictions

Pacific Heights (San Francisco, CA), 13, 33
Pacoima, CA, 39
Palmer case (California), 225
Palo Alto 171, 233, 247
Parent, Tracy, 23
Paris, 172, 195
Park Slope (New York, NY), 210, 212
Parking, 30–31, 101, 115, 164–165, 176, 180, 193–194, 204, 206
Pasadena, CA, 38
Paz Ruiz, Mary, 39–40
Pelosi, Alexandra, 182, 183
Pennrose, 191
People of color, 114, 188, 204, 208, 210
Perea, Margarita, 46, 47
Perturis, Margery, 28
Peters, Nancy, 29
Pettis, Faith, 111, 112, 117
Phillips, Alberta, 83
Pico-Union (Los Angeles, CA), 64
Pilcher, Claire, 198
Pittsburg, CA, 222
Podell Company, 240
PolicyLink, 223
Politico, 220

POOR Magazine, 25
Portland, OR, 2, 5, 9, 11, 105, 171–176, 227, 245; and homeowner opposition to housing, 172, 176–177
Portland for Everyone (P4E), 172, 174–176
Potrero Hill (San Francisco, CA), 132, 135, 139–140
Precita Eyes Muralists, 236
Preston, Dean, 18–20, 23, 25–26
Progress Noe Valley, 197
Proposition 13 (California), 9, 55, 56, 147, 247
Proposition H (Los Angeles, 2014), 60, 70
Proposition H (San Francisco, 1992), 68
Proposition HHH (Los Angeles), 60–62, 70
Proposition M (San Francisco, 1986), 108
Proposition R (San Francisco, 1979), 236
Proposition S (Los Angeles, 2017), 72
Proposition U (Los Angeles, 1986), 62, 63, 72
Prospect Park (New York, NY), 210
Protect Noe's Charm, 157
PSSST gallery, 49–50
Public housing, 94, 144–145, 155, 176, 185, 200
Publicly owned land, 8, 10, 53, 59, 83, 94, 148, 189–190, 211–212, 214, 219–220, 240, 244
Puget Sound Business Journal, 119

Racial diversity, 126, 196, 207, 209–249
Rae, Issa, 37
Rahaim, John, 108, 120
Ramirez, Alejandra, 74
Reagan, Ronald, 130, 239
Real Estate Board of New York, 216
ReBuilding Community, 174
Redack, Xi'An Chandra, 31–33
Redevelopment, 9, 83, 183, 220, 231
Redfin, 54
Redlining, 122, 226
Redmond, WA, 106
Reed, Mary, 101
Regional Transportation District (Denver, CO), 125, 126
Rent control, 5, 12, 14, 22, 26, 32, 34–35, 45–46, 48, 52, 65, 67–78, 73, 75, 93, 116,

120–121, 131, 152–153, 165, 167, 174, 204, 236, 245, 247
Renteria, Sabino "Pio," 83, 101
Renter's tax credit (California), 5
Repeat offender program (Austin, TX), 84–85, 98
Residential Builders Association (RBA), 133–134, 136, 137, 141, 199
Residential Infill Project (Portland), 174
Rezoning, 139, 140, 141, 175, 215; of industrial areas for housing, 132, 135. *See also* Zoning
Rice, Norman, 109, 146
Richmond District (San Francisco, CA), 30, 133, 179; inner Richmond, 13, 133
"Richmond Specials," 133–134, 136
Rios, Michael V., 230
Riverside (Austin, TX), 81
Roadmap toward Equity, A, 223
Robinson, Jackie, 211
Rockridge (Oakland, CA), 160, 162
Roe, Ruby, 80
Rolf, David, 114, 115
Rosas, Maya, 167, 168
Rosedale (Austin, TX), 88
Rosenberg, Mike, 108, 120
Ross, Fred, 42, 58
Rossi, Gary, 29
Rothstein, Richard, 99, 192
Rouleau, Richard, 33–34
Roybal, Ed, 42
Ruiz, Mary, 65
Rumpf, Bill, 110–112, 118, 121
Russian Hill (San Francisco, CA), 195
Ruvalcaba, Arturo, 45, 47, 50
Ruvalcaba, Estela, 45
Ryavec, Mark, 60

Sacramento, CA, 151, 177
Salon, 182
Samaniego, Carlos, 17
Samaniego, Maria, 17, 20
Samaniego, Ricardo, 17, 20, 22
San Diego, CA, 3, 9, 167–168
San Fernando Valley, CA, 38–40, 55, 65
San Francisco, CA, 2–6, 8–36, 40, 45, 48–49, 57, 61, 66, 68, 72–73, 75, 84–85, 98, 102, 106–108, 110–111, 113, 117, 119,

121, 127–156, 157–159, 171, 178–181, 183, 185, 193–200, 204–205, 209, 2018, 221, 223–225, 227–244, 247–248; Board of Permit Appeals, 34; building codes, 32; building permitting process, 141–142, 158; city attorney, 142; county board of supervisors, 14, 28, 138, 139, 140, 142–143, 152, 237, 240; decline in evictions, 154; decline in housing supply, 14; Department of Building Inspection, 18, 135, 236; Department of Public Works, 145; district elections, 137; downtown, 129, 132, 142, 195; economy of, 13; Housing Authority, 145, 228; housing code enforcement/violations, 17–19, 32, 134, 236; housing goals, 146; housing prices, 178–179; loss of public housing units, 145; Mayor's Office of Housing, 154; median rents, 158, 223; moratorium on market rate housing (2015), 240–241; planning code, 32; planning department, 130, 135, 136, 138, 139, 140, 142–144, 18 4, 195–196, 242; Public Utilities Commission, 17–18, 196; redevelopment agency, 17, 24, 110, 183, 198, 231; rent board, 21, 33–34, 154; subsidized housing in, 200; teachers in, 148–149; Unified School District, 148

San Francisco (song), 28

San Francisco 2.0 (film), 182

San Francisco Chronicle, 139, 194

San Francisco Community Land Trust (SFCLT), 23, 150

San Francisco Gray Panthers, 198

San Francisco Housing Action Coalition, 184, 233

San Francisco–Oakland Bay Bridge, 221

San Francisco State University 178,

San Francisco Tenants Union, 20, 23, 25, 27, 149, 236

San Jose, CA, 121, 247

Sanders, Bernie, 165–166

Santa Monica, CA, 56–57, 69, 153, 166–167

Santa Monica for Renters Rights, 69

Santiago, Benito, 150

Satterfield, Vivian, 173

Sauer, Ronald, 28

Savage, Dan, 119, 120

Sawant, Kshama, 116

SB 827 (California), 246

Schaaf, Libby, 161, 223, 225, 227

Schraa, Eugenia, 165*Season of the Witch* (book), 152, 153

Seattle, WA, 2, 5, 8–9, 11, 70, 93, 102–123, 144, 146–147, 149, 162, 165–167, 170, 172, 191, 204, 218, 227, 245, 248; 2017 mayoral election, 122; building codes, 118; chamber of commerce, 112; city council, 118; "Grand Bargain," (2015) 111; median income, 117; planning commission, 118; residential demographics, 114; subsidized housing in, 109, 115; zoning codes, 118

Seattle for Everyone (S4E), 8, 112, 114, 116, 208

Seattle Times, 11, 104, 108, 112–113, 116, 120Section 8 housing, 6, 104

Security deposits, 12

Segregation, 7, 9, 56, 75–76, 90, 93, 96, 100, 117, 164, 192

Selvans, Zane, 168, 169, 192

Senior citizens, 33, 170; affordable housing for, 9, 142, 187–192, 193–195, 211, 215; displacement of, 24–26; and Ellis Act, 20, 27, 31

Service Employees International Union (SEIU) 775, 112, 115

SF Bay Area Renters Federation (SFBARF), 159, 184–185, 202

SF YIMBY Party, 159, 184

Shabu House, 30

Share Better SF, 153

Shaw, Randy: activism of, 5-6; and ACT UP, 51; alliance with builders, 134-135, 137, 240; and proposed national housing trust fund, 177; and proposed small sites program, 149; and Proposition H, 68; and San Francisco Tenants Union, 23; and Tenderloin Housing Clinic, 11

Ships (restaurant), 62, 63

Short-term rentals, 153, 154; ballot measure to regulate (San Francisco, 2015), 153

Showplace Square, 140

Sierra Club, 113–114, 167

Sierra Magazine, 167

Silicon Valley, CA, 15, 134, 149, 152, 181, 197, 199, 232–233, 237; region's effect on San Francisco Bay Area housing prices, 152, 233, 247
Silver Lake (Los Angeles, CA), 40, 44, 53
Single-family homes, 7, 173; density, 162; zoning of, 122, 207, 226, 247
Single room occupancy hotels. See SROs
Skid Row (Los Angeles, CA), 71
Skinner, Nancy, 119, 203
Small Sites Acquisition Program (San Francisco, CA), 23, 149–151, 155, 205, 227, 239, 244
Snapchat, 56
Somers, Susan, 92–93, 98–99
South Bay region, CA, 233
South Berkeley, CA, 202
South Bronx (New York, NY), 12
South by Southwest, 75
South Crown Heights (New York, NY), 219
South Los Angeles, 58, 61
South Minneapolis, 206
South of Market (San Francisco, CA), 6, 13–14, 16–18, 20, 132, 133, 135, 137, 140, 142, 183
South of Market Community Action Network (SOMCAN), 18, 23
South San Francisco, CA, 138
Spain, 11
Speculation, 4, 17, 19, 21–22, 24, 28–29, 34, 35, 42, 52, 65–66, 83–84, 183, 214–215, 219, 226, 234, 247
Spokane, WA, 105
SPUR (San Francisco Bay Area Planning and Urban Research Association), 139
SRO Housing Corporation (Los Angeles, CA), 71
SROs (single room occupancy hotels), 5, 6, 12, 30, 35, 45, 85, 103, 138, 155, 198, 221, 227, 238, 240, 245
St. Louis, MO, 97
St. Paul, MN, 208
St. Paul Community Baptist Church, 215St. Peter's Housing Committee, 236
Starbucks, 106, 217
Starz (TV network), 53
"State of the Nation's Housing" report, 41
"Stay in Place" ordinance (Austin, TX), 91

"Stealth dorm" legislation (Austin, TX), 92
Stock option tax (San Francisco, CA), 144
Stop Diminishing Portland, 176
Stranger, The (newspaper), 119
Strobel, Roger, 28
Suburban sprawl, 97, 164–165
Summer of Love, 13
Sunnyvale, CA, 182
Sunset District (San Francisco, CA), 130, 148, 183–184, 195; inner Sunset, 13, 149
Sunset Strip (Los Angeles, CA), 55
Supportive housing, 51, 57–62

Talbot, David, 152–153
Tang, Katy, 183–185
Teachers, housing for, 243; in San Francisco, 148–149
Tech boom (2011–), 10, 15, 145, 152–155, 158–159, 182, 200, 222, 232, 237–238, 241
Tech companies, 144, 177
Tech workers, 9, 15, 158, 181–182, 197, 232
Temescal (Oakland, CA), 1, 160, 162, 222
Temple Beth Israel, 53
Tenancies in common. See TICs
Tenants: activism of, 25, 66, 74, 80, 81; buyouts, 21, 27–28, 34; protections for, 35, 41, 45, 55, 66–67, 89, 165, 224, 245
Tenants Together, 67
Tenderloin (San Francisco, CA), 6, 11, 26, 34–35, 45, 49, 85, 110, 221, 234, 237, 240; subsidized housing in, 45
Tenderloin Housing Clinic, 3, 6, 11, 16, 18, 20, 25, 27, 30, 32–33, 138, 150–151, 155, 239
Terner Center for Housing Innovation, 141
Texas Association of Builders, 93
Texas Rio Grande Legal Aid (TRLA), 76, 84, 87; TRLA/BASTA Residents Advocacy Project, 85
Texas state legislature, 93–94
TexPIRG, 96–95
TICs (tenancies in common), 19, 22, 24, 27, 29–30, 136, 197
Tovo, Kathie, 83
Transit, 8, 97, 98, 99, 160, 162, 173, 192, 204, 208, 226, 230, 247
Transit-oriented development, 98, 125, 126, 159–160, 167, 175, 184, 244, 246

Trauss, Sonja, 159, 184
Travis County, TX, 75
Triangle Shirtwaist Fire, 2
Trinh, Stephanie, 76
Trulia, 56
Trump, Donald, 75
Turner, B.J., 52
Twitter, 31, 108, 161, 181

Union City, CA, 27, 114
Union de Vecinos, 50, 52
Union Square (San Francisco, CA), 6
Union Station (Los Angeles, CA), 43
United Farm Workers (UFW), 50, 58, 229
United Neighborhoods for Reform, 176
University District (Seattle, WA), 105
University of California, Berkeley, 141,
    177, 201, 203, 241; Urban Displacement
    Project, 241
University of California, Los Angeles
    (UCLA), 37, 63–64
University of Colorado, 168, 170
University of Southern California
    (USC), 64
University of Texas School of Law, 84
University of Washington, 105, 113
Uptown Community Plan (San Diego,
    CA), 168
Uptown Planners (San Diego, CA), 167, 168
Upzoning, 95, 111, 113, 115, 116, 117, 119, 175,
    199, 208, 217–219, 227, 244. *See also*
    Zoning
Urban Institute, 179
Urban Land Conservancy (ULC) (Den-
    ver, CO), 124, 125, 126
Urban renewal, 4, 14, 17, 174, 192–193,
    198, 231
Urbanist, 166

Vacancy control, 152, 153
Van Nuys, CA, 39
Vancouver, BC, 105
Venice, CA, 7, 56–60, 62, 193, 207
Venice Community Housing (VCH), 58,
    59, 60, 62
Venice Stakeholders Association, 60
Venice Vision, 59
Vida (Starz Network program), 53

Vilchis, Leonardo, 50
Villager (newspaper), 190
Visco, Thomas, 95–97

Waiting lists, for housing, 49, 187, 190
Wall Street Journal, 58
Walnut Creek, CA, 118
Washington, DC, 51, 158, 177, 179
Washington Heights/Inwood (New York,
    NY), 218–219
Way, Heather K., 84
Weaver, Celia, 212, 216
Wedge LIVE!, 205
Weird Wave Coffee, 50
Welch, Calvin, 138, 177–178
Wells, Grace, 24–26
West Hollywood, CA, 153
West Indian American Day Carnival
    Association, 219
West Seattle, WA, 106
West Side (Manhattan, NY), 217
Western Addition (San Francisco, CA), 24
Westin, Jonathan, 220
Westside (Los Angeles, CA), 40, 52, 59,
    62–63
Westside (San Francisco, CA), 129, 133–
    134, 183–184, 195
Westwood (Los Angeles, CA), 62–64
Wheelock, Charlotte, 103–104
Wilkins, Robin, 77–82, 100
Williams, Kisha, 87
Williamsburg (New York, NY), 2, 210, 217
World War II, 93, 164, 221
Wrede, Christian, 59
Wright, Ruth, 171

Yakima, WA, 105
Yanez, Leandra, 83
Yañez, René, 150, 239
Yee, Norman, 194
Yelp, 46, 79, 86
YIMBY Democrats of San Diego County,
    168
YIMBYs, 60, 159, 161, 163, 165–168, 171–
    192, 193
Yonkers, NY, 193
YouTube, 86, 189
Yuppies, 14

Zane, Denny, 69
Zendesk, 181
Zillow, 41
Zoning, 3–5, 7–9, 56, 58, 64, 76, 90, 93,
  95–98, 100–101, 122, 142, 153, 158, 161,
  163–164, 171–172, 174–175, 192–193,
  195, 201–203, 206–208, 216, 226,
  246–247; downzoning, 63, 129, 131,
133–134, 163, 201, 218; exclusionary
  zoning, 42, 76, 78, 91, 99, 117, 177,
  226–227, 244–246; upzoning, 95, 111,
  113, 115, 116, 117, 119, 175, 199, 208,
  217–219, 227, 244. *See also* Inclusionary
  housing; Rezoning
Zuniga, Pedro, 46–47
Zynga, 181

Founded in 1893,
UNIVERSITY OF CALIFORNIA PRESS
publishes bold, progressive books and journals
on topics in the arts, humanities, social sciences,
and natural sciences—with a focus on social
justice issues—that inspire thought and action
among readers worldwide.

The UC PRESS FOUNDATION
raises funds to uphold the press's vital role
as an independent, nonprofit publisher, and
receives philanthropic support from a wide
range of individuals and institutions—and from
committed readers like you. To learn more, visit
ucpress.edu/supportus.